# Language and Politics in the United States and Canada

Myths and Realities

# Language and Politics in the United States and Canada

## Myths and Realities

Edited by

**Thomas Ricento**
*The University of Texas at San Antonio*

**Barbara Burnaby**
*Ontario Institute for Studies in Education
University of Toronto*

LAWRENCE ERLBAUM ASSOCIATES, PUBLISHERS
1998   Mahwah, New Jersey                London

Copyright © 1998 by Lawrence Erlbaum Associates, Inc.
All rights reserved. No part of this book may be reproduced in any form, by photostat, microfilm, retrieval system, or any other means, without prior written permission of the publisher.

Lawrence Erlbaum Associates, Inc., Publishers
10 Industrial Avenue
Mahwah, NJ 07430

Cover design by Kathryn Houghtaling Lacey

Library of Congress Cataloging-in-Publication Data

Language and politics in the United States and Canada : myths and realities / edited by Thomas Ricento, Barbara Burnaby.
    p.   cm.
Includes bibliographical references and index.
ISBN 0-8058-2838-9 (alk. paper). — ISBN 0-8058-2839-7 (pbk. : alk. paper)
1. Language policy—United States. 2. Language policy—Canada. I. Ricento, Thomas. II. Burnaby, Barbara.
P119.32.U6L356    1998
306.44'973—dc21                       97-38464
                                              CIP

Books published by Lawrence Erlbaum Associates are printed on acid-free paper, and their bindings are chosen for strength and durability.

Printed in the United States of America
10  9  8  7  6  5  4  3  2  1

# Contents

| | |
|---|---|
| Preface | ix |
| About the Authors | xiii |

**1** Introduction: Respecting the Citizens—Reflections on Language Policy in Canada and the United States    1
*Colin H. Williams*

## Part I   Overviews    33

**2** The Politics of Language in Canada and the United States: Explaining the Differences    37
*Ronald Schmidt, Sr.*

**3** Demographic Considerations in Canadian Language Policy    71
*Roderic Beaujot*

**4** National Language Policy in the United States    85
*Thomas Ricento*

v

## Part II    Forgotten Tongues: Indigenous Languages in North America

113

**5**    Life on the Edge: Canada's Aboriginal Languages Under Official Bilingualism
*Mark Fettes*

117

**6**    Endangered Native American Languages: What Is to Be Done, and Why?
*James Crawford*

151

## Part III    Legal Implications of Official Language Policies

167

**7**    Legal Implications of the Official English Declaration
*Susan Miner*

171

**8**    Language Rights Theory in Canadian Perspective
*Joseph Eliot Magnet*

185

## Part IV    Educational Perspectives

207

**9**    The Imposition of World War I Era English-Only Policies and the Fate of German in North America
*Terrence G. Wiley*

211

**10**    ESL Policy in Canada and the United States: Basis for Comparison
*Barbara Burnaby*

243

# Part V  Focus on Context

**269**

## 11  French-Language Services in Ontario: A Policy of "Overly Prudent Gradualism"?

*Don Cartwright*

**273**

## 12  Quebec, Canada, and the United States: Social Reality and Language Rights

*Calvin Veltman*

**301**

## 13  Partitioning by Language: Whose Rights Are Threatened?

*Thomas Ricento*

**317**

## 14  Conclusion: Myths and Realities

*Barbara Burnaby and Thomas Ricento*

**331**

**Author Index**

**345**

**Subject Index**

**351**

# Preface

Although we usually take our language environment for granted, it becomes a visceral issue when we feel that it is being tampered with. In recent years in Canada and the United States, language policy issues of various sorts have gained considerable profile, and the resulting public and academic discussion has generated at least as much heat as light. Oceans of ink have been spilled in both countries; we have peered across our common border to see if responses to domestic language problems in our neighbor's yard might be relevant to our own situations. Because we are neighbors, we have much in common, but we are different as well. Therefore, we have both profited from and been misled by the examples found in each other's situations.

The aim of this book is to explore parallel and divergent developments in language policy and language rights in the United States and Canada, especially in the past four decades, as a basis for reflection on what can be learned from one country's experience by the other. Effects of language policies and practices on majority and minority individuals and groups are evaluated. Differences in national and regional language situations in the United States and Canada are traced to historical, sociological, demographic, and legal factors that have sometimes been inappropriately generalized or ignored by ideologues. The point of the volume is to show that certain general principles of economics and sociology apply to the situations in both countries, but that differing notions of sovereignty, state and nation, ethnicity, pluralism, and multiculturalism have shaped attitudes and policies in significant ways. Understanding the bases for these varying attitudes and policies provides a clearer understanding of the idiosyncratic, as well as more universal factors that contribute to tensions between groups and to outcomes, many of which are unintended.

This volume is directed toward the attention not only of academics and graduate and undergraduate students, but also of policymakers and those with a general interest in the role of languages in these two countries.

**ix**

# PREFACE

Academic and professional fields addressed include sociolinguistics, demography, political science, applied linguistics, policy analysis, Canadian and American studies, language planning, and bilingual/multicultural education. The book provides background information as well as analyses for the better understanding of current debates, so that the lines of argument are accessible to readers new to these issues and those from other continents. In the United States, we believe that this book makes a major contribution to the polarized debate over declaring English as the official language at the federal and state levels. In Canada, this book brings external perspectives into the controversy over official language policy and its widespread implications for all language situations in the country. This controversy has in some ways immobilized Canada for almost three decades, and fresh approaches are greatly needed. Beneath these overriding debates in both countries, speakers of languages other than English or French, especially Native Americans and Canadians, live their everyday lives influenced by the by-products of official language issues. Although this book is necessarily limited in scope, it represents an attempt to show how all languages and speakers are affected by the manipulation of policies. In particular, policies of neglect and those of overt or barely covert discrimination concerning speakers of languages other than English are given attention.

Preceded by an introduction and followed by a final chapter, five parts structure this volume. In his introduction, Williams draws out major themes raised in the following chapters (such as conceptualizations of nationhood and multiculturalism, the hegemony of English, principles of social justice), raises crucial questions, and looks into the medium term future for languages in the United States and Canada. Part I, Overviews, contains three chapters, by Schmidt, Ricento, and Beaujot, that provide general information and make overarching analyses of language policies in the United States and Canada. Schmidt discusses language diversity within national contexts and describes models of ways in which national governments can approach dealing with such diversity. He then compares the models used in Canada and the United States. Ricento describes four deep values that Americans hold about their country, and argues that these deep values strongly influence what actually happens in language policy-making and implementation. He illustrates the interplay between deep values and the political process that shaped the Bilingual Education Act from its introduction in 1967 until the present day. Beaujot concretizes the picture in Canada by detailing the impact of Canadian federal and provincial policies, showing that, although some objectives appear to have been met, other changes that were perhaps not anticipated have occurred.

**PREFACE**                                                                                                    **xi**

In deliberate contrast to the discussion of high profile issues in the first section, Part II, Forgotten Tongues: Indigenous Languages in North America, contains two chapters on language issues for Native Canadians and Americans. Crawford's chapter offers a brief history of factors contributing to the fact that most indigenous languages in the United States are in danger of extinction. Frameworks for understanding why language death occurs, ways to combat language death, and reasons why people (other than the speakers of the language in question) might care about this threat are given. After a brief discussion which indicates that Aboriginal languages in Canada are in a similar position to those in the United States and for similar reasons, Fettes provides five ways in which Canadian Aboriginal languages are different from the powerful official languages of English and French, and then compares the impact of two recent and startlingly divergent approaches to language policy development for Aboriginal languages in the Yukon and Northwest Territories in light of the five distinctions.

Part III focuses on the law. Miner provides a comprehensive account of the actual outcomes in U.S. courts of "English-only" legislation now in place. From these data, she predicts that further federal and state legislation of this sort is likely to have only minor impact despite rhetoric surrounding their enactment. Magnet appeals more to the philosophy behind Canadian language legislation on English and French. Amid the tensions of conflict and the need for security, Canada has approached French and English relations from a position of binationality and duality. Magnet promotes the principles of duality and accommodation.

Educational perspectives is the theme of Part IV. Education is most often the public institution to which we turn when we manipulate the language situation in our country or local community. Wiley challenges myths surrounding the ways in which new immigrant groups have approached English as the dominant language in the United States, how they have been dealt with in different domains, and the effects on the multilingual reality within U.S. borders. Using the case of the German language in the United States in the earlier part of this century, Wiley shows examples of draconian policies to suppress German, especially through education. Besides closing the door on the value of linguistic diversity, he argues, forced assimilation is not a guarantee of equal participation in society. Burnaby demonstrates that immigrant adults who do not speak English are equally limited in their access to English as a second language (ESL) classes in Canada and the United States through uncoordinated, weak policies. She outlines the development of such policies in Canada in relation to federal official language and multicultural legislation, and makes comparisons between certain structures of government and legislation in the two countries that affect their strategies toward adult ESL.

# PREFACE

Although this theme runs strongly through the whole book, Part V offers a focus on context. Policy creation, implementation, and impact all exist within a social matrix that determines both the rationale for action and the outcomes. Veltman emphasizes the actual, social power of English in North America; that it also has symbolic power as an official language in Canada has little effect in protecting minorities or promoting conformity beyond that which exists. Language communities have mechanisms to subvert government action. Cartwright uses the case of an area in Canada on the border between French-dominant Quebec and the English-dominant regions to the west to show how official language legislation has influenced the course of events. A specific provincial strategy of gradual alignment with the federal legislation appears to have run into difficulties in the tension between pressures concerning French language status and real community needs for institutional support for intergenerational language maintenance. Ricento examines the question of the effects of bilingualism and multilingualism on nations by looking at studies of multilingual countries and at the Canadian situation. He argues that multilingualism in a country is not, in itself, a threat to national unity despite claims by "English-only" advocates, and that "English-only" legislation would have a negative impact on education, voting, public services, and government agencies.

We, the editors, express our deep gratitude to the authors who contributed chapters to this book. We greatly appreciate not only their excellent scholarship, extensive experience, and personal commitment to this project, but also their patience with us through all our delays and demands. It has been a pleasure developing and extending our acquaintance with each of them. The reviewers of the manuscript, Professor James Tollefson of The University of Washington, Seattle, and Professor Lee Gunderson of The University of British Columbia, Vancouver, provided us with many insightful and helpful suggestions, which we acknowledge with much appreciation. We would also like to thank our publisher, Lawrence Erlbaum Associates, and in particular Naomi Silverman whose interest in and support of this project is sincerely appreciated. Finally, we extend our heartfelt appreciation to our families and colleagues for their forbearance and support while we were preoccupied with bringing this project to fruition.

—*Thomas Ricento*
—*Barbara Burnaby*

# About the Authors

**Roderic Beaujot** is Professor of Sociology at the University of Western Ontario. He is Chair of the Advisory Committee on Demographic Statistics and Studies at Statistics Canada, Vice-President of the Federation of Canadian Demographers, and Secretary-Treasurer of the Canadian Population Society. He is the author of *Population Change in Canada: The Challenges of Policy Adaptation*, and co-author (with R. Beaujot, F. Rajulton, E. Gee, and Z. Ravanera) of *Family Over the Life Course*.

**Barbara Burnaby** is a professor in the Department of Curriculum, Teaching, and Learning at the Ontario Institute for Studies in Education of the University of Toronto. Her research and teaching areas include language training for adult immigrants, Aboriginal and official languages in education for Canadian Aboriginal peoples, and adult literacy. Her recent work includes "Literacy in Athapaskan Languages in the Northwest Territories, Canada: For What Purposes?" published in *Written Language and Literacy*; she is second editor (with M. Herriman) of *Language Policies in English Dominant Countries: Six Case Studies* and first editor (with A. Cumming) of *Socio-political Aspects of ESL in Canada*.

**Don Cartwright** is a professor in the Department of Geography at the University of Western Ontario, London, Canada. His areas of interest lie in social geography, ethnic conflict, and minority-language policy, and he has a number of publications in these areas. Before joining the faculty at Western he was Director of Research for the Bilingual Districts Advisory Board, Ottawa, Canada.

## ABOUT THE AUTHORS

**James Crawford**, former Washington editor of *Education Week*, is an independent writer specializing in language policy. His books include *Bilingual Education: History, Politics, Theory, and Practice*; *Hold Your Tongue: Bilingualism and the Politics of "English Only"*; and *Language Loyalties: A Source Book on the Official English Controversy*.

**Mark Fettes** is a doctoral student at the Ontario Institute for Studies in Education, University of Toronto. In recent years he has worked on language policy issues with the Assembly of First Nations, the Canadian Centre for Linguistic Rights, and the Center for Research and Documentation on World Language Problems. He is currently developing a theory of linguistic ecology to be used in formulating and evaluating language policies.

**Joseph Eliot Magnet** is a professor of law at the University of Ottawa. He has been Distinguished Visiting Professor at the University of California, Berkeley, Crown Counsel in Ottawa, and law clerk to the Chief Justice of the Canadian Supreme Court. He has litigated many language cases in the Supreme Court of Canada and advised Canadian governments and minority groups on language matters. He is the author of nine books and eighty scholarly articles.

**Susan Miner** holds a law degree from the University of California, Hastings College of Law, and has worked for the past 20 years as a staff attorney for the California Court of Appeal in San Francisco. In 1993 she earned a master's degree in linguistics from San Francisco State University.

**Thomas Ricento** is Associate Professor in the Division of Bicultural-Bilingual Studies, The University of Texas at San Antonio. He received his Ph.D. in Applied Linguistics from UCLA, and was a Fulbright scholar in Colombia, S.A., in 1989. His research interests are in the areas of language policy and the analysis of discourse. His recent work includes "Language Policy in the United States," for *Language Policies in English Dominant Countries: Six Case Studies*, edited by M. Herriman and B. Burnaby; he is also co-editor (with N. Hornberger) of a special topic issue of *TESOL Quarterly* (Language Planning and Policy).

**Ronald Schmidt, Sr.** is Professor of Political Science at California State University, Long Beach, where he teaches minority politics, political theory, and California politics. He has written and published numerous essays on Latino politics and the politics of language in the United States, and is

## ABOUT THE AUTHORS

completing a book manuscript tentatively titled *Cultural Pluralism and the Politics of Language in the United States*.

**Calvin Veltman** is Professor of Urban Studies at the University of Quebec in Montreal. A native of Chicago, he obtained a Ph.D. in sociology at New York University and has also taught in the SUNY and CUNY university systems. He teaches and does research in the areas of urban residential segregation, linguistic demography, and the language shift of immigrants in the United States and Canada, with particular attention to Quebec.

**Terrence G. Wiley**, Joint Professor of Linguistics and Education at California State University, Long Beach, specializes in language policy, literacy/biliteracy, multicultural/multilingual education, and social, philosophical, and historical foundations of education. His most recent book is *Literacy and Language Diversity in the United States*.

**Colin H. Williams** is Research Professor in Sociolinguistics in the Department of Welsh, The University of Wales, Cardiff, UK, and Honorary Professor in the Department of Geography, The University of Western Ontario, Canada. He has previously taught in universities in Canada, England, and the United States. His main scholarly interests include sociolinguistics and language policy in multicultural societies, ethnic and minority relations, and political geography.

# 1

# Introduction: Respecting the Citizens—Reflections on Language Policy in Canada and the United States

Colin H. Williams
*University of Wales, Cardiff*

A pressing issue all over the contemporary world is the recognition of the cultural worth of its inhabitants. Managing cultural diversity as a permanent feature of the international social order is among the most taxing of political issues. Having failed to control, if not always contain, intercultural conflict through traditional means, we are now searching for new means of social integration. New methods for tackling the old problem of intergroup tensions will have to look beyond the conventional academic disciplines and ideologies drawing on economics, psychology, and political science and seek to incorporate more poignant radical ideas and insights in a more syncretic manner. In this chapter I raise several issues of substance that inform the detailed, critical debate maintained by my colleagues elsewhere in this volume. Drawing on issues raised in the following chapters, I reflect here on managing classic immigrant societies, conceptualizations of nationhood, some dynamics in multicultural societies, the linguistic hegemony of English, principles of social justice, similarities and differences between Canada and the United States, and future possibilities for languages in those two countries. The most significant issue is the question of the distribution of power in society and the encouragement of democratic

1

participation by interest groups who hitherto have felt emasculated within the liberal state, despite the growth of what may be termed the politics of equal recognition in recent decades.

## MANAGING CLASSIC IMMIGRANT SOCIETIES

The foundation of any modern democracy is the ability of its citizens to derive maximum security and satisfaction from contributing to the common wealth of society. The great common wealth of Canada and the United States is the diversity of their peoples. In their attempt to forge a sociopolitical unity from the diversity of multiculturalism, the elite of both societies have been charged with the criticism that the state totality does not reflect the sum of its constituent parts. Hence the contemporary controversies in the United States on the recognition of the worth of, for example, African Americans, Asian Americans, Hispanic Americans, and Native Americans, and in Canada on the appropriate place for Quebecois and francophones, Native Canadians, and "heritage language" Canadians.

Historically these classic immigrant societies have allowed for instrumental pluralism as a societal norm because a broad measure of freedom from state interference provided the necessary breathing space for the peaceful coexistence of citizens. Habermas (1996) averred that such space permitted citizens of widely diverging cultural identities to be simultaneously both members and strangers of their own country. The reproduction of minority cultures was, in part, a function of relatively weak economic-structural assimilation. In time, however, a middle position between assimilation and pluralism came to be appreciated. Advocates of this position claimed that it was possible to participate in mainstream culture and maintain one's heritage language and culture (Edwards, 1985).

Those days are long gone for the majority of Canadians and Americans. Today democratic citizenship is under severe stress. Habermas (1996) argued that the safety curtain of civil religion, which has interpreted a constitutional history of 200 years, may be about to break. His contention was that "a liberal political culture can hold together multicultural societies only if democratic citizenship pays in terms not only of liberal and political rights, but of social and cultural rights as well" (p. 296). Nowhere are these rights so fiercely conjoined and attacked than in the question of ethno-linguistic identities in the modern state. How we promote the mutual respect of individuals as they identify with particular cultural groups is the key difficulty facing us as we grapple with the relationship between language, politics, and identity that is the central theme of this volume.

The challenge to liberal democracies is both real and very pressing for they are committed in principle to equal representation of all. Guttman

# 1. INTRODUCTION

(1992) has asked what equal representation means if public institutions do not recognize particular identities, but only allow for general or universal recognition of shared interests based upon civil and political liberties, education, health care and economic participation:

> Apart from ceding each of us the same rights as all other citizens, what does respecting people as equals entail? In what sense should our identities as men or women, African-Americans, Asian-Americans, or Native Americans, Christians, Jews, or Muslims, English or French Canadians publicly matter? (p. 4)

Public recognition of the worth of constituent cultures, as *permanent* entities in society, is what is at stake in liberal democracies. Indeed for many engaged in the politics of their group's survival, this is precisely what democracy should guarantee in praxis as well as in principle. This, for example, is the nub of the Quebecois argument to be treated as a distinct society, and not one among many provinces within Canada. In various ways it is the preoccupation of all struggling minorities within North America. However, we recognize with Guttman (1992) that "liberal democracy is suspicious of the demand to enlist politics in the preservation of separate group identities or the survival of subcultures that otherwise would not flourish through the free association of citizens" (p. 10). When it refuses to engage in the politics of recognition, liberal democracy appears arrogant and denies the life-enhancing spirit on which all forms of democracy are based. It accentuates fragmentation and anomie within society, ultimately leading to various forms of disengagement from public life and community responsibility. For:

> Democratic citizenship develops its force of social integration, that is to say it generates solidarity between strangers, if it can be recognized and appreciated as the very mechanism by which the legal and material infra-structure of actually preferred forms of life is secured. (Habermas, 1996, p. 290)

North American societies are still in the process of forging an identity that commands the loyalty of the overwhelming majority of citizens. This may seem an odd claim from an international perspective, for both Canada and the United States have virile, recognizable state identities. However, as this volume richly testifies, fundamental issues relating to questions of "national conformity" still animate the myriad political debates on language policy, bilingual education, the limits of tolerance toward the maintenance of a plural society, the reproduction of distinctive core "American" and "Canadian" values and the like.

Of course, such considerations are universal. What makes them critical and arresting within the North American context is the danger posed to democracy by the growth of a perception that citizens are being let down by the performance of the "hollow state" and that a democratic deficit rather than a democratic fulfillment characterizes contemporary politics.

The politics of recognition is a rather belated attempt to compensate for the systematic exclusion of so many groups from the decision-making structures of modern society. Until comparatively recently it was assumed that the clarification of the nature and meaning of minority rights would not overly interfere with mainstream political business and economic development, as witnessed in the impress of the founding peoples on the transformed land.

This mission/destiny view of coast-to-coast nationhood that contributed to the making of America and Canada was predicated on the hegemonic position of the majority nation, which was derived from two variants of a common British, largely English-speaking, political culture. Patriotism is a poor substitute for the initial nationalism of the founding fathers during the process of nation building. Thus we must ask:

> Under what conditions a liberal political culture shared by all citizens can at all substitute for that cultural context of a more or less homogenous nation in which democratic citizenship once, in the initial period of the nation-state, was embedded. (Habermas, 1996, p. 290)

## INCLUSIVE VERSUS EXCLUSIVE NATIONHOOD

Our conceptions of human rights have been formulated in an increasingly comprehensive manner to include elements that earlier theorists would have considered to have lain outside the pale of the citizen–state relationship. This relationship is central to the analysis because democracy avers that citizens are entitled to certain minimum rights, chiefly those of participation in and protection by the state. However, the changing nature of the state, both as ideology and praxis, has encouraged a more pluralist view of its responsibilities.

How do minority interest groups influence the state structure so that it concedes certain rights which are not requested by the majority? Such concessions may be in the field of bilingual education, the legal system, differentiated media and communication systems, or the use of a previously disallowed language within public administration. They may be predicated on the basis of a personality or a territoriality principle or some expedient admixture of both (Nelde, Labrie, & Williams, 1992).

The conventional view, held by many Western states until the early postwar period, was that the state should not discriminate against or in favor of particular subgroups, however they may be defined. This view, termed the *individual rights approach*, is often justified by majoritarian principles of equality of all before the law, and is implemented through policies of equal

# 1. INTRODUCTION

opportunity for socioeconomic advancement based on merit and application. In Europe it is most closely associated with the unwritten constitutional tradition of the British legal system and in North America it was the inspiration behind the rhetoric, if not always the reality, of the melting pot approach to ethnic relations. The fact that many states persistently discriminated, by law, against Jews/Catholics/Protestants and so on in most multifaith societies should never be marginalized in this discussion, for so often the state has exercised a malignant effect on minorities, thereby blighting their historical development. The partial improvement in the treatment of minorities and the resultant constructive dialogue between representatives of the various interest groups and governmental agencies at all levels in the political hierarchy of Europe obviously bodes well for the medium-term future enactment of minority rights.

This presupposes that the state is in some way responsive to the legitimacy of minority demands. Historically, the recognition of linguistic minority demands is a very recent phenomenon. In accordance with the resolutions of the European Parliament (Arfé, 1981; Killilea, 1994; Kuijpers, 1987) the European Commission since 1983 has supported action to protect and promote regional and minority languages and cultures within the European Union. In 1996 some 4 million ecus were expended on European sociocultural schemes (budget line B3-1006 of the European Union Directorate General for Education, Training, and Youth). Equally significant is that we have a raft of recent legislation and declarations upholding the rights of minorities to use their languages in several domains (Williams, 1993). However, linguistic minorities face many structural barriers to their full participation within the E.U. system.

An alternative view, the group rights approach, has found increasing favor of late, for it recognizes that there are permanent entities within society whose potential and expectations cannot be met by reference to the recognition of individual rights alone. In the main, such recognition is offered grudgingly, and reflects a minimalist stance that seeks to extend the individual rights tradition into a multicultural context. Such extensions tend to obscure the key issue of group tension, namely the ability of the minority to preserve, and if possible, develop its own group characteristics and desires, in the face of state inspired assimilation (Williams, 1986).

Glazer (1977) has shown that attempts to institute group rights, in such spheres as government, the civil service, university admission, and business, have already been introduced in as widely varying contexts as Belgium, Canada, Finland, India, and Malaysia. Such reforms have been deliberately aimed at ensuring minority group representation in key areas of social, political, and economic life. Yet in the United Kingdom the attempt to reserve places by a variant on the quota system, or through positive discrimination and affirmative action, have been generally resisted as a subversion of individual rights. Despite the growth in legally enforced particularism and exceptionalism, which recognizes that special circumstances can obtain in minority–majority relations, the general tendency is to play down the group rights approach for it smacks of poor integration in the modern state, where the dominant conformity thesis is paramount.

Two sorts of argument are posed to counter the "special pleading" of constituent differentiated groups in the contemporary world (Williams, 1993, p. 95). The first is well entrenched and argues that the prime duty of the democratic state is to treat all of its citizens equally, regardless of racial, national, ethnic, or linguistic origin. This has been the guiding principle of the American constitutional guarantee of citizen equality. However, even from its earliest days the constitution was subject to constant reinterpretation, as testified by Benjamin Franklin's admission while opening the Federal Convention of Philadelphia in 1787 when, with characteristic modesty and sagacity, he declared:

> I confess that there are several parts of this constitution which I do not at present approve, but I am not sure that I shall never approve them. For having lived long, I have experienced many instances of being obliged by better information, or fuller consideration, to change opinions even on important subjects, which I once thought right, but found to be otherwise. (Farrand, 1966, quoted in Beer, 1993, p. 392)

Of course there are those who hold that minorities should not need "extra rights" if the democratic guarantees are in place. For, as President Vaclav Havel (1991) of the Czech Republic reminded us:

> It seems to me that these collective rights can be accepted and included in the legal system only when we do not understand them as something beyond. As if there were some civil rights that are equal for everybody and then there are some special rights for some special groups of citizens which the others do not share. It is not the case. The right for freedom of speech, the fight to keep their individual culture, the right to education, all these are essential human and citizen rights and in the case of minorities, i.e., communities with their own traditions, spiritual, historic, social and with their own language background, can these general rights be ascertained when they are allowed to be exerted within that frame and in that environment that are genuine to them. And I think that these instrumental functions belong to the collective rights. (p. 15)

Havel's interpretation of democracy is understandable in a political context that stresses the role of the reformed state as the agent and coordinator of radical change, for the growth of democratic representative power in Central Europe enables the state to pose as the guardian of civic rights. Individualism strives to triumph over collectivism, in the matter of human rights as in social justice and economic productivity.

# 1. INTRODUCTION

However, as Phillips (1995) has commented in a different context (while discussing feminism and democracy), institutionalizing group representation appears to be at odds with the main thrust of democracy "which is typically away from group privilege and group representation, and towards an ideal of citizenship in which each individual counts equally as one" (p. 290). The real difficulty for such interpretations is in maintaining the active participation of all citizens in the resultant political process. It is far too tempting for many to yield responsibility and to opt out of formal politics and to opt into informal pressure groups or single-issue movements, leaving proponents of the community drained of their energies to mobilize and agitate on behalf of all.

Phillips (1995) has cautioned that "many contemporary radicals see the ideals of democracy as pointing towards a politics in which people transcend their localized and partial concerns, getting beyond the narrow materialism of special interest to address the needs of the community instead" (p. 290). This concern for an active participatory democracy is surely relevant in most developed societies, where talk of "the hollow state" and of "the democratic deficit" reveal the shallowness of the general public's trust in professional politicians (Williams, 1994).

A return to communitarian democracy has obvious attractions, according to Phillips (1995), when compared with:

> The damming complacancies of twentieth century pluralism, which argued that politics was and always would be a matter of competition between interest groups, and that democracy was sufficiently guaranteed by the chance for groups to compete. But it remains open to precisely the charge that is leveled against pluralism: insufficient attention to political equality. (p. 290)

Societies face two opposing notions of justice. One says that justice is the apportioning of rewards to groups on the basis of proportionality; the other suggests that justice should consider the established rights of individuals, regardless of national origin, language, religion, or any other diacritical cultural marker (Glazer, 1977). In an individualistic society the majority would favor merit as a guiding principle of selection. The various constituent minorities would counter, with some justification, that this merely reproduces their marginalized and pejorative position as a permanent dependency.

Are there thus any guiding principles that suggest which path to follow: whether to reduce discrimination by establishing quotas and preferential places to target-group members, or alternatively to focus on the right of the individual without regard to origin? Again Glazer (1977) is helpful here, for he has suggested it is the model of society the state upholds that determines the choice. If the state adopts a diffusion perspective of ethnic change, viewing group identities as malleable and group membership as a purely private affair, it will conceive of group rights as a barrier to minority assimilation and as a basis for maintaining permanent divisions within the state. However, if the state conceives of its constituent cultural groups as forming part of an established ethnically plural society, then it must legislate and act on what the rights of each group shall be (Williams, 1986).

It is too facile to rest content with either individualist or collectivist paradigms of language contact management. Rather than presume that there exists one universal solution to the question of managing ethnic pluralism, it is more instructive to draw attention to the sheer variety of assumptions about the nature of majority–minority relations inherent in models of ethnic integration. Drawing on Canadian evidence, Kallen (1995) has conceived four models (the melting pot of integration, the mosaic of cultural pluralism, the dominant conformity of absorption, and the paternalism of colonialism), that differentiate between exclusive and inclusive definitions of civil rights. The Western world is facing a period of readjustment following a series of structural transformations that cumulatively have seen a greater recognition being accorded to its indigenous minorities. But just as many autochthonous minorities are finally being treated according to policies predicated on pluralism on the basis of equality, so nonindigenous minorities are treated according to policies predicated on pluralism on the basis of nonequality. How do these two trends impact on each other in language matters?

## THE POLITICS OF EQUAL RESPECT
## IN MULTICULTURAL SOCIETIES

We have been exploring issues of power and social justice that will multiply as the world's states become simultaneously more multicultural, porous, and fragmented. But what sort of multiculturalism are we discussing, and how does it seek to promote the politics of mutual respect? Let us consider the difficulties of operating an ideology of multiculturalism within a model of liberal society that purports to recognize more than the mere survival of cultures by acknowledging their permanent worth.

The seminal work in this field is Taylor's (1992) essay "Multiculturalism and 'The Politics of Recognition.'" Professor Taylor argued that the politics of equal respect embodied within the discourse of recognition does not serve us as well as we imagine. This is because there is:

A form of the politics of equal respect, as enshrined in a liberalism of rights, that is inhospitable to difference, because (a) it insists on uniform application of the rules defining these rights, without exception, and (b) it is suspicious of collective goals.

# 1. INTRODUCTION

Taylor calls it inhospitable because:

> It can't accommodate what the members of distinct societies really aspire to, which is survival. This is (b) a collective goal, which (a) almost inevitably will call for some variations in the kinds of law we deem permissible from one cultural context to another, as the Quebec case clearly shows. (p. 61)

Clearly the dread hand of homogenization, what has come to be called the globalization/localism debate, can lie heavy on any attempt to maintain diversity through an appeal to universal considerations of human dignity and worth. But the filter process by which some decide the relative worth of others is far too imperfect. At its root there is an inherent paradox between the demands for equality and forces for efficiency.

Taylor (1992) argued that the demand for equal recognition is unacceptable. Rather, what we need is a more humble approach that does not imply the pejorativization of all other cultures. It requires "an admission that we are very far away from that ultimate horizon from which the relative worth of different cultures might be evident" (p. 73). This, of course, presumes that cultural diversity is a positive and growing feature of most societies. It has value, not only at the individual level of recognizing human worth, but also at a societal level as legitimizing access to political power and free participation in the democratic process. It follows that the ways of managing cultural diversity will vary according to why we think it has value.

However, a great stumbling block in the recognition of equal worth is the operation of the market and bureaucratic state which in Taylor's (1991) view "tends to strengthen the enframings that favor an atomist and instrumentalist stance to the world and others" (p. 11). Community solidarity and public participation in the decision-making process are weakened and ethnolinguistic groupings, for example, are drawn closer into their own subcultures rather than forming a distinct part of the whole society:

> This fragmentation comes about partly through a weakening of the bonds of sympathy, partly in a self-feeding way, through the failure of democratic initiative itself. Because the more fragmented a democratic electorate is in this sense, the more they transfer their political energies to promoting their partial groupings, and the less possible it is to mobilize democratic majorities around commonly understood program. (p. 113).

Fragmentation and anomie seem to be winning the day for far too many previously committed citizens. And yet they all have, in principle, the right of free association, free speech, and political representation, the hallmarks of a modern democracy:

> A society in which this goes on is hardly a despotism. But the growth of these two facets is connected, part effect and part cause, with the atrophy of a third, which

is the formation of democratic majorities around meaningful programs that can be carried to completion. In this regard, the American political scene is abysmal. (p. 115)

How are these sociopolitical forces played out in linguistic terms and with what consequence for policy and citizenship? We can best address these issues by reference to the place of English within North American society.

## LINGUISTIC HEGEMONY: THE LINGUISTIC IMPERIALISM OF ENGLISH

At the heart of the current debate on the nature of American identity lies a consideration of the official place of the English language as both a symbol and an instrument of American nationhood and state-inspired nationalism. Critics of English as an instrument of imperialism and modernization claim that the spread of English perpetuates an unequal relationship between "developed" and "developing" societies because access to information and power does not depend solely on language fluency. It also depends on institutional structures, economic resources, and relationships. Tollefson (1991) illustrated this need to take account of infrastructural investment when he reminded us that:

> In order to gain access to English-language resources, nations must develop the necessary institutions, such as research and development offices, "think tanks" research universities, and corporations, as well as ties to institutions that control scientific and technological information. From the perspective of "modernizing" countries, the process of modernization entails opening their institutions to direct influence and control by countries that dominate scientific and technical information ... the result is an unequal relationship. (p. 84)

The spread of English is also deeply implicated in the creation of new forms of inequality within societies. Most postcolonial societies are characterized by a dual institutional system, which nevertheless present different ranges of opportunities to their respective members in the conventional and modernized sectors.

In a powerful critique of the role of ELT (English Language Teaching), Phillipson (1992) has demonstrated how arguments used to promote English can be classified into three types, based on the language's:

1. Capacities: English-intrinsic arguments, what English *is*.
2. Resources: English-extrinsic arguments, what English *has*.
3. Uses: English-functional arguments, what English *does*. (p. 270)

# 1. INTRODUCTION

Each element is mediated by the structure of the world order in which English is dominant and each develops its own discourse which locates English vis à vis competing languages. Thus:

English-intrinsic arguments describe English as rich, varied, noble, well adapted for change, interesting, etc. English-extrinsic arguments refer to textbooks, dictionaries, grammar books, a rich literature, trained teachers, experts, etc. English-functional arguments credit English with real or potential access to modernization, science, technology, etc.; with the capacity to unite people within a country and across nations, or with the furthering of international understanding. (pp. 271–272).

The functions of English are nearly always described in positive terms. Whether the arguments for its extension are couched in terms of persuasion, promise or threat, they represent various ways of exerting and legitimating power. This was well understood during colonial times and postcolonially in more subtle, sophisticated ways as is demonstrated in the rhetoric of the British Council. When the British:

Do not have the power we once had to impose our will ("sticks"), cultural diplomacy must see to it that people see the benefits of English ("carrots") and the drawbacks with their own languages, and then, consequently, want English themselves for their own benefit ("ideas"): "the demand is insatiable." And that means that British influence, British power has not diminished, because Britain has this "invisible, God-given asset." Thus "Britain's influence endures, out of all proportion to her economic or military resources." (British Council Annual Report, 1983–1984, p. 9, quoted in Phillipson, 1992, pp. 286–287)

France's "mission to civilize" strategy is a variant on this theme.

Language, and the ideology it conveys, is thus part of the legitimization of positions within the global division of labor. Attempts to separate English from its British and North American value system are misguided, for English should not be interpreted as if it were primarily a tabula rasa. Any claim that English is now a neutral, pragmatic tool for global development is disingenuous because it:

Is part of the rationalization process whereby the unequal power relations between English and other languages are explained and legitimated. It fits into the familiar linguistic pattern of the dominant language creating an external image of itself, other languages being devalued and the relationship between the two rationalized in favor of the dominant language. (Phillipson, 1992, p. 288)

The rise of the Official English movement within the United States is but the latest evidence of a deep-seated tendency to deal with linguistic pluralism by privileging one language as the *only* legitimate language of governance. Miner's discussion in chapter 7 of this volume of the legal implications of the Official English declaration demonstrates how discussions about language policy go to the heart of the debate on what constitutes contemporary American society. Attempts to challenge the hegemony of English by insisting on the right to express oneself publicly in another language and to receive official communications in a language other than English are destined to grow. The state's reaction to such challenges will be a significant test of the extent to which it believes it needs to declare whether or not the English language should be a matter of "official language" legislation. In either case so deeply ingrained is the presumption of unilingual efficiency that it becomes reproduced as a common sense solution, as described by Tollefson (1991):

> The policy of requiring everyone to learn a single dominant language is widely seen as a common-sense solution to the communication problems of multilingual societies. The appeal of this assumption is such that monolingualism is seen as a solution to linguistic inequality. If linguistic minorities learn the dominant languages, so the argument goes, then they will not suffer economic and social inequality. The assumption is an example of an ideology which refers to normally unconscious assumptions that come to be seen as common sense … such assumptions justify exclusionary policies and sustain inequality. (p. 10)

Whether in linguistic affairs or in religious belief systems, common sense explanations so often turn out to make "uncommon sense" (Rogers, 1992), especially to those at the bottom of the pile for whom liberal theories of empowerment through bilingual education programs herald assimilation not integration. In this volume, Schmidt (chapter 2) and Ricento (chapter 4, 13, and 14) trace the growing gap between pluralists and assimilationists who focus on the trigger factor of the English-only campaign but derive their enormous political charge from the precondition of racism and attitudes toward immigration. Ricento recognizes the crux of the debate as stemming from the *deep* level of American national attitudes to language and ethnicity and the *shallow* level of declared public policy. Although this is a useful heuristic distinction, it does not fully capture the inherent antipathy that organized minorities demonstrate toward the hegemonic powers. Schmidt illustrated this when he averred that oppressed minorities, such as Latinos, will seek to reduce structural discrimination by resisting English-only policies and demanding separate status like many francophones in Quebec. This is a modern echo of the civil rights turn of Black Separatists in the 1960s who wished to establish an alternative sociopolitical reality. However, neither the English-only advocates nor the linguistic separatists have a monopoly on truth in interpreting the language issues we are discussing in this volume. Thus the blurring of categorical boundaries through the interpenetration of ethnic and state-wide influences require hybrid and multipolar solutions to language-related conflict.

# 1. INTRODUCTION

Although not wishing to downplay the inherent divisions in American and Canadian society I remain uncomfortable with the underlying assumption that separate sociolinguistic logics can be readily identified and manipulated as if they were incompatible logics of social organization. I am more keen to question the relevance of a state-inspired philosophy for social control based on the recognition of the permanent worth of constituent ethnolinguistic groups. Inherent in this question are the issues of empowerment and social justice.

## PRINCIPLES OF SOCIAL JUSTICE

Several authors in this volume, particularly Burnaby (chapters 10 and 14), Ricento (chapters 4, 13, and 14), and Wiley (chapter 9), are concerned with the moral and political implications of language policy as it effects governmental attitudes and social justice. But it is Crawford (chapter 6) who constructs an eloquent and effective appeal to a higher morality in defense of language variety when he writes:

> We should care about preventing the extinction of languages because of the human costs to those most directly affected ... after all, language death does not happen in privileged communities. It happens to the dispossessed and disempowered, peoples who most need their cultural resources to survive. (p. 163)

Principles of social justice suggest it is desirable that governments accord more recognition to the preferred language choice of their constituent citizens. Principles of state economy suggest that this desire is increasingly conditional on the balance of forces ranged against the advocates of linguistic uniformity. The dilemma facing the United States is aptly summarized thus:

> In multilingual/multicultural societies throughout the world, governments have been forced to come to grips with the difficult task of balancing the interests of the state with the rights of individuals to learn and appreciate their native tongues and cultures, while at the same time being educated in their native, regional and/or national language, and even in a language of wider communication. In the United States, the unreasonable and unfounded fear that linguistic pluralism will weaken national unity may lead to the adoption of policies—language restrictionism, enforced monolingualism in education and voting etc.—that are most likely to promote the disunity that Americans fear. (Ricento, 1996, p. 154)

In tackling both the underlying fears and language-related aspirations of the would-be reformers we need to ask a further set of questions:

1. What are the key needs for language development in the United States and Canada?

2. Whose interests are served in language development?
3. To what extent is democracy undermined by the unsatisfied aspirations of threatened language groups?
4. Are "OLS" (Other Language Speakers) considered as competitors in the crowded arena of minority rights?
5. Are the nonterritorial claims of "OLS" groups sufficiently well developed to have a sociospatial impact in local services and public provision?
6. What is the role of language in education for the adequate rendering of social services? How does one avoid creating a demand for particular languages at the expense of others?
7. What are the different critical masses required for particular services/classes/liaison?
8. In considering various levels of governmental recognition of language needs, in which domains are there well-recognized multicultural rights, in which are differentiated service provision still a privilege, and in which are there unlikely to be any progress whatsoever?
9. How do the central agencies of social reproduction, such as the law, education, and health, relate both to the increased demands of a plural society and strive to satisfy such demands within a predominantly bicultural and bilingual society?
10. How can the historical effects of structural assimilation be mediated so as to allow for a more egalitarian conception of linguistic pluralism?

Until we have adequate answers to these questions it will be extremely difficult to reconcile the differential demands that various interest groups have placed on the American system. Pessimists argue that there is little real chance for the reconciliation of starkly contrasting ethnolinguistic groups. Conflict is inherent in the situation and, far from encouraging the positive aspects of cultural pluralism, the history of American bilingual and multicultural education has been a history of mutual antagonism, begrudging reforms, and geographical ghettoization where spatial segregation and social isolation have become mutually reinforcing patterns in far too many residential communities.

More encouraging signs are detected by experts in comparative bilingualism, such as Baker (1996), who predicted that the outcome of increased awareness of American cultural diversity will mean that "total assimilation and total isolation are less likely than some accommodation of the majority ideology within an overall ideology of pluralism; cultural maintenance within partial assimilation" (p. 378). He based this view on a close reading of the vicissitudes of American bilingual education. He argued that bilin-

# 1. INTRODUCTION                                                                      15

gual education here has gone through four overlapping periods, which began with the permissive period, up until World War I, when society demonstrated an openness to in-migrant languages and, as long as the educational policy was localized in specific districts, the language of instruction did not necessarily figure as an issue in educational provision, as Wiley details later in relation to the experience of German-speaking children in Nebraska's parochial schools as late as December 1917 when *all* foreign languages—not just German—were banned in Nebraska.

However, during the first two decades of this century a profound change in the country's attitudes toward bilingual education overtook America, and heralded Baker's (1996) second phase, namely the restrictive period that lasted up until the 1960s, but resonates even today. This period's antipathy toward bilingual education was triggered by the United State's entry into World War I and the spread of anti-German sentiments that nurtured the melting pot policy which was to be achieved primarily through monolingual education. Wiley's (chapter 9, this volume) carefully argued and clearly documented explication of this episode for the fate of German in North America is a very tangible reminder of the *domestication* of the ethnic-American imagination and soul. It also bears testimony to the diminution of the American spirit by the forced contrivance of the specter of so-called native vulnerability, surely one of the greatest myths to be perpetuated in the modern world!

The third phase was a period of opportunity, which needs to be contextualized in the light of massive social change, best represented by the civil rights movement and its effects on popular consciousness, the development of policies of equal opportunities, and the recognition of race as a factor in American public life. Sundquist (1993) has termed this the tripartite transition of "Slavery, Revolution, Renaissance" where Black literature has shaped the consciousness of cultural identity and familiar patterns of social existence have had to be reconceptualized as reality outpacing the critical imagination of social reformers. Most importantly, Baker (1996) argued that it was during this period that the right to equal opportunity for language minorities was asserted. This took the form of developmental maintenance, bilingual education, and ethnic community mother tongue schools.

The fourth phase was the dismissive period under the Reagan administration that was "particularly hostile to bilingual education" (Baker, 1996, p. 170). It is important to note that although these periods have been used as representative categorical types, the process of bilingual education is always subject to change and dynamic tension. At times restrictive, at others permissive, the opportunities for advancement are epiphenomenal.

Specialists in multiculturalism such as Baker (1996) and Edwards (1985) took great pains to stress the role that educational agencies can play in promoting language awareness programs. Baker suggested that the assumptions of multicultural education include:

1. There is a fundamental equality of all individuals and all minority groups irrespective of language and culture.
2. In a democracy, there should be equality of opportunity irrespective of ethnic, cultural, or linguistic origins.
3. Any manifest or latent form of discrimination by the dominant group against minorities requires elimination.
4. A culturally diverse society should avoid racism and ethnocentrism.
5. While generalizations about cultural behavior may be a natural part of humans making sense of their world, cultural stereotypes are to be avoided.
6. Minority cultural groups in particular need awareness of their culture as a precondition and foundation for building on intercultural awareness.
7. In mainstream monocultural education, language minority parents tend to be excluded from participation in their children's education. In multicultural education parents should become partners.
8. A pluralist integration is established by interaction and not a mosaic, by intermingling and a discovery of others to improve mutual understanding, break down stereotypes, while increasing self-knowledge and self-esteem. (p. 379)

Whether we term such programs multicultural education, citizenship education, or education for cultural pluralism, it is obvious that much of the curriculum and social justification for the promotion or denial of such programs is determined by the prevailing political ideology of the dominant group. In that respect, the United States and Canada have quite different agendas regarding how to manage the central question of honoring pluralism on the basis of equality in society. Let us turn therefore to an examination of how Canada has sought to reconcile several of these preceding issues we have been discussing through a recognition of a group-rights approach to bilingualism and linguistic pluralism.

## CANADIAN MULTICULTURALISM

Having labored for so long under the misapprehension that Canada would evolve toward an amalgam of the British and American social systems, during the early 1960s the Canadian federal government recognized the profound need to create an organic, original basis for Canadian statehood and society. In an attempt to reestablish a more flexible and comprehensive

## 1. INTRODUCTION 17

basis for statehood, the federal government constructed a contemporary official culture that celebrated "unity out of ethnic diversity." On October 8, 1971, then-Prime Minister Trudeau announced that multiculturalism was to become the official government policy. This top-down forging of national identity was based on the institutionalization of multiculturalism that took the form of constitutional reform and the creation of state agencies as, for example, the Canadian Consultative Council on Multiculturalism (1973), the Constitution Act of 1982 together with the Charter of Rights and Freedoms, and the Canadian Multiculturalism Act of 1988.

Multiculturalism, the new national myth and program, was used by the federal government and its supporters as a means of uniting the country and giving it a renewed sense of purpose. In so doing, it sought to challenge the compact theory of state formation as the basis for social unity and intergroup cooperation. Although unlikely to replace the compact theory so long as Quebec remains within the federation, the ideology of cultural pluralism promises to be far more than a symbolic gesture to Canadian progress and evolution. It is also a means by which the central government can advance specific long-term goals and political strategies.

Detractors argue that the multiculturalism policy was an inadequate instrument through which the differences between the two "charter" groups could be rescued from the structural difficulties inherent in the compact theory of government. It asked more questions than it resolved by undermining Quebec's position within Confederation and leaving English Canada perplexed as to its own role and integrity. Critics ridiculed the initiative in the light of Canada's mainly British and French past and overwhelmingly American present, for the new, distinctive face of Canada *was* its government programs and institutions, its multicultural presses and ethnic interest groups, its forced cultural invention, and federalist elite interventionism. If you attacked those, you attacked Canada itself.

The federalist position that the fundamental rights of francophone citizens were best guaranteed within Confederation was given full force under Trudeau's federally inspired and financed policy of bilingualism and multiculturalism. However, the policy provoked a severe backlash in Quebec, where it was emphatically rejected by both the provincial Liberal Party and the Parti Québeçois. Quebec's shift toward territorial unilingualism and a *culture de convergence* was perhaps inevitable given the array of forces ranged against the preservation of a distinctly francophone social order in North America.

A counterresponse, especially strong in the Western provinces, argued that having attempted to appease the French Canadian demands by instituting coast-to-coast bilingualism, the government had in fact reopened the very question it had sought to solve—namely, the essential distinctive nature of Canadian national identity. Its answer was to develop multiculturalism in reaction to hostile responses. In effect multiculturalism was a trade-off against bilingualism for the East.

Recognizing that earlier social paradigms—such as the dual nation theory, the Anglo-conformist hegemony, and the "Bilingual and Bicultural" initiative—had all failed, multiculturalism was proclaimed as having been the "true nature" of Canadian society all along. Revisionists argued that the country had always been an amalgam of disparate groups comprising, among others, the First Nations, the Acadian/Bretons, the Celts, the Germans, the Ukrainians, and the Chinese. The early 20th-century preoccupation with the fusion of Ukrainian, Italian, and German peoples with the "original British and French stock" was but the working out of a multicultural adjustment free from governmental interference. However, for these and all subsequent settlers of non-French, non-English origin it was not their existence that was in doubt, but their relative sociopolitical significance for state formation. Is it too fanciful to suggest that the same distinction holds true today? No one doubts the accuracy of multiculturalism as a *description* of the main current of Canadian society; what is in doubt is what this means in terms of real power to construct a satisfactory framework for policy and as the basis for statehood and full, participative citizenship.

It is claimed that multiculturalism serves as a popular, inclusive, official ideology whereby ethnic, racial, and regional variation can be managed. And yet, unlike earlier ideologies, multiculturalism has no implicit economic mandate, at least not one that is necessarily threatening. At its simplest it is essentially an expression of goodwill and democratic intent, devoid of particular fiscal or regional development implications. Some might argue that multiculturalism also lacks a political mandate—excepting one that subtly reinforces the status quo division of power.

Edwards (1994) argued that attempts to resolve this collectivist/individualist impasse are doomed because they fail to appreciate that the limitations on bilingualism "lie in the structure of Canadian society itself rather than with the policy *per se*" (p. 67; see also McRoberts, 1990).

However, other critics argue that multiculturalism has little real purchase in explaining Canadian history, let alone in regulating its future. McAll (1990), for example, suggested that "while multiculturalism sets out to reinterpret history, therefore, history makes a mockery of multiculturalism" (p. 169). He argued that this is because most nonanglophone, non-British groups have:

> Quietly gone the way of assimilation to the dominant Anglo-Canadian cultural group. Even the most culturally resilient of later immigrant groups, the Ukrainians, has seen facility in the Ukrainian language decline from 92 per cent in 1921 to

# 1. INTRODUCTION

less than 50 per cent in 1971, with a much smaller percentage of the third generation now being able to speak the language. (p. 169)

Similarly, Wilson (1993) discussed a variety of views which coalesce around the notion that the preservation of "symbolic ethnicity ... provides an appearance of democratic pluralism but is in reality a racist policy of assimilation at best and exclusion at worst" (p. 656). Many of the criticisms leveled at multiculturalism, he argued, are exactly those raised against the maintenance of ethnicity as a social category (viz., dual loyalty, the creation of permanent ethnic ghettos, and the handicapping of immigrants in their attempt to learn English or French so as to become economically more useful within the labor market). To artificially perpetuate cultural diversity at the expense of social equality and integration is to deflect attention away from the real centers of decision making and economic power of capitalism in Canada that are still firmly entrenched within establishment networks. "All of this tends to suggest that the ideology of multiculturalism, whether in Canada or elsewhere, is not so much the incubator of a new world as one of the artificial lungs that keeps the old world going" (McAll, 1990, p. 178).

An excellent critique of multiculturalism that involves an examination of the implementation of government policy may be found in Fleras and Elliott (1992). They address four types of criticism that conceive of multiculturalism as (a) socially divisive, (b) regressive, (c) decorative, and (d) impractical. They conclude that much of this criticism is outdated and misinterprets what multiculturalism seeks to achieve. Those who mischievously construe it as a policy that "pays people to maintain their culture and divide Canada" have failed to grasp its role as an instrument to enable immigrants to come to terms with a new environment, to combat racism, and to promote civil liberty and social justice.

Does this imply that Canada will become the first postmodern, multicultural state of the 21st century? For the optimist this emphasis on fluidity, flexibility, accommodation, openness, and diversity is an expression of a highly developed pluralist society that demands *mutual respect and tolerance of its constituent cultures as a structural norm*. To the pessimist such openness is a recipe for continued strife, interregional dislocation, inefficient federalism, and the artificial reproduction of often aggregate cultural identities that deflect attention away from more pertinent social categories. Rather than being a springboard for action, such a conception is seen as an open prison that will hamper the *unfettered development of the individual in a free and burgeoning society*. This is because we are still left with the basic four forces that reflect different sources of political ambition. Russell (1991, 1992) discussed them in terms of Quebec nationalism, aboriginal selfgovernment, regional alienation, and Canadian nationalism. Any attempt to reconcile such disparate challenges requires Herculean stamina.

However, others see hope in a transformed and more thoroughgoing conception of institutional multiculturalism:

> Institutional accommodation to diversity is an idea and practice whose time has come, in light of Canada's multicultural reality. Multiculturalism is no longer about celebrating cultural diversity and intercultural sharing, although many Canadians appear comfortable in limiting it to those roles. ... Multiculturalism is about institutional accommodation and removal of discriminatory barriers that interfere with the integration of minorities into the mainstream. (Fleras & Elliott, 1992, p. 143)

Clearly the goal is not simply to facilitate integration into the mainstream, but to alter what constitutes the mainstream so that the barriers are removed. According to this construction multiculturalism has a very definite political agenda, namely to reconstitute the basis of Canadian statehood.

Despite the fact that elite accommodation has lost ground to a more participatory form of constitution making following the Meech Lake experience and more recent rounds of Canada-making discussions and votes, citizens still face two dangers inherent in the promotion of the multicultural framework. One is cultural dependency and the other is the democratic deficit.

The basic issue relates to the relative autonomy of constituent groups within a policy of multiculturalism. What started as an attempt to celebrate a common Western heritage now has to adjust to the reality of managing divergence in a multiracial society. How vibrant are Canada's constituent cultures? How dependent are they on official patronage? Are they self-sustaining, or are many perpetuating a generation-specific conception of a subculture subsidized by public coffers? Clearly such questions are limiting, but they do draw attention to the dualistic relationship of culture and the modern state. Most minority cultures and languages are increasingly dependent on the state for legitimizing their access to the media, for granting them permission to establish bilingual or religious schools, for upholding in law several of their key fundamental values and principles.

These foci structure the conditions of possibility whereby any language or cultural manifestation may be used in extended domains, and determine the issue of who constructs and shapes the rules that govern language choice. For any specific ethnolinguistic group the following questions are worth asking, although I recognize that they are impossible to answer in any systematic manner. They are worth asking because they point up both the direction of change and the determinants of political power, responsibility, and citizenship rights in Canada:

1. Who shapes the rules of language use and choice?

# 1. INTRODUCTION
21

2. Are these rules fixed and immutable within a "national" bilingual framework, or are other regionally specific options permissible?
3. Who determines the level of public support expended on language maintenance?
4. Who determines the rights and obligations of local, provincial, and federal administrations in establishing relevant multilingual contexts?

Clearly the answers to these questions depend upon a recognition that individuals per se exercising private choice or public rights are incapable of sustaining the infrastructure necessary to support contemporary cultures. It may have been true that, up until circa 1971, voluntary collective action together with autonomous social institutions, such as the Church or an ethnic press, were the cornerstone of any widespread cultural reproduction. Canada is replete with complex and fascinating cameos of ethnic survival, despite the odds. Witness the vicissitudes of the Acadians (Griffiths, 1992; Griffiths & Rawlyk, 1991; Ross & Deveau, 1992), the long-term suffering of the Mennonites (Fretz, 1989; Loewen, 1993) or the application of the Ukrainians (Marunchak, 1970; Woycenko, 1967). It is much harder to sketch successful cameos of First Nation Canadians, although fresh opportunities to develop new identities have been created by the constitutional reform process from the early 1980s onward (Krosenbrink-Gelissen, 1996).

However, when language and the culture it represents becomes institutionalized in new domains via new agencies, such reforms by their very nature change the relationship between the individual and the state, at both federal and local levels. Thus new answers to old questions must focus on the partnership between citizens and government agencies, at whatever level in the hierarchy. Power for enfranchisement is the key to how successful such a partnership will be in serving the needs and expectations of a multicultural society.

But what is the appropriate focus for collective action and social change? McAll (1990) has drawn attention to a basic issue. Should ethnic diversity rather than social inequality be the focus of interest? A multicultural perspective leads one to search for ethnic/cultural interpretations even when there are few determining differences explicable on the basis of ethnicity alone, but many on the basis of economic position. When we move from rhetoric to detailed application, the multicultural framework is being overworked. It may flatter only to deceive.

It may be that McAll underestimated the extent to which reality can be socially constructed. Canada's broad understanding of multiculturalism as a basis for social policy may come to be embraced for more mundane and instrumental reasons as a result of two structural shifts. The first is an increased commercial and trade orientation of the country, whereas the second is a switch from a collectivist to a private rationale.

Fleras and Elliott (1992) commented that initiatives in the 1990s have resulted in a shift away from culture retention and toward the political and commercial exploitation of multiculturalism. They cited as evidence the fact that political authorities have "funded ethnically based commercial ventures at home and abroad rather than simply doling out lump sums of money as in the past to ethnocultural organizations, events, or symbols" (p. 98). Evidence of this shift in commitment was given by Prime Minister Brian Mulroney in his speech at the Multiculturalism Means Business conference in 1986 in Toronto when he stated:

> We, as a nation, need to grasp the opportunity afforded to us by our multicultural identity, to cement our prosperity with trade and investment links the world over and with a renewed entrepreneurial spirit at home ... In a competitive world, we all know that technology, productivity, quality, marketing and price determine export success. But our multicultural nature gives us an edge in selling to that world ... Canadians who have cultural links to other parts of the globe, who have business contacts elsewhere are of the utmost importance to our trade and investment strategy. (Secretary of State, Canada, 1987, quoted in Fleras & Elliott, 1992, p. 98)

From this conception, multiculturalism is a renewable resource. In the globalization/localism debate, Canada can use its heritage as a bridge to other markets worldwide. From the Canadian government's perspective the message is clear; multiculturalism is not only about preserving cultures and improving race relations, it is also about extending trade relations, about employment, about science and technology, global linkage, and yes, even the maintenance of peace and security (Fleras & Elliott, 1992). The subtext is that this version of multiculturalism is also about further differentiating the country from the American mirror held up to Canadian society.

The difficulty is in determining what proportion of the public purse is to be expended on satisfying the legitimate demands of this policy. Dependent cultures are tied inexorably to the largesse of the state. It is the exception rather than the rule for groups to be able to benefit from a large measure of private finance and hence private control so as to further their interests in domains such as education and language planning. Therefore those groups who are at the bottom of the pile now will be further disadvantaged by this switch to private enterprise. Government programs to aid recent refugees notwithstanding, there are severe difficulties in assuming that the private sector will take up the slack of state largesse. For the moment the government is obliged to maintain its support for many multicultural projects

# 1. INTRODUCTION

while simultaneously signaling its intent to withdraw public finances and welcome private sector funding.

An additional criticism is that the multiculturalism policy is narrowly focused, largely Occidental in its infrastructural support, and constitutes one of the social forces marginalizing minority arts and cultures in Canada. Li's (1994) analysis of the art world suggests that Canada's art and multicultural policies reflect and support an Occidental cultural hegemony. In a telling criticism he averred:

> If primordial culture is at work here, it is only in a most remote sense in providing visible minorities with an ancient past and a museum culture from which minority artifacts can be selectively revived to suit the social needs and the political requirements of the time, under the legitimacy of the dominant culture. (p. 385)

Such cultural straightjacketing is a commonly voiced criticism of hegemonic infrastructures as widely variant as Swedish intervention in Lapland, British Council policy in Africa, and French attitudes toward Polynesian cultural reproduction. Either way the language and culture of visible minorities are in danger of being expropriated by external forces and cultural dependency is increased.

However, Canada is also witnessing an increase in mixed marriages, in social and residential mobility, and in the opting out of "given" cultures and the creation of "new" social formations, part of what Rosenau (1993) has described as triumphant subgroups that are "founded on a goal—greater autonomy—that may not be readily met by the accomplishment of a legal status and, thus, needs to be continuously serviced" (p. 77). In most instances the drift toward single-issue politics and fragmentation may not be adequately captured through conventional theorizing and systems based around the grand ideas of the 19th century. This is why much of the earlier discussion centered on Taylor's (1991, 1992) critique of democratic involvement within divided societies is so timely and urgent.

We have already noted that there are clear signs that Canada is moving from a collectivist to an individualist (or private American) conception of social order. This is perceived as a dilution of the commitment to the welfare state and suggests greater disparity between "haves" and "have nots." The individualist emphasis favors the erosion of state intervention in many aspects of socioeconomic life. The keywords of *this* democratic order are initiative, venture, partnership, and flexible accommodation to the global–local nexus. From this perspective identity is not a given; it cannot be taken for granted; it is to be negotiated and reconstructed within each generation. It never *is*, it is always in a state of *becoming*, to paraphrase Heidegger. Similarly, culture has become a commodity to be assessed, priced, served, and repackaged to suit the exigencies of each situation. The competing claims of cultural groups to public recognition and resourcing are increasingly being heard and adjudicated by appointed, nonelected political servants (Williams, 1996).

Clearly the state is deeply implicated also in the direction of change with regard to multicultural policy; as Burnaby (chapters 10 and 14, this volume) makes clear, the Canadian focus on training in official languages to immigrant adults to integrate them into the economy is now in straightened circumstances. As a consequence, the government is trying to find the means to withdraw from the financial implications of support and give back the matter to the provinces and the nongovernmental organizations. The sharp end of this focus is immigration. Any disputes about the presence of immigrants are concentrated on issues such as employment and racism; the profile on language training is low and the language per se is not an issue, only access to it via training is. Such considerations appear to side step the central obligation of the multicultural state to supply an adequate infrastructural support on which may be grafted the aspirations and legitimate expectations of the constituent groups, so that they may flourish because of, not despite, state intervention and sustenance.

Of course, these myriad policies have territorial considerations, and, as I have discussed elsewhere, the linchpin of any development in Canada is the role that the people of Quebec choose for themselves (Williams, 1996). The whole question of language, culture, and values has to be calibrated against what is happening in francophone/anglophone relations. As society becomes more plural, and social mobility increases, there is an increase in the tension between the functional provision of bilingual public services and the formal organization of territory-based authorities charged with such provision. This tension is exacerbated by steady immigration into fragile language areas, for it leads to language-related issues being publicly contested as each new domain is penetrated by the intrusive language group.

In this volume Cartwright (chapter 11) offers a very detailed example of this language contact situation with respect to contemporary Ontario, focusing on the implications of honoring the rights of francophone citizens in a predominantly anglophone society. This, not multiculturalism alone, is the pertinent linguistic reality of Canada. If Quebec becomes more detached from Canada, will this demand for bilingualism decline for all save the social and economic elite? Are we in danger of encouraging class fractions along linguistic lines all in the name of "national unity?"

An overconcern with linguistic categorization and the charting of demolinguistic trends can be dysfunctional and lead to a false impression of the abiding strength of ethnic identity as a social reality with meaning and purchase for everyday life. Critical in this obfuscation and myth perpetuation is that central instrument of Canadian social engineering, the quin-

# 1. INTRODUCTION 25

quennial census. Far from being a neutral instrument of record the census interpretations are used by government to signal key changes in the demolinguistic balance, and it is to independent scrutineers like Castonguay (1992, 1994) that we have to look to find out what is really happening in linguistic matters. In McAll's (1990) view, "These various critiques suggest that the Canadian census has created the impression of continuing multiple ethnic distinctiveness in non-francophone Canada when, in reality, the mosaic has long been subject to a process of melting down" (p. 174).

Traditionally, 80% of Canada's immigrants used to come from countries of European heritage; by 1991 almost 75% came from Asia, Africa, Latin America, and the Caribbean. Currently, Asian-born persons represent half of the immigrants who came to Canada between 1981 and 1991. At the current rate of demographic change the population will start to decline by the 2020s. To avert this contraction—and the accompanying decrease in the size of the economy—it is estimated that Canada needs to increase its population by 1% per annum, hence the federal government's projected immigration target of 250,000 migrants per annum since the end of the 1980s. However, during the first 5 years of this decade the actual immigration figure is approximately half the required total. The suspicion remains that this slow down is a calculated move on behalf of the federal government to appease a Canadian public that has become increasingly hostile toward certain "foreigners" as a result of structural economic difficulties occasioned by the recession(s) of the 1990s.

Coupled with this caution is a shift in emphasis within the federal department responsible for multiculturalism toward combating racism and educating the public in being far more sensitive to the demands of a plural society. The recent mass advertising and consciousness-raising campaign serves two purposes: It seeks to combat racism in a society that is already highly diverse, and it is preparing Canadians for the increase in diversity that will most certainly unfold in the next 20 years (Hopkins, personal communication, June 8, 1995).

Conventionally the concerns of "nonvisible minorities" in the past and visible minorities today are pragmatic and initially have to do with *freedoms from* such features as racism, exploitation, cultural marginalization, and systematic exclusion from the full benefits of citizenship. The resources of multicultural agencies are utilized as a means of redressing past grievances, and serve as a buffer between the subordinate and the dominant organizations and value system. This is essentially the social justice view of multiculturalism we discussed earlier whereby it offers some means of protection from discrimination.

However, as they become better organized, astute groups will press for a greater recognition of their cultural rights, over and above those already recognized, a drive we may call *freedoms to* enjoy such features as mutual respect, equitable employment, comprehensive education, individual choice, and empowerment to decide their lifestyle and future prospects as participative citizens. Multiculturalism, from this perspective, is a set of institutional opportunities for individual and group advancement in a competitive environment. In other words, it becomes a platform for social progress.

I have speculated elsewhere on the increased political and economic salience of Canadian citizens who wish to promote nonofficial state languages, such as Asian-derived languages (Williams, 1996). Among other things my analysis of the impact of Chinese immigrants anticipated the development of heightened tension between the demands of transnational liberalism, which postulates that within an expanding global market all constituent industries (regardless of "national origin") can compete, and geoeconomic discourses, which subscribe to a zero-sum view of economic competition, push for resource supply security, and favor state intervention to guide economic development.

One can well imagine a scenario where Atlantic Canada pushes for geoeconomic policies, whereas Pacific Canada practices transnational liberalism within which the elites of certain cultural groups are hailed as economic power brokers. Such wealth and influence will filter down into social, cultural, and ideological demands for the promotion for the whole of that group. This suggests not only the conventional intergroup tensions so redolent of multicultural societies, but a host of other fracture lines that reflect other aspects of cultural life such as religion, aesthetics, urban segregation and landscaping, popular art, and media representation. Clearly there are other pertinent questions that stand outside the multicultural perspective but have, nevertheless, real influence on intergroup relations. In this introduction I have concentrated on the ethnic/national basis of culture, but what of other bases such as gender, place, new social movements, ecological interests, religious affiliations, special interest groups? How does policy cope with these identities that are becoming more salient?

As multiculturalism is integral to all aspects of society one may be forgiven for speculating in a volume devoted to language policy whether this prevailing ideology is specific enough to inform public policy. Does it have a tendency to absorb all other identities into its own? Is it in danger of becoming a hegemonic paradigm thereby losing its purchase as a guide to action? At present the answer is probably "no," but multiculturalism may push things in this direction, especially when the validity of more flexible and temporary groups (or constituencies) is denied.

All of the aforementioned undergird the central issue of Canada's constitutional future. Russell (1992), in an exasperated tone, has warned:

# 1. INTRODUCTION

No other country in the world today has been engaged so intensively, so passionately, or for so long in searching for the constitutional conditions of its continuing unity. This inward navel-gazing has drained the creative energy of the leaders. It has frustrated, demoralized and, yes, even bored the people. It has undermined Canada's ability to deal with pressing political problems within and to respond to global opportunities without. Canadians simply cannot afford to let the great constitutional debate drag on interminably. It is time to bring it to an end. (p. 193)

In other words, he is asking Canada to settle down and learn to be comfortable with itself. This is not a viewpoint likely to be endorsed by many in Quebec or among the First Nations!

## CANADIAN–U.S. COMPARISONS

As Ricento makes clear in this volume (chapters 4, 13, and 14), the Canadian approach to bilingualism and language policy has been directed toward group rights rather than individual rights. Thus Canada has recognized cultural pluralism and linguistic duality, the latter of which is enshrined in the Charter of Rights and Freedoms. Canada's proactive approach to bilingualism and the promotion of group rights contrasts vividly with the United States, where language differences, by and large, are accepted but do not form the basis of social policy.

It is only when individual rights protected by the constitution are abrogated because of differences of language that remedies are applied as in respect to education policy, voting rights, translation, and government services for LEP (Limited English Proficiency) speakers. Thus in Ricento's interpretation, language in the United States is not viewed as a fundamental constitutional right, but bilingualism and bilingual services are a *means* by which fundamental rights are protected and enforced. At the root therefore is a basic distinction between Canada's perception of bilingualism and America's instrumental view that bilingualism is more often seen as a temporary adjunct to encourage structural assimilation.

## MEDIUM-TERM LANGUAGE TRENDS

Increased interdependence at the North American and global level implies more harmonization and integration for the already advantaged groups. In their attempt to make multiculturalism more accessible and supportive, long-quiescent minorities will be rebuffed as they seek to institutionalize their cultures. However, it is not necessarily a tale of decline and rejection, for there exist some opportunities to influence state and provincial legislatures and metropolitan political systems by appealing to or constructing developments that parallel those created elsewhere in Europe, South East

Asia, and Australasia, where new patterns of intergroup networking are emerging.

First, we have witnessed the emergence of English as the lingua franca of North America, if not of the world. This has caused other international languages such as French and Spanish to jockey for position within the political, educational, and commercial domains of selected territories. Fears over the current dominance of English are well placed. Technology reinforces its utility and the development of an international communication system so vital to commercial and financial transactions underpins its pivotal role as the link language.

Second, francophones have consolidated their position within Quebec and to a lesser extent within New Brunswick and still less within the bilingual belt of the Quebec/Ontario border region. Linguistic territorialization is now a fact of Canadian life, despite the hopes of the original framers of the "Bilingualism and Biculturalism" reforms. However, we should also recognize that there are other aspects to bilingualism which are not territorially manifested but are related to social class. It will be interesting to monitor how both territorial and nonterritorial aspects impact on each other in determining the size, character and location of the bilingual population.

Third, Hispanics are likely to gain greater recognition as an *indigenous* language group in respect of their relative demographic weight, political acumen and contribution to the socioeconomic development of the United States. If Spanish can be seen as a resource for sociocultural growth as well as commercial gain, then as Baker (1996) suggested, national unity and linguistic diversity can coexist. There could be a win–win situation rather than a zero-sum standoff between supporters of English and those of Hispanic-based bilingualism. There is no doubt, however, that the vicissitudes of Spanish will be an important test of the rigors of multicultural democracy in the coming generations.

Fourth, speakers of autochthonous languages in both the United States and Canada, such as the Inuit, the Naskapi, and the Cree, will be further marginalized unless they can significantly influence the patterns of stable bilingualism with a much-reduced language switching in new domains than has hitherto been the norm. Some groups, because of their high fertility rates, are experiencing linguistic reproduction rates greater than one, and their prospects for survival look promising. There is also some evidence that partial success has been made in constructing the appropriate infrastructure, which will support domain extension in education, government, and broadcasting. The key factor is the degree of influence exercised on the local state apparatus to institutionalize patterns of language behavior and service provision in new domains.

# 1. INTRODUCTION

However, one of the great ironies of such developments is that, although sociolinguistically they are influencing the parapublic sector, some autochthonous language speakers are rapidly losing their control in traditional core areas as a result of out-migration, capital-intensive economic development, and the increased mobility requisite of a modern industrial society. The fact that First Nations have become highly politicized in the last 20 years, and look set to be more pivotally involved in determining aspects of Canada's political future, following the fall of Meech Lake and the Oka and Kahnawake episodes, should not divert attention away from their fears of cultural attrition. So much of their collective hopes and aspirations rest on the construction of an appropriate political and socioeconomic infrastructure that can interface with the federal and provincial structure to allay their four principal concerns described as:

> The status and continuity of existing treaties ... the process and outcome of negotiating land claims ... the recognition of the right to self-government, with its constitutional and practical implications ... and the flows of money and programs to Native people, both on and off the reserves. (Young, 1995, p. 224)

Fifth, many of the descendants of European settlers who arrived before World War I, during the settlement of the West, and in the 1920s no longer have the native language of their forebears. For them other diacritical markers, such as diet, music, or the visual arts have replaced language as the link with the wider cultural community. However, fundamental questions surround the symbolic bases of their culture and the degree to which one may characterize residual elements as either authentic or as expressing an integral identity. This is a major feature of North America's cultural heritage and will prove a testing ground for more sensitive and flexible applications of the multiculturalism policy.

Sixth, more recent migrants from Pacific Rim countries will provide the fresh challenges to conceptions of North American identity, especially as economic arguments will reinforce the need for link languages other than English in this realm. Initially this will be a private and commercial-oriented pressure, but as the total size and significance of the Pacific-related link languages grows there will be pressure to reform some of the public agencies, the educational system, and the local state, particularly in California, Washington, Oregon, and British Columbia in order to take account of the new world order.

## CONCLUSION

The politics of recognition presuppose a historically well-entrenched democratic order. The watchwords of the open society are redistributive social justice, participatory democracy, and mutual tolerance. These principles are maintained only in strict proportion to the degree to which we are vigilant defenders of the basic rights of all constituent peoples. I recognize that balancing the rights of minorities, over and against the attempt by the majority to incorporate them within democracy's normative order as individual citizens, is a difficult issue. But we must seek to address the implications of this balancing act if we are to honor the full range of multilingual expectations and needs in our major cities and densely populated regions. This in turn presupposes a political/juridical framework which is adequate to the task in hand for, without this, increased language contact will lead to an escalation of conflict.

Having enshrined multiculturalism as a fundamental characteristic of the Canadian heritage through the "official" framework of English/French linguistic and cultural dualism, the operation of the Multiculturalism Act of 1988 is persistently criticized for not following through with concrete guarantees for implementation (Kallen, 1995). As Canada approaches the next century it faces the specter of fragmentation, which is the enemy of mutual trust in any democracy. And yet, if Canada, with all its benefits, cannot resist the drift toward atomization and polarization, it does not bode well for the much-vaunted principle of mutual interdependence in any other multicultural society on this fragile earth. In similar vein the United States will continue to grapple with its longstanding attitude of ambiguity toward the issues of language policy raised in this volume. Equilibrium or conflict? Integration or cultural pluralism? Combating racism and reducing prejudice or an insistence that *e pluribus unum* can only be realized through a narrowly constructed monolingual straightjacket, called the supremacy of English? These are in rather stark terms the issues of the day. It is my conviction and hope that the deliberations of my colleagues in this volume will contribute to an enlightened position whereby the value of being culturally diverse will not be abandoned for the price of linguistic unity.

## ACKNOWLEDGMENTS

Information germane to this chapter was gathered during my tenure as a Multicultural History Society of Ontario Resident Scholar in 1993. I wish to acknowledge the research support of a 1994 Canadian Studies Faculty Research Award and the intellectual stimulation received from my colleagues Don Cartwright, Jeff Hopkins, and Charles Whebell at the Department of Geography, the University of Western Ontario. I am very grateful for the constructive criticism I received from Charles Castonguay, David Dalby, and Jan Penrose on an earlier version of parts of the Canadian material published as Williams (1996).

# 1. INTRODUCTION

## REFERENCES

Arfé, G. (1981, October). *On a community charter of regional languages and cultures and on a charter of rights of ethnic minorities.* Resolutions adopted by the European Parliament, Strasbourg.

Baker, C. (1996). *Foundations of bilingual education and bilingualism* (2nd ed.). Clevedon, England: Multilingual Matters.

Beer, S. H. (1993). *To make the nation: The rediscovery of American federalism.* Cambridge, MA: Belknap.

Castonguay, C. (1992). *L'orientation linguistique des allophones á Montréal, Cahiers québecois de demographie, 21,* 95–118.

Castonguay, C. (1994). *L'assimilation linguistique: Measure et évolution 1971–1986.* Sainte Foy, Québec: Les Publications du Québec.

Edwards, J. (1985). *Language, society and identity.* London: Longman.

Edwards, J. (1994). Ethnolinguistic pluralism and its discontents: A Canadian study and some general observations. *International Journal of the Sociology of Language, 110,* 5–85.

Farrand, M. (Ed.). (1966). *The records of the Federal Convention of 1787* (Vols. 1–4). New Haven, CT: Yale University Press.

Fleras, A., & Elliott, J. L. (1992). *Multiculturalism in Canada.* Scarborough, Ontario: Nelson Canada.

Fretz, J. W. (1989). *The Waterloo Mennonites: A community in paradox.* Waterloo, Ontario: Wilfred Laurier University Press.

Glazer, N. (1977). Individual rights against group rights. In E. Kamenka (Ed.), *Human rights* (pp. 57–73). London: E. Arnold.

Griffiths, N. E. S. (1992). *The contexts of Acadian history, 1686–1784.* Montreal: McGill–Queen's University Press.

Griffiths, N. E. S., & Rawlyk, G. A. (1991). *Mason Wade, Acadia and Quebec.* Ottawa: Carleton University Press.

Guttman, A. (1992). Introduction. In C. Taylor & A. Guttman (Eds.), *Multiculturalism and "the politics of recognition"* (pp. 3–24). Princeton, NJ: Princeton University Press.

Habermas, J. (1996). The European nation-state: Its achievements and its limits. In G. Balakrishnan & B. Anderson (Eds.), *Mapping the nation* (pp. 281–294). London: Verso.

Havel, V. (1991). A freedom of a prisoner. In J. Plichtová (Ed.), *Minorities in politics* (pp. 14–16). Bratislava: The Czechoslovak Committee of the European Cultural Foundation.

Kallen, E. (1995). *Ethnicity and human rights in Canada.* Don Mills, Ontario: Oxford University Press.

Killilea, M. (1994, February). *On linguistic and cultural minorities in the European Community.* Resolution adopted by the European Parliament, Strasbourg.

Krosenbrink-Gelissen, L. E. (1996). First Nations, Canadians and their quest for identity: An anthropological perspective on the compatibility of nationhood concepts. In A. Lapierre, P. Smart, & P. Savard (Eds.), *Language, culture and values in Canada at the dawn of the 21st century* (pp. 329–345). Ottawa: Carleton University Press.

Kuijpers, W. (1987, October). *On the languages and cultures of regional and ethnic minorities in the European Community.* Resolution adopted by the European Parliament, Strasbourg.

Li, P. S. (1994). A world apart: The multicultural world of visible minorities and the art world of Canada. *Canadian Review of Sociology and Anthropology, 31,* 365–391.

Loewen, R. K. (1993). *Family, church and market: A Mennonite community in the Old and New Worlds, 1850–1930.* Urbana: The University of Illinois Press.

Marunchak, M. (1970). *The Ukrainian Canadians: A history.* Winnipeg: Ukrainian Free Academy of Sciences.

McAll, C. (1990). *Class, ethnicity and social inequality.* Montreal: McGill–Queen's University Press.

McRoberts, K. (1990, March 19–April 2). Federalism and political community. *Globe & Mail.*

Nelde, P., Labrie, N., & Williams, C. H. (1992). The principles of territoriality and personality in the solution of linguistic conflicts. *Journal of Multilingual and Multicultural Development, 13,* 387–406.

Phillips, A. (1995). Democracy and difference: Some problems for feminist theory. In W. Kymlicka (Ed.), *The rights of minority cultures* (pp. 288–302). Oxford, England: Oxford University Press.

Phillipson, R. (1992). *Linguistic imperialism.* Oxford, England: Oxford University Press.

Ricento, T. K. (1996). Language policy in the United States. In M. Herriman & B. Burnaby (Eds.), *Language policies in English-dominant countries* (pp. 122–158). Clevedon, England: Multilingual Matters.

Rogers, J. (1992). *Uncommon sense.* London: HarperCollins.

Rosenau, J. N. (1993). Notes on the servicing of triumphant sub-groupism. *International Sociology, 8,* 77–92.

Ross, S., & Deveau, A. (1992). *The Acadians of Nova Scotia: Past and present.* Halifax, Nova Scotia: Nimbus.

Russell, P. H. (1991). Can the Canadians be a sovereign people? *Canadian Journal of Political Science, 24,* 691–709.

Russell, P. H. (1992). *Constitutional odyssey: Can Canadians be a sovereign people?* Toronto: The University of Toronto Press.

Secretary of State, Canada. (1987). *Multiculturalism: Being Canadian* (Report of the Secretary of State of Canada–Multicultural Division). Ottawa: Department of Supply and Services.

Sundquist, E. J. (1993). *To wake the nations: Race in the making of American literature.* Cambridge, MA: Belknap.

Taylor, C. (1991). *The malaise of modernity.* Toronto: Anansi.

Taylor, C. (1992). Multiculturalism and "the politics of recognition." In C. Taylor & A. Guttman (Eds.), *Multiculturalism and "the politics of recognition"* (pp. 25–74). Princeton, NJ: Princeton University Press.

Tollefson, J. (1991). *Planning language, planning inequality: Language policy in the community.* London: Longman.

Williams, C. H. (1986). Language planning and minority group rights. In W. R. T. Pryce & I. Hume (Eds.), *The Welsh and their country* (pp. 253–272). Llandysul: Gomer.

Williams, C. H. (1993). The rights of autochthonous minorities in contemporary Europe. In C. H. Williams (Ed.), *The political geography of the new world order* (pp. 74–100). London: Wiley.

Williams, C. H. (1994). Development, dependency and the democratic deficit. *Journal of Multilingual and Multicultural Development, 15,* 101–128.

Williams, C. H. (1996). Citizenship and minority cultures: Virile participants or dependent supplicants? In A. Lapierre, P. Smart, & P. Savard (Eds.), *Language, culture and values in Canada at the dawn of the 21st century* (pp. 155–184). Ottawa: International Council for Canadian Studies, Carleton University Press.

Wilson, V. S. (1993). The tapestry vision of Canadian multiculturalism. *Canadian Journal of Political Science, 26,* 645–69.

Woycenko, O. (1967). *The Ukrainians in Canada.* Ottawa: Trident.

Young, R. A. (1995). *The secession of Quebec and the future of Canada.* Montreal: McGill–Queen's University Press.

# I

# Overviews

This book is about language policy. The various authors who have contributed chapters have taken language policy to mean everything from interpretations of national constitutions, through legislation, official statements by governing bodies, government funding of language related activities, and court rulings, to the implications of lack of government action. This book is also a comparison between Canada and the United States. Because the policy focus mainly implies government action or lack of it, this book might have become a forum for discussion of the differences between the structure of governments of the two countries. However, this has not been the result. Language being the pivotal element in human thought and relationships that it is, discussion in this book has turned on intergroup relations in the two countries—in symbolism and communication, in rivalry and cooperation, in rhetoric and action. Of course, the official policies of governments are central to these chapters because they are overarching statements about linguistic relations within the political units, but the real meat lies in analysis of the rich and complex, historical and contemporary networks of human interests that have become associated with language. Yes, these two countries have different histories, population configurations, pressures, and governance, but comparisons between the two are fruitful for both sides because fundamental human dynamics related to identity, power, and justice are common to both. Therefore, this book is about language policies, but it is about much more besides, and the comparison makes new and relevant issues and insights available.

Because the context of language policy dominates discussion in this book, policy is analyzed in terms of its symbolic value to those who make it and those who are affected by its provisions. In Part I, Schmidt (chapter

33

# 34                                                                    I. OVERVIEWS

2) and Ricento (chapter 4) both consider historical and structural matrices out of which language policies have been developed. They see such policies as tools in intergroup relations, with the Canadian record being more one of trying to mediate relations between two groups (see also Beaujot, chapter 3), whereas the U.S. experience is more an attempt by one group to dominate (see also Crawford in Part II, chapter 6). This is not to say that Canada has not had its own history of domination by majorities as well (see Fettes, chapter 5, and Burnaby, chapter 10, this volume), or that the United States does not have significant forces for linguistic and intergroup accommodation, as indicated by Schmidt.

A crucial question is whether language policies have any impact and whether such impacts are in the direction intended. Beaujot's overview of Canadian statistics on language indicates that federal and provincial policies have indeed been followed by an increase in francophones in the federal civil service, numbers of citizens who are bilingual (especially anglophones who have learned French in a proportion larger than before), in immigrant children learning through French rather than English in Quebec schools, and in anglophone children enrolled in French immersion classes. However, he also shows that the relative proportion of the French language in Canada has been reduced and that French/English territorial duality is increasing. Ricento argues that objective evaluation of the efficacy of particular language policies (for example bilingual education) in the United States is problematic because those doing the evaluation employ different assumptions about the purposes, goals, and relative value of such policies. He also raises questions about the potential outcomes of a declaration of English as the official language in that country. He (and Miner, chapter 7, this volume) points out that existing official English laws are mainly symbolic in the face of the fact that English is already dominant in most spheres and areas of life in the United States.

In Part I, there is strong agreement on a growing polarization between pluralist and nativist forces in both countries (but this is a complex relationship with respect to Aboriginal languages). One cannot say that these developments have been a *result* of language policies as much as that they have been central to the climate of intergroup interaction of which language matters have been a part. Beaujot (and Cartwright, chapter 11, this volume) indicates that anglophones and francophones have geographically retreated to their own territories, and that linguistic accommodation has not been enough to mediate the relationship between the two groups; in fact, separation on much more than language grounds is now distinctly possible. Schmidt and Ricento document increasing tension between pluralists and assimilationists in which "English-only" is the rallying cry but immigration and racism are the underlying content.

## I. OVERVIEWS                                                                35

What lessons can be drawn from these events? Ricento draws a distinction between a *deep* level of national attitudes to language and ethnicity and the *shallow* level of declared public policy. His conclusion (echoed by Beaujot's) is that policies are powerless to deal with intergroup tensions until deep attitudes change. Schmidt concludes that increased oppression by the majority will only lead to greater resistance from minorities so that, for example, Latinos in the United States, rather than assimilating faster, may respond to English-only policies by demanding separate status like many francophones in Quebec.

# 2

# The Politics of Language in Canada and the United States: Explaining the Differences

Ronald Schmidt, Sr.
*California State University, Long Beach*

Language policy conflict has reemerged in the United States in recent years with unexpected force and volatility, centering on the three policy issues of bilingual education, linguistic access to voting and other civil and political rights, and the proposal to make English the sole official language of the nation. Uneasy with this seemingly new political terrain, many Americans have looked northward to Canada for insight and example in trying to understand the implications and possible consequences of their own language policy conflict. U.S. proponents of bilingual education and linguistic access measures, for example, have often found inspiration in the pluralistic language policies of Canada's federal government.

American opponents of linguistic pluralism, on the other hand, have found in Canada's political conflicts over language policy clear lessons on what must be avoided in the United States. In 1976, for example, an op-ed piece in *The New York Times* stated: "The disconcerting strength gathered by separatism in Canada contains a lesson for the United States and its approach to bilingual education" ("Bilingual Danger," 1976, p. 46). Although supporting "transitional" bilingual education, *The Times* used the Canadian example to oppose alleged efforts by some educators and Latino political activists to maintain permanent "Spanish-speaking enclaves" because this would lead to "cultural, economic and political divisiveness," and could "only have the effect of condemning to permanent economic and social disadvantage those who cut themselves off from the majority culture."

Canadians, as well, have kept one eye closely on their neighbor to the south as they have sought to find yet another accommodation between Quebec and "English Canada." Indeed, one of the strongest selling points of the failed Meech Lake Accord among many anglophone Canadians was that finding a way to maintain Quebec as a distinct yet integral part of Canada is essential to avoiding the ever-present danger of being submerged under the colossal cultural and economic weight of the United States. Similarly, among Quebecois nationalists the overwhelming "English fact" in North America, generated by the proximity and sheer size of the United States in combination with anglophone Canada, has lent particular urgency to concerns for the survival and prosperity of their ethnolinguistic "island."

The purpose of this chapter is to provide a generalized, although systematic, comparison of language policy conflict in Canada and the United States. In particular, the chapter provides an analytical framework and factual foundation for understanding the degree to which the politics of language in the two countries are truly comparable. In doing so, it poses and sketches out answers to the following questions: To what extent are the dynamics of language policy conflict in the two countries similar? In what important respects are they different? How can the differences be explained? Answers to these questions are essential before one can speak of drawing lessons from one country's experience for the other.

## A FRAMEWORK FOR ANALYSIS

Before proceeding to a comparison of language policy conflicts in Canada and the United States, it will be useful to delineate the analytical frame of reference on which this inquiry will be based. A previous and broader comparative survey of language policy conflicts (Schmidt, 1991) led to four generalizations that will serve as the point of departure for the analysis to follow. *First*, linguistic diversity is the norm and not the exception among states in the contemporary world. Very few states—and no large ones—have monolingual populations.

*Second*, language policy conflict, although not ubiquitous, is increasingly common in the contemporary world, and it has tended to emerge on the political stage under two conditions: (a) when heightened competition between ethnic groups within a polity generates political mobilization and conflict along ethnic lines, and (b) when language is perceived as centrally

## 2. THE POLITICS OF LANGUAGE                                               39

important to the survival, enhancement, or both of the identity and power position of one or more of the ethnic groups in the polity. In this sense, it is important to understand that language policy conflict is not about language per se, but rather its sources are to be found in ethnic group conflict. Language use and language policy come to symbolize a larger conflict between ethnolinguistic groups over their relative power positions within the political community.

A *third* generalization is that the ethnic political conflict at the heart of the politics of language is conditioned by the ideological dominance of two primary public values in the modern world: *equality* and *nationalism*. Thus, the rhetoric of virtually all language policy conflicts centers around the role of the state in resolving disputed interpretations of the impact of language "competition" on (a) the relative degree of "equality" between ethnolinguistic groups and (b) "national unity."

*Fourth,* and finally, language policy approaches employed by states attempting to resolve these political conflicts may be categorized into four types:

1. *Domination/exclusion*, in which a dominant ethnolinguistic group controls the state and aims to maintain its dominance in the political economy through excluding subordinate language groups from learning the "language of power," publicly using it, or both.
2. *Assimilation*, in which the state seeks to eliminate language conflict by inducing members of subordinate language groups to acculturate linguistically by adopting the "national language" as their own.
3. *Pluralism*, in which the state aims to create a climate of acceptance and toleration for multiple languages, through support for the maintenance of several languages existing in the society and encouragement of multilingualism on the part of members of the polity.
4. *Linguistic confederation*, where the several language groups occupy separate subnational territories and in which the state legitimates their linguistic dominance within their respective regions.

Each of the policy orientations listed embodies a different understanding of the proper relationship between language use and ethnic "equality," and each embodies a different understanding of the nature of "national unity" as well.

These four generalizations about the nature and focus of language policy conflicts will form the foundation from which this chapter compares the politics of language in Canada and the United States. As is seen as we turn now to our comparison, the language policy conflicts of both countries fit well within the broad generalizations outlined earlier.

## SURFACE SIMILARITIES

On the surface, there are striking similarities between the recent language policy conflicts in Canada and the United States. Foundational to their language policy strife, both countries began to experience heightened ethnic political conflict in the 1960s, as previously subordinated ethnolinguistic groups mobilized to seek greater "equality" with a dominant anglophone majority. Thus, Quebec's Quiet Revolution of the 1960s, which culminated in the francophone political mobilization of the 1970s, was paralleled in important ways by the Chicano Movement in the U.S. Southwest during the same period.

Similarly, the historical roots of these conflicts may be found in the fact that the territories that became both countries were settled by competing European colonial powers (France and Britain in the case of Canada; Spain and Britain in the United States), leaving distinctly different cultural, social, and political legacies.[1] Further, the subordinated community in each country experienced *conquest* at the hands of the dominant group as a central historical reality, and political activists in each have had occasion to urge "remembrance" of the experience of conquest in the political mobilizations of the contemporary period. Moreover, linguistic and cultural preservation have formed key goals in each subordinated community's political mobilization.

It is also interesting to note the basic similarity in policy issues central to the recent politics of language in each country. Thus, debate and political conflict have centered in each country on official language policy, education policy for language minority children, and linguistic access to political and civil rights vis-à-vis both government and the economy. And, as might be expected from the analytical framework outlined earlier, the key value debates in each case have centered on how to achieve *equality* for the subordinated ethnolinguistic group while maintaining *national unity* in the country at large. Finally, these debates in both countries have involved policy decisions made by both federal and subnational governments (i.e., states and provinces, as well as local governments).

## "PLURALISTS" VERSUS "ASSIMILATIONISTS" IN THE UNITED STATES

Despite these surface similarities, however, there are fundamental differences in the political conflicts over language policy of the two countries. At

---

[1]France too, of course, played an important role in the settlement of the United States, but for purposes of understanding contemporary United States language politics, the most significant settlements were those of Spain and Britain.

## 2. THE POLITICS OF LANGUAGE
41

the broadest conceptual level, the most important contrast is that the sharpest contest in the United States has been between proponents of an *assimilationist* approach versus supporters of linguistic *pluralism*, whereas in Canada the most intense debate has been between *pluralists* and proponents of linguistic *confederation*. Consequently, the policy approaches being pursued and debated by conflicting partisans in the two countries are fundamentally different. After elaborating on these differences, the analysis focuses on how we might best account for this fundamental contrast in the focus of debate.

### Pluralists in The United States

As noted earlier, recent language policy conflict in the United States began in the 1960s in conjunction with the rise of a new political assertiveness on the part of the Latino communities in the nation, and particularly by Chicanos in the Southwest. This movement, in turn, was partially stimulated by the Civil Rights Movement for minority group equality initiated by African Americans in the South. By the time the first "new" national language policy, the Bilingual Education Act of 1968, was adopted by Congress, more than 10 years of the civil rights struggle had passed through the television screens and before the eyes of the American public, and much of the worldview animating the political support for bilingual education had been stimulated by that struggle for racial equality.

In reviewing their own power positions and histories in the American political economy, however, Chicanos and Puerto Ricans (as well as many Native Americans and some Asian American groups) focused not only on racial and economic subordination but on cultural and linguistic discrimination as well. In the field of education, for example, Latinos could recount numerous instances in which their names had been anglicized by teachers, and punishment for speaking Spanish on playgrounds was routine policy in many Southwestern public schools. In charting their own course toward greater equality, therefore, most Latino activists placed a central importance on respect for and retention of their language and culture.

Many Chicanos in the Southwest took their ideological bearings in the late 1960s and early 1970s by recounting the military conquest through which this region became part of the United States. Following its humiliating defeat in 1848, Mexico was forced to cede nearly half of its territory to the United States under the sway of what the activists viewed as the racist and imperialistic Manifest Destiny doctrine of the 19th century. In view of the patent illegitimacy of that conquest from their perspective, many Chicanos argued that the Spanish language and their *mexicano* culture were more "native" to and legitimate in the region than the English language and anglo culture, and that being stripped of these prized aspects of their identities by the public schools was tantamount to cultural genocide by the state. In seeking bilingual education policies, therefore, most Chicano activists sought public schooling that would aim at helping them to retain their linguistic and cultural distinctiveness in the U.S. polity. At the same time, however, Chicanos and other Latino activists recognized English as the longstanding and probably unchangeable lingua franca of the U.S. political economy. In the educational field, therefore, they sought a "maintenance" bilingual education policy aimed at helping their children master both languages and cultures. Possessed of a pluralistic vision of U.S. society, they wanted their children to feel "at home" in both their own ethnolinguistic communities, and in the larger anglo public world (Hernandez-Chavez, 1978, 1984).

In addition, in the early 1970s Latino activists (led by the Mexican American Legal Defense Fund, or MALDEF) mounted a related campaign for linguistic access to political and civil rights guaranteed under the U.S. Constitution and by certain legislation. Their first and most controversial step was to mount a lobbying campaign to persuade Congress to amend the Voting Rights Act of 1965 to include protections for linguistic minorities. With virtually no organized opposition, and citing numerous examples of American citizens (mostly Chicanos in the Southwest) unable to vote because they could not read and write the English language, a parade of witnesses testified before Congress in favor of exorcising language as a barrier to this central democratic right. Accordingly, Congress did find in its 1975 Extension of the Act " that voting discrimination against citizens of language minorities is pervasive and national in scope" (U.S. Commission on Civil Rights, 1981, p. 120). Titles II and III of the amended law required that registration forms, ballots, and election materials in a language other than English must be provided if more than 5% of the voters in an election district spoke the same non-English language and if the English illiteracy rate in the district was greater than the national illiteracy rate (Leibowitz, 1982). Although watered down in a compromise amendment forced by the Reagan Administration in 1982, the non-English ballot provisions were subsequently expanded to include even more eligible voters than the original version in 1992 amendments to the law.

Further, the same logic was used by Latinos and other language minority activists to argue that access to other political and civil rights should not be denied simply because the client, citizen, or both spoke a language other than English. Among the rights targeted were full access to public social services in a language the client understands, to a defendant's full understanding of courtroom proceedings in cases against him or her, and to protection against public and private employment discrimination under

## 2. THE POLITICS OF LANGUAGE                                          43

the guise of linguistic uniformity rules. In none of these cases did the
Congress, state legislatures, or state and federal courts subsequently develop and implement an unambiguous right to linguistic access, but many
partial victories were won by language minority activists (Piatt, 1990). And,
although the political momentum on linguistic access issues seemed to be
in the pluralists' favor in the early 1990s, the election of a Republican
Congress in 1994 swung that momentum in a contrary direction.

To summarize, the position at the heart of these struggles for linguistic
access has been that unless persons in the U.S. political community have an
*equal* right to all other civil and political rights without regard to their
English language facility, they will have been treated unjustly. From this
*pluralist* perspective, "English-only" government in the multilingual
United States is a violation of the civil and political rights of members of
language minority groups.

### Assimilationists in the United States

The principal source of opposition to the pluralist position in the United
States has come from supporters of linguistic and cultural *assimilation*. From
the very beginning of the contemporary period, for example, assimilationists were uncomfortable with the concept of bilingual education. Although
conservatives opposed the 1968 bilingual education bill on fiscal grounds,
many liberals supported it only as an antidote to the disproportionately
greater school dropout rates among Latino youths, and not as a measure to
help maintain non-English languages and cultures. During most of the
1970s, in fact, bilingual education policies at all levels of government were
subject to an intense debate over whether the programs should be *transitional* or *maintenance* in aim. Whereas "maintenance" programs would aim
at making students bilingual adults in English *and* their native language,
"transitional" programs were designed to teach students in their native
languages *only* until they had mastered English well enough to be transferred to an "English-only" mainstream classroom. From the transitional
(assimilationist) point of view, the students' native languages were viewed
as "crutches" to be overcome as quickly as possible, whereas from the
maintenance (pluralist) perspective the native language was seen as a
precious national resource to be developed and nurtured for the well-being
of both student and society. Supporters of the transitional approach sought
to provide linguistically "deprived" youth (i.e., deprived of English in their
homes) with an "equal opportunity" to succeed in what was conceptualized normatively as a monolingual English-speaking American society. By
the end of the 1970s, legislatures at all levels of government had made it
clear that there was little support among elected officials for a straightfor-

ward maintenance approach: Most legislation became increasingly clear in restricting publicly funded programs to the transitional approach.

By the beginning of the 1980s, further, many assimilationists—citing disputed program evaluations showing poor results for the predominantly transitional programs being implemented by public schools—began to argue that the existing Federal legislation and regulations were too restrictive, and that school districts should have more flexibility in experimenting with approaches other than bilingual education for teaching limited English proficient (LEP) students. Among the programs cited most frequently as models to be emulated were the French immersion programs popular among anglophone parents in Quebec.

The arguments made most often by assimilationists at this stage, therefore, were (a) that bilingual education programs were not successful in helping language minority students master English, thereby impeding the schools' efforts to help these students attain greater equality of opportunity in the (anglophone) society, and (b) that as a consequence of the programs' failure, a growing number of undereducated, non-English-speaking language-minority persons (mainly Latinos in the southwest and northeast) would pose an increasing threat to the national unity of the country. A subsidiary position pushed by the Reagan Administration in the 1980s was that education programs rightfully should be designed and funded by the states, and therefore the states should have maximum flexibility in designing and funding programs for language minority (and all other) students. Convinced that so-called "bilingual" education programs would necessarily result in monolingual, non-English-speaking adults, assimilationists pushed increasingly for "more successful" ways of teaching English to LEP students.

Many assimilationists were even more disturbed by the implications of the concept of linguistic access, and especially by so-called bilingual ballots. The idea that citizens of the United States should be under no obligation to learn the English language before being allowed to exercise their rights as citizens was anathema to many anglophone Americans. In California (the state with by far the largest number of Latinos and Spanish speakers), for example, voters in 1984 overwhelmingly approved (by a 71% to 29% margin) an initiative that ordered the governor to send a letter to the President of the United States expressing the state's opposition to the inclusion of language minorities in the protections of the Voting Rights Act. Clearly reflecting the assimilationist positions on the equality and national unity debates on language policy, the initiative measure read, in part:

> The United States Government should foster similarities that unite our people, and the most important of which is the use of the English language.

## 2. THE POLITICS OF LANGUAGE                                    45

Multilingual ballots are divisive, costly and often delay or prevent our immigrant citizens from moving into the economic, political, educational and social mainstream of our country. (quoted in Pitt, 1985, p. 295)

This measure, along with others like it, was sponsored and supported by a new, nationwide lobbying group known as "U.S. English," which became the primary organizational basis for the assimilationist position on language policy issues. Organized in 1983 by former U.S. Senator S. I. Hayakawa (R-California) and John Tanton (a Midwestern physician also associated with immigration restriction organizations), the primary agenda of U.S. English was to support efforts to declare English as the only official language of the United States and its political subdivisions. By 1990, U.S. English claimed a nationwide membership of over 400,000, and had been joined in 1987 by another lobbying group—more militant in tone—known as "English First." Hayakawa had initiated this movement in 1981 by introducing a proposed amendment to the U.S. Constitution to the Senate. After his retirement from the Senate in 1982, others took up the cause and similar proposed amendments have been introduced in each Congress since 1981. By 1996, proponents of official English had managed to get a bill passed in the Republican-controlled House of Representatives that would have declared English the country's only official language, as well as wiping out all linguistic access provisions of the Voting Rights Act. The Senate, however, failed to act on the bill before the 104th Congress adjourned.

The central positions in the literature of both organizations sponsoring the "Official English" (or "English-Only") Movement are that the policies of bilingual education and bilingual ballots threaten the unity of the United States, and that declaring English as the sole "official language" is a necessary countermeasure to these wrongheaded policies. Although unsuccessful thus far in Congress, the campaign has won some important votes at the state and local levels. By lopsided margins, for example, state initiatives for official English were successful in California (1986), Colorado (1988), and Florida (1988). A hotly contested measure with far-reaching implementation language was narrowly approved by voters in Arizona (1988). Victorious elections were achieved as well in several notable local jurisdictions, including Miami (1980) and San Francisco (1984). Each of these jurisdictions had experienced rapid growth of non-English-speaking immigrant populations in recent years. By 1990, moreover, 17 states had designated English as their sole "official" language through either voter initiative or legislative action.

Meanwhile, however, linguistic pluralists had become alarmed at the "divisiveness" and "racism" of the "English-Only" movement, and they organized (in 1987) a new counteroffensive coalition of Latino, civil rights, and language education organizations known as "English Plus." As denoted by its title, the aim of English Plus is to support the mastery of English by all residents of the U.S., *plus* the retention of other languages, learning of other languages, or both (Henry, 1990). This coalition has claimed successes in turning back Official English campaigns in several states (including Texas), and it supported a successful suit in the Arizona U.S. District Court overturning that state's Official English law as a violation of the First Amendment to the U.S. Constitution (*Yniguez and Gutierrez v. Mofford, et al.,* 1990). Although this decision was upheld by the Ninth Circuit Court of Appeals in 1994, it was under review by the U.S. Supreme Court as recently as early 1997.

Further, linguistic pluralists in the educational field have mounted a new campaign of intellectual and political support for a maintenance approach to bilingual education. The controversial negative program evaluation studies of bilingual education, they have argued, were defective in that they were poorly designed, based on sloppily collected data, and ignored or distorted more positive data (see, e.g., U.S. General Accounting Office, 1987). Their most important argument, however, has been that the programs evaluated were almost entirely transitional in nature, whereas a growing volume of *basic* research indicates that maintenance programs are necessary to build a strong and continuing foundation in the student's native language in order to support their mastery of English as a *second* language. Only by mastering your first language, pluralists increasingly argue, can you truly master another language. Transitional programs fail to do this because they are bent on moving students into "English-only" classrooms as quickly as possible. Interestingly, among the most important contributors to this line of argument in the United States has been a Canadian educational researcher, Jim Cummins (1981, 1984, 1986, 1989).

Through the decade of the 1990s, therefore, the controversy over language policy has showed no signs of abating. Indeed, with high rates of immigration continuing to swell the populations of non-English speakers in the United States, political conflict between *assimilationists* and *pluralists* over language policy issues seems assured for the forseeable future.

## CANADA: "PLURALISTS" VERSUS "LINGUISTIC CONFEDERATIONISTS"

In Canada, as noted earlier, the recent debate over language policy has had a fundamentally different focus, although the policy issues in conflict have been very similar. Canada's contemporary politics of language began with Quebec's Quiet Revolution of the 1960s, and the federal government's response thereto. Prior to that decade, Canada's francophones were a distinct, and largely isolated subcommunity concentrated mostly in Que-

## 2. THE POLITICS OF LANGUAGE 47

bec and in contiguous portions of New Brunswick and Ontario. Although they held formal power in Quebec's local politics, the francophones were clearly a subordinate group economically and culturally in both province and country. During the 1960s, however, English-speaking Canada became aware that significant changes were taking shape in the francophone community. Their French-speaking neighbors (composing about 25% of the country's population) were becoming increasingly secular and expansive in their outlook, increasingly dissatisfied with their "allotted" share of the material bounty produced in Canada's expanding economy, and especially, increasingly nationalistic and assertive politically (Levine, 1990; McRoberts, 1988).

### Federal Government Pluralism in Canada

In partial response to the new force of Quebec's cultural nationalism in Canadian public life, the federal government appointed a Royal Commission on Bilingualism and Biculturalism in 1963. The Commission's primary purpose was to seek out a new, more "modern" solution to the perennially difficult relationship between Canada's two dominant ethnolinguistic groups. By the time the Commission issued its final report and recommendations in 1969, Canada had a new Liberal Party government at the federal level, headed by Prime Minister Pierre Elliott Trudeau. Trudeau, who would dominate Canadian federal politics for much of the next 16 years (he was Prime Minister from 1968 to 1984, except for a few months), adopted the *pluralistic* philosophy of the Royal Commission report as his own, and became its principal champion in Canadian politics.

In its 1969 report, the Royal Commission set out as the proper goal for Canada an "equal partnership not only of the two peoples which founded Confederation but also of each of their respective languages and cultures" (Canada, Royal Commission on Bilinguilism and Biculturalism, 1973, 4–5). In its articulation of the meaning of this "equal partnership," the Royal Commission forthrightly espoused the values of linguistic *pluralism*. Cultural and linguistic equality, according to the Commission:

> … Means essentially that everybody has the same access to the various benefits of a society without being hindered by his cultural identity. Thus, it is not enough for members of a minority group to have access to the same activities, institutions, and benefits as the members of the majority group; that simply requires the absence of discrimination against individuals as such. The equality to which we refer requires that a person who engages in some activity or associates with some institution need not renounce his own culture, but can offer his services, act, show his presence, develop, and be accepted with all his cultural traits. (p. 5)

In short, Canada must become a truly bilingual nation so that each individual member of the two founding peoples can feel "at home" in all of the public spheres of his or her country.

Following this personality principle, the Commission recommended a variety of measures that can be categorized as four types of essentially *pluralistic* remedies: (a) ensuring equal linguistic access to institutions of the Federal government (and to provincial governments in certain bilingual districts) for members of both founding communities; (b) ensuring that parents in each language group enjoy the right to have their children educated in their own language; (c) equalizing employment and advancement opportunities in the Federal government between the two founding groups, including the right to work for the government in the official language of their choice; and (d) equal consumption opportunities, ensuring that members of both groups would find labels and advertising information available in their own language.

Although the first and fourth categories of remedy were to be national in scope, the second and third were to be constrained by the "territorial principle" requiring that sufficient numbers of each language group were available to make them practicable. Finally, Canada was to declare itself *officially bilingual*. The original formulation was that the country should be officially "bicultural" as well, but opposition from a variety of quarters (e.g., aboriginal peoples and several European-origin immigrant communities) resulted in a compromise formula designated as *"multiculturalism within a bilingual framework."* This separation of language from culture was to contribute to continued hostility toward the pluralistic framework within Quebec. In addition to the official language designation, in any case, the Commission recommended a pluralistic approach both to education policy for language minority children and their parents, and to the issue of equal linguistic access to political, civil and certain economic rights.

As noted earlier, Prime Minister Trudeau enthusiastically endorsed the liberal pluralist philosophy of the Royal Commission report and many of its specific recommendations. Accordingly, many of the report's recommendations were incorporated in the Official Languages Act, which was adopted by Canada's Parliament in 1969. In addition to outlining Canada's new federal linguistic regime, the Act also established a Commissioner of Official Languages, who was given the task of serving as an "ombudsperson" for official language "minority" communities and as the language "conscience" of the country (Canada, Commissioner of Official Languages, 1991).

In an apparent effort to head off the rising tide of francophone independence sentiment in Quebec, following the adoption of the 1969 Act Trudeau's government set out to convince all Canadians that they should become bilingual individuals, as well as to see themselves as members of a

## 2. THE POLITICS OF LANGUAGE 49

bilingual nation. Thus a 1977 Federal government brochure, explaining and defending the nation's new language policy in both English and French, declared that learning both official languages:

> Is desirable as a personal and national asset so that members of the two official language groups may be able to communicate with each other, understand and cherish each other's diverse ways of life, and serve as a natural link between the two linguistic communities. (Government of Canada, 1977, p. 43)

In addition, Prime Minister Trudeau spent considerable time and political energy attempting to persuade Canada's 10 provincial governments (which have substantially more independent policy-making authority than do U.S. state governments) to adopt the bilingual, multicultural *pluralist* philosophy and policies embodied in his vision of the "new" and evolving *nation* of Canada.

Finally, as its crowning language policy achievement, the Trudeau government's "patriation" of the Canadian Constitution in 1982 included several specific protections of individual linguistic rights in the document's Charter of Rights and Freedoms (roughly analogous to the U.S. Constitution's Bill of Rights). Section 16 of the Charter, for example, declared that "English and French are the official languages of Canada and have equality of status and equal rights and privileges as to their use in all institutions of the Parliament and government of Canada" (Jackson, Jackson, & Baxter-Moore, 1986, p. 747). With respect to the issue of "linguistic access," Section 20 stipulates further that "any member of the public in Canada has the right to communicate with, and to receive available services from" (p. 747) a central office of the federal government in English or French, and from regional offices where there is a sufficient language minority population to make it desirable and practicable. In a nation with a significantly more expansive public sector (proportionately) than is true in the United States, providing this degree of linguistic access has been a formidable undertaking. Finally, Section 23 of the Charter spells out extensive "minority language educational rights" through the secondary level for citizens of Canada who are members of either of the two "foundational" ethnolinguistic groups. The basic principle embodied in Section 23 is that members of an official language group have the right to see their children educated in their own language at public expense, even if they are in the minority in any given province, subject to the constraint that sufficient numbers of them are concentrated to make such an educational approach practicable.

In sum, therefore, by the time Prime Minister Trudeau left office in 1984, his government had wrought profound changes in Canada's federal language policy. In the implementation of the Official Languages Act, the federal government had become far more bilingual than it had been before

1969. Even in the prairie and western provinces (with relatively few francophones in residence), Canadians were reminded daily by their federal government of the fact that French is one of the nation's two official languages. Moreover, under comparatively aggressive affirmative action policies, in which an ever-larger number of federal government employees were required to be bilingual, francophones found increased opportunities for employment by the federal government (i.e., francophones are far more likely to be bilingual in Canada than are anglophones). Further, Trudeau's regime kept provincial governments under some federal pressure to adopt educational policies protective of the rights of their official-language-minority populations.

Nevertheless, despite the Trudeau government's prodigious efforts to persuade all Canadians to see themselves as bilingual, multicultural nationals in an increasingly bilingual and multicultural nation, opposition to its *pluralist* philosophy and policies was strong from several quarters. In the end, although the Progressive Conservative Party opted for the most part to continue (and even strengthen in some respects) Trudeau's language policy after its election to power in the federal government in 1984, this ambitious program failed to win a new national consensus for Canada. As a result of this failure language policy conflict has continued to dominate much of the country's political agenda into the 1990s.

Opposition to the federal government's bilingual, bicultural policy of pluralism came from three sources: (a) from *assimilationists* in the English-dominant provinces, (b) from *pluralists* who wanted a multilingual, multicultural policy that would include the languages and cultures of native peoples and so-called "allophone" (i.e., non-English- and non-French-speaking) immigrants, and (c) from *linguistic confederalists* in Quebec who wanted that province to be officially monolingual in French, and to be recognized as a truly distinct nation in the Canadian confederation.

*Assimilation* to the English language and to the Anglo culture had long been a preferred option among some anglophones in Canada. Indeed, from the Conquest in 1763 to at least the Confederation agreement in 1867, British policy toward the French-speaking settlers in Canada alternated between attempts at assimilation and a kind of "separate and *un*equal" toleration of the language and Roman Catholic religion of the French (a relatively mild version of the "domination/exclusion" policy approach). And, although the Federal government after Confederation was at least nominally bilingual, many of the English-dominant provincial governments were straightfowardly assimilationist in policy approach. Jackson et al. (1986) summarized the historical pattern:

> In the other provinces [i.e., other than Quebec, which *did* have an operationally bilingual policy] … the practice until the 1940s was for English-speaking Canadi-

## 2. THE POLITICS OF LANGUAGE 51

ans, wherever they were in the majority, to deprive French-speaking minorities of public school facilities in their native language, and to refuse them the use of their language in government institutions. (p. 240)

In part because of this historical experience, francophones outside of Quebec found it increasingly difficult to maintain their language and culture. As Bourassa (quoted by Cook in Mallea, 1984) put it early in this century: "French Canadians, like Canadian Indians, can only exercise their treaty rights when they remain on 'the reserve' in Quebec" (p. 229). Accordingly, a review of census patterns over the 20th century shows a steady decline of French-speaking ability and use outside of Quebec.

Although former Prime Minister Trudeau managed to get "foundational" minority language rights included in the 1982 Constitution, as noted earlier, he did not succeed in eliminating all assimilationist sentiment from the anglophone provinces. Indeed, despite the language rights guaranteed in the 1982 Charter of Rights and Freedoms, a kind of "English-only" movement has swept some provinces in recent years, and opposition to the federal government's bilingual policy has been on the rise. By February 1990, for example, and despite a pluralistic provincial policy, 28 local governments in Ontario (which has more than half a million francophones) had declared themselves to be officially unilingual in English. The largest of these was Thunder Bay, a municipality of 113,000 people in the northwest part of the province (Walsh, 1990). It is doubtful that even the most ardently monolingual Canadian anglophones seriously expect to assimilate all the country's francophones to English at this late date. Nevertheless, among the English speakers there appears to be a growing sentiment that they have a right to be "fed up" with the seeming truculence of and constant necessity to negotiate with the Quebecois, a sentiment that pits them against the efforts of the Federal government to find a workable pluralist solution for the country's future.[2] Insofar as it opposes further efforts to negotiate an agreement with Quebec, this rising English-only sentiment may be seen as a (negative) kind of support for a final "divorce" between English and French Canada. Nevertheless, English assimilationism continues to represent a distinctly minority position in contemporary Canadian language politics, articulated most frequently in private rather than openly in the political arena.

A *second* form of opposition to the Federal government's bilingual policy has come from *pluralists* who seek a broader definition of and official support for the country's mosaic of multilingualism and multiculturalism. As noted earlier, some of this opposition has come from Canada's aboriginal peoples (Amerindian and Inuit), who argue that *their* languages and

---

[2]Although not himself an assimilationist, Resnick (1990) articulated forcefully some of this sentiment on the part of anglophones.

52                                                                                        SCHMIDT

cultures are more "foundational" than either English or French, and should
be officially recognized and protected in public policy and by the Constitution. Indeed, it was a filibuster along these lines by a Cree Indian member
of Manitoba's legislature that managed to delay a vote long enough to block
that province's approval of the Meech Lake Accord in June 1990 (Burns,
1990; see also Hall, 1989; Purich, 1989).

In addition, some immigrant communities in Canada have sought to
have their languages and cultures included in a pluralist language policy.
During several periods, Canada has pursued an aggressively positive
immigration policy, and its 1981 census identified over 70 ethnic groups
(apart from the anglophones and francophones). Some of these groups
constitute significant subcommunities in several large cities (e.g., Toronto,
Montreal, Vancouver, Edmonton, and Winnipeg) and in rural areas (particularly in the prairie provinces). The 1981 census showed that among the
most significant "other" ethnolinguistic groups in Canada are those from
Germany (5% nationally), Italy (3%), Ukraine (2%), and Asia (14% from all
Asian countries combined; Jackson et al., 1986). Immigration from Asia has
been steadily increasing, and from 1981 to 1986 43% of all immigrants to
Canada came from that continent (Malcolm, 1990). The 1981 census also
found that the following provinces had relatively high proportions of
"allophone" residents: the Northwest Territories (43.2%), Manitoba
(23.1%), Saskatchewan (17.7%), Ontario (17.2%), British Columbia (16.5%),
and Alberta (16.2%; Jackson et al., 1986). This list includes the most populated and fastest growing provinces in the country, with the exception of
Quebec (which reported only 6.7% allophones). In any case, for activists
representing a multicultural perspective on Canada's ethnolinguistic mosaic, the bilingual pluralist language policies embodied in the 1969 Official
Languages Act and the 1982 Charter of Rights and Freedoms are seriously
deficient in their narrowness.

## Quebec and Canadian Linguistic Confederalism

By far the most serious opposition to the Federal government's bilingual
policies, however, has come from the increasing consensus within francophone Quebec in favor of some form of *linguistic confederation*. At first
glance it may appear ironic that just as Canada's federal government began
to take stronger steps in support of a bilingual, bicultural nation-state at the
end of the 1960s, Quebec's increasingly nationalistic francophone majority
moved toward a monolingual French policy for their own province. Reacting to serious concerns about the survival of French in predominantly
anglophone North America, Quebec's National Assembly adopted a series
of three policies under three successive party governments from 1969 to

## 2. THE POLITICS OF LANGUAGE

1977 that chronicle the shift away from a bilingual policy and toward provincial *"francisation"*:

1. Bill 63 in 1969 (under the last Union Nationale government, headed by Jean-Jacques Bertrand), which "established the principle of the priority of the French language," but also "confirmed the right of parents to choose French or English schools for their children" (d'Anglejan, 1984, pp. 36–37).
2. Bill 22 in 1974 (under Robert Bourassa's first Parti Liberal du Quebec government), which made French the sole "official" language of Quebec and sought to require "allophone" parents to educate their children in French schools, but retained certain protections for anglophones (pp. 37– 39).
3. Bill 101 in 1977 (under Rene Levesque's Parti Québécois government), the "Charter of the French Language," which was "designed to make Quebec both institutionally and socially a unilingual French state [and] ... to curb the growth of the English-speaking community and to diminish its status" (p. 40).

Concern for the survival of French derived from the decreasing birthrate among French Canadians, the small number of French-language immigrants to Quebec, and the assimilation of nearly all other immigrants into the English-speaking population of the province. By the 1971 census, the combined effect of these forces had reduced the francophone population significantly below its historical proportion of the Canadian population (i.e., from one third to a little over one fourth). In addition to this issue of linguistic *survival*, an important motivation for the increasingly restrictive language policy of Quebec was the continuing *inequality* of francophones, and especially their continued economic subordination in "their" province (d'Anglejan, 1984; Lemco, 1987; Levine, 1990). The latter was particularly important in view of the urbanization and increasing integration of Quebec's francophones into the North American and global economies, a phenomenon that linked in the public mind the two issues of cultural survival and equality (Levine, 1990).

Thus Quebec's 1977 Charter of the French Language, which remains virtually unassailable politically within the province, departed from the federal government's *pluralist* language policy in several respects. In addition to reiterating that French is the only official language of the province, it (a) restricted the right of anglophone parents moving into Quebec to have their children educated in English (in theory "allophone" parents had already lost this right under Bill 22, and their free choice is not covered by Federal policy either), (b) imposed a series of sanctions designed to advantage francophones in economic and professional activities (e.g., "francisa-tion" programs for business and the professions designed to ensure that French is the dominant language used in these domains), and (c) provided measures designed to ensure a French *visage* in the province (e.g., monolin-gual French outdoor commercial signs and billboards, "francisation" of geographic designations, etc.). Quebec's government also adopted several additional programs aimed at ensuring the integration of adult immigrants into the francophone community of the province. These were recently codified into a formal policy statement (Government of Quebec, 1990), and have been buttressed by a new agreement negotiated between the federal government and Quebec expanding the province's control over immigra-tion (*Canada–Quebec Accord*, 1991).

In short, Quebec has attempted to implement a policy of *linguistic confederation* based on the proposition that, because the rest of Canada is de facto virtually monolingual in English, the country—if it is to remain a single country—must acknowledge the reality that Quebec is and will remain a distinctly francophone province. In turn, the federal government should continue toward *bilingualism*, as is the case in other linguistically federated countries (e.g., Belgium, Switzerland, etc.), but should not ex-pand its own linguistic powers at the expense of Quebec's program. As summarized shortly after its adoption by Pierre Laporte, a language plan-ning official in Quebec, the Charter gives the province's language policy:

> A completely new political significance: Bill 101 is more than a language legisla-tion; it is an attempt by the new [Parti quebecois] government to move political consciousness away from its previous content to a Quebecois content. Language legislation in Quebec, as it is in many "new nations" of Africa and Asia, is now a nation-building mechanism. (quoted in d'Anglejan, 1984, p. 43)

Quebec's rationale for Bill 101's relatively "illiberal" policy of restrictive-ness is based on its understanding of the seriousness of the linguistic and cultural crisis faced by francophones in overwhelmingly anglophone North America, and on its understanding of the meaning of its own distinctiveness as a society. The rationale begins from the fact that franco-phones throughout Canada, even in Quebec, were relegated historically to a subordinate position in the political economy. Because inequality between the two language groups was a fact of life from the time of the Conquest, there were reasons to believe that the individualistic premises of the liberal pluralist policy of the federal government would not succeed in protecting the survival of the Quebecois language and culture, much less ensure their elevation to a position of equality.

The logic of this part of the argument is as follows: If the most favored opportunities (employment, status, power) in a society are in the hands of one language group, individual responses to "equal opportunity" policies

## 2. THE POLITICS OF LANGUAGE                                    55

will be shaped by that very social context toward conformity with the dominant language and culture. That is, individuals making "free" choices to improve their own life chances will choose, other things being equal, to conform with those aspects of the social context (e.g., language use and cultural identification) that will improve their own power positions. If the language of power is English, individuals will choose English in the pursuit of their own advantage. Because the language of power prior to the reconquest of the province *was* English, it was not surprising that allophone migrants to Quebec would choose English rather than French as the preferred language for their children's education, or that francophones "allowed" into the corridors of (English-dominant) power would gradually acculturate into anglophone North America.

In short, the leaders of Quebecois nationalism believed that liberal pluralism provided an inherently unstable foundation for a bilingual country. Languages are naturally in competition, and one language or the other would inevitably dominate in any given territory (Laponce, 1987). The pluralist policies of official bilingualism espoused by the federal government provided no protection against the destructive effects of this seemingly inexorable logic of individual free choice on the language and culture of the francophone community. The only way to alter this logic, in turn, was to make French the indisputable language of power in the province, a social transformation that could not be accomplished through policies based on free market principles.

The second major rationale for Bill 101 is based on the requisites for francophone cultural distinctiveness within a dualistic country. That is, if francophones are to feel "at home" in "their" province (i.e., to be "masters of their own house"), then Quebec's need to be an essentially *distinct* society must be recognized by all of Canada. Simply "translating into French" an evolving *Canadian* national culture would not accomplish this, because the "feel"—the cultural "soul"—of the province in that case would still be predominantly anglophone. This is an apparently subtle point, and lies at the heart of the contemporary Constitutional stalemate between Quebec and "English Canada."

In any case, there is evidence that more than a decade of implementation of Bill 101 has brought measurable results. Indeed, a 1991 comprehensive survey by Quebec's public administrative agencies responsible for language policy indicated steady, although incremental progress toward the francization of the province on virtually every measure of language use (Dumas, personal communication, May 27, 1991). Not surprisingly, therefore, reports from Quebec by outsiders in recent years have been virtually unanimous in their perception that francophones have come to feel that they are at last in control of their own cultural and economic destiny (see, e.g., Francis, 1990; Stanley, 1990; Uchitelle, 1990).

The contradiction between the *pluralist* policy of the federal government and the *linguistic confederationist* policy of Quebec has kept Canada in a state of political instability throughout the last several decades. As noted earlier, a key component of this contradiction is the conflict between the "individual" rights enshrined in Canada's 1982 Charter of Rights and Freedoms, and the "collective" francophone rights being sought through Quebec's Bill 101. One of the arenas for the playing out of this conflict in recent years has been Canada's Supreme Court, which "has told Quebec that it may not print its laws or conduct its parliamentary debates or operate its courts in French only; [and] that it may not require Canadian citizens to send their children to francophone schools" (Frum, 1988, p. 10). Although Quebec revised Bill 101 to conform to these rulings, in late 1988 another Court decision led to the province's invocation of the "notwithstanding" clause of the 1982 Constitution, thereby overturning (at least temporarily) that decision.

The conflict in this case involved the provision of Bill 101 which restricted most commercial signs in the province to the French language. The Court found this provision in violation of the Canadian Charter of Rights and Freedom's protection of free expression (and in violation of Quebec's Charter as well). The "notwithstanding" clause, which was included in the 1982 Constitution at the insistence of several western provinces, is roughly analogous to the nullification doctrine proposed by U.S. southern states prior to the Civil War in that it enables a Canadian province to substitute its own policies for those of the federal government (although with prescribed limits on scope and duration). Under intense francophone political pressure, Premier Bourassa invoked the clause and pushed Bill 178 through the National Assembly in late 1988 in very short order. The bill was aimed at a compromise in that it restricted outdoor commercial signs to French, but allowed bilingual signs inside business establishments. Initially, however, Bill 178 succeeded only in reigniting the language issue within Quebec and throughout Canada, and in demonstrating anew the depth of the country's division on the language issue (Levine, 1990).

In a genuine sense, therefore, language policy conflict is central to Canada's current constitutional crisis. Former Prime Minister Trudeau's insistence on enshrining individual language rights in the country's 1982 Charter of Rights and Freedoms was a principal factor in Quebec's decision to be the only province to refuse to sign the 1982 Canadian Constitution Act. (Quebec argued that these individualistic provisions, along with significant shifts of power from the provincial to the federal government, violated the spirit and the letter of the Confederation agreement that had created the country of Canada in 1867.)

ism that the replacement of Pierre Trudeau by
finister of Canada in 1984, and of Rene Levesque
:mier of Quebec in 1985, would facilitate a new
ment on the Constitution. The two new leaders
egree of confidence, and Mulroney's success in
ie provincial leaders to agree in 1987 to the Meech
ld have satisfied Quebec by giving it a Constitu-
nct" status, along with several other concessions)
:ling in Canada that the constitutional crisis had
t happened, however, two of the nine anglophone
ies to the agreement were out of office shortly
provinces of Newfoundland and Manitoba ulti-
: agreement before it expired in June 1990. As a
ntinued unresolved through the 1990s, and the
country's ability to put this fundamental conflict to rest remains highly
problematic.

As an attempt to win a new ethnolinguistic consensus in Canada, then,
the Federal government's *pluralist* language policy seems to have been a
clear failure. Although there is a growing number of bilingual Canadians,
especially among the young, overall both English and French Canada are
becoming more unilingual within their own spheres (Albert, 1989). At the
provincial political level, moreover, both English and French Canada seem
to be increasingly intransigent in their positions with respect to the constitutional crisis. At a countrywide level, therefore, the real alternative seems
not to be a choice between a pluralist and a linguistically confederate
Canada, but between the latter policy approach and some form of political
"divorce" between the two Canadas.

## TOWARD EXPLAINING THE DIFFERENCES

In view of the foregoing, it is clear that there are fundamental differences
between the politics of language in the two countries. As noted at the outset
of these descriptions, the most obvious difference is that U.S. partisans on
this issue have been fighting between "assimilationist" and "pluralist"
language policies, whereas Canadians have been in conflict over the Federal government's "pluralist" policy versus Quebec's insistence on a "confederal" resolution to the language issue.

How do we account for this basic difference in policy debate and political
alignment? Despite the seeming similarity in ethnolinguistic situation in
the two countries, why is it that in Canada the federal pluralist approach
to language policy is viewed by most as a moderate, middle-of-the-road
position (supported by both the Federal Liberal and Progressive Conserva-

58                                                                                    SCHMIDT

tive ruling parties for over a generation), whereas in the United States the same policy goals have remained very much on the political defensive and are viewed by most political elites as potentially dangerous? Why is it that in the U.S. linguistic assimilation is the preferred policy of the vast majority of Anglos, whereas in Canada assimilationism is viewed as so extreme that publicly advocating this position is seen as virtual political suicide in most areas? How do we explain the fact that U.S. Latinos (who have consistently expressed a strong preference for linguistic and cultural maintenance) have not pushed for a confederal policy in light of the near-consensus among francophones in Canada that any other approach threatens the very survival of non-English ethnolinguistic communities in overwhelmingly anglophone North America?[3]

Pursuing answers to these questions will shed some light on important differences between ethnolinguistic politics in the two countries. Although there is not space to develop complete answers in this chapter, it is possible to briefly outline the historical and structural factors that seem most compelling in accounting for the differences sketched out earlier.

## The Legacies of History

Insofar as the past helps to shape the present political dynamic of any society, it is instructive to review important historical differences in the ethnolinguistic relationships of the United States and Canada. Although, as noted early in this chapter, both countries have legacies of dualistic European colonization and the conquest of one group by another, closer inspection reveals substantial differences between their historical experiences that have helped to shape quite disparate ethnolinguistic relationships in the present.

The historical experiences that molded nationalistic sentiment and Anglo behavior toward ethnolinguistic minorities, for example, were quite different between the two countries. Canada did not become a single country until 1867, nearly a century after the United States began its process of nationalization. Prior to Confederation in that year, Canada was a group of individual colonies ruled somewhat separately by British colonial authorities. In contrast, by 1867 the United States had fought a bitter war of independence, another war against the mother country in 1812, had experienced the surge of westward expansion (including propagation of the Manifest Destiny doctrine and the war against Mexico), and had survived a traumatic and bloody civil war—each of which had contributed to

---

[3]On the consistent Mexican American desire for linguistic and cultural maintenance, see Garcia (1989), Southwest Voter Research Institute, Inc. (1988), and de la Garza, DeSipio, Garcia, Garcia, and Falcon (1992). Several arguments for a kind of *linguistic confederation* policy for Latinos have been made (e.g., Barrera, 1988; Castro, 1976), but this remains a distinctly minority position among Latino activists.

## 2. THE POLITICS OF LANGUAGE 59

a high degree of nationalistic sentiment in the country. Until relatively recently, on the other hand, Canadians have self-consciously contrasted themselves to the United States on this point, priding themselves on their relative lack of nationalistic fervor.

In a provocative analysis, Lipset (1965, 1985, 1990) has provided other historical grounds for explaining the relatively higher degree of nationalistic sentiment in the United States that may, in turn, help to account for its historically lower levels of tolerance for ethnolinguistic diversity. Borrowing from the work of Louis Hartz, Lipset has argued that the American Revolution is the single most important historical event dividing the subsequent national experiences and political cultures of the two countries. It was the American Revolution, Lipset insisted, that set the United States in the direction of complete hegemony by the political culture of Lockean liberalism described by Louis Hartz (i.e., a highly individualistic liberalism with universalistic aspirations, unconstrained by a more corporate feudal tradition). In contrast, Lipset continued, it was the Canadian response to and rejection of the American Revolution that charted that country's development along a more corporatistic cultural path. Adding to the seminal importance of Canada's rejection of the revolutionary liberalism of the United States, Lipset suggested, were the incorporation of expatriate Loyalist colonists who migrated from the United States in the years immediately following the Revolution, and the fact that the Canadian religious tradition in its formative years was heavily Catholic (Anglo-Catholic for the British settlers and Roman Catholic for the French Canadians), whereas that of the United States was strongly influenced by the congregational organizational base of the Protestant dissenting tradition.

In partial consequence of these historical dissimilarities, Lipset argued, the political cultures of the two countries were very different. Until recently, the political culture of Canada has been relatively traditionalist, hierarchical, establishmentarian, deferential toward authority, statist, and corporatist. In comparison, that of the United States has been more anti-authoritarian, populist, egalitarian, free-market-oriented, minimalist toward government, and individualistic. Although Lipset's contrast between political cultures may be overstated, and has resulted in considerable criticism (see, e.g., Brym, 1989), to the extent that it contains some degree of descriptive historical validity his account may help to explain the relatively greater degree of intolerance for diversity and commitment to assimilationism in the United States as contrasted with Canada.

In any case, it is surely significant that the populistic nativist movement that swept through the United States several times between the mid-19th century and the 1920s, has no real parallel in Canadian history (Higham, 1963). Attempting to eliminate all "foreign" influences from the country (through "Americanization" campaigns and exclusion of most immigrants except those from Britain and northern Europe), the nativist movement demanded a relatively high level of cultural and linguistic conformity and was politically successful on many fronts. Accordingly, U.S. policymakers have faced far more grass-roots pressure for assimilative ethnolinguistic policies than has been true for their Canadian counterparts.

In addition to these contrasts in political culture, it is also relevant that English Canadians throughout their history have had a strong motive to accommodate their francophone compatriots, whereas in the United States there has been no comparable motivational force. That is, numerous scholars have emphasized that the fear of U.S. encroachment (militarily, economically, culturally, politically) has provided English Canadians with a strong motive to be accommodative toward their francophone "cousins" for over 200 years. Anglos in the United States, in contrast, had no self-interested motive to placate the wishes of the conquered Mexicans in their midst. Indeed, motivated by strong beliefs in their racial as well as cultural superiority, American settlers in the territories ceded by Mexico moved as quickly as possible to expropriate the land holdings of those they had defeated.

In summary, each of these contrasting historical experiences—the different timing of nationhood and of the development of nationalistic fervor, the differing degrees of liberal individualism as a central foundation for political culture, and the disparate self-interested motivations regarding the treatment of the conquered minority—may help to account for the relatively greater degree of anglophone political elite openness to continued ethnolinguistic diversity in Canada as compared to the United States.

In addition, the experiences of history have provided quite different foundations for the development of group consciousness between the two conquered minorities. To begin, the wars of conquest and their aftermaths contained quite different historical "lessons" for the conquered groups. Canada's war of conquest (1763) was, in truth, a colonial battlefront in a larger war between the two original European powers, Britain and France. The United States' conquest, on the other hand, occurred nearly a century later (1848) between two New World nations—the United States and Mexico—in which the conqueror annexed a large portion of its neighboring country.

Viewing the Canadian conquest as an episode in European colonialist competition introduces a potentially important difference in psychohistorical consciousness between the two experiences of conquest. That is, the nationalistic rivalry between Britain and France, although not always ideological in the modern sense, was longstanding, dating back at least to the Norman invasion of 1066. Over the centuries each side could claim significant victories, and the era of colonialism ended without decisive superiority

## 2. THE POLITICS OF LANGUAGE 61

by either power. The point of this discussion is to indicate that Canadian francophones, viewing themselves as members of an important "world power" culture, may not have experienced their conquest as quite so humiliating in the sense of raising questions about the possibility and meaning of genuine "equality" between national groups. That was not the case with respect to the war between the United States and Mexico. As numerous accounts attest, the contrast between Mexico and its superpower northern neighbor—in respect to military might, cultural penetration, economic domination, material prosperity, and so forth—long ago gave rise to a sense of disproportionality between the two countries with no real parallel in the relationship between the French and English Canadas. Thus, whereas Mexicans often have been preoccupied with the perils and dilemmas of living "so far from God and so close to the United States" (as have Canadians), most *norteamericanos* and their political leaders have been able to ignore the very existence of their southern neighbors much of the time. Putting the point differently, the impact on all of Canada of President Charles de Gaulle's defiant 1967 declaration of support for a "free" Quebec—based as it was on an implicit and proportionate rivalry between French and British cultures—has no psychological parallel for the United States in any conceivable declaration by a president of Mexico.

A related historical disproportion has to do with the demographic strengths of the conquered peoples in Canada and the United States. At the time of the Canadian conquest in 1763, French settlers outnumbered the British by a wide margin, and it was not until the mid-19th century that anglophones outnumbered francophones to any significant degree. In the American southwest, by contrast, 19th-century Anglo agricultural expansion into Texas and the Gold Rush to California, almost simultaneously with the area's annexation, meant that Mexico's previously pastoral *mestizos* were quickly outnumbered by a vast margin, with the sole exception of the Santa Fe region in what would become New Mexico.

In part as a consequence of these demographic realities, the historical experiences of ethnic group development by French Canadians and Mexican Americans were to be quite different. Barred from continuing their lucrative trading practices by their new British "masters," the French Canadians largely withdrew to self-sufficient agriculture as a means of ethnocultural survival, aided by a highly nationalistic francophone Roman Catholic clergy. Thus began Canada's "two solitudes"—two founding peoples coexisting quite separately under British colonial rule. In addition, Canada's conquest resulted in few francophones immigrating to "British North America" for nearly two centuries. Although the francophones' famous "revenge of the cradle" meant that French Canadians would remain some one third of the country's population until well into the 20th century, the point here is that nearly 200 years of relatively isolated ethnocultural development facilitated the creation of a cohesive, insular, and quite self-conscious ethnic group with a long history of distinctive identity. Although the modernization and economic integration of francophone Canada in the mid-20th century would involve vast and astoundingly rapid political and social change, the historical "group base" from which the "Quiet Revolution" began was never really in doubt (despite several futile 19th-century British efforts at assimilation).

In contrast, the historical development of Mexican Americans (and, more recently, Latinos) as an ethnic group in the United States was very different. Vastly outnumbered in most areas and stripped of their land, Mexican Americans found themselves quickly transformed from a pastoral people to an agricultural, mining, and industrial proletariat throughout the region (Barrera, 1979). Simultaneously, Mexican Americans were subjected to two powerful forms of U.S. cultural and political influence: (a) they were treated in many areas as *racially* inferior along patterns that had been evolved for African Americans, Asian Americans, and American Indians (e.g., dual labor markets, segregated public schools), and (b) pervasive and insistent demands for linguistic and cultural assimilation were made as a condition for acceptance as genuine "Americans." In the face of these forces, moreover, the conquered *mexicanos* lacked two important structural supports for ethnocultural prosperity that were available to francophones in Quebec: For the most part they did not own their own land in the southwest (as noted earlier), and the church played a very different role for Mexican Americans as compared to French Canadians. Whereas Mexican Americans also were overwhelmingly Roman Catholic, the church in the Southwest was led by a largely anglophone (especially Irish) clergy that urged ethnocultural assimilation and politicoeconomic accommodation rather than group "survival" through self-isolation.

In addition, the relative insularity of French Canada for almost two centuries was unmatched in other ways among Mexican Americans in the southwest. A relatively porous border between the U.S. Southwest and the mother country, for example, meant that periodic economic or political upheaval to the south brought a sure influx of newcomers to alter the nature and cohesion of the group at regular intervals. In the 20th century, moreover, Mexican Americans were joined by a growing number of other newcomers from distinct yet related "Latin" countries (e.g., Puerto Rico, Cuba, El Salvador, Guatemala, Nicaragua), who generated a neverending discussion over the appropriate ethnic boundaries that were to "count" in the ethnocultural politics of the United States.

As a result of these forces—early numerical "minorization," early economic integration in a subordinate position, "racial" discrimination, pres-

## 2. THE POLITICS OF LANGUAGE 63

sures to assimilate, lack of insularity and ethnic boundary definition—Mexican Americans have found it much more difficult to achieve
consensus on the bases and meaning of their own identity as an ethnocultural group or on the import of that identity for greater equality within the
larger society. In short, the relative paucity of structural support for ethnolinguistic maintenance among Mexican Americans—to be outlined here
later for the contemporary period—has deep historical roots and may help
to account for the near-absence among them of political demands for either
a confederal policy or for the repatriation of *Aztlan* to Mexico. A more
complete account, however, requires an examination of important contemporary differences in the *structural* supports for ethnolinguistic diversity
between the two countries, a subject to which we now turn.

### Structural Contrasts

As noted earlier, one of the most important contrasts between recent
Canadian and U.S. language policy conflicts is the fact that the goal of
ethnolinguistic equality being sought by the subordinate group in each
country has been defined quite differently. Although the Quebecois have
coalesced around a *confederal* definition of equal status, U.S. Latinos have
sought a *pluralist* approach that recognizes English as the dominant language of the country. Thus, most U.S. Latinos and their allies have argued
for an "English-Plus" goal and have not mobilized for the creation of
political jurisdictions in which Spanish would be the dominant and official
language. In addition to the historical disparities outlined earlier, several
important contemporary *structural* differences in the power positions of the
two conquered groups exist that help to explain this apparently fundamental contrast in ethnocultural aspiration.

The first, and most obvious, structural difference between the power
position of Latinos in the United States and francophones in Canada is their
respective *geodemographic* locations in the two countries, a difference rooted
in the past as noted earlier. Francophones have always been a larger
percentage of Canada's population than have been Latinos in the United
States. However, more important for grasping the underlying factors influencing their policy aims is the fact that francophones have been the overwhelming majority of Quebec's population since the province was
established in the 19th century. Although they too have been concentrated
geographically (particularly in the southwestern states), Latinos have been
a minority population in every state in the Union. Indeed, New Mexico's
admission into the Union as a state was delayed until enough Anglos had
settled there to relegate the *hispanos* to a minority of the population (Kloss,
1977). Although the Latino population has been growing faster numerically than any other racial or ethnic group in the United States in recent

decades (due, in roughly equal amounts, to relatively high birthrates and international migration), they are not projected to be a majority in any state before the end of the 21st century. Anglos are expected to become a minority population in California by the year 2000, but rapid growth among the Asian American and Latino populations accounts for this projection. Latinos are expected to equal Anglos in numbers in California by about 2030, but no one ethnic group is expected to become a majority as far into the future as demographers have been willing to project (Bouvier & Gardner, 1986). Under the rules of majoritarian democracy, therefore, the power position of francophones in Quebec (with more than 80% of the population) is far different from that of Latinos in any U.S. state now or in the forseeable future.

Moreover, the apparent ability of Quebec's francophones to capture control of their own economic destiny by using their numerical superiority in provincial politics (Levine, 1990) has no forseeable parallel for Latinos in the United States. Political analysts of both the right (Phillips, 1990) and the left (Zeitlin, 1990) have recently emphasized that one of the most important changes in the U.S. political economy in the last decade was a significant growth of *economic inequality* and a decline of the middle class as a proportion of the U.S. population. Along with the African American population, Latinos have been particularly affected by these economic changes. A 1989 report issued by the National Council of La Raza found a significant drop in Latino family income in the 1980s and a concomitant increase in the proportion of Latinos living below the poverty line. Most discouraging to Latino activists was the finding that poverty had increased even among two-parent Latino families, from 13.1% to 16% (Davis, 1989). Insofar as economic and political power are mutually reinforcing, therefore, the power position of Latinos seems unlikely to take the trajectory experienced by Quebec's francophones during the past three decades. Indeed, with the U.S. economic position projected to continue its decline relative to the world economy in the years to come, the central dynamic of the U.S. political economy does not appear to give grounds for optimism to U.S. Latinos bent on gaining their "fair share" of the nation's shrinking political and economic bounty. Instead, some analysts are projecting a developing two-tiered political economy in the United States, with a shrinking middle class and Latinos relegated once again to the lower class along with African Americans (Hayes-Bautista, Schink, & Chapa, 1989). The greatly different "location" of Latinos in the U.S. economy and francophones in Canada's economy in the 1990s, therefore, is a second important structural difference in the power position of the two language minority groups.

A third important structural difference is *political*, embedded particularly in the contrasting federal systems of the two countries. Although both

## 2. THE POLITICS OF LANGUAGE

countries have federal governments, Canada's federal system has been far more decentralized than has that of the United States. Despite presidential rhetoric of decentralization from Reagan to Clinton, and Canadian provincial concerns about that country's centralization (particularly under Trudeau), these differences remain substantial and are not likely to change dramatically in the near future. This is an important dimension for the politics of language because only a highly decentralized federal system could possibly accommodate the degree of autonomy proposed by the Quebecois in their "linguistic confederalist" approach to language policy. Trying to imagine a state government successfully overriding a U.S. Supreme Court decision protecting the rights of language minority persons explicitly written into the Constitution is sufficient to grasp one aspect of the important difference being highlighted here. Another aspect of the difference is illuminated by imagining the president of the United States calling together the governors of all the states for a conference to negotiate a settlement to important differences between them, and expecting that their agreement would have a good chance of being implemented to end a major constitutional crisis. The structural differences between the two systems embedded in these hypothetical examples are enormous.

Yet another important political structural variable derives from the relative size of the state apparatus in the two countries being compared here, particularly at the subnational level of government. As an entire literature recently developed by political scientists attests, "the state" acts as an independent variable shaping the political economy of any society. We may expect, therefore, that a more developed state will have a greater impact on the socioeconomic reality and political dynamic of any particular jurisdiction than will a smaller state apparatus. Here it is important that the welfare state of the Canadians, particularly at the subnational level, is relatively more developed and more extensive than that of the United States. That is, Canada's provincial-level public sectors tend to be larger in proportion to their private sectors than is true of state and local governments in the United States.

As Levine (1990) has documented in great detail, the Quebecois were able to make use of the state apparatus in their province to bring about profound changes in the relative distribution of economic power (ranging from huge economic development programs to control of employment opportunities throughout the relatively more extensive public sector) from the 1960s through the 1980s. Latinos in the United States, in contrast, have lacked this structural support both because their relative numerical political strength is far less and because the state governments of the U.S. operate in a much different political climate vis-à-vis state intervention in the private sector. The only comparable structural support in the United States is the population of bilingual education teachers, a much less significant force in American political life for a variety of reasons. The relatively small state in American politics also gives greater ideological credence to and enhances the power position of assimilationists who argue that the retention of minority languages and cultures, although necessarily allowed under liberalism's individual freedoms, is a private matter and is not a proper subject of public policy (see, e.g., Epstein, 1977).

Finally, a fourth structural variable that throws into relief important differences between the two countries might be termed *organizational*. Drawing on the work of Raymond Breton, for example, Brym (1989) has emphasized that francophones in Canada have a much higher level of ethnolinguistic "institutional completeness" than is true of any minority group in the United States. As Brym explained, "'institutional completeness' refers to the number and type of formal organizations in an ethnic community that service ethnic-group members: schools, churches, sports clubs, mutual-aid societies, credit unions, employment agencies, and so forth" (p. 117). Further, the greater the degree of ethnolinguistic institutional completeness in the society, the greater will be the effect of an individual's ethnic group membership on that individual's socioeconomic standing in the larger society. Thus, with a far more extensive organizational base, francophones in Quebec have a much greater incentive to identify themselves in ethnolinguistic terms than do Latinos in the United States. The operation of this structural variable, of course, parallels the argument made by Quebecois proponents of linguistic confederation. Further, it is in accord with the generalization of sociolinguists that the viability of a language in competition with other languages normally depends on the degree to which it operates in a variety of institutional domains (Fishman, 1972). Although francophones in Quebec have been dominant in a wide variety of these domains, increased significantly in recent years by Bill 101, Spanish speakers in the United States have had far fewer "public spaces" in which to interact and reinforce their own language.

Together with the important historical differences outlined earlier, the net result of these structural considerations should be instructive to Americans concerned about the likelihood that Latinos will follow the path of the Quebecois. To imagine that prospect as a serious possibility, it is necessary to project a series of interrelated and highly unlikely developments. First, Latinos would have to form an overwhelming political majority in a political jurisdiction with real effective control over domestic public policy, even if their policy positions flew in the face of longstanding national policies and political values. Second, Latinos would have to be able to translate their numerical strength into enough political power to gain some measure of effective control over their economic future, which could, in turn, be used

## 2. THE POLITICS OF LANGUAGE 67

to extend an organizational base for their own cultural and linguistic development. This scenario is so unlikely that it is not difficult to understand why Latinos have not mounted a campaign for a policy of linguistic confederation, especially in a context that also includes a pervasive liberal individualistic political culture and the virtually hegemonic position of the English language in North America. Further, in view of these structural political facts of life in the United States, it seems apparent that Latinos have had a surer grasp of their political reality than have the assimilationist pundits seeking to generate widespread alarm over the separatist implications of pluralistic language policy proposals.

This is not to say, of course, that language policy conflict will not be rancorous or volatile in the United States in the years to come. Indeed, one possible scenario is that Anglos will become increasingly anxiety-ridden over their apparent loss of status in a nation that is increasingly racially and ethnically diverse. Unprepared for a pluralist understanding of their national identity, some Anglos may also continue to perceive state support for bilingualism and biculturalism as an important threat to their *personal* identity as Americans as well. To the degree that anxiety finds political expression, it is possible that there will be increased Anglo support for a relatively aggressive and restrictive policy of assimilation. This development, in turn, could very well trigger a backlash of ethnic political cohesion in the now much larger minority populations of the country. As one social scientist recently concluded in his survey of literature on ethnic solidarity in the contemporary world:

> The degree of an ethnic group's identity will vary in direct proportion to the amount of opposition encountered by the group; the greater the opposition, the greater the degree of identity, and conversely, the lesser the amount of opposition, the lesser the degree of identity. (Scott, 1990, p. 163)

Ironically, then, the most important lesson that may be derived from this analysis is that an aggressive policy of linguistic assimilation in the United States may be more likely to push Latinos in the direction of increased separatism than any desire on their part to emulate the example of the Quebecois in Canada. Which lessons Canadians may wish to learn from the example of language policy conflict in the United States will be left to their own political analysts.

### ACKNOWLEDGMENTS

An earlier version of this essay was presented at the 1991 Annual Meeting of the American Political Science Association. I am grateful for assistance from the Government of Quebec, federal Government of Canada, and

California State University, Long Beach in the preparation of this chapter; in addition, I wish to thank Charles Noble, George Scott, Louis Balthazar, John Mallea, and Barbara Burnaby for critical comments on earlier versions of this chapter.

## REFERENCES

Albert, L. (1989, Spring). Language in Canada, *Canadian Social Trends*, pp. 9–12.

Barrera, M. (1979). *Race and class in the Southwest: A theory of racial inequality*. Notre Dame, IN: University of Notre Dame Press.

Barrera, M. (1988). *Beyond Aztlan: Ethnic autonomy in comparative perspective*. New York: Praeger.

Bilingual danger. (1976, November 22). *New York Times*.

Bouvier, L. F., & Gardner, R. W. (1986). Immigration to the U.S.: The unfinished story. *Population Bulletin, 41*(4), 3–50.

Brym, R. J., with Fox, B. J. (1989). *From culture to power: The sociology of English Canada*. New York: Oxford University Press.

Burns, J. F. (1990, June 24). Canadian leader appeals for calm on Quebec dispute. *New York Times*, pp. A–1,4.

Canada, Commissioner of Official Languages. (1991). *Annual report 1990*. Ottawa: Minister of Supply and Services Canada.

Canada, Royal Commission on Bilingualism and Biculturalism. (1973). *Bilingualism and biculturalism: An abridged version of the royal commission report*. Canada: McClelland and Stewart Limited, in cooperation with The Secretary of State Department and Information Canada.

*Canada–Quebec Accord Relating to Immigration and Temporary Admission of Aliens*. (1991). (mimeographed document).

Castro, R. (1976). Shifting the burden of bilingualism: The case for monolingual communities. *The Bilingual Review, 3*(1), 3–30.

Cummins, J. (1981). The role of primary language development in promoting educational success for language minority students. In *Schooling and language minority students: A theoretical framework*. Los Angeles: California State University Evaluation, Dissemination, and Assessment Center.

Cummins, J. (1984). The language minority child. In S. Shapson & V. D'Oyley (Eds.), *Bilingual and multicultural education: Canadian perspectives* (pp. 71–92) Clevedon, England: Multilingual Matters.

Cummins, J. (1986). Empowering minority students: A framework for intervention. *Harvard Educational Review, 56*(1), 18–36.

Cummins, J. (1989). *Empowering minority students*. Sacramento: California Association for Bilingual Education.

d'Anglejan, A. (1984). Language planning in Quebec: An historical overview and future trends. In R. Y. Bourhis (Ed.), *Conflict and language planning in Quebec* (pp. 29–52). Clevedon, England: Multilingual Matters.

Davis, K. (1989, December 16). Latino poverty grew over decade, study finds. *Los Angeles Times*, p. A28.

de la Garza, R., DeSipio, L., Garcia, F. C., Garcia, J., & Falcon, A. (1992). *Latino voices: Mexican, Puerto Rican, and Cuban perspectives on American politics*. Boulder, CO: Westview.

Epstein, N. (1977). *Language, ethnicity and the schools: Policy alternatives for bilingual-bicultural education*. Washington, DC: Institute for Educational Leadership, George Washington University.

Fishman, J. A. (1972). *The sociology of language*. Rowley, MA: Newbury House.

## 2. THE POLITICS OF LANGUAGE 69

Fishman, J. A. (1987). What is happening to Spanish on the U.S. mainland? *Ethnic Affairs, 1,* 13–23.

Francis, D. R. (1990, June 21). Why one Canadian province quarrels with the rest. *Christian Science Monitor,* 10.

Frum, D. (1988, October). Who's running this country, anyway? *Saturday Night,* pp. 56–66.

Government of Canada. (1977). *A national understanding: Statement of the government of Canada on the official languages policy.* Ottowa: Minister of Supply and Services Canada.

Government of Quebec. (1990). *Vision: A policy statement on immigration and integration.* Quebec City: Department of Communications, Quebec Ministry for Cultural Communications and Immigration.

Garcia, M. T. (1989). *Mexican Americans: Leadership, ideology, & identity, 1930–1960.* New Haven, CT: Yale University Press.

Hall, T. (1989, February 27). Fed up with being left out in the cold. *The Toronto Globe and Mail.*

Hayes-Bautista, D. E., Schink, W. O., & Chapa, J. (1988). *The burden of support: Young Latinos in an aging society.* Stanford, CA: Stanford University Press.

Henry, S. (1990, March). English only: The language of discrimination. *Hispanic: The Magazine for and About Hispanics,* 28–32.

Hernandez-Chavez, E. (1978). Language maintenance, bilingual education and philosophies of bilingualism in the United States. In J. E. Alatis (Ed.), *GURT 1978: International dimensions of bilingual education* (pp. 527–550). Washington, DC: Georgetown University Press.

Hernandez-Chavez, E. (1984). The inadequacy of English immersion education as an educational approach for language minority students in the United States. In *Studies on immersion education: A collection for United States educators* (pp. 144–183). Sacramento: California State Department of Education.

Higham, J. (1963). *Strangers in the land: Patterns of American nativism 1860–1925* (2nd ed.). New York: Atheneum.

Jackson, R. J., Jackson, D., & Baxter-Moore, N. (1986). *Politics in Canada: Culture, institutions, behavior and public policy.* Scarborough, Ontario: Prentice-Hall Canada.

Kloss, H. (1977). *The American bilingual tradition.* Rowley, MA: Newbury House.

Laponce, J. A. (1987, December). *What kind of bilingualism for Canada: Personal or territorial? The demographic evidence.* Paper presented at the Conference on Ethnic and Racial Minorities in Advanced Industrial Democracies. University of Notre Dame, Notre Dame, IN.

Leibowitz, A. H. (1982). *Federal recognition of the rights of minority language groups.* Rosslyn, VA: National Clearinghouse for Bilingual Education.

Lemco, J. (1987, September). *The implications of an "official" language: The cases of Quebec's Bill 101 and California's Proposition 63.* Paper presented at the Annual Meeting of the American Political Science Association, Chicago.

Levine, M. V. (1990). *The reconquest of Montreal: Language policy and social change in a bilingual city.* Philadelphia: Temple University Press.

Lipset, S. M. (1965). Revolution and counterrevolution: The United States and Canada. In T. R. Ford (Ed.), *The revolutionary theme in contemporary America* (pp. 21–64). Lexington: University of Kentucky Press.

Lipset, S. M. (1985). Canada and the United States: The cultural dimension. In C. F. Doran & J. H. Sigler (Eds.), *Canada and the United States: Enduring friendship, persistent stress* (pp. 109–160). Englewood Cliffs, NJ: Prentice-Hall.

Lipset, S. M. (1990). *Continental divide: The values and institutions of The United States and Canada.* New York: Routlege.

Malcolm, A. H. (1990, July). Beyond vanilla: Immigration has accentuated Canada's diversity. *New York Times,* p. IV–2.

Mallea, J. R. (1984). Minority language education in Quebec and anglophone Canada. In R. Y. Bourhis (Ed.), *Conflict and language planning in Quebec* (pp. 223–260). Clevedon, England: Multilingual Matters.

McRoberts, K. (1988). *Quebec: Social change and political crisis* (3rd ed.). Toronto: McClelland & Stewart Inc.

Phillips, K. (1990, June 17). Reagan's America: A capital offense. *New York Times Magazine*, 26–28, 40, 64.

Piatt, B. (1990). *Only English? Law and language policy in the United States.* Albuquerque: University of New Mexico Press.

Pitt, L. (Ed.) (1985). *California controversies.* San Rafael, CA: ETRI Publishing Co.

Purich, D. J. (1989). Treatment of Aboriginal peoples. In Lorne Ingle (Ed.), *Meech Lake reconsidered* (pp. 47–52). Hull, Quebec: Voyageur.

Resnick, P. (1990). *Letter to a Quebecois friend, with a reply by Daniel Latouche.* Montreal & Kingston: McGill-Queen's University Press.

Schmidt, R. J. (1991, March). *Sources of language policy conflict: A comparative perspective.* Paper presented to the Annual Conference of the Western Political Science Association, Seattle, WA.

Scott, G. M., Jr. (1990). A resynthesis of the primordial and circumstantial approaches to ethnic group solidarity: Towards an explanatory model. *Ethnic and Racial Studies, 13*(2), 147–171.

Southwest Voter Research Institute, Inc. (1988). Southwest Latino voters speak with single voice. *Southwest Voter Research Notes, 2*(6), 1, 4.

Stanley, A. (1990, June 25). Autonomy's cry revived in Quebec. *New York Times*, p. A3.

Uchitelle, L. (1990, June 24). Quebec could easily prosper on its own, economists say. *New York Times*, pp. A1,A4.

U.S. Commission on Civil Rights. (1981). *The voting rights act: Unfulfilled goals.* Washington, DC: U.S. Government Printing Office.

U.S. General Accounting Office. (1987). *Bilingual education: A new look at the research evidence.* Washington, DC: Author.

Walsh, M. W. (1990). A tongue lashing in Canada. *Los Angeles Times*, p. A1.

Zeitlin, M. (1990, May 20). U.S. misery in inequality: Ignoring the grim truths. *Los Angeles Times*, pp. M4, M8.

# 3

# Demographic Considerations in Canadian Language Policy

Roderic Beaujot
*The University of Western Ontario*

The population of Canada has become increasingly diverse in terms of ethnic origin. Immigration has ensured that no one ethnic group constitutes a majority, and intermarriage has resulted in more than one fourth of the population citing more than one ethnic origin. Except in the cases of First Nations (Native Canadian) peoples and visible minorities, the very concept of *ethnicity* has lost much of its earlier significance.

On the other hand, language concepts remain very relevant, and the two official languages have come to dominate. The focus here is on the national languages of English and French, their relative magnitude, the dynamics of change, and associated policy questions. In 1991, 7.7% of the population spoke languages other than English or French at home and 1.4 % knew neither of the official languages. The largest component of the latter are recent immigrants who are likely to learn one of the languages, as well as First Nations peoples in remote regions.

Recent censuses have included three language questions. Mother tongue is the language first spoken and still understood. Home language is the language used most often in the home. Knowledge of official languages asks if people know either or both English and French sufficiently well to be able to carry on a conversation. The comparisons of mother tongue and home language provide a measure of language retention or transfer. The

1991 census added a question on the languages known well enough to be able to carry on a conversation.

## DEMOGRAPHIC TRENDS

In 1760, the French population of the current territory of Canada amounted to at least 80% of the total non-Native population (Lachapelle & Henripin, 1980). It is estimated that by around 1805 the English group attained the majority. By 1850 the French group had fallen to 30% of the total, a level that would remain almost constant for the next 100 years (Review of Demography, 1989). By 1991, the French group comprised less than 25% of the Canadian population.

Issues of English–French relations have been a recurring theme in Canada. It is more than a question of language and communication; these relations involve "recurrent power struggles for the control of the means required for society building in its economic, cultural and linguistic dimensions" (Breton, 1988, p. 557). In effect, there is competition for resources and for control of institutions, along with the opportunities that these provide. Breton further observed that new rounds of competition have been triggered by changes in relative size of the groups, political mobilization, and unresolved contradictions. The development of policies of accommodation between English and French has been a constant challenge (Cartwright, 1988b).

The relatively stable balance of the period between 1850 and 1950 was largely maintained by the underlying demographics; higher French fertility compensated for immigration that largely supported the English group. This dynamic was broken in the 1960s when all factors played against the relative size of the French group. Most importantly, the French lost their fertility advantage while the English maintained their immigration advantage and language transfer favored English over French, especially outside of Quebec. As a result of the operation of these factors, 23.1% of the population spoke mostly French at home by 1991, whereas 68.7% spoke mostly English, with another 0.5% declaring both as the language spoken most often at home (Table 3.1).

Assessing the relative importance of the various factors, Lachapelle (1988a, 1988b) concluded that international immigration plays the largest role in the relative decline of the French group in Canada. Fertility and mortality differences are small. Linguistic transfers are not that common; the net transmission of French from mother to child is rather constant at about 95% in recent decades. In contrast, international migration reinforces the English group. For instance, in the cohort who were aged 0–4 in 1941 and 45–49 in 1986, the proportion French mother tongue fell from 36 to 26% over this 45-year period. Three quarters of this observed difference is due

## 3. DEMOGRAPHIC CONSIDERATIONS

**TABLE 3.1**

Distributions by Mother Tongue, Home Language, and Official Languages, 1991

|  | Canada | Quebec | Rest of Canada |
|---|---|---|---|
| *Mother Tongue* |  |  |  |
| English | 60.6 | 9.0 | 78.0 |
| French | 24.2 | 81.8 | 4.7 |
| Both English and French | 0.4 | 0.6 | 0.3 |
| Other | 14.9 | 8.6 | 17.0 |
| Total | 100.0 | 100.0 | 100.0 |
| *Home language* |  |  |  |
| English | 68.7 | 10.9 | 88.2 |
| French | 23.1 | 82.8 | 3.0 |
| Both English and French | 0.5 | 1.0 | 0.3 |
| Other | 7.7 | 5.4 | 8.5 |
| Total | 100.0 | 100.0 | 100.0 |
| *Official languages* |  |  |  |
| English only | 67.1 | 5.5 | 87.9 |
| French only | 15.2 | 58.1 | 0.7 |
| Both English and French | 16.3 | 35.4 | 9.8 |
| Neither English nor French | 1.4 | 0.9 | 1.6 |
| Total | 100.0 | 100.0 | 100.0 |

*Note*: Multiple responses including English, French, and other languages have been included with English and French. From *1991 Census* (catalog Nos. 93–317 and 93–318), by Statistics Canada, 1992. Copyright 1992 by Ministry of Industry, Science, and Technology. Adapted with permission.

to international migration. Besides international migration, the differences in fertility and mortality, along with language shifts, all play against the French group for the country as a whole (Lachapelle, 1987). In terms of births, those of French mother tongue represented 36% of the total in 1941, compared to 29% in 1961 and 23% in 1986 (Lachapelle, 1988c).

### Official Language Minorities

It is often said that the linguistic minorities involve over 1 million French outside of Quebec and another million English in Quebec. However, this generalization is based on old statistics and the concept of mother tongue, which may not be the most accurate indicator of linguistic identity. In 1991, there were only 667,000 persons outside of Quebec who indicated French as their home language and 810,000 persons in Quebec indicating English as their only home language.

The French language minorities outside of Quebec and New Brunswick have typically undergone considerable erosion. Language transfer has played a major role in the decline of French outside of Quebec and New Brunswick. As long as they could maintain a certain isolation, often in rural areas or in extractive industries, and maintain communities around religious affiliations, there was considerable persistence of these minorities. However, with the broader scale of social interaction and the reduced role of religion in defining communities, the French minorities have been undermined (Beaujot & McQuillan, 1982). Thériault (1989) maintained little hope for the French-speaking communities outside of Quebec and Acadia. The rural isolation, often based on a parish identity, is no longer available. The groups no longer have the necessary "compact relationships" that would assure their long-term existence as language communities. Intermarriage has also played a significant role, because in most cases English is adopted as the home language (Castonguay, 1979; Robinson, 1989). As a result of these factors, Cartwright (1988a) spoke of the bilingual "belt" around Quebec having become a series of "pockets." For all persons of French mother tongue outside of Quebec, more than 30% do not cite it as the language used most often at home (Bourbeau, 1989). Beyond New Brunswick and Ontario, this figure rises to 50%. In families outside of Quebec where one parent is of French mother tongue and the other is English, over 80% of children have English as their mother tongue (Harrison & Marmen, 1994).

In Quebec, the English mother tongue group has been declining as a proportion of the total population for more than a century. In 1844 they comprised one fourth of the population, compared to less than 10% in 1991 (Caldwell, 1988; see Table 3.1). Since 1971, the English mother tongue group has also declined in absolute numbers and is increasingly concentrated in Montreal. Fertility is very low, measured at 1.2 births per woman in 1981 or close to half of the replacement level (Tremblay & Bourbeau, 1985). Compared to the past, the English group is now benefiting less from language transfers and it continues to suffer substantial departures to other provinces. In the period between 1976 and 1981, close to 20% of the English home language population left the province. Given other factors such as aging and internal ethnic diversity, there is concern about the viability of what was once an important community in the province. This concern applies especially to the English youth who are particularly prone to leave and who, although heavily concentrated in Montreal, are very heterogeneous in ethnic origin (Harrison, 1996).

It is also noteworthy how internal migration is selective of English and other languages in leaving Quebec and of French in going to Quebec. In the period between 1976 and 1981, the rates of out-migration for Quebec were

## 3. DEMOGRAPHIC CONSIDERATIONS                                        75

1.7 per 1,000 for French, 7 per 1,000 for other, and 39 per 1,000 for English home language (Termote & Gauvreau, 1985). Thus the English out-migration rate was 23 times that of the French. The rates of out-migration from the rest of Canada (to Quebec) were: 13.1 for French, 0.4 for other, and 0.5 per 1,000 for English. This time the French rate is 26 times as high as the English rate. The relative lack of migratory interaction between the English outside of Quebec and the French in Quebec suggest that the provincial boundaries are acting as a national boundary (Termote, 1995).

Consequently, since 1961, and especially since 1971, the linguistic duality has increasingly involved a territorial duality. The French majority has increased in Quebec whereas the English majority has increased outside of Quebec. Official languages are increasing where they are in the majority and decreasing where they are in the minority. In terms of home language, 90% of francophones lived in Quebec in 1991, where they account for 84% of the population. In contrast, 96% of anglophones lived in other provinces, accounting for 89% of the population.

At the same time, official language bilingualism has increased from 13.5% in 1971 to 16.3% in 1991 (Albert, 1989). Bilingualism is four times as high in the French than in the English mother tongue population of Canada, but anglophones have made progress especially in Quebec and the contact regions (Grenier & Lachapelle, 1988). The rise in the status of the French language has promoted a greater number of nonfrancophones to learn the language.

### The French Language

Although the proportion with French mother tongue or home language has continued to decline at the national level, Lachapelle (1989a) noted other data suggesting that French has improved in status since the early 1970s. There is an increase in the extent to which parents pass the French language on to their children. Outside of Quebec, the knowledge of French has increased, especially among younger cohorts. French has increased as a proportion of the population of Quebec due to the departure of other groups and due to the increased rate at which these groups transfer to French (see Veltman, chapter 12, this volume). The proportion of the non-French mother tongue group of Quebec who can speak French increased from 33% in 1961 to 64% in 1986.

As a result of these various factors, the proportion of the Canadian population that is able to speak French has remained stable, measuring 32% both in 1951 and 1991 (Grenier & Lachapelle, 1988; Statistics Canada, 1993, Table 3). Although French is declining as a language spoken at home, it is increasing as a second language.

## Quebec

Focusing on Quebec in particular, the main positive result for the French language is that its proportion has increased, especially since 1966. The 1986 level of 83% French mother tongue is the highest level in a century and a half (Lachapelle, 1989b). However, a major component of the changing proportions results from net departures of non-French groups. In the period between 1966 and 1986, the departures of English from Quebec were more than sufficient to compensate for the transfers to English from French and other groups (Lachapelle, 1988c). Persons who transfer to English are also more likely to leave the province. In effect, this has meant that the increasing French predominance in Quebec has been at the expense of a decreasing relative size of the Quebec population in Canada.

Factors other than migration have played less significant roles in affecting the French majority in Quebec. Language transfer produces a result that is basically neutral for the French language; there are about as many French mother tongue people who speak other languages at home as there are people from other mother tongues who speak French at home. However, at ages under 30, the transfers involve a net deficit for the French language (Bourbeau, 1988). Veltman (1988) also observed that anglicization has not stopped for the French-born of Quebec.

Although recent international migrants to Quebec are more likely to associate with the French than the English group, the English group continues to gain more immigrants than its relative share in the base population (Beaujot, 1997; Termote & Gauvreau, 1988). The geographic concentration of immigration in Montreal also presents a problem with regard to the assimilation to the French language. Most immigrant groups, except Haitians and Portuguese, are in residential locations of English concentration. Veltman (1986, 1988) found that even if the schools are French, English is used extensively and the children continue to identify with the English language. Only when the children go to schools with high proportions of French, as in the case of the Portuguese, do the recent immigrant children adopt French as their main language of interaction. Veltman also observed that the immigrants who arrive as adults are less likely to switch languages. When they do transfer, those who know French, or neither English nor French, are more likely to transfer to French. Those who know English on arrival are more likely to integrate into the English group or leave the province. It can be seen that a variety of factors are important in the linguistic choices of immigrants: age at arrival, knowledge of official languages at arrival, linguistic concentration of the chosen residential location, language of instruction in the schools, and linguistic composition of the school population itself. Nonetheless, Veltman (1988) found that the second

# 3. DEMOGRAPHIC CONSIDERATIONS                                        77

generation from abroad or from outside Quebec are tending to adopt French as their home language.

Paillé (1989a) expressed concern about the potential for the French language to maintain its own on the Island of Montreal. Representing 40% of the population of the metropolitan area, it is here that immigrants are most likely to initially arrive. High non-French immigration, combined with low French fertility, is expected to reduce the French mother tongue concentration below the 60% level that it has maintained over the period between 1976 and 1986. For instance, in the school population, the French mother tongue represented 63.8% of the total in 1971 compared to 54.2% in 1986. As of 1987, there have been more non-French mother tongue immigrants than births to French home language mothers on the Island of Montreal. However, these statistics are based on residential locations. During the workday, the presence of persons from outside of the Island produces a greater concentration of French than that implied in these data.

## NATIONAL POLICY ISSUES

Language policy issues are particularly complex; views can be rather different at the national than at provincial levels, and there is a tension between alternative orientations. Breton and Breton (1980) referred to the contrast between the pan-Canadian and segmentalist perspectives. The pan-Canadian approach argues for promoting the two languages across the country through institutions that are able to operate in both languages, whereas the segmentalist or territorial approach argues for building on the strength of majority languages in given areas. Clearly, there is more than just language at stake, but basic conceptions of the society, including approaches to maintaining unity in the face of diversity, or for creating a different form of association across the two major parts of the country.

The federal policy has largely adopted a pan-Canadian approach, especially through ensuring that the national-level civil service operates in the two languages and by supporting official language minorities and second language education (Pal, 1993). The proportion of French mother tongue in the civil service in effect increased from 21.5% in 1965 to 27.0% in 1986 (Brooks, 1989). Official bilingualism increased the value of French language proficiency for entry and mobility within the federal bureaucracy. Funding for second language education, along with parental demand, have increased the knowledge of French among children outside of Quebec. Enrollment in French immersion programs increased from 65,000 in 1980–1981 to 250,000 in 1990–1991 (Harrison & Marmen, 1994). By the early 1990s, 6.8% of eligible students were enrolled in such programs (Bourbeau, 1989).

Other observers of the demographic trends are more critical of the thrust of federal language policy. Cartwright (1988a) was concerned that the bilingual zone that provides for a transition between English and French Canada has withered. Canada could be becoming more like Belgium in terms of the geography of language, with Ottawa and Montreal being somewhat equivalent to Brussels as the only area where the two languages effectively coexist. Reflecting in general on languages that are in geographic contact, Cartwright (1989) further observed that in the war of languages, contact and interaction will eventually lead to unilingualism. Possibly a minority language can withstand the assimilative pressures only if it is sufficiently concentrated to reduce such contact (Laponce, 1988).

It can be argued that the Royal Commission on Bilingualism and Biculturalism (1967) made a serious mistake in not adopting the territorial principle as a basic underlying approach to language policy (McRoberts, 1989). A territorially based bilingualism may make it more likely that Canada could survive as a bilingual nation (Polèse, 1990). The idea of promoting the two languages across the country has been counter to the aspirations of Quebec and it makes little sense in large parts of English Canada (Guindon, 1988). Two attempts to establish "bilingual districts" across the country, as suggested by the Royal Commission and adopted as part of the 1969 Official Languages Act, were doomed to failure because there was no clear social consensus supporting this approach.

## PROVINCIAL ISSUES

Quebec policy has been aimed at supporting the French language. In the late 1960s, the Royal Commission on Bilingualism and Biculturalism had observed that francophones controlled little of the economic activity in Quebec. The better educated French population who were upwardly mobile had little opportunity to work in French in the private sector. In terms of public institutions, Quebec had developed into "two solitudes" each with control over its own education systems, hospitals, and social service agencies (Coleman, 1983). In addition, most immigrant children were going to English schools. The aim of policies adopted in 1974 (Bill 22) and 1977 (Bill 101, Chartre de la langue française) was to reverse these trends. In particular, the policies sought to expand the use of French as the language of work at middle and senior levels of management in the private sector. Second, there was an attempt to integrate the linguistically separate education, hospital, and social service agencies. Finally, there was the requirement that immigrant children go to French schools. Besides these specific objectives, these policies in effect helped to improve the social mobility prospects of the new francophone middle class that had emerged during

## 3. DEMOGRAPHIC CONSIDERATIONS

the Quiet Revolution (Brooks, 1989). Francophones gained greater access to economic structures, and almost exclusive control over state agencies.

In further assessing the demographic impact of language legislation, Paillé (1989b) noted first that the trends in the language of education have been reversed. In 1976–1977, 38% of the foreign born students were in French schools compared to 78% in 1985–1986 and 90% in 1992–1993. The array of language policies in Quebec that have made French effectively the language of the society, including policies regarding language use in the schools and the Quebec government involvement in immigrant selection, is having the impact of promoting a greater association to the French language among more recent immigrants and their children (Vaillancourt, 1989). In addition, the proportion of the population with no knowledge of French was reduced from 11.6% in 1971 to 6.4% in 1991. The various policies have contributed to a reversal of previous trends that involved a decline in the proportion French in the province over the period between 1951 and 1971.

The Royal Commission on Bilingualism and Biculturalism had also suggested an official bilingual status for Quebec and the bordering provinces of Ontario and New Brunswick. However, only New Brunswick adopted official bilingualism. Consequently, Canada is a bilingual country with only one bilingual province. The linguistic composition in Acadia (northern and eastern New Brunswick) is very stable with 58 to 59% of the population of French mother tongue over the period between 1951 and 1986 (Lachapelle, 1989a, p. 13). In other provinces, the orientation has been to increase French services in specific areas. For instance, in Ontario this applies especially to an area of eastern and northern Ontario, where 65% of persons of French mother tongue live. The proportion of French in the small population of this region ranges from 25 to 75% of given counties (Cartwright, 1988b).

## SUMMARY AND CONCLUSION

The general linguistic trends in Canada therefore involve decreases in the official language minorities—that is, English in Quebec and French in the rest of Canada. Partly because of anglophone control over economic opportunity, at least in provinces other than Quebec, immigrants and their descendants are primarily oriented to the anglophone society in Canada (Reitz, 1980). Outside of Quebec, the influence of immigration is simple; it contributes to the English rather than to the French official language (Beaujot, 1997). In Quebec, immigration enhances the English minority because there is more English among immigrants than in the native born, and a sizable proportion of third-language migrants continue to transfer to the English language.

Although language policy in Quebec has promoted a greater association of immigrants to the French language, it must be noted that this is at the expense of departures of English and other linguistic groups. Therefore, it is at the expense of a lower total weight of Quebec in the population of Canada. Lachapelle (1988c) has put it well; it is hard to envisage scenarios that would both sustain the weight of Quebec in the Canadian total and increase the proportion French in Quebec. The rest of Canada does not have such a problem; more of its international arrivals are English to start with, immigrants retain their languages less, and almost all transfers favor English.

A variety of factors therefore contribute to the enhancement of the demographic boundary between Quebec and the rest of Canada (Termote, 1995). This includes the reduced demographic weight of Quebec in Canada, the reduced relative size of the French minority outside of Quebec and of the English minority in Quebec, the increased concentration of Canada's French population in Quebec, the contribution of immigration to the English language outside of Quebec along with a greater ambivalence in the linguistic role of immigrants to Quebec, and the lack of migratory exchange between the French of Quebec and the English of the rest of Canada.

Clearly the politics of language do not simply involve language as a means of communication. It is an aspect of personal identity and institutional affiliation, and it sets certain parameters to collective aspirations as a society. Constitutionally, it involves a search for a means to reflect the dualistic nature of the country.

One problem is the reduced relative size of the French language, which had stood at close to 30% over the period between 1850 and 1950 and has since been reduced to less than 25%. More than any other factor, this growing disequilibrium between Canada's two language communities could eventually contribute to the demise of a bilingual Canada and to the political separation of Quebec (Polèse, 1990).

Second, the increasing territorial duality means that most people live in regions where their language is in the majority. This is the case for 90% of the French home language and 96% of the English home language. It is only in Ottawa, Montreal, and Acadia that the two languages effectively coexist. Consequently, there is reduced potential for the minorities, English in Quebec and French in the rest of Canada, to provide a real presence and a viable community that would help to define the nature of the country. In terms of home language, these minorities comprise only some 5% of the population of the whole country. In a segmentalist or territorial model, linguistic minorities are less relevant because one builds on the regional distribution of the two languages. However, in a pan-Canadian model that seeks to achieve institutional bilingualism throughout the country, the

## 3. DEMOGRAPHIC CONSIDERATIONS 81

linguistic minorities in each region play an important role. In some ways, they are the very reason for applying an institutional model that seeks to make them feel at home in any part of the country. If it is the minorities that are to hold an institutionally bilingual country together, this glue is becoming weak. In particular, the orientation in Quebec is increasingly in favor of developing a distinct society, rather than building a bilingual country (Bastarache, 1989).

However, increased individual bilingualism in the official languages, from 12% in 1961 to 16% in 1991, may provide a substitute to the unifying role of linguistic minorities. Ultimately, it is also a question of values, aspirations, and economic potential for defining the society in which people want to live.

### ACKNOWLEDGMENT

Parts of this text are taken from Beaujot (1991), with permission from Oxford University Press. Statistics Canada information is used with the permission of the Minister of Industry, as Minister responsible for Statistics Canada. Information on the availability of the wide range of data from the Statistics Canada can be obtained from Statistics Canada's Regional Offices, its World Wide Web site at http://www.statcan.ca, and its toll-free access number 1-800-263-1136.

### REFERENCES

Albert, L. (1989). Language in Canada. *Canadian Social Trends, 12,* 9–12.

Bastarache, M. (1989). Will current demographic trends jeopardize Canada's evolution towards official languages equality? In *Demolinguistic trends and the evolution of Canadian institutions* (pp. 121–129). Ottawa: Secretary of State.

Beaujot, R. (1991). *Population change in Canada: The challenges of policy adaptation.* Toronto: Oxford University Press.

Beaujot, R. (1997). *Comportements démographiques et statut socio-économique des immigrants Canadians.* In J. L. Rallu, Y. Courbage, & V. Piché (Eds.), *Old and new minorities* (pp. 147–163). Montrouge, France: Editions John Libbey Eurotext.

Beaujot, R., & McQuillan, K. (1982). *Growth and dualism: The demographic development of Canadian society.* Toronto: Gage.

Bourbeau, R. (1988). Trends in language mobility between English and French. In J. Curtis, E. Grabb, N. Guppy, & S. Gilbert (Eds.), *Social inequality in Canada: Patterns, problems, policies* (pp. 221–229). Scarborough, Ontario: Prentice-Hall.

Bourbeau, R. (1989). *Canada: A linguistic profile* (Cat. No. 98–131). Ottawa: Statistics Canada.

Breton, A., & Breton, R. (1980). *Why disunity? An analysis of linguistic and regional cleavages in Canada.* Montreal: Institute for Research on Public Policy.

Breton, R. (1988). French–English relations. In J. Curtis & L. Tepperman (Eds.), *Understanding Canadian society* (pp. 557–585). Toronto: McGraw-Hill.

Brooks, S. (1989). *Public policy in Canada: An introduction.* Toronto: McClelland and Stewart.

## 82 BEAUJOT

Caldwell, G. (1988). L'avenir de la communauté anglophone du Québec. *L'Action Nationale,* *78*, 359–365.

Cartwright, D. (1988a). Linguistic territorialization: Is Canada approaching the Belgian model? *Journal of Cultural Geography, 8*, 115–134.

Cartwright, D. (1988b). Language policy and internal geopolitics: The Canadian situation. In C. H. Williams (Ed.), *Language in geographic context* (pp. 238–266). Clevedon, England: Multilingual Matters.

Cartwright, D. (1989). Languages in contact: Is conflict inevitable? *Journal of Canadian Studies, 23*, 130–135.

Castonguay, C. (1979). Exogamie et anglicisation chez les minorités canadiennes-française. *Canadian Review of Sociology and Anthropology, 16*, 21–31.

Coleman, W. D. (1983). A comparative study of language policy in Quebec: A political economy approach. In M. M. Atkinson & M. A. Chandler (Eds.), *The politics of Canadian public policy* (pp. 21–42). Toronto: University of Toronto Press.

Grenier, G., & Lachapelle, R. (1988). *Aspects linguistiques de l'évolution démographique.* Ottawa: Report for Review of Demography, Health and Welfare.

Guindon, H. (1988). *Quebec society: Tradition, modernity and nationhood.* Toronto: University of Toronto Press.

Harrison, B. (1996). *Youth in official language minorities* (Cat. No. 91–545–XPE). Ottawa: Statistics Canada.

Harrison, B., & Marmen, L. (1994). *Languages in Canada* (Cat. No. 96–313). Ottawa: Statistics Canada.

Lachapelle, R. (1987). *L'avenir démographique du Canada et des groupes linguistiques.* Ottawa: Report for Review of Demography, Health and Welfare.

Lachapelle, R. (1988a). *L'immigration et le caractère ethnolinguistique du Canada et du Québec* (Documents de Recherche No. 15). Ottawa: Statistics Canada, Direction des études analytiques.

Lachapelle, R. (1988b, June). *Ethnic diversity and the evolution of language groups.* Paper presented at the Canadian Population Society, Windsor, Ontario.

Lachapelle, R. (1988c). Quelques tendances démolinguistiques au Canada et au Québec. *L'Action Nationale, 78*, 329–343.

Lachapelle, R. (1989a). Evolution of language groups and the official languages situation of Canada. In *Demolinguistic trends and the evolution of Canadian institutions* (pp. 7–34). Ottawa: Secretary of State.

Lachapelle, R. (1989b, April). *Evolution démographique des francophones et diffusion du français au Canada.* Paper presented at Université Laval, Quebec.

Lachapelle, R., & Henripin, J. (1980). *La situation démolinguistique au Canada: Évolution passée et prospective.* Montreal: Institute for Research on Public Policy.

Laponce, J. A. (1988). Conseil au Prince qui voudrait assurer la survie du français en Amérique du Nord. *Cahiers Québécois de Démographie, 17*, 35–48.

McRoberts, K. (1989). Making Canada bilingual: Illusions and delusions of federal language policy. In D. P. Shugarman & R. Whitaker (Eds.), *Federalism and political community* (pp. 141–171). Peterborough, Ontario: Broadview.

Paillé, M. (1989a). *Nouvelles tendances démolinguistiques dans l'Ile de Montréal 1981–1996* (Notes et documents No. 71). Quebec: Conseil de la langue française.

Paillé, M. (1989b). Aménagement linguistique et population au Québec. *Journal of Canadian Studies, 23*, 54–69.

Pal, L. A. (1993). *Interests of state: The politics of language, multiculturalism, and feminism in Canada.* Montreal: McGill–Queen's University Press.

Polèse, M. (1990). Misplaced priorities: A review of demolinguistic trends and the evolution of Canadian institutions. *Canadian Public Policy, 16*, 445–450.

## 3. DEMOGRAPHIC CONSIDERATIONS 83

Reitz, J. G. (1980). Immigration and inter ethnic relationships in Canada. In R. Breton, W. Isajiw, W. Kalbach, & J. Reitz (Eds.), *Cultural boundaries and the cohesion of Canada* (pp. 337–362). Montreal: Institute for Research on Public Policy.

Review of Demography. (1989). *Charting Canada's future*. Ottawa: Health and Welfare.

Robinson, P. (1989). French mother tongue transmission in mixed mother tongue families. *Canadian Journal of Sociology, 14*, 317–334.

Royal Commission on Bilingualism and Biculturalism. (1967). *Report* (Vol. I). Ottawa: Queen's Printer.

Statistics Canada. (1992). *1991 census home language and mother tongue* (Cat. No. 93–317). Ottawa: Author.

Statistics Canada. (1992). *1991 census knowledge of languages* (Cat. No. 93–318). Ottawa: Author.

Termote, M. (1995). Tendances démolinguistiques au Canada et implications politiques. In Federation of Canadian Demographers, *Towards the XXIst century: Emerging socio-demographic trends and policy issues in Canada* (pp. 161–172). Ottawa: Federation of Canadian Demographers.

Termote, M., & Gauvreau, D. (1985). Le comportement démographique des groupes linguistiques du Québec pendant la période 1976–1981: Une analyse multirégionale. *Cahiers Québécois de Démographie, 14*, 31–58.

Termote, M., & Gauvreau, D. (1988). *La situation démolinguistique du Québec*. Quebec: Conseil de la langue française.

Thériault, J.-Y. (1989). Lourdeur ou légèreté du devenir de la francophonie hors Québec. In *Demolinguistic trends and the evolution of Canadian institutions* (pp. 135–144). Ottawa: Secretary of State.

Tremblay, M., & Bourbeau, R. (1985). La mortalité et la fécondité selon le groupe linguistique au Québec, 1976 et 1981. *Cahiers Québécois de Démographie, 14*, 7–30.

Vaillancourt, F. (1989). Demolinguistic trends and Canadian institutions: An economic perspective. In *Demolinguistic trends and the evolution of Canadian institutions* (pp. 73–92). Ottawa: Secretary of State.

Veltman, C. (1986). *L'impact de la ségrégation résidentielle sur l'équilibre linguistique au Québec* (report for review of demography). Ottawa: Health and Welfare.

Veltman, C. (1988). *L'impact de l'immigration internationale sur l'équilibre linguistique à Montréal* (report for review of demography). Ottawa: Health and Welfare.

# 4

# National Language Policy in the United States

Thomas Ricento
*The University of Texas at San Antonio*

Chapter 2 of this volume describes central differences between U.S. and Canadian approaches to cultural and linguistic diversity, arising from important differences in the sociopolitical histories of the two countries. There are, of course, many similarities; both countries, historically, have favored conformity to English, and, especially in the case of Canada, to British sociocultural norms. The francophone community in Quebec was able to withstand absorption into the dominant anglo culture, although the dream expressed by Pierre Elliot Trudeau of individual French/English bilingualism (the personality principle) for all Canadians is dead. In both countries, nondominant or, in the case of Canada, nonofficial (so-called allophone) languages have been in the shadows because English and French have dominated the stage. Although the survival of French in Quebec was greatly enhanced by the Quiet Revolution of the 1960s and 1970s, the English "fact" in North America continues to favor shift from French to English outside Quebec (see Beaujot, chapter 3; Cartwright, chapter 11; and Veltman, chapter 12, this volume), and from Spanish to English in the United States. In the United States, English achieved its unchallenged status as the national language through custom; from the earliest days of the republic, speaking English was understood to be a sine qua non for membership in the polity known as the United States. This was

**85**

so not because repressive laws were passed limiting the public utility of other languages, but due to social pressure to conform (cf. Schmidt, chapter 2, this volume). As Heath and Mandabach (1983) noted: "It has not been the law which has repressed language diversity, but society" (p. 101). In Canada, the fact that 90% of all Canadians live within 200 miles of the United States border has influenced its economic as well as cultural development; American movies, literature, and music—all in English—have permeated Canadian life. Indeed, one of the reasons French nationalism is possible in Quebec is because Canadian nationalism is so loosely defined, if it has been defined at all (McNaught, 1988). For some Canadians, English-speaking Canada has more in common with the United States than with any notion of Canadian nationalism; for others, Canadian nationalism is defined as the right *not* to be American.

In this chapter, I provide a selective analysis of language policy in the United States.[1] Using a case-study approach, I examine a particular aspect of policy, the Bilingual Education Act of 1968, as modified in subsequent reauthorizations, to illustrate how policy is developed within the political culture of the United States. I will also explain why there has been, and continues to be, great resistance to linguistic and cultural pluralism in the United States.

## DEVELOPMENT AND PERCEPTION OF NATIONAL POLICIES: THE CASE OF THE BILINGUAL EDUCATION ACT OF 1968

Unlike Canada, which passed the Official Languages Act of 1969, and Australia, with its National Policy on Languages (1987) and the Australian Language and Literacy Policy (1991), the United States has never attempted to articulate, let alone implement, a national language policy[2]. When language matters are addressed at the federal level, usually in legislation or in higher court rulings, the goals usually center around the solution of long-standing social problems, most frequently to redress violations of constitu-

---

[1]I limit coverage in this chapter to national policy and politics, and largely to issues relating to the relative status of languages and their speakers. This focus is not intended to minimize the complexity or multilayered nature of policy issues. For example, I refer to English as a single variety, when in fact there are many varieties of English, including many so-called nonstandard varieties, the speakers of which are penalized much the same way speakers of non-English languages are penalized. Degree of literacy in standard English (and other languages) also plays a determinative role in the life chances of persons who may speak English without having practical skills in reading or writing it. Ricento (1996a) provided a more comprehensive treatment of U.S. language policy issues.

[2]The U.S. Congress has passed laws, such as the Native American Language Act of 1990 and the National Literacy Act of 1991, among others. However, no attempt has been made to develop an integrated long-term policy; laws are often not funded or receive only token support.

# 4. NATIONAL LANGUAGE POLICY 87

tional and statutory civil rights.[3] Therefore, to accurately characterize *language* policies, one must situate such government actions within broader *social* policy issues and sociohistorical processes. For example, to understand the goals of the Bilingual Education Act of 1968, one needs to understand why that legislation was passed when it was passed, whose interests were being served, what the general policy framework was with regard to the status of minority languages and speakers of those languages, what sort of support was or wasn't provided to implement the legislation, what the prevailing social attitudes were at the time regarding bilingual education, and so on. To illustrate the complexity involved, I offer three interpretative frameworks (others could be cited) that implicitly or explicitly have informed public (including academic) discourse on bilingual education:

1. *The Remediation Framework* would suggest that the Bilingual Education Act (BEA) of 1968 and the accompanying May 25, 1970 memorandum of the Department of Health, Education, and Welfare, the *Lau v. Nichols* Supreme Court decision of 1974, and the Office of Civil Rights' proposed Lau Regulations (1980) all sought to ensure that "students will not be excluded from participation in, be denied benefits of, or be subjected to discrimination in education programs and activities because they have a primary language other than English" (from proposed regulations, U.S. Department of Education, Aug. 5, 1980); that the beneficiaries were language minority children; that the implementing language was vague;[4] and that there was great resistance to bilingual education (especially beginning in the 1970s), as well as a lack of qualified personnel and expertise in the construction and implementation of bilingual education programs. Although originally conceived as a research and demonstration program, in subsequent years, the program moved toward a service emphasis (Leibowitz, 1980). Research has been published that suggests quality bilingual education programs have more than achieved the goal of promoting proficiency in English plus another language (e.g., Ramírez, Yuen, & Ramey, 1991).

---

[3]For example, the goal of the Bilingual Education Act of 1968 was to improve educational access and attainment among Spanish-speaking Mexican American children in the southwest who had either been segregated in inferior schools or had been placed in English-only (submersion) classes (Lyons, 1992). The Voting Rights Act of 1965 suspended literacy tests and other educational prerequisites for voting, and amendments to that act in 1975 required bilingual ballots in those districts in which at least 5% of the population belonged to a single-language minority group.

[4]An example of vagueness is in the definition of limited English-speaking ability children as "children who come from environments where the dominant language is other than English" (Fernández, 1987, 92–93). Such a definition could include English monolingual children as well as children with different degrees of fluency in English and in their native language.

2. *The Poverty Program Framework* would see the Bilingual Education Act of 1968 as one of several relatively inexpensive Congressional measures designed to relieve social and political pressure among certain marginalized populations (primarily Spanish-speaking) in particular regions of the country. From the beginning, it was a "poverty program" rather than an innovative and experimental approach to language instruction; the modest initial funding of $7.5 million in 1969, serving only 27,000 children nationally, reflects the low importance attached to the program; and lack of implementing legislation as well as lack of funding for research in the early years of the program indicate low expectations for achieving even the narrow goal of promoting proficiency *only* in English. Some researchers have found that although some programs have been successful, bilingual education programs in general have not proven to be superior to programs that do not employ the child's native language in instruction (e.g., Baker & de Kanter, 1983).

3. *The Failed Attempt at Social Engineering Framework* interprets the Bilingual Education Act of 1968 as a well-intentioned but misguided attempt to promote linguistic and cultural assimilation among language-minority populations. Self-serving ethnic leaders, not language minority children, were the principal beneficiaries; the real goal of the BEA was to strengthen the political power of Spanish-speaking elites by promoting a policy of Spanish language maintenance and loyalty to cultural values alien to mainstream American values; separatism, jobs, and political power were either the hidden goals behind the lofty ideals expressed in the BEA, or became the goals soon after programs were implemented. Porter (1990) and Imhoff (1990), in part, made this argument.

Which view is descriptively accurate? Which can be supported by the factual record? The answer is that evidence for each position has been adduced by different interested constituencies. How one regards the *results* of 30 years of federal support for bilingual education will depend, in part, on which *framework* one uses in evaluating the results. One could conclude that too much or too little money was spent; one might find the goal of promoting competency in English *and* another language laudable, or not worthy of support at all; one might view the federal role to have been appropriate, or to have been anemic, short-sighted, wrong-headed, too little too late, or some or all of the aforementioned.

Framework 1 seems to reflect the original intent of the BEA, if one wishes to be a "strict constructionist," relying on the original legislation and Congressional testimony to understand the intent of the legislators when

# 4. NATIONAL LANGUAGE POLICY

they crafted the legislation. Frameworks 2 and 3 have been adopted mostly by individuals and groups philosophically opposed to bilingual education—and especially to so-called "maintenance" programs—and more broadly, to governmental attempts to solve entrenched social problems. A conventional view would see Framework 1 as "liberal" and Framework 3 as "conservative" with Framework 2 occupying the middle ground; that is, government intervention to solve social problems *can* be a good thing in theory, but all too often inappropriate and costly programs only make matters worse. This liberal to moderate to conservative analysis, however, masks a common underlying assumption in all of the frameworks: Cultural and linguistic assimilation into the American "mainstream" should be the goal of policy. They differ with regard to how this goal can best be achieved.

I find that although the BEA was flawed in its design and implementation, the federal role has been but one of many variables deciding the fate of bilingual education (Grades K–12) in the United States, or more broadly, the fate of the education of language-minority (i.e., non-English-speaking or non-English-dominant) children. Given that bilingual education entails language status issues, the two most significant generalizations that can be made with regard to language policies which deal with language status (the functional distribution and use of a language in society) in the United States are that:

1. The symbolic and functional role of (standard) English as the national language permeates all policies dealing with issues of *status*.
2. Policies that violate *deep values* will be difficult, if not impossible, to implement. Deep values represent an accretion of national experiences, influenced by certain intellectual traditions, which together create underlying, usually unstated or hegemonic frameworks within which policies evolve and are evaluated. In this chapter, deep values refers to attitudes and beliefs about language and cultural (including national) identity.

Deep values vary from society to society and over time; in the case of the United States, a unique set of historical circumstances of nation building, from the colonial era through the 1920s, has resulted in a set of beliefs and attitudes toward English, non-English languages, and bi- and multilingualism that are universally understood, if not universally accepted. Examples of these dominant—although not universally held—values in the United States include, but are not limited to:

1. *The notion that Americans have a common national experience, which has created particular values understood to be essential "American" values.* This is expressed in *The Federalist* by Alexander Hamilton, John Jay, and

James Madison (1788), who characterized the nation as "one united people—a people descended from the same ancestors, *speaking the same language* [italics added], professing the same religion ...very similar in their manners and customs" (Jay, quoted in Crawford, 1992, p. 32). Being American means speaking English, among other things.

2. *The notion that the unity and cultural integrity of the United States cannot abide cultural, including linguistic, pluralism.* This view has been stated often by national leaders, but perhaps never more succinctly than by Theodore Roosevelt in a message to the American Defense Society in 1919:

> For it is an outrage to discriminate against any such man because of creed or birthplace or origin. *But this is predicated* [italics added] upon the man's becoming in very fact an American and nothing but an American. If he tries to keep segregated with men of his own origin and separated from the rest of America, then he isn't doing his part as an American. ... We have room for but one language here, and that is the English language, for we intend to see that the crucible turns our people out as Americans, of American nationality, and not as dwellers in a polyglot boardinghouse. (cited in Crawford, 1992, p. 59)

3. *The notion that the federal government should not intrude into matters of language or culture directly, because these matters are best left to the family and communities.* Of course, in fact the government *does* intrude on behalf of English and acquiesces (i.e., is silent) vis-à-vis other languages and non-English-speaking ethnolinguistic groups, generally. Another, and perhaps more negative, way to put this is government should *only* intrude when the dominant language (English) and culture ("American") are in need of protection from real, or perceived, threats. During the Americanization campaign (1914–1924), both the federal and state governments passed laws to promote the learning of English and American civic values in communities across the United States. In the current period, legislation declaring English the official language of government has been introduced in every session of Congress since 1981, a consequence (in part) of fears that the increase in immigration from non-European and non-English-dominant countries, which began in 1965, could threaten the hegemony of "American" culture. In most cases, federal involvement in language policy is a response to pressures from the grassroots.

4. *The notion that ethnolinguistic groups merit no special protections that might ensure their continued existence as groups.* The idea that the maintenance of immigrant and indigenous languages and cultures[5] is

---

[5]For non-English languages to thrive in North America, they must be functional in all domains of daily life, such as education, the media, and the workplace. As Schmidt (chapter 2, this volume) notes, French has thrived in Quebec because it is the language of daily life, public and private. This is certainly not the case with Spanish in the United States, and this situation is not likely to change any time soon.

## 4.  NATIONAL LANGUAGE POLICY                                                                 91

intrinsically valuable, let alone that it makes social and economic sense, is a relatively alien notion for most native, and even assimilated, Americans.

These values have corresponding antipodes reflecting differing readings of the American experience, in some sense seeking to demythologize the misty past. For example, Jay's statement in *The Federalist* (1788) cannot be accepted as accurate, because he referred to a *subset* of the nation (mostly males born in England or in the colonies of English ancestry), whose status as the Founding Fathers allowed them to define the "nation" as they saw fit. In this context, perhaps another of Jay's maxims, said to be one of his favorites, is more revealing: "The people who own the country ought to govern it" (Monaghan, 1935, p. 323). Jay was a realist, and saw no need to broaden the concept of nation to encompass groups he probably never imagined would be capable of understanding the principles, or methods, of enlightened self-government (e.g., African Americans and Native Americans). It should be noted that according to Pitt (1976), about 49% of the national population at the time of the 1790 census was of English origin; nearly 19% was of African origin; 12% was Scotch or Scotch Irish; Irish accounted for about 3%. Dutch-, French-, and Spanish-origin peoples accounted for about 14%, and Native Americans were largely ignored by the Census (cited in Wiley, 1996b). One hundred and thirty years later, Theodore Roosevelt's 1919 recapitulation of Jay's dictum revealed that (a) differences *did* exist and could no longer be ignored, and (b) it was all right to discriminate against persons if they refused to become "anglified," that is, English-speaking "Americans." It would not be until passage of the 1964 Civil Rights Bill that legally sanctioned discrimination against African Americans, whose presence on the North American continent dates back to the early 1600s, would be abolished, fully 176 years *after* the publication of *The Federalist* (Hamilton, et al., 1788). Myths may have their place in nation building, but mature societies that have been built largely by immigrant muscle and infused with indigenous and immigrant cultures and languages cannot abide myths that no longer apply, indeed that were never intended to embrace the entire population.

## HOW DEEP VALUES INFLUENCE
## LANGUAGE POLICY DEVELOPMENT

Awareness of the dominant values listed earlier helps us better understand how the political process has engaged issues such as the education of language minority children. The Bilingual Education Act of 1968 was an attempt to improve the socioeconomic status of a segment of the American population that had been denied access to meaningful education, not a blueprint to promote societal, or even individual, bilingualism. The aims were very pragmatic, and noncommittal with regard to whether bilingualism is good or bad in itself. Dropout rates among Spanish-speaking students were unacceptably high, a result, in part, of discriminatory educational practices (Weinberg, 1995). The BEA was a relatively modest experimental program designed to provide seed money to schools to help them develop bilingual education programs.

Although the notion of deep values helps us better interpret why particular policies, be they explicit or covert, official or unofficial, national or local, are devised and supported (or not), other factors play important roles as well. At various times in U.S. history, deep values have been transmuted into virulent strains of nativism, xenophobia, and blatant racism, leading to restrictive laws and practices that have contravened constitutional civil rights. In a number of instances, courts—including the U.S. Supreme Court in several cases, most notably *Meyer v. Nebraska* (1923)—have provided a counterbalance to extremist policies and practices (see Wiley, chapter 9, this volume, for a discussion of *Meyer v. Nebraska*). Courts have also served to advance the rights of non-English speakers in more calm times, in order to address issues of access in specified public domains, such as education (e.g., *Lau v. Nichols*, 1974). Legislatures have also served as arenas for policy development, providing a mechanism for grassroots movements to modify the majoritarian dominant values to reflect their values, needs, or both. This is seen clearly in the Bilingual Education Act and the Voting Rights Act of 1964, amended in 1975 to allow for bilingual ballots in districts with substantial numbers of voters who speak non-English languages. The point is that the political system in the United States does allow for nondominant interests to get a hearing, and to propose legislation that reflects minority views on important issues. However, to the extent that such legislation contravenes one or more deep values (or is perceived to violate those values), it will be resisted at the local level, or even abandoned or reversed by courts or other legislatures. For example, in recent years, efforts at the state level (e.g., in California) to scale back, or eliminate entirely, affirmative action policies begun in the 1970s, have achieved some success. The movement to declare English the official language of the United States, beginning in the 1980s, emerged, in part, to repeal federal support of bilingual education and bilingual voting ballots, considered by official English supporters to be illegitimate "ethnic entitlements." This alternation between policies of governmental intervention to remediate social inequalities followed by weakening or withdrawal of such policies is interpreted in some quarters as a cynical manipulation of the social agenda by dominant elites in order

## 4. NATIONAL LANGUAGE POLICY

to placate popular discontent when it is expedient to do so, and otherwise ignoring it when the cost of maintaining the status quo is acceptably low. In this analysis, elite attitudes toward language in education policies, for example, can appear to be variable and shallow, changeable, reflecting realignment of political parties and shifts in voter demographics. Such short-term changes in overt policies, however, do not fundamentally alter deep values or the attitudes that are informed by those values.

Staying with the example of the BEA, we can see how deep values interacted with political currents in the period between 1967 and 1995 in determining the evolution of the BEA. In 1967, Texas Senator Ralph Yarborough introduced S. 428, a bill designed to address "the special educational needs of the large numbers of students in the United States whose mother tongue is Spanish and to whom English is a foreign language" (quoted in Lyons, 1990, p. 66). Yarborough cited high dropout rates among Spanish-speaking students in the five southwestern states, and believed measures were needed to improve the educational attainment of these children. Authorized activities in the bill included:

1. Bilingual-education programs,
2. The teaching of Spanish as a native language,
3. The teaching of English as a second language,
4. Programs designed to impart to Spanish-speaking students a knowledge of and pride in their ancestral culture and language,
5. Efforts to attract and retain as teachers promising individuals of Mexican or Puerto Rican descent,
6. Efforts to establish close cooperation between the school and the home.

The limitation of the bill to the Spanish-speaking was criticized by members of Congress and educators. Representative Henry B. González (D-Texas), argued:

The most serious defect of S. 428 is that it recognizes only the problems of the Spanish-speaking population. There are many other groups across the land who have the very same problem who would be ignored by this legislation. There are, for example, French-speaking people in Louisiana and the far northeast. There are Indians scattered throughout the country, some on reservations, and others, in fact some twelve thousand or more organized groups in this country with ethnic interests of one kind or another. ... The bill as drawn ignores these interests and denies to these other groups what it gives to the Spanish-speaking. I believe that this is unjust, and may very possibly be unconstitutional. It appears to me that in view of our long history of pluralism, and in view of our continuing efforts to promote mutual respect and tolerance, we would be inviting grave and justly deserved criticism from many ethnic groups if we recognize the problems of only one. (1967 Senate Hearings, Bilingual Education, p. 600, cited in Leibowitz, 1980, p. 16).

Schmuel Lapin, General Secretary of the YIVO Institute of Jewish Research, doubted a bill as restrictive as Yarborough's could succeed:

> It is most doubtful whether the goals of these measures can be attained if its provisions are limited to one language and one culture alone. Unless all Americans regardless of their national origin are made to feel that the preservation of the various languages and cultures brought here by immigrants is important to the United States, there is little reason to believe that such a program restricted to Spanish alone can be successful. (1967 Senate Hearings, Bilingual Education, p. 602, cited in Leibowitz, 1980, p. 16)

During Congressional hearings on the bill, more than 100 witnesses, nearly all supportive of bilingual education, argued that bilingual education would not only help improve academic achievement among Spanish-speaking students, but it would "prevent the loss of potential bilingualism among Spanish-speaking students" (Lyons, 1990, p. 67). Others argued that bilingual education would be beneficial to the nation's linguistic and cultural resources. The program at the Coral Way Elementary School in Miami, Florida, was cited as a successful two-way bilingual program that had provided bilingual instruction to both Spanish- and English-language background students since 1963.

Because the concept of bilingual education was popular in 1967, more than three dozen other bills were introduced into the House of Representatives (Lyons, 1990). Two bills sought to expand coverage to other language groups: The Hawkins–Roybal bill included assistance to the French-speaking in addition to the Spanish-speaking and the Scheuer bill authorized bilingual instruction for all children whose native languages were not English (Leibowitz, 1980). The final bill that emerged differed in crucial ways from the one Senator Yarborough introduced. Rather than focusing on Spanish-speaking children, the bill focused on "children who come from environments where the dominant language is other than English" (p. 17). Children were seen as deficient (in English ability) rather than as proficient in another language. Another important change was that "the teaching of Spanish as the native language," which could have been changed to "home languages," was dropped, lessening the possibility that native language skills of non-English-speaking students would be developed. Finally, the provision regarding "efforts to attract and retain as teachers promising individuals of Mexican or Puerto Rican descent" (which could have been modified to include non-English speakers) was dropped. In January 1968, Public Law 90–247, which added Bilingual Education Programs (the BEA) under Title VII of the Elementary and Secondary

## 4. NATIONAL LANGUAGE POLICY

Education Act (ESEA), was signed by President Johnson. Although it was recognized at the time that the primary beneficiaries of the bill would be Spanish-speaking children given their numbers and needs, it was expected that the number of children from other linguistic groups would increase in the following years as a result of passage of the Immigration and Nationality Act of 1965, which gave preference to immigrants who already had families in the United States (1967 Senate Hearings, Bilingual Education, cited in Leibowitz, 1980).

Ambiguities over the objectives of the BEA continued until Title VII was reauthorized in 1974. Although some early versions and interpretations of the BEA supported an enrichment model for developing fluency in two languages (between 1967 and 1974), by the 1974 reauthorization process, the BEA had come to reflect a philosophy of remediation designed to mainstream "disadvantaged" children into "mainstream" (i.e., English-only) classrooms as quickly as possible.[6] In that year, Frank Carlucci, Undersecretary of the Department of Health, Education, and Welfare (HEW) said "the goal of Title VII [under which the BEA was funded] is to assist children of limited or non-English speaking ability to gain competency in English—and **not** to require cultural pluralism." In amendments to the 1974 reauthorization of the BEA, a "program of bilingual education" was defined, stating in part that "there is instruction given in, and study of, English and, to the extent necessary to allow a child to progress effectively through the educational system, the native language of the children of limited English-speaking ability" (cited in Lyons, 1990, p. 69). The 1974 amendments also authorized "the voluntary enrollment to a limited degree" of English-speaking children in bilingual education programs, noting that "in no event shall the program be designed for the purpose of teaching a foreign language to English-speaking children" (p. 69).

Why the changes? In the mid-1970s, a backlash was developing against preserving minority languages and cultures. Noel Epstein (1977) a journalist for the *Washington Post*, wrote a book in which he criticized not bilingual education, but the role of the federal government in financing and promoting it. As he put it, "The overriding question is whether the federal government is responsible for financing and promoting student attachments to their ethnic languages and cultures, jobs long left to families, religious groups, ethnic organizations, private schools, ethnic publications and oth-

---

[6]The real goal of the BEA, according to the implementing legislation, was to improve the educational opportunities of poor children. In the original legislation in 1968, children from low- income families ($3,000 per year or less) were targeted for enrollment in "new and imaginative elementary and secondary school programs designed to meet [their] special educational needs" (Fernández, 1987, p. 91). The 1971 guidelines and a 1973 position paper developed by the U.S. Office of Education suggest that native language maintenance was the government policy. However, the 1974 reauthorization of the BEA made it clear that the goal of the BEA was to develop English proficiency and not to develop the child's native language.

ers" (Epstein, 1977, quoted in Crawford, 1992, p. 87). This line of reasoning was adopted by groups such as U.S. English and English First, who argued against the notion of "affirmative ethnicity." Although the original goal of the BEA was to enhance the educational attainment of (largely) Spanish-speaking students in the Southwest—*not* to promote "student *attachments* to their ethnic languages and cultures," as was claimed by Epstein—the charge of "affirmative ethnicity" stuck, largely because deep value #3 (nongovernment intervention into matters of language and culture) had been violated. This led to attacks on bilingual education from political elites and even from "assimilated" members of language-minority groups who by now had appropriated the dominant culture's mindset with regard to at least some aspects of its deep values.

At about the same time as this nascent anti-affirmative action movement was gaining attention, the first large-scale study of bilingual education, conducted in the mid-1970s by the American Institutes for Research (AIR), was released. It found "no consistent significant impact" for bilingual instruction (Crawford, 1992, p. 219). Although the study had serious methodological flaws, the results were hailed by opponents of the BEA as providing evidence that bilingual education was no better than traditional submersion, or "sink or swim," programs. Language-acquisition scholars who examined the AIR report and another study by Baker and de Kanter (1983)[7] found "logical contradictions and the denial/distortion of evidence" (Cummins, 1994). Contrary evidence was ignored, and in 1978, Congress, reacting to the shifting political winds and relying, in part, on questionable research, amended the BEA, declaring that the child's native language would be used *only* to facilitate achieving competence in English.

After his election in 1980, President Ronald Reagan came out strongly against bilingual education, which he interpreted to mean native language maintenance[8] (a view that bore no resemblance to the actual policy or existing practice). As a result of a technicality, the so-called Lau Regulations,[9] which were extremely unpopular by then, were withdrawn. In 1984,

[7]In the Baker and de Kanter study, the authors culled the research literature of more than 300 studies, decided 28 were methodologically sound, and based on data from those studies concluded that there was no difference in outcomes between bilingual education and other types of programs. Because differences in qualities of programs, instructional methods used, characteristics of students, length of programs, and many other variables were not controlled for in reviewing the 28 studies, most language acquisition scholars give little credence to the Baker and de Kanter study (see, e.g., Willig, 1985, for a critique).

[8]In a spring 1981 speech, President Reagan said: "It is absolutely wrong and against American concepts to have a bilingual education program that is now openly, admittedly dedicated to preserving their [LEPs'] native language and never getting them adequate in English so they can go out into the job market and participate" (quoted in Fernández, 1987, p. 96).

[9]In 1980, as part of a settlement of a case in Alaska, the Office of Civil Rights published official regulations that spelled out the obligations of school districts to LEP students (Fernández, 1987). Students with greater proficiency in their native language than in English had to be in bilingual programs, whereas students demonstrating superior proficiency in    (cont.)

## 4. NATIONAL LANGUAGE POLICY 97

President Reagan, courting the Hispanic vote in his bid for reelection, backpedaled, praising "effective bilingual education programs." In the 1984 reauthorization legislation of the BEA, a compromise was fashioned between supporters and opponents of bilingual education. The bill allowed for experimentation with alternatives to transitional bilingual education, such as ESL and structured immersion, as well as maintenance programs that included foreign language instruction (Fernandez, 1987). However, by the early 1990s, the voices advocating transitional bilingual, structured immersion, and ESL programs were prevailing in the Congress. The Fiscal Year 1992 appropriation for the BEA contained some notable changes from the 1984 bill; Special Alternative Instruction—programs that did not require the use of the LEP's (limited English proficient) native language—increased from 6% (FY 1988) to 23% (FY 1992), under part A appropriations (grants to Local Education Agencies—(LEAs). Funding levels for personnel training, multifunctional resource centers, data collection, evaluation assistance centers, and a fellowship program to support doctoral students in bilingual education were decreased between 12% and 20% over 1988 levels, after adjusting for inflation (Ricento, 1996a).

The changes that occurred in the BEA beginning in 1967 through 1992 paralleled social and political changes sweeping the country. By 1994, the widespread antiimmigrant backlash in California led to passage of Proposition 187, which cut off many public services, including education, to undocumented Americans.[10] Picking up on the national trend, and as part of a desire to reduce government spending on social programs, the 104th Republican-led Congress reduced funding for the BEA, passed immigration reform legislation, and for the first time in U.S. history passed a bill (in the House of Representatives only) declaring English the official language of government. Provisions of the bill include repeal of the Bilingual Election requirements of the Voting Rights Act of 1965 (section 203), and a prohibition against federal employees communicating in writing in non-English languages, although they may communicate orally in languages other than English.[11] Although a number of factors contributed to passage of these bills, the deep values discussed earlier, no less than

---

[9](cont.) English could receive instruction in English. Students with equal ability in two languages could choose either an English-only or bilingual program.

[10]Immediately following the passage of Proposition 187 in 1994, the constitutionality and legality of the measure was challenged in federal court. Several rulings have found most of the provisions of the measure to be unconstitutional, relying in part on earlier Supreme Court decisions which have found statutes that treat members of a suspect class differently in the absence of a compelling government interest to be in violation of the equal protection clause of the 14th amendment of the U.S. Constitution (cf., e.g., *Plyler v. Doe*, 1982).

[11]The U.S. Senate failed to act on a similar bill in the 104th Congress; therefore, the Congress failed to enact an official English law. However, it is expected that similar legislation will be introduced in future sessions.

98                                                                                    RICENTO

current political winds, played a crucial role. Further support for this view is provided in the transcript of the debate that took place in the House of Representatives on August 1, 1996 (see Congressional Record–House, August 1, 1996, pages H9726 to H9772).

## LESSONS FROM THE BEA

The history of the BEA, a particular piece of language-in-education legislation, can serve here to illustrate some of the attributes of federal approaches to language policy development:

1. Complex problems, involving language, are reduced in legislation that is unrealistic in its expectations, goals, methods, or any combination thereof: (for example, poverty among Mexican Americans has many causes and would not have been reduced even if bilingual education had early on been successful in achieving its modest goals; the goals enunciated in the Native American Language Act of 1990 could be made only because many Native languages were by then moribund, or nearly so, well past the point of realistic recovery (see Crawford, chapter 6, this volume). Furthermore, the bill requires government agencies to ensure that their activities promote the goal of preserving indigenous languages, although they provide no guidelines on how to do this, or realistic funding levels (an example of symbolic language policy, perhaps?); had bilingual–bicultural education among Natives been allowed to continue a century earlier, it is much less likely that such legislation would have been necessary in 1990.
2. There has been inadequate planning and allocation of resources to effectively implement legislative or judicial remedies.
3. English-only hegemonic values that permeate the political culture make it difficult to fashion policies, especially in education, that promote (or at least do not penalize) bi- or multilingual competence, whether individual or societal.

However, despite the shortcomings of federal support for programs designed to provide access to quality education for language minority children, there have been many success stories. Since 1963, the Coral Way Elementary School has enabled children "to operate effectively in two languages and two cultures" (from a 1966 report by the school district). The only disappointment was that Anglo children did not reach national norms in Spanish reading achievement[12] (although such an outcome is to be

_____

[12]It should be noted that the Spanish-speaking children in the Coral Way program were largely middle-class, light-skinned Cubans who had fled Cuba after the 1959 revolution (cont.)

# 4. NATIONAL LANGUAGE POLICY

expected given that English is the dominant language outside of school). The Oyster Bilingual School, a public elementary school in Washington, DC that serves an ethnically, racially, and economically diverse student population, with 74% of the student population being language minorities representing over 25 countries, has been in operation since the early 1970s. The program is successful, according to Freeman (1996), because:

> Language minority and language majority members of the Oyster community collaborate in their efforts to define bilingualism and cultural pluralism as resources to be developed. The Spanish–English language plan is revealed to be one part of a larger identity plan that aims to promote social change by socializing children differently from the way children are socialized in mainstream U.S. educational discourse. (p. 557)

In a study of 2,000 English-language learners students in California, Florida, New Jersey, New York, and Texas, Ramírez et. al. (1991) found one of the best schools in Brooklyn, New York, where 99% of the students were poor African-Americans and Latinos. They cite the reasons for the success of the program: "supportive atmosphere. Children ... grow at their own pace. ... Where learning Spanish is encouraged, they [students] don't feel like outsiders" (cited in Crawford, 1992, p. 231). Other factors were a well-trained staff, fluent bilingual teachers, and involved parents who are more likely to help children with schoolwork in a language they understand. A number of other successful two-way bilingual education programs have been locally funded, including one serving 3,000 students in San Diego, California (Lyons, 1990). Overall, based on data compiled for the 1994–1995 school year, there were 182 two-way bilingual education programs in 100 school districts in 18 states and the District of Columbia, according to a recent report published by the Center for Applied Linguisitcs (Christian & Whitcher, 1995). Although 167 programs used Spanish as one of the instructional languages, two-way programs were also offered in Cantonese (3), Korean (4), Navajo (2), French (2), Arabic (1), Russian (1), and Portuguese (1). The goal of these programs is to enroll equal numbers of monolingual English students and students monolingual in the non-English language to facilitate true bilingual proficiency.

The success or failure of bilingual education in the United States did not, and does not, depend entirely on the stated policies of the federal government; however, lackadaisical enforcement by the federal government sends the message that such policies are not to be taken seriously. For example,

---

(cont.) (although some have questioned this assertion). Darker skinned Mexican-descent children in Texas and California were generally much poorer, and had more of the attributes of caste-like minorities (Ogbu, 1978) than of voluntary immigrants, as the Cubans were. This helps explain, in part, why bilingual education worked in Dade County at that time.

even though federal guidelines for compliance under Title VI of the Civil Rights Act of 1964 have been in effect since 1970, school district compliance with the guidelines has been poor. School districts around the country were nine times less likely to be monitored for compliance under the Reagan administration than under the Ford or Carter administrations (Lyons, 1990). During the Reagan administration, 58% of the reviews found districts to be in violation of the provisions of the Lau guidelines, but follow-ups were rare (Crawford, 1986). In such an environment, local school districts have the ability to circumvent federal policy with relative impunity. Clearly, successful programs (e.g., the Oyster Bilingual School) have gone beyond minimal statutory requirements and have enlisted broad-based community support. Although local autonomy has its advantages over centralized control, there can be confusion as to what constitutes bilingual education and how to implement appropriate programs—in short, how to ensure compliance with federal mandates. Because school districts and boards have usually been given wide latitude in setting up their own language programs (Fernández, 1987), there is enormous variation in what passes for bilingual education in the United States, and hence a high probability that compliance with federal mandates will not be achieved. In some schools, merely having non-English speakers in a classroom is considered bilingual education, whereas in other schools a program of mainstream English-only classrooms with a pull-out ESL component is labeled bilingual education by principals and other administrators. Without monitoring, resources to develop appropriate programs, and local support, it cannot be assumed that federal policy will be translated into effective programs, *even assuming broad societal support* for such programs.

## OTHER FACTORS THAT INFLUENCE POLICY DEVELOPMENT

Deep values develop over long periods of time and are closely tied to important historical documents (e.g., The Declaration of Independence, The U.S. Constitution, *The Federalist*) and national/international events (the Revolutionary War, the Spanish–American War, large-scale immigration at the end of the 19th and beginning of the 20th century, World War I, the International Communist movement) that contribute to a collective sense of nationhood and national identity. Events or processes that threaten to modify the existing social order—that is, that are viewed by dominant groups as assaults (real or imagined) on national identity (which really means the power of those groups that are dominant in the national political culture)—are identified as "national problems" requiring remediation;

## 4. NATIONAL LANGUAGE POLICY

citizens are told that failure to "control" the problem could result in serious harm to national identity, national values, and the common good.

Historically, linguistic, cultural, and religious diversity in the United States has often been characterized by elites from the mainstream political culture as detrimental to national identity. Higham (1971) chronicled the various nativist movements from 1860 to 1925 that resulted in widespread, if not universal, acceptance (or at least awareness) of English monolingualism, Anglo-Saxonism, and Protestantism as national behavioral and cultural norms. McClymer (1982) detailed how federal and state governments, along with major corporate interests, sponsored a national program to Americanize immigrants. Although the program was by most measures a failure,[13] it succeeded in politicizing American cultural values. The model of appropriate American behavior, attitudes, and beliefs was spelled out in curricula, pamphlets, and text books produced during this period (Ricento, 1996b).

In recent years, groups such as U.S. English in the United States and APEC (Alliance for the Preservation of English in Canada) in Canada have restated the same fears voiced during the Americanization era, that is, that relatively high rates of immigration (or migration in Canada) and fertility among non-English speaking groups threaten the future of American (or Canadian) society (i.e., the dominance of [largely] White English speakers). The first president of U.S. English, the political lobbying group that, since 1983, has advocated the passage of laws making English the official language of the United States, was very active in the zero population growth movement and the immigration reform movement.[14] Here we see a link between desires to preserve deep values (the roots of national identity) by limiting immigration and strengthening a potent symbol of national identity through official English legislation. It is true that in Quebec, as Beaujot (chapter 3, this volume) and Veltman (chapter 12, this volume) point out,

---

[13]The Carnegie Corporation's Study of the Methods of Americanization found the federal Bureau of Naturalization had exaggerated the number of Americanization programs and participants in the period from 1914 to 1925. More reliable estimates suggest about 1 million immigrants enrolled in formal public school Americanization classes sponsored by the Bureau of Naturalization; however, high attrition rates, ranging from 30 to 80%, meant that the true minimum number of adult immigrants effectively reached by the public schools was around 400,000 in the period from 1914 to 1925 (McClymer, 1982).

[14]John Tanton founded the Federation for American Immigration Reform (FAIR) in 1979. Tanton joined Zero Population Growth and became its national president in the mid-1970s. In a memo written for a study group composed of members of U.S. English and similar groups, Tanton wrote:

Is apartheid in Southern California's future? The demographic picture in South Africa now is startlingly similar to what we'll see in California in 2030. … A white majority owns the property, has the best jobs and education, has the political power, and speaks one language. A non-white majority has poor education, jobs, and income, and speaks a different language … Will there be strength in this diversity? Or will this prove a social and political San Andreas fault? (quoted in Crawford, 1992, p. 155)

# 102                                                      RICENTO

patterns of migration have been influenced by language policies that support French in education and government. However, in Quebec as in the United States, in the long term it is fertility rates, coupled with macroeconomic and cultural forces, that tend to determine whether a language and its cultural moorings will survive, and what its status will likely be vis-à-vis other languages. Thus, even though French was declared the *only* official language of Quebec in 1977 with the passage of Bill 101, the importance and utility of English in public—as well as private—domains continues unabated. In the United States, English has no real competition; yet the passage of an immigration reform bill (which reduced immigration quotas and modified selection criteria) in 1996 by the U.S. Congress, coupled with the passage of an official English bill by the U.S. House of Representatives (also in 1996) signals a concern among elites that deep values (or "American" values) are in some jeopardy, and if American values (i.e., dominant interests) are to be maintained, they need to be "protected."

Deep values are shaped over decades and even centuries of lived experience in communities throughout the nation. We can see how the existence of these values has led to conflicts between segments of majoritarian (or dominant) groups and minority (or marginalized) groups. Many minority groups have suffered generations of humiliation in educational and other public settings whereas other groups, most of whose members were later structurally assimilated (such as German Americans), have experienced episodes in which their language and culture have been attacked. Spanish in the Southwest has been under pressure for nearly a century and a half, largely as a consequence of discrimination toward people of Mexican and Latin American origin. It was a crime in Texas until 1973 to use a language other than English as the medium of public instruction; the Texas Department of Education encouraged teachers to punish children who used Spanish in the classroom or the playground (see Crawford, 1992). So-called "Spanish detention" was enforced even after passage of the BEA in some places. Anti-Hispanic attitudes go back a long way; in 1855, legislation was passed in California mandating English-only instruction in both public *and* private schools. Racism against Mexicans was continuous, persistent, blatant, sanctioned in law. Even the state constitutional requirement that all state laws be published in Spanish was often ignored in California (Crawford, 1992). That history lingers.[15]

---

[15]Evidence that anti-Spanish attitudes still exist in Texas, at least, is not difficult to find. In a child custody case in Amarillo, Texas, August 16, 1995, State District Judge Sam Kiser ordered Marta Laureano, a bilingual Mexican native, to speak more English to her 5-year-old daughter. In oral comments, the judge told Laureano that speaking only Spanish was a form of child abuse, and that not knowing English threatened to "make her [daughter] a maid for the rest of her life" (cited in Williams, 1995, p. B1). The judge later apologized for his choice of words, but stood by his written orders requiring Laureano to speak more English to her daughter.

## 4. NATIONAL LANGUAGE POLICY

Native Americans were systematically robbed of their languages and cultures by anglo-conformity policies (see Fettes, chapter 5, and Crawford, chapter 6, this volume). Many tribal elders remember a time when speaking their native language resulted in punishment and shame. The policy of destroying Indian languages and cultures, beginning with Congressional appropriation of funds in 1802 to promote "civilization among the aborigines" (Leibowitz, 1971), has meant that bilingual programs have been very difficult to implement. Under Title VII funding, only about 11% of bilingual education grants to school districts were set aside for Indian children in 1986–1987 (about $10 million; Crawford, 1989). Lack of qualified bilingual teachers for many languages means programs are simply not available.

The patriotism of Japanese, Chinese, and German Americans has been called into question at various times in U.S. history simply because they used their language in community publications and maintained private schools to teach their languages and cultures. After U.S. entry into World War I, Americanizers attacked the foreign language press in many states and territories. In Hawaii, for example, the Japanese press was singled out, in part because of its large circulation, in part because of the strong anti-Japanese racism of anglo-Hawaiians. Edward P. Irwin, editor of the *Pacific Commercial Advertiser*, wrote in 1920 that: "Here in Hawaii today, there are Japanese papers that do not actively teach anti-Americanism, but they do teach Japanism, and that amounts to the same thing" (cited in Tamura, 1993, p. 41).

Germans, too, were victims of vicious hate campaigns throughout the United States during the Americanization campaign. Laws were passed banning German speech in the classroom, on the street, in church, in public meetings, and even on the telephone. In the Midwest, at least 18,000 persons were charged with violations by 1921 (Crawford, 1992; see also, Wiley, chapter 9, this volume, for a more detailed discussion). As a result of anti-German hysteria during the World War I era, enrollments in German foreign language classes decreased from a record high of nearly 24% in 1915 to less than 1% in 1922 (Wiley, chapter 9, this volume). In fact, the association of English with patriotism had a chilling effect on the study of all modern languages among U.S. high school students, declining from 36% (1915) to 14% (1948) of that population; it was not until 1994 that foreign language enrollments among high school students would exceed the enrollment rate of 1928 (Draper & Hicks, 1996). At the postsecondary level, registrations in modern foreign languages per 100 college students since 1977 has ranged from 7.3 to 8.2, with enrollments in French, German, and Russian declining an average of 32% since 1990. Although enrollments in Chinese and Japanese have increased during the same period, the actual numbers of college

**104**                                                                                     **RICENTO**

students studying these languages is still modest (Chinese—26,471, 2.3%; Japanese—44,723, 3.9%; Brod & Huber, 1997).

Those who spoke so-called nonstandard varieties of English, such as Gullah and Louisiana Creole, were often as marginalized socially and economically as those who did not speak English. This continues to be an issue today. Americans who could not read or write (enslaved African Americans were denied literacy through compulsory ignorance laws) were further marginalized by the use of literacy tests.[16] As Wiley (1996a) pointed out, "Privileged varieties of language become a kind of social capital facilitating access to education, good grades, competitive test scores, employment, public office and [other] economic advantages for those who have mastered the standard language" (p. 515).

## SUMMARY

In evaluating the effectiveness or fairness of language policies, whether explicit or covert, planned or accidental, national or local in scope, the analyst must consider a broad range of variables and outcomes. The analyst must bear in mind that choice with regard to language acquisition (including the variety acquired, e.g., standard vs. nonstandard dialects) and use is constrained by many factors, including ethnicity/race, socioeconomic status, and the effects of contact situations. So long as access to standard English, a necessary but not sufficient prerequisite for socioeconomic integration and mobility, is not universally available (or attainable), policies that privilege one variety (standard English) over all other languages and varieties used by significant numbers of people help perpetuate social divisions along lines of social class, race/ethnicity, and cultural background.

Historically, assimilation into the mainstream culture among immigrant groups has been predicated, in general, on the suppression, and eventual loss, of non-English languages and nonmainstream cultures. Where structural (including legal) barriers blocked mobility to the middle class (for example, with Mexican Americans, Native Americans, and African Americans), or in cases where economically self-sufficient communities existed (e.g., with German Americans in many midwestern communities in the early to mid-19th century), non-English languages and nonstandard English dialects have been maintained. In some cases, continual migration from

---

[16]Literacy as a requirement for voting was suspended in the Voting Rights Act of 1965. The Act was amended in 1975 to provide for ballots in non-English languages in districts where at least 5% of the population belonged to a single minority group. In 1982, the criterion was narrowed to 5% of potential voters who "do not speak or understand English adequately enough to participate in the electoral process" (Crawford, 1992, p. 272n). This reduced the number of districts required to provide bilingual ballots from 369 to 160.

## 4. NATIONAL LANGUAGE POLICY                                                   105

other countries has replenished speech communities (as with Spanish in the Southwest, California, Florida, and parts of the Northeast). In these communities, complex continua of bilingualism and, for example, Spanish monolingualism exist (Baugh, 1984), although shift to English monolingualism by the third generation is the norm (Veltman, 1983). In some communities, non-English languages have found a niche in the local or regional political economy, as has happened with Spanish in Dade County, Florida over the past several decades. In other contexts, speech communities have been relatively successful in transmitting and maintaining non-English languages intergenerationally for private or specialized uses, as with Chinese in parts of California and New York, and Hebrew in many Jewish communities. In the case of Native Americans, government policy not only destroyed Native cultures and languages, it impeded assimilation into mainstream culture.

This brief survey of the experiences of immigrant and indigenous populations throughout U.S. history points out the variability in treatment of different groups and relative degree to which assimilation (behavioral, structural, or both) occurred. The process of assimilation for European groups varied; southern and eastern Europeans encountered more barriers than did those from northern Europe and the British Isles (except for the Irish); those from Asia (especially China, Korea and Japan) were initially given higher status than African Americans, but soon came to be lumped with other non White groups at the bottom of the social pecking order, especially in the west and south.[17]

Today, culture is often a surrogate for race in public debate on immigration and language matters, such as occurred with the "ebonics" controversy in Oakland, California in December 1996 (this is taken up in chapter 14 of this volume). However, politically conservative journalists and pundits continue to publish articles that make clear the degree to which culture is tied to race in their thinking.[18] Suppression of difference—linguistic and cultural—appears to be the goal today among a vocal, but influential,

---

[17]Between 1893 and 1903, seven immigration restrictionist bills were passed in at least one of the houses of Congress (Hartmann, 1967). The racial basis of the literacy provision in the bills was evident. In discussing the immigration issue in Congress in 1905, Congressman Oscar W. Underwood (D-Alabama) "instructed the House on the pure whiteness of the old immigration in contrast to the mixture of Asiatic and African blood coursing in the veins of southern Europeans" (Higham, 1971, p. 164). In defending a literacy test as a condition of admission to the United States, Senator F. M. Simmons (D-North Carolina) appealed to the preservation of the Anglo-Saxon civilization against immigrants who "are nothing more than the degenerate progeny of the Asiatic hoards which, long centuries ago, overran the shores of the Mediterranean ... the spawn of the Phoenician curse" (p. 164, 165).

[18]Two examples will suffice: In an op-ed piece, columnist Don Feder (1997) wrote, "Over 90% of new immigrants are 'non-white'." Many come from caudillo cultures where corruption is pervasive. Most have a mañana work ethic. Their customs and traditions are as alien to our own as sushi to kosher cuisine" (p. 7B). In another op-ed column, well-known conservative commentator William F. Buckley (1992) wrote a column in which he explained why    (cont.)

minority as it was (explicitly) in the first two decades of this century, and as it was (often implicitly) during the colonial era. In that sense, at least, nothing has changed.

The tumultuous history of the BEA illustrates how difficult it is to implement a policy when the dominant national culture is not receptive to it at some deep level, and where a long history of antagonisms between majority/minority groups exists. The best available research suggests that late-exit bilingual education programs are superior to weak transitional models, or English immersion (submersion) programs, as measured by the academic achievement of language minority students. However, opposition to "folk" bilingualism—whether individual or societal—is so deeply held in the dominant political culture that anything other than elite bilingualism (i.e., for the most highly educated) will not be tolerated.

## CAN LANGUAGE BE PLANNED IN THE UNITED STATES?

Because the U.S. political culture resists social planning generally, the likelihood that language planning agencies or commissions would be established is very remote. Further, there are structural and philosophical reasons to account for the limited proactive role the federal government has played, and continues to play, in policy development: The states retain primary jurisdiction with regard to education policy; issues of language status in public and most private domains have been settled by consensus of the dominant political culture over the course of generations of lived experience. Given these constraints and realities, the task of justifying *why* language should be planned, *how* it should be planned, and to *what ends* becomes an even more daunting challenge. In this section, I suggest possible answers to these questions.

### Why Plan Language? (An Economic Argument)

Language has intrinsic and extrinsic value; it is a marker of individual and group identity and a means of exchange between groups or individuals (Carr, 1985). Economists who specialize in the economies of language have investigated issues such as language and earnings and costs and benefits of multilingualism (see Grin & Vaillancourt, 1997). Studies by sociolinguists have been conducted in the United States which suggest Spanish language maintenance correlates with low income; however, some scholars have questioned the results because they overlook important variables, and

---

[18](cont.) it is easier to assimilate British immigrants than African Zulus; the former "speak English ... are by and large Christians ... and they are white-skinned. The Zulus speak no English, know nothing of democracy, and are black-skinned" (p. 9A).

## 4. NATIONAL LANGUAGE POLICY 107

because correlational studies do not support cause and effect (García, 1995, p. 146). Nonetheless, economic analysis can provide tools to aid social (including language) planning, enhance its effectiveness, and measure the degree to which changes in language policy have achieved stated objectives. For example, the effects of language policies in Canada on income has been investigated (e.g., Beach & Vaillancourt, 1996). Studies such as these validate extant policies or provide information to justify modifications in current policy.

A shortcoming of economic approaches is that they are not able to capture the complexity of language behavior and attitudes, or the contexts of language behavior. On the other hand, such complexity is often minimized by supporters of linguistic diversity who tend to view language as a "resource," that is, as a form of human capital. Following this analogy, pluralists argue that language should be managed (like other "material" resources) to maximize the greatest social good at the most reasonable cost, which entails some sort of planning. This view of language is not widely shared by the dominant political culture, which tends to view language as an instrument for communication with little intrinsic value. A quantitative economic model that reflects such a view is the rational-choice paradigm in which individuals adopt behaviors (linguistic and otherwise) based on self-interest (or perceptions of what constitutes one's best interests) "to maximize their satisfactions" (cited in Lane, 1996, p. 113), and the "marketplace" is responsive to individual choices over a period of time. With regard to language-related issues, the evidence provided in this chapter suggests that so-called market forces do not provide for an equal distribution of optimum choices for individuals because of differences in socioeconomic status, ethnicity/race, religion, status as a member of an indigenous or immigrant language minority group, or some combination thereof. For example, bilingualism for the well-educated middle and upper classes is generally considered an asset, whereas bilingualism among the poor is seen as a liability by mainstream society. In order to counterbalance inequities resulting from discriminatory policies and practices in education and the workplace, economic approaches in language planning need to factor in social attitudes and structural barriers that limit choices among diverse populations. American society continues to diversify linguistically and culturally, and in the absence of planning in education (especially with regard to literacy at all levels), in public services (to ensure communication between citizens and governments works smoothly), and in business and industry (with regard to workplace training and the transnational economy), the economic and concomitant social consequences of ignoring the central role of language in national life could be severe.

## How Should Language Be Planned?

Given the historical disinclination against actively prescribing language policies, the powers and responsibilities of, for example, a planning agency constituted by the federal government would likely be very restricted and closely supervised by Congress or the executive branch. When the federal government has entered into the language policy arena, it usually has done so in response to some social pressure (e.g., to pass restrictive literacy tests, to ameliorate a problem that had not been addressed by local or state educational institutions, as in the case of the Bilingual Education Act, or to ensure compliance with court rulings or legislative edicts, such as Title VI of the Civil Rights Act of 1964, or in modifying the Voting Rights Act in 1975 to include provisions for bilingual ballots). The evidence provided in this chapter, however, suggests that a quasi-independent, publicly funded agency could provide policy makers at federal, state, and local levels better and more detailed information on national language needs and resources than is currently available. To the extent that national language policy goals are achievable, decision making at the local and state levels requires the availability of relevant data and policy options. For example, projections on the economic benefits of increasing the pool of fully bilingual persons with specific types of skills would be valuable information for individuals and policy makers. Schools and universities might use such information in decision making with regard to curriculum and hiring decisions. Government support of such an agency could indirectly stimulate broad-based investment in the private sector to develop national language resources.

Realistically, what is needed more than a centralized effort at the national level is the political will and popular support to invest in human resources. The best approach to planning language will involve coordinated efforts among researchers (linguists, educationists, policy scientists, demographers, sociologists, anthropologists), community organizations (educational, ethnic, religious, philanthropic, business), and government (legislators, politicians, policy experts, legal experts). Planning, to be effective, should involve all stakeholders in the process, implementation, and evaluation of policies. Planning must be ongoing and periodically reevaluated, and it should always reflect the peculiar needs of defined contexts and communities. Although the development of national goals may be helpful to set a direction and endpoint, policies must be worked out "on the ground" to meet local needs.

## To What Ends Should Language Be Planned?

This question has been partially addressed in the previous section. However, because this chapter has focused on a particular policy, the Bilingual

## 4. NATIONAL LANGUAGE POLICY 109

Education Act, it might be useful to consider how a different approach to language-in-education policy might result in a different outcome with regard to the issues that motivated the BEA in the first place.

I have argued that deep values have shaped the goals and influenced the outcomes of bilingual education for language minority children in the United States. Let us suppose that states required elementary schools to offer nonexploratory foreign language instruction in Grades K through 6, and by high school graduation, all students would be required to pass an exit exam in a foreign language. The federal government would subsidize the additional costs of these programs for some period of time. Throughout the United States, in every state and community, two-way bilingual education programs for majority and minority language students would be available; students would be motivated to enroll in these programs because of the exit exam in a foreign language necessary to graduate. Minority language students would be able to improve their English skills while maintaining and developing their native non-English language; majority-language students would acquire an additional language; all students would develop literacy in two languages while learning in culturally diverse classrooms. The nation would be provided with individuals competent in two (or more) languages, which would contribute to the Gross Domestic Product, as well as enhance national security by providing a cadre of fully bilingual persons for work in highly specialized government (including military) agencies. Bilingualism would be normal, rather than a temporary state preceding English monolingualism. English would continue to be the public language, but through common agreement (not coerced through legislation), and in communities and homes throughout the country, no one would feel ashamed or the need to apologize for speaking, writing, and reading other languages in addition to English. As more Americans develop literate and oral competence in two (or more) languages, they would be more likely to value other cultures, instead of seeing them as aberrations from the "norm," (whether overt or covert norms). This would benefit the United States in international relations and trade.

This scenario could happen; indeed, several states have passed legislation requiring foreign language instruction from elementary grades through high school, with some states requiring foreign language fluency for graduation from secondary school (see Ruíz, 1994; Tucker, 1994). But the trend is not widespread, funding of such programs has been limited, and the federal government has not supported ambitious national goals in this area. However, this is precisely the sort of policy that could lead to broad-based improvements in the education of language minority individuals as well as mainstream monolingual English speakers. It is a "win-win" policy, but without vocal political support from the grass roots and at the national level, it will not happen. Perhaps it will not be until deep values are significantly modified (or until the education crisis becomes too critical to ignore) that the political will to foster such policies will emerge. Let us hope that with increased awareness through education, dialogue and debate, Americans will come to see diversity as normal and beneficial, a central element of national identity. If that were to happen, terms such as bilingual education would become obsolete because monolingual education would no longer exist.

## ACKNOWLEDGMENTS

I would like to thank Barbara Burnaby, Nancy Hornberger, and Terrence Wiley for their very helpful comments and suggestions on earlier drafts of this chapter.

## REFERENCES

Baker, K. A., & de Kanter, A. A. (Eds.). (1983). *Bilingual education: A reappraisal of federal policy.* Lexington, MA: Lexington.

Baugh, J. (1984). Chicano English: The anguish of definition. In J. Ornstein-Galicia (Ed.), *Form and function in Chicano English* (pp. 3–13). Rowley, MA: Newbury House.

Beach, C., & Vaillancourt, F. (1996). *Income and language skills of Canadians, 1970–1990* (Mimeographed document). Ottawa: Statistics Canada.

Brod, R., & Huber, B. (1997). Foreign language enrollments in United States institutions of higher learning, Fall 1995. *ADFL Bulletin 28,* 2.

Buckley, W. F. (1992, February 12). Brits, Zulus, Buchanan, and politics. Detroit Free Press, p. 9A.

Carr, J. (1985). Bilingualism in Canada. Is the use of the English language a natural monopoly? In F. Vaillancourt (Ed.), *Economie et langue* (pp. 27–37). Québec: Conseil de la langue française.

Christian, D., & Whitcher, A. (1995). *Directory of two-way bilingual education programs in the United States.* Santa Cruz, CA: National Center for Research on Cultural Diversity and Second Language Learning.

Crawford, J. (1986, June 4). U.S. enforcement of bilingual plans declines sharply. *Education Week,* p. 1.

Crawford, J. (1989). *Bilingual education: History, politics, theory and practice.* Trenton, NJ: Crane.

Crawford, J. (1992). *Hold your tongue: Bilingualism and the politics of "English Only."* Reading, MA: Addison-Wesley.

Cummins, J. (1994). The discourse of disinformation: The debate on bilingual education and language rights in the United States. In T. Skutnabb-Kangas & R. Phillipson (Eds.), *Linguistic human rights: Overcoming linguistic discrimination* (pp. 159–177). Berlin: Mouton de Gruyter.

Draper, J. B., & Hicks, J. H. (1996). Foreign language enrollments in public secondary schools, Fall, 1994: Summary report. *Foreign Language Annals, 29,* 303–306.

Epstein, N. (1977). *Language, ethnicity, and the schools: Policy alternatives for bilingual–bicultural education.* Washington, DC: Institute for Educational Leadership.

## 4. NATIONAL LANGUAGE POLICY 111

Feder, D. (1997, March 19). America's future gradually darker. *San Antinio Express-News*, p. 78.

Fernandez, R. R. (1987). Legislation, regulation, and litigation: The origins and evolution of public policy on bilingual education in the United States. In. W.A. Van Horne (Ed.), *Ethnicity and language* (pp. 90–123). Milwaukee: The University of Wisconsin System Institute on Race and Ethnicity.

Freeman, R. D. (1996). Dual-language planning at Oyster Bilingual School: "It's much more than language." *TESOL Quarterly, 30,* 557–580.

García, O. (1995). Spanish language loss as a determinant of income among Latinos in the United States: Implications for language policy in schools. In. J. Tollefson (ed.), *Power and inequality in language education* (pp. 142–160). Cambridge, England: Cambridge University Press.

Grin, F., & Vaillancourt, F. (1997). The economics of multilingualism: Overview and analytical framework. In W. Grabe (Ed.), *Annual review of applied linguistics* (pp. 43–65). New York: Cambridge University Press.

Hamilton, A., Jay, J., & Madison, J. (1788). *The federalist.* New York: The Modern Library.

Hartmann, E. G. (1967). *The movement to Americanize the immigrant.* New York: AMS.

Heath, S. B., & Mandabach, F. (1983). Language status decisions and the law in the United States. In J. Cobarrubias & J. A. Fishman (Eds.), *Progress in language planning: International perspectives* (pp. 87–105). Berlin: Mouton.

Higham, J. (1971). *Strangers in the land: Patterns of American nativism 1860–1925.* New York: Atheneum.

Imhoff, G. (1990). The position of U.S. English on bilingual education. In C. B. Cazden & C. E. Snow (Eds.), *English plus: Issues in bilingual education, the annals, 58* (pp. 48–65). Newbury Park, CA: Sage.

Lane, R. E. (1996). What rational choice explains. In J. Friedman (Ed.), *The rational choice controversy: Economic models of politics reconsidered* (pp. 107–126). New Haven & London: Yale University Press.

*Lav v. Nichols,* 414 U.S. 563 (1974).

Leibowitz, A. H. (1971). *Educational policy and political acceptance: The imposition of English as the language of instruction in American schools.* (ERIC Document Reproduction Service No. ED 047 321)

Leibowitz, A. H. (1980). *The bilingual education act: A legislative analysis.* Rosslyn, VA: National Clearinghouse for Bilingual Education.

Lyons, J. J. (1992). Secretary Bennett versus equal educational opportunity. In J. Crawford (Ed.), *Language loyalties: A source book on the official English controversy* (pp. 363–366). Chicago: The University of Chicago Press.

Lyons, J. J. (1990). The past and future directions of federal bilingual-education policy. In C. B. Cazden, & C. E. Snow, (Eds.), *English plus: Issues in bilingual education, the annals* (pp. 66–80). Newbury Park, CA: Sage.

McClymer, J. F. (1982). The Americanization movement and the education of the foreign-born adult, 1914–25. In B. J. Weiss (Ed.), *American education and the European immigrant: 1840–1940* (pp. 96–116). Urbana: University of Illinois Press.

McNaught, K. (1988). *The Penguin history of Canada.* London: Penguin.

Monaghan, F. (1935). *John Jay.* New York: Bobbs-Merrill.

*Meyer v. Nebraska,* 107 Neb. 657, 187 N.W. 100 (1922), rev'd, 262 U.S. 390 (1923).

Ogbu, J. U. (1978). *Minority education and caste: The American system in cross- cultural perspective.* New York: Academic Press.

Pitt, L. (1976). *We Americans: Vol. I. Colonial times to 1877.* Glenview, IL: Scott, Foresman.

*Plyer v. Doe,* 457 U.S. 202 (1982).

Porter, R. P. (1990). *Forked tongue: The politics of bilingual education.* New York: Basic Books.

Ramírez, J. D., Yuen, S. D., & Ramey, D. R., (1991). *Final report: Longitudinal study of structured immersion strategy, early-exit, and late-exit transitional bilingual education programs for language-minority children*. San Mateo, CA: Aguirre International.

Ricento, T. K. (1996a). Language policy in the United States. In M. Herriman & B. Burnaby (Eds.), *Language policy in English dominant countries: Six case studies* (pp. 122–158). Clevedon, England: Multilingual Matters.

Ricento, T. K. (1996b, April). *The role of English language education in the Americanization campaign of 1890–1920*. Paper presented at the American Educational Research Association National Convention, New York.

Ruíz, R. (1994). Language policy and planning in the United States. In W. Grabe (Ed.), *Annual review of applied linguistics* (pp. 111–125). New York: Cambridge University Press.

Tamura, E. H. (1993). The English-only effort, the anti-Japanese campaign, and language acquisition in the education of Japanese Americans in Hawaii, 1915–40. *History of Education Quarterly, 33*, 37–58.

Tucker, G. R. (1994). TESOL and NAFTA: Challenges for the 21st century. *TESOL Matters 4*, 1,4,5.

Veltman, C. (1983). *Language shift in the United States*. Berlin: Mouton.

Weinberg, M. (1995). *A chance to learn: A history of race and education in the United States* (2nd ed.). Long Beach: California State University Press.

Wiley, T. G. (1996a). English-only and standard English ideologies: Two dimensions of status ascription in language planning and policy formation. *TESOL Quarterly, 30*, 511–535.

Wiley, T. G. (1996b). *Literacy and language diversity in the United States*. Washington, DC and McHenry, IL: The Center for Applied Linguistics and Delta Systems.

Williams, J. (1995, September 17). Alteration of language order hailed. *San Antonio Express News*, p. B1.

Willig, A. C. (1985). A meta-analysis of selected studies on the effectiveness of bilingual education. *Review of Educational Research, 55*, 269–317.

# II

# Forgotten Tongues: Indigenous Languages in North America

The two chapters in Part II consider Aboriginal languages in Canada and the United States. This focus serves as a strong reminder that issues of French and English in North America exist within a larger local and world context in which thousands of other languages struggle in their unique circumstances. Whereas Wiley and Burnaby (chapters 9 and 10 of this volume) draw attention to issues relating to immigrants to the two countries and the ways in which they have been treated (or mistreated) linguistically, Fettes and Crawford (chapters 5 and 6 in this part) show what a desperate condition most of the indigenous languages north of Mexico have been reduced to. In comparison with such conditions, the linguistic problems facing English and French speakers seem paltry and self-serving.

The Aboriginal languages of North America must be appreciated for policy purposes in a very special light. They are the indigenous languages of the land and therefore have a major symbolic importance in the context of the language heritage and resources of what are now Canada and the United States. As the original languages of the continent, they have no sources of external support if they languish here. If Basque or Swedish or even Spanish-speaking communities in North America are at risk of losing their languages, there are human and other linguistic repositories elsewhere from which new resources can be drawn, but if Tlingit or Potawatomi or even Navajo decline to a dangerous point, there is no external support.

Fettes, briefly, and Crawford, in some detail, discuss some of the language and other policy history that has contributed to pushing the majority of Aboriginal languages in Canada and the United States to the point of

113

extreme danger and some to extinction. Although there has been some variation in Canadian and U.S. approaches to Aboriginal peoples and their languages, there are more similarities than differences. Crawford not only details the "English-only" policies of forced schooling for indigenous children and other measures that were repressive of their languages, but he also shows the complex relationship between English and the indigenous languages that has come out of the isolation, dislocation, and economic exclusion forced on Aboriginal groups. Both genocide and linguicide were involved, so now language loss, economic marginalization, and crises of social identity are realities.

In terms of the implications for language planning, Fettes and Crawford take different approaches to delineating issues, but these perspectives are complementary. Crawford, focusing on the imminent death of many of the indigenous languages in the United States, explores various conceptual frameworks that have been used to account for language death—survival of the fittest (or extinction of the weakest), suicide, murder, or interaction in the complex ecology of communities. He places the plight of these languages in the context of the interests of the non-Aboriginal population, asking why we should care about the continued survival of these languages. The scientific interest of linguists, the value of linguistic diversity, the value of cultural pluralism, and social justice are raised as considerations.

Fettes takes a different perspective on framing language policy issues by showing why Aboriginal languages in North America are not like the much-discussed languages of English, French, or even Spanish. First, there are a lot of languages to be attended to, most with a small number of speakers (even in the largest language groups). Because the number of speakers within each Aboriginal group is dwindling (some at an alarming rate), all of the languages need to be supported in terms of preservation and revitalization. Virtually none of the languages has a tradition of writing that functions in the ways that literacy operates in English, French, or Spanish. Several centuries of contact with the immigrants to this continent has meant that the Aboriginal languages have maintained or been confined to certain domains of use and development. In light of these kinds of differences, a radically different mindset of language policy development is required when dealing with these languages in comparison with dealing with English, French, or Spanish.

Fettes illustrates his points lavishly by comparing the responses made in Canada's two northern territories in the 1980s and 1990s to a policy initiative that arose as a spin-off from the federal Official Languages Act. In one case, the federal model of official language status and focus on central government services was followed; in the other, a community-based process was used. Fettes contrasts the outcomes of these policies in

## II. FORGOTTEN TONGUES                                                115

light of the needs and characteristics of the speakers of the Aboriginal languages involved.

Both Fettes and Crawford make as their main points the essential role of community if initiatives to support, maintain, and revive Aboriginal languages are to be effective. Without community support, other efforts will be ineffective. In dire linguistic, economic, and social circumstances, identity and spirituality are at stake, and choices are made in a complex matrix of strongly competing economic and political demands for attention and resources. Other authors in this volume point out the importance of the family and community and their crucial roles in the future of French and minority immigrant languages in Canada and the United States. The two chapters in Part II, however, take this consideration to its limits because they are talking about languages that have been themselves thus pressed.

# 5

# Life on the Edge: Canada's Aboriginal Languages Under Official Bilingualism

Mark Fettes
*University of Toronto*

For many in and out of Canada, Canadian "language policy" refers to the country's struggles with the relative status of English and French. There is little doubt that this national preoccupation has hindered the development of a more comprehensive approach to linguistic issues. In modern times, the defining step was taken by the Trudeau government of 1968–1972, which established the policy of "multiculturalism in a bilingual framework," arbitrarily divorcing cultural and linguistic rights. Through the Official Languages Act, (Canada, 1988) and the language clauses of the Constitution Act (1982), the federal government guarantees the rights of English and French speakers in the areas of law, education and government services. This is the meaning of "bilingualism" in official policy, a pragmatic solution to the fact that of Canada's 28 million people, 63% report English as a mother tongue and 25% report French (Statistics Canada, 1991b). The remaining 12% of the population enjoy no such guarantees,[1] and must

---

[1]An exception is the general guarantee of the right to an interpreter in court proceedings under the 1982 Charter of Rights and Freedoms. The Official Languages Act may not be interpreted "in a way that is inconsistent with the preservation and enhancement of the use of languages other than English and French," nor "abrogate or derogate from any legal or customary right"; these clauses are clearly intended to rule out the active suppression of non-official languages, without committing the government to any form of support.

**118**                                                                                                                          **FETTES**

generally struggle along on volunteer efforts and tiny amounts of funding
if they wish to provide even the most basic services in a nonofficial language
to their children or their community.

Such exclusionary policies are particularly bitter for many of Canada's
Aboriginal people. Of approximately one million Canadians claiming Aboriginal descent, some 650,000 choose to identify themselves as Indian/First
Nations, Métis, or Inuit; over 80% of this group report an attachment to their
ancestral language, even if they no longer speak it (Statistics Canada,
1991a).[2] Dakota elder Eli Taylor gives a sense of how deep this bond runs:

> Our native language embodies a value system about how we ought to live and
> relate to each other ... It gives a name to relations among kin, to roles and
> responsibilities among family members, to ties with the broader clan group ...
> There are no English words for these relationships ... Now, if you destroy our
> languages you not only break down these relationships, but you also destroy
> other aspects of our Indian way of life and culture, especially those that describe
> man's connection with nature, the Great Spirit, and the order of things. Without
> our languages, we will cease to exist as a separate people. (cited in Shkilnyk,
> 1986, p. 31)

The same idea is expressed in the Declaration on First Nations Languages by the Assembly of First Nations, Canada's largest Aboriginal lobby
group:

> Language is our unique relationship to the Creator, our attitudes, beliefs, values,
> and fundamental notions of what is truth. Our languages are the cornerstones of
> who we are as a people. Without our languages our cultures cannot survive ...
> The right to use our Aboriginal languages, and the right to educate our children
> in our languages, is an inherent Aboriginal and treaty right. The federal govern-
> ment has a legal obligation through various treaties, and through legislation, to
> provide adequate resources that will enable us to exercise this right. (Assembly of
> First Nations, 1990, p. 39)

There is sadness, anger, and urgency in such calls. For several generations, beginning in the mid-19th century, Aboriginal languages were systematically excluded from Canadian schools and public life; especial havoc
was wreaked by Aboriginal boarding schools, where children were separated from their families for 6 months or more per year and forced to use
English even among themselves (Tschanz, 1980). In the 1960s, this policy of
linguicide was abandoned for the practice of neglect, leaving children,
parents and grandparents to cope as best they could with psychological
scars, linguistic handicaps, and an institutional framework built on French
and English. The result has been continued language loss in most commu-

---

[2]The figure of 650,000 includes an estimated 30,000 people living on incompletely enumerated reserves. The data on language attitudes are based on the adult population (15 years and
over).

## 5. LIFE ON THE EDGE 119

nities, but also the slow development of effective language programs, largely through trial and error. The latter's accelerating growth in the decade since 1985, coupled with calls to recognize Aboriginal languages at the federal level, represent the greatest challenge to Canada's current linguistic regime (see Crawford, chapter 6, this volume, for U.S. parallels).

### THE STATE OF ABORIGINAL LANGUAGES IN CANADA

Aboriginal languages in Canada consist not of one nor half a dozen tongues, but of 60 or more, commonly grouped in 11 linguistic families. The families typically include dialect chains reaching over considerable distances (varieties of Cree are spoken from northern Alberta to the east coast of James Bay), so that there is no simple way to decide where one language ends and the next begins; the standard linguistic sourcebook Ethnologue (Grimes, 1988) lists 70 Aboriginal languages for Canada, another source (Foster, 1982) only 53. At the political level, the defining unit may be a band or nation (of which there are more than 600) or even a single community[3] (which number over 2,000). Some implications of this are taken up here later.

The languages vary greatly not only in phonology, vocabulary, and syntax, but in size, distribution, and vitality (Burnaby & Beaujot, 1986; Kinkade, 1991; Statistics Canada, 1991a). The three most widely dispersed languages are among the most robust: the Inuit (or Canadian Eskimo) language, with some 21,000 speakers, and the Algonquian languages Cree and Ojibway (72,000 and 27,000 respectively). Other Algonquian languages include Micmac and Montagnais-Naskapi (sometimes known as Innu), with 5,000 to 7,000 speakers each, and a number of smaller ones, some robust, some almost extinct; all together this language family accounts for approximately 60% of the entire Aboriginal population.

The Athapaskan or Dene family (of which Navajo and Apache are also members) is spread across Western Canada from the Alaskan border to southern British Columbia and northern Manitoba. None of the 14 or more languages in this group has more than a few thousand speakers, but several continue to flourish in their native communities. The southern language families of the Iroquois (Mohawk and five smaller languages along the St. Lawrence River) and the Sioux (Dakota, Assiniboine, and related tongues scattered across the Prairies) have been eroded drastically, but in most cases a larger speaker population exists across the border in the United States.

Finally, British Columbia, the westernmost province, is a world unto itself. Five language families (Haida, Kutenai, Salishan, Tsimshian, and

---

[3]This position is implicitly adopted by the Assembly of First Nations (1990) when it declares that "language is a community resource, to be developed at the community level" (p. 39).

Wakashan), accounting for some 20 languages, are unique to British Columbia although they are shared with adjoining regions in the United States. Most languages in these families have a population base of no more than 2,000 or 3,000, sometimes fewer than 1,000, and many communities appear to be on the verge of losing their last speakers.

This brief overview highlights the following challenges to policy makers in the area of Aboriginal languages:

1. Policy must be based on the realities of small numbers and great diversity, in contrast to Canada's present official languages,
2. Erosion of the base of fluent speakers means that language preservation and revitalization may be primary policy goals in many communities.

A further important challenge is in the area of literacy. Canadian Aboriginal languages do not have a strong written tradition; although orthographies began to develop in some Inuit, Cree, Ojibway, and Micmac communities before this century, the introduction of compulsory schooling in English generally ensured the restriction of native language literacy to informal and religious domains. In some communities the tradition virtually disappeared, and in others it seems never to have put down strong roots (Burnaby, 1985). Today only 13% of Aboriginal adults in Canada claim to be able to read, and 9% to be able to write, in their ancestral language (Statistics Canada, 1991a). Many dialects do not have a standard written form that is accepted by the community.[4] Hence:

3. Aboriginal language policies that are limited to written domains and do not build on existing, primarily oral, traditions are likely to be ineffective.

An important corollary is that different kinds of knowledge are accessible in Aboriginal and official languages, and inter-translatability is highly problematic. In the area of law, for instance, fundamental concepts such as "guilty" and "not guilty," or "justiciability," are extremely difficult to render intelligible in an Aboriginal semantic framework (Henderson, 1995). A question of great importance for Aboriginal languages is the extent to which inter-translatability is necessary, or desirable, which is equivalent to asking whether they must become "modern" languages in order to continue to serve their communities. Although strong statements

---

[4]Interestingly, the highest rates of Aboriginal literacy are reported among regions using the syllabic writing system originally developed for the Ojibwe, and subsequently adapted for the eastern dialects of the Inuit language and some of the northern Dene languages. For more information see Burnaby (1985).

# 5. LIFE ON THE EDGE

may be found on both sides of the issue, they are bound up in a web of assumptions and ideological convictions that, in situations of language shift, often take precedence over rational policy development (Langgaard, 1992; McConvell, 1991);

4. Both "full modernization" and "domain separation" need to be considered as a potential basis for Aboriginal language policy and related to the wider developmental context of the groups involved.

Although the close study of language use and language attitudes in individual communities would provide an invaluable resource for formulating Aboriginal language policy, relatively few data are available. The Canadian census did not start collecting information on individual Aboriginal languages until 1981, and even its most extensive study (Statistics Canada, 1991a) is limited in its usefulness. In recent years, however, detailed surveys have been conducted in some areas of the country by Aboriginal organizations and the Territorial governments (Assembly of First Nations, 1990, 1992; Cottingham & Tousignant, 1991; Fredeen, 1991).

Although these studies have employed widely varying methodologies, they confirm a further fact of vital importance for Aboriginal language policy: even within a single language, individual bands or communities display widely differing rates of language retention. For instance, the Atahkakohp reserve in Saskatchewan has nearly lost its use of Cree (Fredeen, 1991), whereas 50 kilometers away the same language flourishes in the Whitefish reserve, as measured by its use in a variety of social settings and across all generations. This confirms that important dimensions of Aboriginal language policy must be formulated and implemented at the local level;

5. Policies aimed at aiding *languages* rather than *communities* cannot take into account important variables that influence local outcomes.

These challenges are rarely confronted by policy makers. It is easier to ignore Aboriginal languages, to attempt to fit them into the framework of existing language policy, or to respond on an ad hoc basis to local initiatives than to develop a coherent approach based on separate principles. Examples of each of these approaches are mentioned in the following review.

Aboriginal language policy does not develop in a vacuum, of course. In the past, it was one aspect of a general effort to assimilate Aboriginal people into "mainstream" Canadian society. Today, at its best, it provides a linguistic dimension to the system of self-government that is slowly

# 122                                                                    FETTES

taking shape in various parts of the country.[5] The relationship between linguistic and political self-determination is a complex one, but many of the Aboriginal groups who have gained the greatest control over their own lives have also gone the furthest in developing language policies to suit their needs.

## FEDERAL POLICY: A FAILURE OF NERVE

Toward the end of the 1960s, as the federal government was coming to grips with the need to accommodate francophone linguistic rights at the national level, realization was also spreading of the inequity of Aboriginal educational policies, divorced as they were from Aboriginal languages and cultures. A turning point came in 1972, when a relatively new Aboriginal organization, the National Indian Brotherhood, published *Indian Control of Indian Education*, a clear and moving call for an education system based on Aboriginal values and priorities. The paper was subsequently accepted by the federal government as the basis for national policy. In the following years many Aboriginal communities began to experiment with various forms of bilingual and bicultural programs, both within the formal school system and outside it; for many, this still represents the only context in which linguistic policies are explicitly debated and defined.

Progress has been slow and uneven, however. Because education in Canada is under provincial jurisdiction, but Aboriginal peoples have a direct relationship with the federal government, the evolving network of band-controlled and federal schools has been plagued by a lack of both expertise and consistency. In terms of language policy, each Aboriginal community and school board has essentially set about reinventing the wheel, usually with little technical or financial support. A 1990 survey by the successor organization to the National Indian Brotherhood reported that few bands offered a language program past the first 3 years of schooling, even though "all bands responding to the survey stressed the need to have their language taught in school from nursery to grade 12" (Assembly of First Nations, 1990, p. 24). Communities have also been slow to appreciate the fact that school-based programs alone do little or nothing to slow language shift; their effectiveness depends on the use of the language in the home and community, and on deliberate efforts to restore its importance and prestige. Although this point was strongly emphasized in a number of studies distributed to more than 600 bands across the country (Assembly of First

---

[5]Canada's Aboriginal people are still governed by the Indian Act, an outdated, racist set of laws that regulates nearly every aspect of an Aboriginal person's life. Following many years of promises, the federal government has at last moved to begin dismantling the Act province by province, transferring its responsibilities to Aboriginal political institutions. Some provincial governments have also moved to share jurisdiction in education, health, and natural resources.

## 5.  LIFE ON THE EDGE                                                123

Nations, 1990, 1992; Fettes, 1992), there is little evidence that this led to a more comprehensive approach to language policy at the grass-roots level.

Many barriers do indeed stand in the way of the development of consistent and effective maintenance strategies for Aboriginal languages, including the political weakness of national Aboriginal organizations, the presence of many competing priorities on local and national agendas, and the extremes of poverty and social dysfunction that characterize many Aboriginal communities. Another major stumbling block is the attitude of the federal government. Up until the 1980s, little attention was paid to the languages (the 1981 census was the first to ask for data on specific languages and language families), beyond their occasional teaching in band or federal schools. The first move toward recognizing the political significance of Aboriginal languages stemmed from the debate over the 1982 Constitution, which led to much greater political recognition for First Nations throughout the following decade.[6] As is described here later, the patriation of the Constitution gave rise to important language policy initiatives in the Yukon and Northwest Territories. For a brief period it even appeared that federal language policy as a whole would evolve to accommodate Aboriginal languages, in accordance with Article 35 of the Constitution Act guaranteeing "existing Aboriginal and treaty rights".[7] Although ultimately inconclusive, this episode is worth recounting in some detail.

At the 1984 First Ministers Conference on Aboriginal Constitutional Matters (bringing together the leaders of the federal government and the 10 provinces), the outgoing Canadian Prime Minister, Pierre Trudeau, "directed the federal government to 'preserve and enhance the cultural and linguistic heritage of Canada's Aboriginal people.' This directive resulted in a major review of the state of affairs pertaining to Aboriginal languages" (Jamieson, 1988a, p. 90). Studies commissioned by the Department of Secretary of State confirmed ongoing language shift in the Aboriginal population (Burnaby & Beaujot, 1986) and revealed huge discrepancies in federal and provincial funding for Aboriginal language programs (Phillips, 1985). They also demonstrated remarkable depths of commitment and resourcefulness on the part of Aboriginal language activists across the country (Shkilnyk, 1986). A proposal for a comprehensive federal policy was developed and circulated by the Department (Secretary of State, Can-

---

[6]Aboriginal leaders argue that the "First Nations" constitute a separate order of government within the Canadian Confederation, as recognized in the 11 treaties signed by the British Crown, the Government of Canada, or both between 1871 and 1921, in subsequent agreements such as the James Bay Treaty (1973), and in international law. This viewpoint won growing, if qualified, public acceptance throughout the 1980s, but is still tenaciously resisted by the federal and provincial governments.

[7]The relevance of this section to linguistic rights has been argued by several scholars (e.g., Nahanee, 1992; Varennes, 1993). However, the existence and extent of protection for Aboriginal languages under Article 35 has yet to be tested in the courts.

ada, 1985; Shkilnyk, n.d.), and two national Aboriginal organizations were funded to develop their own policy proposals.[8] As late as January 1988, Secretary of State David Crombie could tell the Aboriginal Language Policy Conference: "Every community and every Indian community in particular wants to have its language survive; if you will work in your communities, we in the federal government will support you to the very best of our ability" (Jamieson, 1988a, p. 91).

Yet by this time the process of federal policy development had in fact stalled. In the same year, 1988, a proposal to establish a National Aboriginal Language Institute, extensively discussed and endorsed by Aboriginal organizations, failed to elicit an official response from the Secretary of State. In October 1989 the government unexpectedly included Aboriginal languages in its bill to establish a Heritage Languages Institute, focusing on minority immigrant languages; this aspect of the bill was subsequently withdrawn in the face of united opposition from Aboriginal groups, and demonstrates the government's utter failure to build on the work of the previous few years. A Private Member's Bill to establish a separate Aboriginal Languages Institute, sponsored by an Aboriginal member of the Opposition, drew sympathetic noises at its first reading but was not taken up by the government (Assembly of First Nations, 1990).

With the advent of International Literacy Year in 1990, a number of studies and conferences on Aboriginal languages and literacy were funded. Along with several strong language policy statements from Aboriginal and educational organizations, the Parliamentary Standing Committee on Aboriginal Affairs included a recommendation to support Aboriginal languages in its major literacy report (Standing Committee on Aboriginal Affairs, 1990). Yet the net effect of this activity on federal policy was virtually nil. Indeed, the early 1990s saw the major federal source of

---

[8]The Assembly of First Nations (AFN), which represents some 650 on-reserve bands across the country, produced *The Aboriginal Language Policy Study* (Jamieson, 1988a, 1988b) and organized a national Aboriginal Language Policy Conference in January 1988. The Native Council of Canada (NCC), which represents urban Indians, produced a separate *Language Retention Project Report* (Dunn, 1989). The NCC commitment appears to have been superficial, the AFN continued its policy work and established some fundamental guidelines for Aboriginal language planning (Assembly of First Nations, 1990, 1992; Fettes, 1992). They include: (a) the primacy of the community in determining the direction and pace of its own language program; (b) a restricted role for national institutions; (c) the importance of integrating Aboriginal culture and values into any language program; (d) the key role of Elders in language development. These policy studies show an acute awareness of the language status problem, calling for Aboriginal and public governments at all levels to develop language policies and include the languages within the framework of negotiations on self-government. They also avoid the trap of concentrating exclusively on the schooling issue, noting that "the fact that First Nations languages are not used in most of the communities surveyed effectively negates efforts of language personnel. The need to promote language use in the home is therefore critical" (Assembly of First Nations, 1990, p. 37). At the same time, it is recognized that most Aboriginal language teachers are undertrained, undersupported, and underpaid, and that this situation, too, must change.

# 5. LIFE ON THE EDGE 125

discretionary funding for Aboriginal community based linguistic and cultural activities, the Native Social and Cultural Development Program, cut back from $2 to $1 million in annual funding—a return to pre-1983 levels. By 1994, federal policy toward Aboriginal languages, with two important exceptions, had returned to the limbo of 10 years earlier.

These exceptions were the Aboriginal Language Agreements with the Yukon and Northwest Territories. In the whole of Canada, the Territories provide the only examples of a sustained attempt by public government to develop a coherent and supportive Aboriginal language policy. Among the provinces, only Quebec has developed such a policy on paper (Sécretariat des affaires autochtones, 1989)—without, however, putting it into practice. The remaining provinces have limited such intiatives to the formal education system, usually by establishing guidelines for the limited instruction of Aboriginal languages as "second" or "heritage" languages, without any broader policy objectives. Although in itself worthy of critical review, this form of language policy is not covered further here, particularly as it does not differ markedly from practices in other OECD countries (Churchill, 1986). Instead, I focus on the two remarkable experiments being conducted "north of 60."

## THE NORTHWEST TERRITORIES: PUTTING THE COURT BEFORE THE HORSE?

The Northwest Territories (NWT) is a vast region stretching across 3.4 million square kilometres of land north of the 60th parallel. The area is home to fewer than 60,000 people, of whom 35,300 (61%) are of Aboriginal descent. In the east, 87% of the population are Inuit; in the west, 49% are either Inuit (Inuvialuit) or Dene-Métis (comprising five different language groups), with a small number of Cree speakers in the south. The Inuit and Dene are separated by a cultural and linguistic gulf, a fact soon to be reflected in the creation of the new Inuit-led territory of Nunavut in the Eastern Arctic.

The NWT is a creation of the federal government, subject to the authority of the Minister of Indian Affairs and Northern Development, and for most of its existence was administered from Ottawa. Over the last 30 years, however, it has evolved a largely autonomous government based on an elected 24-seat Legislative Assembly. Members run for election on an individual platform and choose the Executive Council from among themselves, in a unique consensus-based form of decision making that owes much to Aboriginal traditions. Since 1979 a majority in the Legislative Assembly has been Aboriginal, with 10 of the seats representing the pre-

**126**                                                                                                   **FETTES**

dominantly Inuit population of the eastern territories (Indian and Northern Affairs Canada [INAC], 1992).

Aboriginal languages in the NWT have suffered in much the same way as in the rest of Canada, particularly in the western region. It is the resistance of Inuktitut in the east that has done most to change the situation. From 1975, as unilingual Inuit began to take their seats in the Legislative Assembly, it became increasingly clear that an English-only policy was not appropriate. An Interpreter Corps was established, while limited financing for the development and use of Aboriginal languages was made available through the Indigenous Language Development Fund (Harnum, 1993). In a historic irony, however, radical change came as a consequence of the entrenchment of *French* language rights in Canada's 1982 Constitution Act. Faced with a potential court challenge to the English-only status of the Yukon and Northwest Territorial governments, in March 1984 the federal government put forward an amendment to the NWT Act that would have made French a full official language (New Economy Development Group [NEDG], 1994). This move sparked off a series of important steps:

1. In the area of *legislation*, the Legislative Assembly successfully negotiated approval for an alternative Official Languages Act, which besides recognizing English and French gave all[9] of the Aboriginal languages of the NWT official status,
2. In terms of *programs*, a separate funding agreement was negotiated with the federal government, whereby $16 million were provided over five years for activities "to preserve, develop and enhance" Aboriginal languages,
3. A task force on Aboriginal languages was formed to carry out *consultations* in all NWT communities and report back to the Assembly.

This crystallization of NWT language policy as a response to federal legislation has had a decisive (and not necessarily beneficial) influence on its subsequent development, as can be shown by examining each of these areas in turn.

---

[9]The definition of "all" Aboriginal languages illustrates some of the difficulties of classification referred to earlier. The 1984 version of the Act named Cree, Chipewyan, Dogrib, Gwich'in, North Slavey (Hare), South Slavey, and Inuktitut. The present (1990) version specifies "Cree, Chipewyan, Dogrib, Gwich'in, Slavey (including North and South Slavey) and Inuktitut (including Inuvialuktun and Inuinnaqtun)," thereby reducing the number of "languages" to six but recognizing nine linguistic traditions, which are frequently treated as separate languages for the purposes of translation, signage, and so on. The usage of "Inuktitut" in the NWT generally refers to the Eastern Arctic tradition, written in syllabics, as separate from Central Arctic Inuinnaqtun and Mackenzie Delta Inuvialuktun, both of which use the Roman alphabet. In the rest of Canada "Inuktitut" is used as a generic term for the Inuit language, along with the local variants "Inuttitut" (Northern Quebec) and "Inuktut" (Labrador).

## 5. LIFE ON THE EDGE
127

### Legislation: Symbols Versus Substance

The Official Languages Act for the NWT was passed in 1984 and subsequently amended (Northwest Territories, 1988). From the beginning it was modeled on the federal Official Languages Act, (Canada, 1988), and thus shares many of its assumptions. In summary, the Act is based on the principle that a citizen should not be obliged to speak and use more than one official language in order to communicate with the government or the courts, or to represent his or her community in the Legislative Assembly. Accordingly, the Act specifies the circumstances in which services or translation in all or some official languages must be provided. Although the Government of the Northwest Territories continues to function primarily in English, as it has done since its inception, all bills, acts, regulations and documents for wide public use must be published in both English and French. Simultaneous translation in all official languages is provided for the proceedings of the Legislative Assembly, and is available on request for any court hearing. Sound recordings of both Assembly debates and court proceedings are available in any official language "upon reasonable request." Government services must be provided in official languages "where there is a significant demand ... or where the nature of the office makes it reasonable to expect to communicate or receive services in that language." Regulations and guidelines may further define the meaning of "reasonable," although none had been developed as late as 1994 (Harnum, 1994, p. 5).

The irony of the Act as it pertains to Aboriginal languages is that the domains of use to which it refers have little to do with Aboriginal culture or the unique circumstances of small, declining, oral-language communities. Although the Act's first key objective for Aboriginal languages is "their preservation, development and enhancement," no provision whatsoever for this is made in the substantive articles that follow. It seems likely that the Languages Act was initially perceived as a symbolic gesture by the Legislature, directed toward raising the *status* of Aboriginal languages rather than responding to more concrete *needs*. Subsequently, the adoption of a framework based on federal language policy inevitably focused attention on the planning issues associated with modern languages of administration. Considerable effort has been put into developing standardized writing systems, terminology in areas such as health and law, and trained interpreters and translators for all six Aboriginal languages. By contrast, the absence of any recognition for educational rights or collective rights means that the Act is irrelevant to the most crucial and pressing linguistic issues confronting Aboriginal communities.

The symbolic intent of the Act is confirmed by the results of various independent assessments. The amended Act of 1990 created, among other things, the office of Languages Commissioner, who, like her federal counterpart, acts as a linguistic ombudsman, clarifying and evaluating the workings of the Official Languages Act. The annual report of the Commissioner tabled in 1993 gave a picture of a government that was far from committed to the goals laid out in the Act's preamble. Information about the Act had not been made public, departments had received no guidelines on its implementation, and numerous details had remained undefined or unregulated throughout the many years since the first version of the Act was passed. Major questions remained concerning the Act's effectiveness in such areas as the courts (e.g., tape recordings of final decisions, orders, and judgements), government institutions (e.g., the language of work, or the provision of services), and the authority of the Commissioner (Harnum, 1993).

Substantial delays have also characterized the government's approach to the position of Aboriginal languages under the Education Act. In the early 1980s, the Special Committee on Education recommended the development of a comprehensive system of bilingual bicultural education, claiming that it would strengthen "students' general use of languages, and enable them to learn more effectively about every subject in the curriculum" (Special Committee on Education, 1982, quoted in Department of Education, Northwest Territories, 1990, p. 6). Territorial education policy, however, continued to be based on a classic "transitional" approach, whereby languages other than English were taught and used in the earliest years only as a prelude to full English immersion. When the 1977 Education Act was consolidated in 1988, 4 years after the adoption of the first Official Languages Act, its linguistic provisions remained as originally drafted:

- English as compulsory, either as a language of instruction or as a second language, from kindergarten to Grade 2,
- The first language of the majority as compulsory, either as a language of instruction or as a second language, from kindergarten to Grade 2,
- The language of instruction from kindergarten to Grade 2 to be determined by the local or regional education authority, which is to be "consulted" by the Minister of Education in determining the language of instruction for higher grades. Teaching of the first language after Grade 2 is optional (Northwest Territories, 1988).

For the first decade of the Official Languages Act, Territorial laws governing education were thus compatible with Aboriginal children being taught entirely in English from the time they entered kindergarten, although for 3 years they must have a class in their first language. Individual linguistic rights were not recognized; the collective linguistic rights of the majority of children in a class were limited to learning their language as a

# 5. LIFE ON THE EDGE                                                129

"second" language for 3 years. These provisions are far weaker than the guarantee of publicly funded K–12 first-language instruction "where numbers warrant," provided to English and French speakers under the Canadian Charter of Rights and Freedoms. Not surprisingly, following the passage of the revised Official Languages Act in 1990 this section of the Education Act came in for repeated criticism; eventually these concerns were addressed in a thorough revision (see later discussion). Yet the long delay reinforces the impression that the Official Languages Act itself was not part of a thought-out policy on Aboriginal languages, but a symbolic gesture whose long-term implications have still to be faced.

## Programs: Communities Come Last

The framework of the Official Languages Act is given effective force through programs and expenditures under the Canada–NWT Aboriginal Languages Agreements (1984–1991, 1991–1994, and 1995–1997), which have collectively provided the NWT with $45 million for Aboriginal language development, plus a number of contributions under the regular GNWT budget in the areas of language services and education. Since July 1992, responsibility for coordination of official language programs has been vested in the Official Languages Unit, Department of the Executive. In spite of this centralized office, two comprehensive evaluations, and the reports of the Languages Commissioner, no clear overview is available to describe what has been achieved in the past 10 years. However, in recent years the allocation of funds between different program areas has remained fairly consistent (NEDG, 1994). Table 5.1 shows a breakdown between three broad areas.

Further insight may be gained from a breakdown between different Aboriginal languages. Although this information is not readily available from government reports, the 1994 evaluation report gives a partial analysis according to the three language families involved—Inuit, Dene, and Cree (NEDG, 1994)—and observes:

> The demand for Language Bureau services for Inuit languages was significantly higher than for Dene languages with twice as much interpretation and eight times the amount of translation being carried out. Inuit language programming for broadcast in 1992–93 (84 hours of original programming) was much higher than for Dene languages (one hour). Participation in literacy awareness programs and in the Teacher Education Program by Inuit language speakers was also much greater than by Dene language speakers. (p. 31)

It may first be noted that these trends are no more than one would expect, given the very different demographic profiles of the Dene and Inuit languages. Inuktitut, the standard Eastern Arctic form of the Inuit language, is spoken by some 80% of eastern NWT residents; from 1999 it will be a major language of government and administration in the Nunavut Territory, even if English continues to play an important role (Foot, 1993; INAC, 1992). The Baffin Divisional Board of Education has worked systematically since its formation toward developing a K–6 Inuktitut curriculum in all Eastern Arctic schools, with the long-term goal of establishing a bilingual (Inuktitut–English) curriculum for the remaining grades. In contrast, only one of the Dene languages, Dogrib, displays retention rates[10] similar to Inuktitut, and none has been developed as a language of instruction past Grade 3; the same is true for NWT Cree and the eroding western dialects of the Inuit language. (The Dene Kede and Inuuqatiglit curricula provide guidelines on culturally appropriate materials for school programs, but do not include a strong language component.)

With this in mind, the allocation of resources displayed in Table 5.1 takes on new significance. The development of language services and the inte-

**TABLE 5.1**

Allocations for Aboriginal Language Programs in the Northwest Territories, 1993–1994

| | Agreement | % | Regular budget | % | % of total |
|---|---|---|---|---|---|
| Language services (interpretation/translation, terminology, standardization, signs) | 1,779,000 | 32.0 | 1,990,000 | 421.3 | 36.4 |
| Education, training (curriculum development, teacher education, certificate programs) | 2,520,000 | 45.5 | 2,830,000 | 58.7 | 51.6 |
| Community programs (language camps, publications, traditional knowledge, adult literacy, broadcasting, etc.) | 1,245,000 | 22.5 | — | — | 12.0 |

Note. Figures (in Canadian dollars) are calculated from Tables 1.4 and 1.17c in New Economy Development Group (NEDG), 1994 (Section II-1).

---

[10]According to the 1991 census, 77% of Inuit in the NWT speak an Inuit dialect; only 38% of Dene and 13% of Metis speak a Dene language. A more detailed (although less exhaustive) survey is reported in NEDG (1994), according to which the percentages of self-reported first-language speakers (i.e., with a current preference for their Aboriginal language) are Chipewyan 52%, Cree 44%, Dogrib 83%, Gwich'in 9%, Inuktitut 91%, Inuinnaqtun 76%, Inuvialuktun 19%, North Slavey 54%, and South Slavey 55%. Every language group, including Inuktitut and Dogrib, shows a potential shift toward English in the younger age groups, although this may be avoided if Aboriginal language use increases at a later age.

## 5. LIFE ON THE EDGE                                                                131

gration of Aboriginal languages within the formal education system are appropriate measures for well-established community languages; in keeping with the philosophy of the Official Languages Act, they aim to bring Aboriginal languages as close as possible to the situation and status of English and French. Yet the only obvious beneficiary of this approach is Inuktitut, the language at the center of the NWT's linguistic policy reforms. Far more important for the Dene languages, as well as for Inuvialuktun and Inuinnaqtun and Cree, is the mobilization of individual commitment to learning, using, and transmitting each language—a goal that can only be addressed through "community programs," even though other measures may help to make the languages more visible and to reduce some of the barriers to their use in public life.

Astonishingly, in the first 10 years of the language program the NWT carried out neither a systematic sociolinguistic survey nor a comprehensive community needs assessment. It may safely be assumed that such data would throw several of the assumptions behind the language program into doubt. For instance, although hospitals and other government institutions have made services in Aboriginal languages more readily available, only a small proportion of NWT residents are aware of the increased services and make use of them (NEDG, 1994). Nearly all government departments routinely spend less than their budget on Aboriginal language services (Harnum, 1993). These observations strongly suggest that the programs under the Aboriginal Languages Agreement are poorly matched with community demand. Equally noteworthy is the fact that funds destined for community use have been held back. According to the Language Commissioner's first annual report, "In 1991–92, of the $500,000 available [for] other organizations and community projects, $148,734 was unspent, despite the fact that proposals were received totaling $1,603,262" (Harnum, 1993, p. 152). Taken together, the evidence points overwhelmingly to a lack of government interest in community language use, an interpretation reinforced by the evaluation report:

> Much [community] involvement has been passive in nature, with communities present as recipients of services. ... Key stakeholders hold different opinions about the Agreement's contribution to any long-term objectives for Aboriginal languages. Some recognize that the provision of language services and infrastructure has been the major thrust to date and, as a result, some community members and groups feel that their language-related needs are not yet satisfactorily met. (NEDG, 1994, pp. xxii-xxiii)[11]

---

[11]Of interest is also the following comment from the Languages Commissioner:
The government fosters this passive service-recipient role in most of its activities, but the communities have very clearly stated to me that they are dissatisfied with this role and want control. The Premier has openly stated that this [i.e., community control over the language program] is unacceptable to her. (B. Harnum, personal communication, April 20, 1995)

132                                                                                      FETTES

The Northwest Territories, therefore, are the scene of a sustained and costly effort to apply to Aboriginal languages the basic tenets of federal official language policy. Although lip service is paid to the unique features and problems of these languages, none of the five challenges identified in the first section of this chapter has been effectively addressed by government programs. Instead, policy is divided between symbolic recognition (such as the use of Aboriginal languages on signs, and the provision of simultaneous translation in the Legislative Assembly),[12] limited services in the fields of health and education, and initiatives based on a classic "language planning" model focused on written standards. The speakers of Inuktitut have gained most from this situation; the speakers of the weaker languages such as Gwich'in and Chipewyan have gained least.

## Consultation: Groping Toward a Vision

The fragmented, top-down nature of NWT language policy documented here earlier is particularly puzzling in light of extensive consultations held since the first Official Languages Act in the NWT was passed. In 1985, the Task Force on Aboriginal Languages (1986) traveled to communities across the NWT and produced a balanced and visionary report. As a first principle, the report recommended the establishment of separate guidelines for the different languages, through the input of two regional advisory councils (Dene and Inuit) into a Ministry of Aboriginal Languages and Culture. Additional monitoring would be provided by Dene and Inuit Language Commissioners and their staff. Concrete measures included the development of a K–9 bilingual bicultural education system over 10 years (echoing the earlier report of the Special Committee on Education, 1982), and programs to "ensure and enhance" the use of Aboriginal languages in the daily life of communities. The Task Force on Aboriginal Languages (1986) was emphatic in stating that, on the one hand, "Aboriginal peoples must be recognized as having the ultimate right and responsibility for the future of their languages and cultures"; on the other, "Northern society as a whole has responsibility for actively supporting and encouraging Aboriginal peoples in exercising these rights" (p. 23).

The recommendations of the Task Force were widely quoted, yet even more widely ignored. To date, no community advisory councils have been established; in fact, the efforts of the present Languages Commissioner to form such a council have been resisted by the government (B. Harnum, personal communication, April 20, 1995). Aboriginal languages continue

---

[12]Simultaneous translation is provided in Inuktitut and the five Dene languages 6 hours a day, 5 days a week, although the Dene languages are rarely used in the Assembly. Tapes of the proceedings are made available in all six of these languages; to date there have been approximately six requests. (B. Harnum, personal communication, April 20, 1995)

## 5. LIFE ON THE EDGE 133

to be administered along with English and French, rather than within a separate framework that might enable their unique characteristics to be addressed. A later consultation, the 1991 Aboriginal Languages Conference, demonstrated the success of the government in focusing attention on its institutional agenda; where the Task Force had put forward a broad, community-centered vision, discussion at the conference was limited to "the roles and policies of fourteen government departments" in providing services in Aboriginal languages (*Bringing Our Languages Home*, 1991). This condemned to irrelevance the inaugural challenge of the organizers:

> We need to strengthen our own commitment to Aboriginal languages. We must involve our Elders for their essential knowledge and level of language. Aboriginal people must take back control of Aboriginal languages and find ways to determine our needs ourselves. (p. 9)

It could be argued, in fact, that the narrow frame of reference of the Official Languages Act and the bureaucratic focus of government policy together make a meaningful response to such concerns impossible, unless one or the other is changed. At the time of writing (1995) it appears that the most powerful engine of such change will be a new Education Act, whose draft text has been submitted to the Legislative Assembly following a 4-year process of revision. Linguistic issues were one of the major concerns which prompted this review; the enshrinement of official language minority rights in the Charter of Rights and Freedoms, coupled with the adoption of the NWT Official Languages Act, had rendered the older text wholly inappropriate. At the same time, changes in the structure and philosophy of education had made a redraft highly desirable. Accordingly, in 1990 an intensive consultation process was launched, focusing both on the Act as a whole and on the language provisions in particular (Department of Education, Northwest Territories, 1990).

As early as November 1990, responses from school boards and cultural institutions had demonstrated a common will to give Aboriginal languages and cultures a far more prominent place in the school system (Kakfwi, 1990). From the responses it seems clear that the symbolic value of making all Aboriginal languages "official" had a powerful effect; no one was willing to argue that some official languages should be less accessible to their speakers than others. When the government's proposals for changing the Act were finally published, over 3 years later, it identified four guiding principles, or "directions," based on the feedback received (Department of Education, Northwest Territories, 1994). One of these stated simply: "Education must be based on the languages and cultures of the north." Whether or not that was meant literally (English, and southern culture disseminated through it, continue to exert enormous influence in the NWT), it represented a radical departure from earlier policy; the suggestions put forward in the discussion document were even strengthened in some respects during the subsequent drafting process.

In March 1995 the new draft, Bill 25, was tabled in the Legislative Assembly. Its linguistic provisions include:

70. The language of instruction of the education program must be an official language. There may be more than one language of instruction in an education district and more than one language of instruction in a school.
71 Subject to the approval of the Minister, a District Education Authority shall determine the language of instruction to be used in the education district. ... A District Education Authority may choose a language as the language of instruction if (a) there is significant demand for the language in the education district; (b) there are a sufficient number of teachers who are fluent in the language available to teach in the language in the education district; and (c) there are sufficient and suitable school program materials available in the language.
73. Subject to [the following restrictions], a District Education Authority shall, in accordance with any directions of the Minister, determine the language to be taught as part of the education program. ... If an official language other than English is the language of instruction, English must be taught as a language as part of the education program. If English is the language of instruction, an official language other than English must be taught as part of the education program.

It will be noted that the Bill avoids defining individual and collective linguistic rights altogether (apart from those mandated under the Charter of Rights and Freedoms, which are recognized in Section 72). Under the new Act, a District Education Authority would not be required to provide instruction in a particular Aboriginal language, even if that was the first language of all of its pupils. This pragmatic approach, which would delegate important aspects of language policy to the regional and community levels, is in striking contrast with the centralist, rights-based philosophy of the Official Languages Act. Although concerns over the potential costs of mandatory multilingual education were repeatedly expressed in the prior discussion documents, one is tempted to question whether any detailed estimates were ever prepared or compared with the $4 million currently spent, for marginal benefits, on interpretation and translation services.

On the other hand, the Bill would create a framework for language policy that is, at least, compatible with a multilingual, multicultural vision of the NWT. The parallelism between Aboriginal languages and English, as well

## 5. LIFE ON THE EDGE 135

as the obligation to combine the teaching or use of English with at least one other official language, would imply support for widespread bilingualism in English and an Aboriginal language as a long-term goal, even if this is not spelled out. Concomitantly, the transfer of primacy in linguistic decisions to local and regional education authorities would place greater responsibility on the shoulders of parents, Elders, and community leaders. This new dynamic in education could lead, in the right circumstances, to greater community involvement in the language program as a whole—thereby achieving what a decade of consultation has otherwise failed to do.

Before considering the likelihood of such a development, we turn to the NWT's western neighbor for an entirely different perspective on Aboriginal language policy.

### THE YUKON: A SEARCH FOR SUSTAINABILITY

The Yukon is approximately one-third the size of the NWT, with half of the population (29,000 people). Aboriginal people, nearly all of them Dene, comprise just under 20% of the population; they belong to eight different language groups, organized in 14 First Nations.[13] The political development of the Territory followed the southern pattern more closely than the NWT: Massive immigration following World War II reduced Aboriginal people to a minority, while paternalistic policies—first under direct federal control, later under an increasingly independent territorial government—disrupted their traditional way of life. Extensive self-government and land claims negotiations have been carried out over the past 20 years, culminating in the so-called Umbrella Final Agreement signed by the Council of Yukon Indians and the federal and territorial governments in 1992 (INAC, 1992).

Following the patriation of the Constitution in 1982, the government of the Yukon, like that of the NWT, resisted the imposition of federal official language policy. Its compromise, however, took the form of an agreement to provide services in English, French, and Aboriginal languages separately, on their own terms, without declaring any of them official. For this purpose the Yukon sought and received exclusion from the scope of the federal Official Languages Act. In 1988 the Yukon passed its own Languages Act and signed the Canada–Yukon Language Agreement, which provided $4.2 million for Aboriginal languages over 5 years (Gardner, 1993).

---

[13]The Dene languages are Gwich'in, Han, Kaska, Tagish, Upper Tanana, and Northern and Southern Tutchone; the two latter are the largest groups, comprising eight First Nations and about half of the Aboriginal population. Tagish was replaced as the first language of the Tagish people by the unrelated coastal language, Tlingit, in the course of the past century; only three fluent speakers of Tagish were identified in a 1991 survey.

The single most important difference between the language profiles of the NWT and the Yukon is that the latter has no equivalent of Inuktitut (i.e., a still-vital Aboriginal language spoken by 15% of the total population, significantly standardized, and with effective political representation in the Legislative Assembly). No single Aboriginal language in the Yukon has more than 1,000 speakers; the overall fluency rate is only 30%, with rates for individual languages ranging from 75% (Kaska) to 13% (Southern Tutchone; Cottingham & Tousignant, 1991). From the beginning of the Yukon language program, then, policy was formulated on the basis of quite different premises than in the NWT. This is apparent in all three areas discussed previously: legislation, programs, and consultation.

## Legislation: Keeping All Options Open

The Languages Act (Yukon Territory, 1988) is framed to leave a wide array of policy choices in the hands of the Yukon government. On Aboriginal languages, it declares, "The Yukon recognizes the significance of aboriginal languages in the Yukon and wishes to take appropriate measures to preserve, develop, and enhance those languages in the Yukon." It guarantees the right to use "a Yukon aboriginal language in any debates and other proceedings of the Legislative Assembly" and provides that the government "may make regulations in relation to the provision of services ... in one or more of the aboriginal languages of the Yukon." Compared with the NWT Official Languages Act, the Yukon Languages Act commits the government to very little. Even the clause pertaining to the Legislative Assembly need not mean a great deal in practice, and certainly does not imply the routine use of costly interpretation services. The Yukon appears to be determined to avoid the pitfalls of the *rights*-based approach adopted in the NWT, in favor of a flexible response based on expressed *needs*—thereby allowing the unique circumstances of each language and language community to be taken into account.

A similarly cautious approach is evident in the Yukon Education Act (1990), whose main Aboriginal language provisions run as follows:

### Language of instruction
50. 1. The Minister may authorize an educational program or part of an educational program to be provided in an aboriginal language after receiving a request to do so from a School Board, Council, school committee, Local Indian Education Authority or, where there is no Local Indian Education Authority, from a Yukon First Nation.

2. In deciding whether to authorize instruction in an aboriginal language, the Minister shall consider (a) the number of students to be enrolled in the instruction, (b) the availability of resources and per-

## 5. LIFE ON THE EDGE

137

sonnel for the instruction, (c) the educational feasibility of providing the instruction, and (d) the effect of the instruction on students who receive their instruction in English.

### Aboriginal languages

52. 1. The Minister shall provide for the development of instructional materials for the teaching of aboriginal languages and the training of aboriginal language teachers.

2. The Minister shall employ aboriginal language teachers to provide aboriginal language instruction in schools in the Yukon. [Two paragraphs follow defining the status of aboriginal language teachers.]

5. The Minister shall establish policies and guidelines on the amount of instruction and the timetabling for the instruction of aboriginal languages in consultation with appropriate Local Indian Education Authorities, School Boards, and Councils.

6. The Minister shall meet on an annual basis with the Central Indian Education Authority to review the status of aboriginal language instruction in Yukon schools and make appropriate modifications where necessary. [Article 54 further details the responsibilities of the Central Indian Education Authority, to be established by the Council of Yukon Indians.]

Like the Languages Act, the Education Act is not based on a defined language policy, but on its *absence*. Although stopping short of delegating full authority to local authorities, the Act differs notably from the NWT model in explicitly basing government decisions on the results of consultation with First Nations. In the NWT, not only is this term avoided because it traditionally excludes the Inuit, but the entire concept of sovereign peoples is eschewed in favor of the domesticated notion of "communities." In the Yukon's Education Act, as in the NWT's Bill 25, no Aboriginal linguistic rights are recognized; implicit, however, is the collective right of Aboriginal people to include their own language in the curriculum, and to use it as a language of instruction where the necessary personnel, resources, and students exist. On the other hand, the Yukon government is not committed in any way to training such personnel or funding curriculum development; these remain policy decisions to be taken outside the legislative framework.

The Umbrella Final Agreement on land claims, signed in May 1992 between the Yukon and Canadian governments and the Council for Yukon Indians, represents the most important development in the legal framework relating to Aboriginal peoples. The UFA sets out the general principles of the relationship between First Nations and the public government

138                                                                                    FETTES

of the Territory, and establishes the means for individual First Nations to negotiate self-government including the "authority for the design, delivery and management of Indian language and cultural curriculum." The UFA also commits the Yukon to recognizing and recording oral histories and place names, and foresees the possible use of Aboriginal languages by First Nations representatives on Territorial Boards (Gardner, 1993, Appendix K). The agreement is generally premised on the long-term devolution of services to First Nations governments, so that day-to-day life in Aboriginal communities comes to be increasingly controlled by the communities themselves, in a microcosm of the Canadian federal system.

## Programs: Nurturing the Language Tree

The Canada–Yukon Language Agreement (1988), which like its NWT counterpart is largely focused on ensuring French-language rights in the North, also commits the federal and territorial governments to the preservation, development, and enhancement of Aboriginal languages "as an important long-term goal." Within this general framework, more specific Cooperation and Funding Agreements on the Development and Enhancement of Aboriginal Languages have been negotiated for 5-year periods (1988–1993 and 1993–1998). These set out the following objectives:

> To preserve, develop and enhance Aboriginal languages in the Yukon, by providing funding and support for:
>
> (a) Ensuring the perpetuation, revitalization, growth and protection of Aboriginal languages; and
>
> (b) Responding to the language needs of Aboriginal communities in the Yukon; and
>
> (c) Providing public services in the Aboriginal languages of the Yukon in accordance with the Languages Act (Yukon).

The first Funding Agreement provided $4.25 million for Aboriginal languages over 5 years. The second established a maximum of $5.59 million for the next 5-year period, but the federal government, facing across-the-board budget reductions, has already made it clear that cuts of 10% or more will be made. On the other hand, Yukon government investment in Aboriginal language programs outside the framework of the Language Agreement has steadily increased, totaling over $1.6 million in 1992–1993. These expenditures include Aboriginal language instructor training, curriculum development, the Aboriginal Language Certificate and Diploma program, adult and college courses, and technical assistance for oral history and other

## 5. LIFE ON THE EDGE

language-related cultural projects (Gardner, 1993). In proportion to the Aboriginal population base, Language Agreement funds are roughly equivalent to those of the NWT (approximately $200 per person per year), whereas the proportion of other government expenditures related to language programs (as assessed by the evaluators) is significantly higher in the Yukon.

Aboriginal Language Services (ALS), the coordinating center for Aboriginal language policy in the Yukon, has been located in the Executive Council Office since it was established in February 1989. With the field of action left open by the wording of the Languages Act, the first initiative of ALS was to develop a strategic plan in consultation with the Aboriginal community, government departments, and the Yukon Native Languages Centre (an impressive source of linguistic expertise whose development, from 1976, in many ways paved the way for the success of the Yukon program). This led directly to the most comprehensive Aboriginal language survey ever carried out in Canada. A random sample of Aboriginal respondents from every First Nation was tested for fluency and analyzed according to age, sex, education, occupation, and use of the language in a variety of domains (Cottingham & Tousignant, 1991).

Among other findings, the report concluded that about 30% of the aboriginal people speak their ancestral language; that many more people wish to learn it than are now learning it; that the home environment is preferred for learning the languages; that all types of school experiences have had a negative impact on language retention; that oral traditions are passed on by only about 21% of the population; and that those who pursue traditional occupations are more likely to be fluent. This situation, the report argued, calls for a measured government response:

> Language policy is inseparable from economic policy in the same way that sustainable environment policy is inseparable from economic policy ... [T]he priority for government aboriginal language initiatives must be on preservation, development and enhancement activities rather than on the provision of a broad range of aboriginal language services to the Indian public at this time ... [T]he first priority is clearly to fully support the Indian people in taking self-determined initiatives to ensure the aboriginal languages of the Yukon survive into the 21st century. (pp. 13–15)

In conjunction with an earlier report (Tlen, 1986), this survey analysis set the Yukon on a policy course diametrically opposed to that of the NWT. Provision of services in Aboriginal languages was established as a relatively low priority. In addition, the key role observed for the home and community environment made it clear that school programs in Aboriginal languages, no matter how well intentioned, would not be adequate to ensure language retention. Finally, the goal of long-term sustainability, coupled with the evolving land claims process, made it imperative that each First Nation take responsibility for its own language program. The paradox now faced by ALS was that its status, as a branch of central government, ran essentially counter to its own policy goals. Somehow accountability and overall policy direction would have to be maintained while the initiative was gradually transferred to the Aboriginal communities themselves.

Two important developments immediately followed the survey. In one, a field network of eight community-based Interpreters/Territorial Representatives was established in consultation with the First Nations. These representatives have a broad mandate: selected in part for their fluency in the local language, they are trained in the interpretation of Territorial government services, and additionally are expected to work as a "local language promotor, model and resource/facilitator for community-based retention activities" (Gardner, 1993, p. 32). This unique combination of roles is very much in keeping with the Yukon's policies of decentralization and cost-effectiveness, and is proving increasingly useful to the language program as time goes by. The sudden expansion of ALS staff from 2 to 13 in the 1991–1992 fiscal year did cause certain administrative problems, which have since been eased.

As discussions on the field network proceeded, the Director of Aboriginal Language Services and the author of the survey report held meetings with each Yukon First Nation to go over its findings. These consultations led in turn to the April 1991 Aboriginal Languages Conference, planned and executed with full involvement of the First Nations. As well as attending plenary sessions, where Elders, linguists, and others shared their concerns and ideas, participants met in Language Circles to develop "preservation strategies," identifying overall goals and concrete objectives for the maintenance or revitalization of their particular language (*Voices of the Talking Circle*, 1992).[14] This marked the first step toward direct involvement of the communities in planning the language program, and was followed by the establishment of the Community Initiatives Funding Program by ALS.

Although the conference was considered a great success, momentum slipped over the next year as publication of the proceedings was delayed. The First Nations also needed time to adjust to a new cycle of policy development at the level of the language groups. Because the latter "are not homogenous, but include collections of families, clans, and autonomous First Nations representing a broad range of possibly divergent interests," all of the ideas and projects arising from the first cycle of policy development needed to be talked over and reworked to ensure support (Gardner,

---

[14]According to the evaluator, "The real flavor and spirit of the conference was captured in a video production ... by the NEDAA arm of Northern Native Broadcasting Yukon" (Gardner, 1993, p. 22).

## 5. LIFE ON THE EDGE                                                    141

1993, p. 31). Inevitably this proved to be a slow and uneven process: in August 1992, 16 months after the conference, no community was identified as having an operational language retention plan focused on definite outcomes. Another difficulty lay in the funding approval process, in which First Nations initially felt they had little say. Finally, ALS itself had difficulty in adapting to the new set of goals, particularly in terms of planning and administration.

It was at this juncture that the evaluation of the Funding Agreement at the end of its 5-year term provided an opportunity to rethink program strategy. In contrast to the NWT, where the evaluations have been notable for their lack of clarity and focus, ALS established a long-term relationship with a professional consultant, Dr. Leslie Gardner, who soon became a valued advisor. Her work has helped to clarify the strengths and weaknesses of the program, and has been "particularly helpful in keeping [ALS] focused on the objectives of the agreement, and in developing plans which have some evaluability" (L. Carberry, personal communication, May 5, 1995). Gardner's first report provided a more explicit conceptual framework and some theoretical underpinnings for the "Yukon Model," as the program had come to be known. It included the principles of: the people being the proper stewards of their languages; the goal of creating a critical mass of real interaction in each language to sustain it and carry it forward; an emphasis on home and community-based initiatives (with school initiatives dependent on these); and increased stakeholder involvement (Gardner, 1993).

Although strongly supportive of most aspects of the Yukon program, Gardner emphasized the need to carry through with the transfer of ownership to First Nations. She noted the dilemma of the ALS as a government agency in its mandate to promote stakeholder involvement above all. As such, the ALS was "somewhat the victim of its own success" and would have to sustain both its work and its accountability (Gardner, 1993, p. 41).

### Consultation: Widening the Circle

Taking the evaluator's recommendations into account, the second Funding Agreement, signed on May 23, 1993, set out new priorities for the Yukon program:

> The major strategy implicit in the second Agreement, and its corresponding activities, is that the specific work within each Aboriginal language will be determined by each of the language groups. The nature of this work will be different for each language group. However, there will still be common thrusts to language work supported by the Agreement:
>
> 1. Preservation of the languages (for example, oral history work),

2. Promotion of the languages (for example, delivery of language products including media),

3. Encouragement of everyday language use (for example, delivery of public services in the languages).

Specific areas for improvement (related to *how* the work of the Agreement is carried out) were derived directly from the values contained in the Yukon model, the issues raised in the evaluation report, and direction from elders. These three areas of improvement for work during 1993–1994 are:

1. Emphasis on improved communication, cooperation and partnership,

2. Increased accountability to the languages and to the people,

3. Continued facilitation of self-determination and choice by each language group. (*1993–94 Annual Report*, 1994, p. 2)

These program revisions were paralleled by various changes in ALS staff and infrastructure, including the move to a new storefront office, improvements in planning and reporting procedures, and the recruitment of a former chair of the Council for Yukon Indians as the new Director of ALS, following a 9-month vacancy. A new policy of regular press releases on the Community Initiatives Program was instituted, and contacts with key bodies such as the First Nations Elders Council, the First Nations Education Commission, and Northern Native Broadcasting Yukon were strengthened (*1993–94 Annual Report*, 1994, pp. 3–4). The years 1993 and 1994 also saw sustained efforts to strengthen the network of Interpreters/Territorial Representatives, whose wide dispersion, broad mandate, and requirements for professional training and career development posed a considerable administrative challenge. This period of internal consolidation, according to one participant, "was a turning point for the program ... because if we had not addressed the issues [raised by staff] appropriately, we would not have been able to move forward on any of the subsequent programming directions and activities" (L. Carberry, personal communication, May 5, 1995).

The central component of the renewed strategy was the Community Intiatives Program (ALCIP). In its first year, following the conference in 1991, the ALCIP had attracted 25 funding proposals from First Nations, ranging from the recording of oral history to the provision of interpretation or translation for political gatherings (Gardner, 1993, Appendix I). A perceived lack of input into the funding approval process by First Nations themselves led to some frustration and disillusionment in the communities. Beginning in 1993, this was addressed both through stronger ties with Yukon-wide organizations, as mentioned earlier, and through the network of Interpreters/Territorial Representatives. These initiatives included in-

## 5. LIFE ON THE EDGE
143

creased contact with other resource agencies (e.g., police, schools, and social workers), modeling of language use by ALS staff among themselves and in their work with others, and the design and implementation of adult classes in several languages (*1993–94 Annual Report*, 1994).

In addition, "the program began a concerted attempt to distribute the dollars among the language groups." Increased efforts were made to inform First Nations of the program, and to assist them in developing suitable proposals. Thirty-one projects were funded in 1993–1994 for a total of $374,000 in grants, almost 30% of the Agreement budget. Activities included "the promotion and facilitation of everyday language use and of Elder outreach, language and media, and language preservation and documentation projects" (*1993–94 Annual Report*, 1994, p. 8). Oral history projects were the most widespread, accounting for approximately a third of program expenditures. Although language camps, courses, and other forms of instruction were also funded, not all language groups had them, and the emphasis clearly remained on strengthening the position of the present users and ensuring the preservation of traditional knowledge.

Another major category of expenditure was directed at promoting the language program in visible ways. In cooperation with the First Nations Education Commission, an inventory of oral history resources was prepared, as a first step toward a complete database and clearinghouse. A project was initiated with the Elders' Council "to obtain high quality recordings of elders' legends, songs and music in all eight languages" (*1993–94 Annual Report*, 1994, p. 5), and a book entitled *Ditth'ek Ts'a' Tr'etadal: Walking Together; Words of the Elders* was funded. Northern Native Broadcasting Yukon was supported in the production of a 26-part television series focusing on Aboriginal languages and cultures, *Haa Shagoon*, in which Elders spoke their native languages. "Pride in Culture" radio spots, conceived along similar lines, were also funded and aired. Language promotion materials were produced in different languages (e.g., a Kaska calendar and a Tlingit genealogy booklet). Together these measures were intended to raise the status of the languages and encourage their everyday use in the lives, homes, and communities of Aboriginal people and in Yukon society.

Although ALS has now succeeded in making its presence felt throughout the Yukon, its major challenge remains. With the threat of further funding cuts looming, and with four individual land claims agreements already signed, the ultimate success of the Yukon Model depends on the will of the First Nations to develop, fund, and implement comprehensive language plans for their communities. As of mid-1995, all eight language groups were still at an early stage in this process. According to the ALCIP Program Manager, "the ball is really rolling at this point and the language agenda is starting to clarify in a number of ways;" however, funding cuts in the final two years of the current Funding Agreement could threaten "our ability to keep even minimum levels of work going until the language groups and First Nations are able to carry it forward on their own" (L. Carberry, personal communication, May 5, 1995). A visit to the Yukon in February 1997 confirmed this precarious balance. Although a solid base of community language renewal projects has been established, it has yet to find a stable niche in the rapidly evolving political relationship between First Nations and the federal and territorial governments.

## SUMMING UP: A REFLECTION ON MODELS AND STRATEGIES

In weighing the merits of the two approaches described earlier, it is illuminating to consider the success of the Northwest Territories and the Yukon in addressing the five challenges outlined in the first section of this chapter.

The NWT has never really come to grips with the specific needs of small languages, nor their different stages of development. By insisting on treating Inuktitut like English and French, and all other Aboriginal languages like Inuktitut, the NWT government risks winning the symbolic battle but losing the sociolinguistic war. The stated goal of language preservation in the Official Languages Act has never been properly conceptualized; instead policy appears to be based on a trickle-down concept, where money is poured into high-prestige activities such as interpretation and formal education, in the hope that this will encourage speakers to retain and transmit the languages. Although some positive psychological effects are likely, the absence of any focus on language use in the home and community makes them largely irrelevant to the issue of linguistic survival.

The most remarkable failing of the NWT approach is the lack of serious and long-term consultation with Aboriginal communities. At best, as in the revised Education Act, linguistic decisions are devolved to local Boards of Education. However, this is not necessarily in agreement with the central government's commitment to promote the preservation and development of the languages, which would require an active and lasting dialogue with parents, teachers, local governments, and the Boards themselves. At worst, there is no consultation at all in relation to important policy decisions within the central administration (e.g., the negotiation of the Funding Agreements) or the Legislative Assembly (e.g., the provision of full interpretation in six Aboriginal languages, at enormous cost, but not in Inuinnaqtun, Inuvialuktun, or Cree). These failings are compounded by the lack of guidelines or regulations for the application of the Official Languages Act, and the limited information made available on both the Act and the

## 5. LIFE ON THE EDGE                                                          145

Languages Agreement. Rather than advancing Aboriginal communities' sense of ownership of the languages, the Government of the NWT seems bent on expropriation, making it impossible for any of the five challenges to be adequately addressed within the overall policy framework.

The NWT, however, faces fundamental changes as the Eastern Arctic prepares for devolution to the new Nunavut Territory in 1999. With Inuktitut secure within its own borders, the speakers of the remaining languages, all of them small and threatened, may be able to recast language policy in a mould more suited to their capabilities and needs. The new Education Act may represent a first step in this process; it must be followed by acknowledgment of the importance of community ownership and the centrality of the home environment, and their integration into language policy. If this takes place, the painstaking development of interpretation skills, terminology, and curricula, in which the NWT has invested so much, may at last take its place in a comprehensive strategy for language maintenance and development.

In contrast to the NWT, which has based its language program on the symbolism of the Official Languages Act, the Yukon Model represents a carefully thought-out attempt to design an Aboriginal language program around the goals of language preservation and renewal. In the context of the language survey and the subsequent conference, undertaken early in the life of the program, ALS confronted all five of the policy challenges listed in the first section of this chapter, and attempted to formulate a response to each. The result was a funding program focused on small, community-based projects, involving both oral and written language, developed and carried out on a local basis. This approach is remarkable not only for its decentralist philosophy, but for its ability to encompass noninstitutional policy issues such as language use in the home—thereby accurately reflecting the recommendations of Fishman (1991) in his landmark study of minority language retention, *Reversing Language Shift*. There can be few, if any, public governments which have succeeded in addressing these issues to a similar degree.

The ultimate success of the Yukon Model remains an open question. Ironically, its small-scale, grass-roots approach to language policy, although both cost-effective and adapted to the needs of Aboriginal languages, lacks the political clout of the NWT's high-profile official languages legislation, and may therefore be more susceptible to government cuts. Yet it would be unwise for any language community to base its continued existence on support from a geographically and culturally distant capital. The completion of the land claims process in the Yukon poses the question of domain separation versus modernization at the most fundamental level; can the traditional First Nations way of life, with its rich tapestry of knowledge and

**146**
FETTES

values derived from the land, retain a significant place in the lives of Aboriginal people, and what concessions, compromises and forms of resistance may be necessary to ensure its survival? The language question, although requiring its own answers, is but one aspect of this larger challenge.

The same challenge is repeated across Canada, which in turn represents but one small window on the threat that the international development paradigm poses to cultural and linguistic diversity everywhere (see Crawford, chapter 6, this volume). As First Nations from British Columbia to Newfoundland move toward various forms of self-government, it remains unclear how the issue of Aboriginal linguistic rights will play out at the federal and provincial levels. The orthodoxy of official bilingualism has ensured the continuing marginalization of Aboriginal languages in both discourse and practice (Fettes, 1994); the federal government, which could have built on the achievements of the mid-1980s by developing a language policy in conformity with Article 35 of the Charter of Rights and Freedoms, has failed utterly to do so. On the other hand, the sensitivity of Canadians to linguistic issues, the increasing recognition of Aboriginal economic and political rights, and the precedents set by the Territorial Language Agreements suggest that real change could still come about, provided that First Nations are prepared to raise the language banner high and keep it there.

If the preservation and development of Aboriginal languages is eventually adopted as a policy goal by other levels of public government in Canada, on what should such a policy be based? The preceding analysis strongly suggests the adoption of the Yukon Model as a general approach. Naturally, many of the specifics of the program would vary from language to language and community to community; this, indeed, is one of the central features of the Yukon Model. Yet the core values remain constant and universal:

> Self-determination and choice; inclusiveness, widening the circle, every part is important; synergy; diversity, flexibility and responsiveness; openness; participation, partnership and working together; experiential learning and action; people own the language; continual dialogue and exchange; integration and cross-cultural bridging; recognition, respect and celebration by honoring stature in the community; observing proper protocol and tradition; carrying the message; storytelling; facilitating growth and change; concrete benefit to the community; and government as catalyst and facilitator. (Gardner, 1993, pp. 14–15)

Anyone who has worked with Aboriginal communities will recognize the appropriateness of such principles, and may well reflect on the benefits they would bring to the practice of government as a whole. Yet a place may be seen, as well, for the rights-based approach so haphazardly applied in the NWT. Any language program, whether based on the Yukon model or

# 5. LIFE ON THE EDGE 147

not, would be strengthened by the passage of legislation guaranteeing, for instance, the right to education in an Aboriginal language where numbers warrant. Before such policies are dismissed as both expensive and unnecessary, the critics should question the assumptions behind the present linguistic regime in Canada, with its implicit imposition of functional monolingualism on the greater part of the population. If the "aboriginal and treaty rights" guaranteed in Section 35 of the Charter are to mean anything at all, they must surely imply equal opportunities for Aboriginal languages within a policy of "multiculturalism in a *multilingual* framework." This is the experiment that both of the Territories have had the courage to assume, and whose continuing progress should be followed closely by all those committed to working for a multilingual world.

## ACKNOWLEDGMENTS

My thanks in particular go to Barbara Burnaby, for suggesting I write this chapter and for providing encouragement and advice as it proceeded; Audrey Greyeyes, for assistance in obtaining many of the necessary documents; Lesley Carberry and Betty Harnum, for feedback on an early draft; and Ruth Norton, whose guidance provided me with invaluable insights and opportunities.

## REFERENCES

*1993–94 annual report. Canada–Yukon Cooperation and Funding Agreement on the Development and Enhancement of Aboriginal Languages.* (1994). Ottawa/Whitehorse: Government of Canada/Government of the Yukon.

Assembly of First Nations. (1990). *Towards linguistic justice for First Nations.* Ottawa: Assembly of First Nations.

Assembly of First Nations. (1992). *Towards rebirth of First Nations languages.* Ottawa: Assembly of First Nations.

*Bringing our languages home.* (1991). Yellowknife: Government of the Northwest Territories.

Burnaby, B. (Ed.). (1985). *Promoting native writing systems in Canada.* Toronto: Ontario Institute for Studies in Education.

Burnaby, B., & Beaujot, R. (1986). *The use of Aboriginal languages in Canada: An analysis of 1981 census data* (Doc. No. S2–176). Ottawa: Department of Secretary of State.

Canada. (1988). *Official Languages Act.* Ottawa: Registered Statutes of Canada 1985 (4th Supplement), c. 31.

Churchill, S. (1986). *The education of cultural and linguistic minorities in the OECD countries.* Clevedon, England: Multilingual Matters.

Consolidation of Education Act, Northwest Territories, Registered Statutes of the Northwest Territories 1988, c. E-1.

Constitution Act, Canada, Schedule B to the Canada Act, 1982 (U.K.), c. 11.

Cottingham, B. E., & Tousignant, J. P. (1991). *A profile of Aboriginal languages in the Yukon.* Whitehorse, Yukon Territory: Aboriginal Language Services.

Department of Education, Northwest Territories. (1990). *Help improve the Education Act.* Yellowknife: Government of the Northwest Territories.

Department of Education, Northwest Territories. (1994). *Voices: Direction for improving the Education Act.* Yellowknife: Government of the Northwest Territories.

de Varennes, F. (1993). *La protection constitutionelle des droits linguistiques des autochtones.* Moncton, New Brunswick: University of Moncton Law School.

Dunn, M. (Ed.). (1989). *Language retention project report.* Ottawa: Native Council of Canada.

Fettes, M. (1992). *A guide to language strategies for First Nations communities.* Ottawa: Assembly of First Nations.

Fettes, M. (1994). Linguistic rights in Canada: Collisions or collusions? A conference report. *Bulletin of the Canadian Centre for Linguistic Rights, 1,* 18–20.

Fishman, J. A. (1991). *Reversing language shift: Theoretical and empirical foundations of assistance to threatened languages.* Clevedon, England: Multilingual Matters.

Foot, R. (1993, April–May). Arctic life, arctic language: Language and politics in Nunavut. *Up Here,* 14–17.

Foster, M. K. (1982). *Indigenous languages in Canada.* Ottawa: Commissioner of Official Languages.

Fredeen, S. (1991). *Sociolinguistic survey of indigenous languages in Saskatchewan: On the critical list.* Saskatoon: Saskatchewan Indigenous Languages Committee.

Gardner, L. (1993). *Walking the talk. Implementation evaluation of the Canada–Yukon Funding Agreement on the Development and Enhancement of Aboriginal Languages, 1988/89–1992/93.* Edmonton, Saskatchewan: Leslie Gardner & Associates.

Grimes, B. F. (Ed.). (1988). *Ethnologue* (11th ed.). Dallas: Summer Institute of Linguistics.

Harnum, B. (1993). *Eight official languages: Meeting the challenge. First annual report of the Languages Commissioner of the Northwest Territories.* Yellowknife: Government of the Northwest Territories.

Harnum, B. (1994). *Together, we can do it! Second annual report of the Languages Commissioner of the Northwest Territories.* Yellowknife: Government of the Northwest Territories.

Henderson, S. (1995). Governing the implicate order: Self-government and the linguistic development of Aboriginal communities. In S. Léger (Ed.), *Les droits linguistiques au Canada: Collusions ou collisions?* (pp. 285–316). Ottawa: Canadian Centre for Linguistic Rights, University of Ottawa.

Indian and Northern Affairs Canada. (1992). *The evolution of public governments in the North and the implications for Aboriginal peoples.* Ottawa: Indian and Northern Affairs Canada.

Jamieson, M. E. (1988a). *The Aboriginal language policy study. Phase II: Implementation mechanism.* Ottawa: Assembly of First Nations.

Jamieson, M. E. (1988b). *National Aboriginal language policy study* (draft). Ottawa: Assembly of First Nations.

Kakfwi, S. (1990). *Language rights in education in the Northwest Territories. Recommendations tabled by the Minister of Education, the Honourable Stephen Kakfwi* (Tabled Doc. 54-90, 2). Yellowknife: Government of the Northwest Territories.

Kinkade, M. D. (1991). The decline of native languages in Canada. In R. H. Robins & E. M. Uhlenbeck (Eds.), *Endangered languages* (pp. 157–173). Oxford, English: Berg.

Langgaard, P. (1992). Greenlandic is not an ideology, it is a language. In N. Graburn & R. Iutzi-Mitchell (Eds.), *Language and educational policy in the North* (Conference proceedings) (pp. 167–178). Berkeley: Canadian Studies Program, University of California at Berkeley.

McConvell, P. (1991). Understanding language shift: A step towards language maintenance. In S. Romaine (Ed.), *Language in Australia* (pp. 143–155). Cambridge, England: Cambridge University Press.

## 5. LIFE ON THE EDGE 149

Nahanee, T. (1992). *Aboriginal language rights in Canada.* Unpublished discussion paper for the Assembly of First Nations, Ottawa.

National Indian Brotherhood. (1972). *Indian control of Indian education.* Ottawa: National Indian Brotherhood.

New Economy Development Group. (1994). *Evaluation of the Canada–NWT Cooperation Agreement for French and Aboriginal Languages in the NWT. Final report.* Yellowknife: Government of the Northwest Territories.

Northwest Territories. (1988). *Official Languages Act.* Yellowknife: Registered Statutes of the Northwest Territories 1988, c. O–1.

Phillips, S. (1985). *Aboriginal languages in Canada: A research report.* Ottawa: Department of Secretary of State.

Sécretariat des affaires autochtones, Québec. (1989). *Safeguarding and promoting Aboriginal languages in Quebec.* Québec: Social and Cultural Development Committee, Aboriginal Affairs Secretariat.

Secretary of State, Canada. (1985). *A proposal for an Aboriginal languages policy: Discussion paper.* Ottawa: Department of Secretary of State.

Shkilnyk, A. M. (n. d.). *Progress report—Aboriginal language policy development.* Unpublished internal memo for the Department of Secretary of State, Ottawa.

Shkilnyk, A. M. (1986). *Canada's Aboriginal languages: An overview of current activities in language retention.* Ottawa: Department of Secretary of State.

Special Committee on Education. (1982). *Learning, tradition and change in the Northwest Territories.* Yellowknife: Government of the Northwest Territories.

Standing Committee on Aboriginal Affairs. (1990). *"You took my talk": Aboriginal literacy and empowerment. Fourth report of the Standing Committee on Aboriginal Affairs.* Ottawa: House of Commons.

Statistics Canada. (1991a). *Aboriginal peoples survey: Language, tradition, health, lifestyle and social issues* (Cat. No. 89–533). Ottawa: Author.

Statistics Canada. (1991b). *The nation: Mother tongue* (Cat. No. 93–313). Ottawa: Author.

Task Force on Aboriginal Languages, Northwest Territories. (1986). *The report of the Task Force on Aboriginal Languages.* Yellowknife: Government of the Northwest Territories.

Tlen, D. L. (1986). *Speaking out: Consultations and survey of Yukon Native languages planning, visibility and growth.* Whitehorse: Government of the Yukon/Council for Yukon Indians.

Tschanz, L. (1980). *Native languages and government policy: An historical examination.* London, Ontario: Centre for Research and Teaching of Canadian Native Languages, University of Western Ontario.

*Voices of the talking circle.* (1992). Whitehorse, Yukon Territory: Aboriginal Language Services.

Yukon Territory. (1988). *Languages Act.* Whitehorse: Statutes of the Yukon 1988, c. 13.

Yukon Territory. (1990). *Education Act.* Whitehorse: Statutes of the Yukon 1989–1990, c. 25.

# 6

# Endangered Native American Languages: What Is to Be Done, and Why?

James Crawford
*Silver Spring, MD*

The threat to linguistic resources is now recognized as a worldwide crisis. According to Krauss (1992b), as many as half of the estimated 6,000 languages spoken on earth are "moribund"; that is, they are spoken only by adults who no longer teach them to the next generation. An additional 40% may soon be threatened because the number of children learning them is declining measurably. In other words, 90% of existing languages today are likely to die or become seriously embattled within the next century. That leaves only about 600 languages, 10% of the world's total, that remain relatively secure—for now. This assessment is confirmed, with and without such detailed estimates, by linguists reporting the decline of languages on a global scale, but especially in the Americas, Africa, Australia, and Southeast Asia (Brenzinger, 1992; Robins & Uhlenbeck, 1991; Schmidt, 1990).

   In formulating a response to this crisis, there are three questions that need to be explored: (a) What causes language decline and extinction? (b) Can the process be reversed? And (c) why should we concern ourselves with this problem? Before attempting to provide answers, it would be helpful to look in detail at the situation of Native American languages in the United States.

**151**

## THE CRISIS

Language loss has been especially acute in North America. No doubt scores, perhaps hundreds, of tongues indigenous to this continent have vanished since 1492. Some have perished without a trace. Others survived long enough for 20th-century linguists to track down their last speakers and partially describe their grammars—for example, Mohican in Wisconsin, Catawba in South Carolina, Yahi in California, Natchez in Louisiana, and Mashpi in Massachusetts (Swadesh, 1948).

While Krauss (1995) estimated that 175 indigenous languages are still spoken in the United States, he classified 155 of these—89% of the total—as moribund. Increasingly, young Native Americans grow up speaking only English, learning at best a few words of their ancestral tongue. Out of 20 native languages still spoken in Alaska, only Central Yupik and St. Lawrence Island Yupik are being transmitted to the next generation. Similarly, in Oklahoma only 2 of 23 are being learned by children. All of the nearly 50 languages indigenous to California are moribund; most are kept alive by small groups of elders (Hinton, 1994). Few of Washington State's 16 Indian vernaculars are spoken by anyone under the age of 60. Krauss (1995) projected that, nationwide, 45 of today's Native American languages will lose their last native speakers by the year 2000; 125 by 2025; and 155 by 2050. Most of the 20 that remain, while viable at present, will soon be fighting to survive.

The imminence and scale of language extinction are well illustrated by the U.S. Census Bureau's (1993) estimate that more than one-third of American Indian and Alaska Native tongues had fewer than 100 home speakers in 1990.[1] And this is probably a conservative estimate of the threat, because the Census has no way of knowing whether these are fluent speakers. It simply asks the rather vague and ambiguous question: "Does this person speak a language other than English at home?" But not "How well?" "How often?" or "Under what circumstances?"[2]

---

[1] "Native North American languages" comprised 136 different groupings; of these, 47 were spoken in the home by fewer than 100 persons; an additional 22 were spoken by fewer than 200.

[2] Without an interviewer to explain the purpose of the home-language question, it has elicited unintended responses. The extent of language shift may be understated through misinterpretations, such as: "Can this person speak, at any level of proficiency, a language other than English?" and "Does this person ever speak another language at home?" So persons with limited proficiency, such as those who have studied a foreign language in school, are often counted as minority language speakers. For example, the 1980 Census found that a substantial minority of "Spanish speakers" in the home were not of Hispanic ethnicity—a "totally untenable ... conclusion," according to Veltman (1988, p. 19).

Moreover, self-reports have been shown to be unreliable when compared with objective measures of language proficiency (see, e.g., Hakuta & D'Andrea, 1992), often contaminated by ethnic feelings, such as pride in the native language. Ambiguous questions provide even more room for subjective assessments. (cont.)

# 6. ENDANGERED NATIVE AMERICAN LANGUAGES 153

Rapid shift to English is evident even among speakers of the healthiest indigenous languages such as Navajo, a group that was historically isolated and thus among the slowest to become bilingual. As late as 1930, 71% of Navajos spoke no English, as compared with only 17% of all American Indians at the time (U.S. Census Bureau, 1937). The number who speak Navajo in the home remains substantial—148,530 in 1990, or 45% of all Native American language speakers (Census Bureau, 1993). But the percentage of Navajos who speak only English is growing, predictably among those who have migrated from their tribal homeland, but also among those who have remained. For Navajos living on the reservation, ages 5 and older, the proportion of English-only speakers rose from 7.2% in 1980 to 15% in 1990. For those ages 5–17, the increase was even more dramatic: from 11.8% to 28.4% (see Table 6.1).

Among school-age children living on the reservation, the number of monolingual English speakers more than doubled, from 5,103 to 12,207.

A 1992 tribal survey suggests even more rapid erosion. Among 3,328 Navajo kindergartners at 110 schools on or near the reservation, 32% spoke Navajo well, whereas 73% spoke English well. Only 16% were rated higher in Navajo than in English (Holm, 1993). These figures are quite ominous

**TABLE 6.1**

Tribal Population and Home Language Speakers, Age 5+, Navajo Reservation and Trust Lands (AZ, NM, & UT), 1980–1990

|  | Age 5-17 | % | Age 18+ | % | Total | % |
|---|---|---|---|---|---|---|
| **1980** |  |  |  |  |  |  |
| Population | 43,121 | 100.0 | 65,933 | 100.0 | 109,054 | 100.0 |
| *Speak only English* | 5,103 | 11.8 | 2,713 | 4.1 | 7,816 | 7.2 |
| Speak other language | 38,018 | 88.2 | 63,220 | 95.9 | 101,238 | 92.8 |
| **1990** |  |  |  |  |  |  |
| Population | 42,994 | 100.0 | 81,301 | 100.0 | 124,295 | 100.0 |
| *Speak only English* | 12,207 | 28.4 | 6,439 | 7.9 | 18,646 | 15.0 |
| Speak other language | 30,787 | 71.6 | 74,862 | 92.1 | 105,649 | 85.0 |

Source: Census Bureau, 1989, 1994.

[2](cont.) On the other hand, the Census has acknowledged a significant undercount of minority groups, including Native Americans. Those living in remote areas are least likely to be counted; in the past, large numbers of census forms have piled up, unclaimed, at reservation trading posts (D. Waggoner, personal communication, 1994). Such Indians are less likely to speak only English in the home; so undercounting them tends to overstate the extent of language shift.

Another possible distortion, especially for small populations, is that language estimates are based on a 12% sample. A survey conducted by linguists and indigenous speakers in California turned up several Indian languages missed entirely by the 1990 Census (Hinton, 1994).

On balance, however, the last two decennial censuses probably overstate the extent of proficiency in (and usage of) languages other than English. Fortunately, the questions were asked consistently in 1980 and 1990. So at least the trends of language shift may be reliably plotted on the basis of comparable data. Unfortunately, no home language question was asked before 1980.

154                                                                      CRAWFORD

for the future viability of Navajo, long considered the most secure indigenous tongue in the United States.

The crisis of Native American languages can be summarized as follows:
Unless current trends are reversed, and soon, the number of extinctions
seems certain to increase. Numerous tongues—perhaps one-third of the
total—are on the verge of disappearing along with their last elderly speakers, and many others are not far behind. Even the most vigorous 10% have
a weakening hold on the young. In short, Native American languages are
becoming endangered species.

## WHAT CAUSES LANGUAGE DEATH?

Obvious parallels have been drawn between the extinction of languages and
the extinction of plants and animals. In all probability, like the majority of
creatures in natural history, the majority of languages in human history have
passed from the scene;[3] they have fallen victim to predators, changing
environments, or more successful competitors. Moreover, the pace of extinction is clearly accelerating both for languages and for biological species. In
the past, despite a few exceptional periods (e.g., the late Mesozoic era, when
the dinosaurs died out), the process has proceeded discretely and locally.
Today, by contrast, it is proceeding generically and globally. We appear to
have entered a period of mass extinctions—a threat to diversity in our
natural ecology and also in what might be called our cultural ecology.

Wilson (1992) has estimated that before industrialism began to affect
tropical rain forests, roughly one in a million plants and animals there
became extinct each year; today the rate is between 1 in 1,000 and 1 in 100.
Instead of individual species facing difficulties in particular habitats, suddenly we are seeing a generalized threat to many species, such as the
well-publicized extinction of frogs in diverse environments.

Naturally, we do not have similar estimates for the rate of language
extinction. Because languages leave no fossil record, there is no way to
calculate the rate at which they died out in the past. But the phenomenon of
language death is strikingly similar—and causally linked—to the death of
biological species. Modern cultures, abetted by new technologies, are en-
croaching on once-isolated peoples with drastic effects on their way of life
and on the environments they inhabit. Destruction of lands and livelihoods;
the spread of consumerism, individualism, and other Western values; pressures for assimilation into dominant cultures; and conscious policies of
repression directed at indigenous groups—these are among the factors
threatening the world's biodiversity as well as its cultural and linguistic
diversity.

---

[3]Krauss speculated that 10,000 years ago, there may have been as many as 15,000 languages
worldwide—2.5 times as many as today (cited in Schwartz, 1994).

## 6. ENDANGERED NATIVE AMERICAN LANGUAGES    155

How does a language die? One obvious way is that its speakers can perish through disease or genocide. This was the fate, for example, of most languages spoken by the Arawak peoples of the Caribbean, who disappeared within a generation of their first contact with Christopher Columbus. But such cases are relatively rare. More often language death is the culmination of language shift, resulting from a complex of internal and external pressures that induce a speech community to adopt a language spoken by others. These may include changes in values, rituals, or economic and political life resulting from trade, migration, intermarriage, religious conversion, or military conquest. Some describe these as "changes in the ecology of languages" (Wurm, 1991, p. 2)—continuing the comparison with natural species—a Darwinian model suggesting that languages must adapt or perish.

Here the analogy begins to become misleading. Unlike natural species, languages have no genes and thus carry no mechanism for natural selection. Their prospects for survival are determined not by any intrinsic traits, or capacity for adaptation, but by social forces alone. As a practical matter, in discussing language shift it is probably impossible to avoid biomorphic metaphors like *ecology, survival, death, extinction,* and *genocide* (certainly if one judges from this chapter thus far). But unless we remain vigilant, such metaphors can lead us into semantic traps, and these traps have political consequences.

Conceiving language loss as a Darwinian process implies that some languages are fitter than others, that the "developed" will survive and the "primitive" will go the way of the dinosaurs. Although I know of no linguist who makes such an argument, there are plenty of laypersons who do. (And such voices are heeded by legislators, as testified by the advance of the English Only movement since the mid-1980s.) Some scholars of "language death" have helped to perpetuate this misunderstanding by ignoring its social and historical causes. By focusing exclusively on "structural-linguistic" factors, they imply "that a language can 'kill itself' by becoming so impoverished that its function as an adequate means of communication is called into question" (Sasse, 1992, pp. 10–11). The research literature demonstrates precisely the opposite: such structural changes are the result, not the cause, of language decline.

In a related vein, several writers have raised the question: "Language murder or language suicide?" (e.g., Edwards, 1985)—as if it were possible to separate external and internal factors in language loss and thereby assess blame. According to the "suicide" model, a language community (say, the Irish) opts to abandon its native tongue out of self-interest (to enjoy the superior opportunities open to English speakers) rather than in response to coercion. As Denison (1977) asserted, a speech community:

**156**                                                                                                              **CRAWFORD**

sometimes "decides," for reasons of functional economy, to suppress a part of itself. ... There comes a point when multilingual parents no longer consider it necessary or worthwhile for the future of their children to communicate with them in a low-prestige language variety, and when children are no longer motivated to acquire active competence in a language which is lacking in positive connotations such as youth, modernity, technical skills, material success, education. The languages at the lower end of the prestige scale retreat from ever increasing areas of their earlier functional domains, displaced by higher prestige languages, until *there is nothing left for them to be appropriately used about.* In this sense they may be said to "commit suicide." (p. 21)

Certainly language choices are made, in the final analysis, by speakers themselves. But this "explanation" of language death explains little about the social forces underlying such choices. Whether deliberate or not, the notion of language suicide fosters a victim-blaming strategy. It reinforces the ethnocentric prejudice, all too common among dominant groups, that certain languages are unfit to survive in the modern world. At best, it encourages the prevalent worldwide response to threatened cultures: malign neglect.

Yet "murder," too, has been overrated as a cause of language extinction. This is due in part to the popular notion that conquerors "naturally" force their languages on others. But scholars have also favored the murder hypothesis, for example, in explaining the spread of Indo-European languages. The traditional account is that, over a relatively brief period—roughly the 4th millennium B.C.—bands of warriors armed with superior technology (and in some versions, with superior "racial" traits) charged out of the Russian steppes (or Asia Minor or Northern Europe) to defeat indigenous peoples from India to Ireland and impose their own Proto-Indo-European vernacular(s).[4]

---

[4]Of course, this idea predates the advent of linguistic archaeology. In 1492, Antonio de Nebrija completed a Castilian grammar book, the first ever completed of a European language. When he presented it to Queen Isabella and she asked, "What is it for?" the Bishop of Avila answered for him: "Your Majesty, language is the perfect instrument of empire." Thus began a 300-year attempt by Spanish monarchs to repress and replace indigenous languages in the New World. Yet despite repeated edicts from Madrid, the policy was frequently ignored by Spanish priests and civil officials, who found it easier to pursue their work through indigenous lingua francas like Nahuatl and Quechua (Heath, 1972).

A U.S. Commissioner of Indian Affairs similarly invoked the conqueror's prerogative to justify linguistic repression in North America:

All are familiar with the recent prohibitory order of the German Empire forbidding the teaching of the French language in either public or private schools in Alsace and Lorraine. Although the population is almost universally opposed to German rule, they are firmly held to German political allegiance by the military hand of the Iron Chancellor. If the Indians were in Germany or France or any other civilized country, they should be instructed in the language there used. As they are in an English-speaking country they must be taught the language which they must use in transacting business with the people of this country. No unity or community of feeling can be established among different peoples unless they are brought to speak the same language, and thus become imbued with like ideas of duty. (Atkins, 1887, p. xxii)

## 6. ENDANGERED NATIVE AMERICAN LANGUAGES                                  157

Renfrew (1987) recently cast strong doubts on this hypothesis. Invoking archaeological as well as linguistic evidence, he argued that Proto-Indo-European advanced more gradually through the expansion of agriculture, beginning as early as 6500 B.C. Farming supports considerably larger populations than hunting and gathering, but also requires constant migration in search of arable land. Thus, instead of spreading their language(s) primarily by conquest, it is more likely that Indo-Europeans overwhelmed other language communities with superior numbers. Europe's original inhabitants (with exceptions, e.g., the Basques) either adopted the newcomers' way of life, including their speech, or perished trying to compete with it. In this scenario demographic, cultural, and economic changes, rather than military factors played the key roles in language extinction. While the debate over Indo-European origins continues, Renfrew's hypothesis is more consistent with sociolinguistic evidence about language shift.

In sum, the murder versus suicide dichotomy is simplistic in the extreme. And it lends support to those who would either justify the colonizer's prerogative to coerce assimilation or blame the victims for acquiescing. Languages die from both internal and external causes, operating simultaneously. On the one hand, the process always reflects forces beyond its speakers' control: repression, discrimination, or exploitation by other groups (and, in many situations, all three). On the other hand, except in the case of physical genocide, languages never succumb to outside pressures alone. There must be complicity on the part of speech community itself, changes in attitudes and values that discourage teaching its vernacular to children and encourage loyalty to the dominant tongue.

Take the example of Native American languages, which were targeted by the U.S. government in a campaign of linguistic genocide. In 1868, a federal commission on making peace with the plains Indians concluded: "In the difference of language to-day lies two-thirds of our trouble ... Schools should be established, which children should be required to attend; their barbarous dialects should be blotted out and the English language substituted" (quoted in Atkins, 1887, p. xx).

By the 1880s this policy was institutionalized in the boarding school system established by the Bureau of Indian Affairs (BIA). Under strict English Only rules, students were punished and humiliated for speaking their native language as part of a general campaign to erase every vestige of their Indian-ness. A BIA teacher in the early 1900s explained that the schools

> went on the assumption that any Indian custom was, per se, objectionable, whereas the customs of whites were the ways of civilization. ... [Children] were taught to despise every custom of their forefathers, including religion, language, songs, dress, ideas, methods of living. (Kneale, quoted in Reyhner, 1992, p. 45)

Lieutenant Richard Henry Pratt (1892/1973) architect of the BIA school system, summed up its educational philosophy succinctly: "Kill the Indian ... and save the man" (p. 261).

When John Collier was appointed commissioner of Indian Affairs in 1933, he condemned and prohibited these ethnocentric practices, going so far as to experiment with vernacular instruction in Navajo and other languages (Szasz, 1977). Nevertheless, English Only rules and punishments persisted unofficially for another generation, as many former students can attest.

In the short term, the coercive assimilation policy met with limited success in eradicating Indian languages. Brutality of this kind naturally breeds resistance and determination to defend the culture under attack. Moreover, the isolation and exclusion of most Indians from the dominant society made assimilation seem like a poor bargain indeed. Even when students excelled in BIA schools and embraced the dominant culture, on graduation they were usually shunned by white society.

Over time, however, the English Only policy did take a toll on the pride and identity of many Indians, alienating them from their cultural roots and from their tribes, and giving them little or nothing in return. Being punished for speaking the ancestral language often devalued it in their own minds, and some accepted the dominant society's judgments. This has left a legacy of opposition to bilingual education among not a few Indian parents, who vividly remember the pain they suffered in school and hope to shield their children from the same experience (Crawford, 1995).

Yet while the English Only boarding schools did damage to the status of indigenous languages within their own communities, other factors may have exerted a stronger influence. The advent of a cash economy, government services, and in some cases industrial employment, along with the penetration of once-remote reservations by English-language media (especially television and VCRs), have created new pressures and enticements for Native Americans to enter the wider society, or at least to abandon their old ways.

Returning again to the example of the Navajo, we can see that language shift began to accelerate after the BIA abandoned its punitive English Only policy. That is, linguistic assimilation seems to have proceeded more efficiently on a laissez-faire basis than it did through coercion. Pragmatic parents tend to see advantages in raising their children mostly or entirely in English, the language of social and economic mobility. Thus every step toward modernization puts the indigenous tongue at a greater disadvantage. Gradually its sphere of usage contracts to home and hearth, religious rituals, and traditional ceremonies. In theory, stable bilingualism (diglossia) offers a possible antidote to language loss, but the odds for maintaining this

# 6. ENDANGERED NATIVE AMERICAN LANGUAGES

balance decline to the extent that traditional cultures decline, thereby shrinking the domains of the ancestral tongue.

How should we conceptualize the causes of language shift? Rather than relying on Darwinian metaphors, Fishman (1991) offered criteria with fewer semantic pitfalls. In place of changing "ecology," he cited "dislocations"—physical, economic, social, and cultural—affecting a language community. These include a group's dispersal from its historic homeland, subordination to a socioeconomic system in which its tongue commands limited power and prestige, and the weakening of traditional bonds through contact with modern, atomized democracies that elevate individual freedom over communal values. Although a comprehensive theory of language loss remains to be developed, Fishman's categories provide a useful framework for investigation.

## IS THERE A CURE?

What, if anything, can be done to cope with this crisis? Is it possible to rescue languages now on the brink of extinction, or perhaps even to resuscitate some that are no longer spoken? This latter idea is not so farfetched when one considers the example of Hebrew—a "dead" language for nearly 2,000 years when it was brought back to life in modern Israel; Hebrew today has several million speakers. Some Native American groups have expressed interest in doing the same thing. Recently the Coquille tribe of Oregon sought funding for a project to revive the Miluk language, using tape recordings from the 1930s of its last living speakers (Farley, 1992).

Of course, it would be hard to find a community whose language is threatened today that commands the level of resources the State of Israel devoted to the cause of reviving Hebrew. So the question of whether this kind of effort can succeed is very relevant. If there is little hope of preventing the extinction of a language, a revitalization project may be ill-advised; scarce funds might be better spent on other social and educational programs. On the other hand, if endangered languages can be saved, there is little time for delay in the name of budgetary constraints.

In the 1980s several tribes recognized the urgency of this task. The Navajo, Tohono O'odham, Pasqua Yaqui, Northern Ute, Arapaho, and Red Lake Band of Chippewa were among those that adopted policies designed to promote the use of their ancestral tongues in reservation schools and government functions. Ironically, in most cases the English Only movement sounded the alarm bells that energized Indian leaders (Crawford, 1992a).

While these tribal language policies were an important first step, their implementation has been uneven. To succeed, language renewal projects require not only good intentions but enormous practical efforts. Some tribes still need expert help to complete orthographies, grammar books, and dictionaries. Virtually all need assistance in developing and publishing curriculum materials. Bilingual education programs—for example, at community-run schools like Rough Rock on the Navajo reservation—are a major (if underutilized) tool for promoting native-language literacy (McLaughlin, 1992). Another key task is teacher training, complicated by the fact that Indian language speakers often lack academic credentials, while outsiders lack essential cultural and linguistic knowledge. As a result, these projects must draw on cultural resources available on reservations, relying especially on elders, the true experts in these languages.

Tribal initiative and control are essential to the success of revitalization efforts because language choices are a matter of consensus within each community. They are very difficult to impose from without. "All-important is the peoples' will to restore their native languages," Krauss (1992a) maintained, citing his experiences at the Alaska Native Language Center in Fairbanks. "You cannot from the outside inculcate into people the will to revive or maintain their languages. That has to come from them, from themselves" (p. 21). If endangered languages are to be saved, it is crucial for native speakers to see the value of doing so and get actively involved in the process.

At the same time language renewal faces a perennial barrier to social progress on Indian reservations: scarce resources. Such projects must compete with other, usually more pressing priorities like health care, housing, schooling, and economic development. Most tribes, lacking a local tax base, have historically relied on federal funding for these needs. But since 1980 the federal government has cut back substantially on its support of Indian programs generally (a trend that continues under the Clinton Administration).

Congress recently passed the Native American Languages Acts of 1990 and 1992,[5] laws that, respectively, articulate a government policy of protecting indigenous languages and authorize a grant program for that purpose. Although some federal help was previously available through the National Science Foundation, the National Endowment for the Humanities, and the Department of Education, for the first time the 1992 Act made tribes eligible for funding to carry out language conservation and renewal. Yet Congress has been slow to fund the program. Finally, in the fall of 1994, the Clinton Administration awarded $1 million in grants to launch 18 language revitalization projects nationwide—a meager amount, but still a beginning.[6]

---

[5]Thanks to the efforts of the American Indian Language Development Institute and Native American Language Issues Institute. (For the text of the 1990 Act, see Crawford, 1992b, pp. 155–57.)

[6]The Administration for Native Americans, a branch of the Department of Health and Human Services, issued regulations governing this grant program in the *Federal Register* on March 25, 1994.

# 6. ENDANGERED NATIVE AMERICAN LANGUAGES    161

Implementation of the 1990 Act has also been disappointing. Among other things, it called upon all agencies of the federal government—including the Departments of Interior, Education, and Health and Human Services—to review their activities in consultation with tribes, traditional leaders, and educators to make sure they comply with the policy of conserving Native American languages. By the fall of 1991, the president was required to report back to Congress on what was being done and to recommend further changes in law and policy. But the Bush Administration ignored these provisions and the Clinton Administration has similarly failed to conduct the mandated review. After some prodding by the Senate Select Committee on Indian Affairs, the matter was referred to the BIA, whose only response has been to compile a list of bilingual education programs in its schools (a rather short list, at this writing). So, although the federal government now has a strong policy statement on file favoring the preservation of indigenous tongues, its real-world impact has thus far been limited.

So the question remains: Is there a realistic chance of reversing the erosion of Native American languages? In theory, this goal is quite possible to achieve, as we know from the miraculous revival of other languages. Heroic efforts are now being made on behalf of languages with only a few elderly speakers, for example, by the Advocates for Indigenous California Language Survival (Feldman, 1993; Hinton, 1994). For other languages—especially those still being learned by children, taught in bilingual education programs, and receiving tribal support—there is considerable hope. In practice, however, limited progress is being made in retarding the pace of language shift overall. This bleak situation is unlikely to change without a stronger commitment at all levels and without a substantial infusion of new resources. To put it bluntly, the decisive factor in the survival of Native American languages will be politics—the final subject of this chapter.

## WHY SHOULD WE CARE?

Why concern ourselves with the problem of endangered Native American languages, to the extent of investing the considerable time, effort, and resources that would be needed to save even a handful of them? Posing the question in this way may seem callous, considering the shameful history of cultural genocide practiced against indigenous peoples in this country. But, for many non-Indians, who tend to view linguistic diversity as a liability rather than an asset, the value of these languages is not self-evident. Knowledge about Native American issues in general is limited. Meanwhile, assimilationist biases remain strong; hence the symbolic opposition these days to any kind of public expenditure aimed at preserving "ethnic" cultures (Crawford, 1992a). Until such attitudes are changed—by effectively answering the question, "Why should we care about preserving Native American languages?"—there will be limited progress in conservation and renewal.

Advocates have advanced a variety of answers. Let us consider them on their scientific merits and on their political appeal:

1. Linguists, who are increasingly vocal on this issue, have warned that the death of any natural language represents an incalculable loss to their science. "Suppose English were the only language available as a basis for the study of general human grammatical competence," wrote Hale (1992). Although "we could learn a great deal ... we also know enough about linguistic diversity to know that we would miss an enormous amount" (p. 35). No doubt few who are acquainted with this problem would disagree: From a scientific standpoint, the destruction of data is always regrettable. Losing a language means losing a rare window on the human mind. But from the perspective of the public and policymakers, this argument smacks of professional self-interest; it is hardly a compelling justification for new spending in times of fiscal austerity.

2. Others have argued that the loss of linguistic diversity represents a loss of intellectual diversity. Each language is a unique tool for analyzing and synthesizing the world, incorporating the knowledge and values of a speech community. Linguistic "categories [including] number, gender, case, tense, mode, voice, 'aspect,' and a host of others ... are not so much discovered in experience as imposed upon it" (Sapir, 1931, p. 578). Thus to lose such a tool is to "forget" a way of constructing reality, to blot out a perspective evolved over many generations. The less variety in language, the less variety in ideas. Again, a Darwinian analogy:

> Evolutionary biologists recognize the great advantage held by species that maintain the greatest possible diversity. Disasters occur when only one strain of wheat or corn, a "monoculture" is planted everywhere. With no variation, there is no potential to meet changing conditions. In the development of new science concepts, a "monolanguage" holds the same dangers as a monoculture. Because languages partition reality differently, they offer different models of how the world works. There is absolutely no reason why the metaphors provided in English are superior to those of other languages. (Schrock, 1986, p. 14)

Theoretically this sounds plausible; yet such effects are impossible to quantify. Who can say whether a concept that evolved in one language would never have evolved in another? The extreme version of the Sapir–Whorf hypothesis—that perception and cognition are

## 6. ENDANGERED NATIVE AMERICAN LANGUAGES        163

determined by the structure of whatever language one happens to speak—has been demolished by Chomskyan linguistics (see, e.g., Pinker, 1994). Its more flexible version, "linguistic relativity," is another matter. Few would dispute that culture, influenced by language, influences thought. Yet the impact remains too elusive, too speculative, to rally public concern about language loss.

3. Then there is the cultural pluralist approach: language loss is "part of the more general loss being suffered by the world, the loss of diversity in all things" (Hale, 1992, p. 3). While this argument is politically potent—with lots of cosmopolitan appeal—it is scientifically dubious. For at least one linguist working to save endangered languages, such "statements ... are appeals to our emotions, not to our reason" (Ladefoged, 1992, p. 810). Again the biological analogy breaks down. From the loss of natural species scientists are continually documenting ripple effects that harm our global ecosystem. No such evidence is available for the loss of linguistic species, which are not physically interdependent and which "evolve" in very different ways. No doubt it would be interesting to know more about extinct languages like Sumerian, Hittite, Etruscan, and even Anglo-Saxon. But how can we regard their disappearance as a global "catastrophe"? As for the threat to human diversity in general, Ladefoged continued: "The world is remarkably resilient; ... different cultures are always dying while new ones arise." Indeed, this resilience is the basis for linguistic diversity itself.

4. A final—and, in my view, the most effective—line of argument appeals to the nation's broader interest in social justice. We should care about preventing the extinction of languages because of the human costs to those most directly affected. "The destruction of a language is the destruction of a rooted identity" (Fishman, 1991, p. 4) for both groups and individuals. Along with the accompanying loss of culture, language loss can destroy a sense of self-worth, limiting human potential and complicating efforts to solve other problems, such as poverty, family breakdown, school failure, and substance abuse. After all, language death does not happen in privileged communities. It happens to the dispossessed and the disempowered, peoples who most need their cultural resources to survive.

In this context, indigenous language renewal takes on an added significance. It becomes something of value not merely to academic researchers, but to native speakers themselves. This is true even in extreme cases where a language seems beyond repair. As one linguist summed up a project to revive Adnyamathanha, an Australian aboriginal tongue that had declined to about 20 native speakers:

It was not the success in reviving the language—although in some small ways [the program] did that. It was success in reviving something far deeper than the language itself—that sense of worth in being Adnyamathanha, and in having something unique and infinitely worth hanging onto. (Tunbridge, quoted in Schmidt, 1990, p. 106)

## AUTHOR'S NOTE

Copyright © 1998 by James Crawford. All rights reserved. An earlier version of this chapter was presented at the annual conference of the American Educational Research Association, New Orleans, April 5, 1994, and published in the *Journal of Navajo Education* and the *Bilingual Research Journal*.

## REFERENCES

Atkins, J. D. C. (1887). *Report of the commissioner of Indian affairs* (House Exec. Doc. No. 1, Pt. 5, 50th Cong., 1st Sess). Washington, DC: U.S. Government Printing Office.

Brenzinger, M. (Ed.). (1992). *Language death: Factual and theoretical explorations with special reference to East Africa*. Berlin: Mouton de Gruyter.

Crawford, J. (1992a). *Hold your tongue: Bilingualism and the politics of "English Only."* Reading, MA: Addison-Wesley.

Crawford, J. (Ed.). (1992b). *Language loyalties: A source book on the Official English controversy.* Chicago: University of Chicago Press.

Crawford, J. (1995). *Bilingual education: History, politics, theory, and practice* (3rd ed). Los Angeles: Bilingual Educational Services.

Denison, N. (1977). Language death or language suicide? *International Journal of the Sociology of Language, 12*, 13–22.

Edwards, J. (1985). *Language, society, and identity.* Oxford, England: Basil Blackwell.

Farley, J. (1992). Statement of Jerry Farley, executive vice president, Coquille Economic Development Co. In U.S. Senate, *Native American Languages Act of 1991: Hearing before the Select Committee on Indian Affairs* (p. 29). Washington, DC: U.S. Government Printing Office.

Feldman, P. (1993, July 12). Breathing new life into dying languages. *Los Angeles Times*, pp. A1, A20–21.

Fishman, J. A. (1991). *Reversing language shift: Theoretical and empirical foundations of assistance to threatened languages.* Clevedon, England: Multilingual Matters.

Hakuta, K., & D'Andrea, D. (1992). Some properties of bilingual maintenance and loss in Mexican background high-school students. *Applied Linguistics, 13*, 72–99.

Hale, K., (Ed.). (1992). Endangered languages. *Language, 68*, 1–42.

Heath, S. B. (1972). *Telling tongues: Language policy in Mexico, colony to nation.* New York: Teachers College Press.

Hinton, L. (1994). *Flutes of fire: Essays on California Indian languages.* Berkeley, CA: Heyday.

Holm, W. (1993). *A very preliminary analysis of Navajo kindergartners' language abilities.* Window Rock, AZ: Navajo Division of Education, Office of Diné Culture, Language and Community Services.

Krauss, M. (1992a). Statement of Mr. Michael Krauss, representing the Linguistic Society of America. In U.S. Senate, *Native American Languages Act of 1991: Hearing before the Select Committee on Indian Affairs* (pp. 18–22). Washington, DC: U.S. Government Printing Office.

## 6. ENDANGERED NATIVE AMERICAN LANGUAGES 165

Krauss, M. (1992b). The world's languages in crisis. *Language, 68,* 6–10.

Krauss, M. (1995, February 3). *Endangered languages: Current issues and future prospects.* Keynote address, Dartmouth College, Hanover, NH.

Ladefoged, P. (1992). Another view of endangered languages. *Language, 68,* 809–811.

McLaughlin, D. (1992). *When literacy empowers: Navajo language in print.* Albuquerque: University of New Mexico Press.

Pinker, S. (1994). *The language instinct: How the mind creates language.* New York: Morrow.

Pratt, R. H. (1973). Official report of the nineteenth annual Conference of Charities and Correction. In F. P. Prucha (Ed.), *Americanizing the American Indians: Writings by the "Friends of the Indian," 1880–1900* (pp. 260– 71). Cambridge, MA: Harvard University Press. (Original work published 1892)

Renfrew, C. (1987). *Archaeology and language: The puzzle of Indo- European origins.* Chicago: University of Chicago Press.

Reyhner, J. (1992). Policies toward American Indian languages: A historical sketch. In J. Crawford (Ed.), *Language loyalties: A source book on the official English controversy* (pp. 41–47). Chicago: University of Chicago Press.

Robins, R. H., & Uhlenbeck, E. (Eds.). (1991). *Endangered languages.* Oxford, England: Berg.

Sapir, E. (1931). Conceptual categories in primitive languages. *Science, 74,* 578.

Sasse, H.-J. (1992). Theory of language death. In M. Brenzinger (Ed.), *Language death: Factual and theoretical explorations with special reference to East Africa* (pp. 7–30). Berlin: Mouton de Gruyter.

Schmidt, A. (1990). *The loss of Australia's Aboriginal language heritage.* Canberra, Australia: Aboriginal Studies Press, 1990.

Schrock, J. R. (1986). The science teacher and foreign languages. *Kansas Science Teacher, 3,* 12–15.

Schwartz, J. (1994, March 14). Speaking out and saving sounds to keep native tongues alive. *The Washington Post,* p. A3.

Swadesh, M. (1948). Sociologic notes on obsolescent languages. *International Journal of American Linguistics, 14,* 226–235.

Szasz, M. C. (1977). *Education and the American Indian: The road to self-determination since 1928* (2nd ed). Albuquerque: University of New Mexico Press.

U.S. Census Bureau. (1937). *The Indian population of the United States and Alaska.* Washington, DC: U.S. Government Printing Office.

U.S. Census Bureau. (1989). *1980 census of population: Characteristics of American Indians by tribes and selected areas* (PC80–2–1C). Washington, DC: U.S. Government Printing Office.

U.S. Census Bureau. (1993, April 28). *Number of non-English language speaking Americans up sharply in 1980s, Census Bureau says* [Press release].

U.S. Census Bureau (1994). *1990 census of population: Social and economic characteristics for American Indian and Alaska Native areas* (1990 CP-2-1A). Washington, DC: U.S. Government Printing Office.

Veltman, C. (1988). *The future of the Spanish language in the United States.* Washington, DC: Hispanic Policy Development Project.

Wilson, E. O. (1992). *The diversity of life.* Cambridge, MA: Harvard University Press.

Wurm, S. A. (1991). Language death and disappearance: Causes and circumstances. In R. H. Robins, & E. Uhlenbeck (Eds.), *Endangered languages* (pp. 1–18). Oxford, England: Berg.

# III

# Legal Implications
# of Official Language Policies

In affairs of state as well as everyday life, actions are taken with certain implicit or explicit intentions. Also, actions often have unintended outcomes, even with respect to the explicit intentions, and not all of these outcomes are beneficial. In Part III, the matter of official language legislation in Canada and the United States is considered. Neither of the chapters in Part III makes a direct comparison between Canada and the United States on this topic, not only because the United States does not (yet) have such a piece of legislation, but more important because there are many contextual factors that would make such a comparison very difficult. Nonetheless, both chapters raise crucial matters that are intrinsically interesting and that provoke reflection on circumstances in the other country. Both chapters focus not on the act (or potential act) itself but on issues that have arisen or would arise in implementation. Thus, Miner (chapter 7) discusses court decisions in the United States that would have to be taken into consideration in the framing of an official language act in that country. Magnet (chapter 8) takes lessons for legal theory from the experience of implementing the Official Languages Act in Canada. Although most other chapters in this book also reflect on this topic in one way or another, Fettes' (chapter 5) and Cartwright's (chapter 11) chapters are especially germane.

In Canada, the Official Languages Act of 1969 was created to assist in the mediation of relationships between the country's largest linguistic population, anglophones, and its second largest group, francophones. Thus, although language is in focus in the Act, all other aspects of relations, frictions, competition, and conflicts between the two groups are implied.

**167**

**168**                                               **III. LEGAL IMPLICATIONS**

Magnet discusses how the Act has been used by governments to manage linguistic conflicts in the country, and argues that the principles behind the Act have not been clear enough for the purposes of the bureaucracies and courts that have had to administer it. He proposes principles of duality and accommodation to clarify future work in this area. His accounting of the price paid for the confusion caused by such a nonspecification of principles is important as an object lesson to the United States and other countries considering official language legislation.

Miner addresses a similar matter in her chapter. In anticipation of the development of an official language law for the United States, she examines court decisions—already taken on the basis of existing legislation and constitutional provisions—that would impinge on either the framing or implementation of such a piece of legislation, or both. Presumably, the new legislation would have to be formulated to skirt these existing factors or else these factors, some of them constitutional, would have to be altered. Her major headings deal with two questions: (a) Is there a right to express oneself in a language other than English? and (b) Is there a right to receive communications in a language other than English? Like Magnet, Miner takes the complex of real-life outcomes back to principles—in her case, orientations toward language as language-as-problem, language-as-right, and language-as-resource.

Reading these two chapters gives readers plenty to think about with respect to official language legislation in general and comparison between such efforts in the two countries in particular. The most profound matter is probably the contrast between the fact that Canada's legislation concerns two languages, whereas the potential American bill would name just one language. As Magnet points out, Canada's Act has been less than successful as a negotiation tool between the two language groups involved, and other groups associated with languages not named as official have been made anxious about their status and support, as discussed, for example, by Burnaby (chapter 10, this volume) and Fettes. In other words, legislation on official languages that is not crystal clear does not necessarily quell tensions between linguistic groups and may well provoke problematic reactions from groups not named. It is not surprising, therefore, that Miner's chapter considers the impact of language legislation not on speakers of English but on speakers of other languages. If the United States declares English to be the official language, it must be prepared to state its intentions clearly. If the real intentions are, in fact, racist, classist, or both, these will have to be defended in order to make the law in the first place. To put a more positive slant on things, the benefits of such legislation will have to be identified and demonstrated. Finally, the consequences in terms of conflict between the interests of English speakers and those of speakers

## III. LEGAL IMPLICATIONS                                                                 169

of languages not named in the legislation will have to be anticipated and provided for.

These two chapters implicitly demonstrate how difficult it is to compare government policy in Canada and the United States. The history and structure of the U.S. Constitution and governance are such that a great deal is resolved through the courts. This type of resolution to problems only in fact began in Canada with the Constitution Act of 1982. The content of Miner's and Magnet's chapters is a clear demonstration of the kinds of action that are in focus when policy is discussed in the respective countries. Magnet demonstrates how lack of clarity in legislation has led to problems even in the relatively small role that the Canadian courts have had in its implementation. How much more important will clarity be to the potential U.S. legislation because the courts will play a greater role?

Finally, both authors make it clear that language legislation is about intergroup tensions and conflicts—civic, educational, and especially economic. Miner points out that courts in the United States have not used the official language declarations of states significantly in issues concerning minority language rights. It seems that official language acts can be framed either to wade into the fray of intergroup tensions or they can be so general as to be symbolic. However, the power of symbols is not to be taken lightly. Once raised, they can be invoked in every aspect of life.

# 7

# Legal Implications of the Official English Declaration[1]

## Susan Miner
*State of California Court of Appeal, First Appellate District*

According to recent census figures (McLeod, 1993), an increasing proportion of the U.S. population speaks a language other than English. In
California that proportion is nearly one in three. So far, the United States
has been spared the difficulties experienced in other parts of the world,
where bitter cultural, ethnic, and class divisions have been exacerbated by
linguistic differences. At least one commentator attributed this relative
calm to the dominance of a single, national language (English), coupled
with the appearance of tolerance from the absence of any official language
(Ruiz, 1990).

Yet that appearance of tolerance is threatened by the strength of the
English-only movement. Legislation is pending in Congress to establish
English as the official language, and 18 states have already adopted Official
English Declarations. In California, the voters in 1986 overwhelmingly
approved an amendment to the state constitution declaring English to be
the official language of the state (Cal. Const., art. III, §6).[1]

---

[1] Article III, section 6, of the California Constitution provides as follows:

(a) *Purpose.* English is the common language of the people of the United States of America
and the State of California. This section is intended to preserve, protect and strengthen the
English language, and not to supersede any of the rights guaranteed to the people by this
Constitution.

(b) *English as the Official Language of California.* English is the official language of the State
of California. (cont.)

**171**

The proliferation of Official English Declarations raises two broad legal questions concerning the rights of language minorities (Piatt, 1992): (a) Is there a right to express oneself in a language other than English? (b) Is there a right to receive communications in a language other than English?

## RIGHT TO EXPRESSION IN OTHER THAN ENGLISH

At present, certain federal constitutional and statutory provisions shield speakers of other languages from being compelled to speak English, or, put another way, from being denied the right to use their language of choice (Chen, 1992).

### Freedom of Speech

The First Amendment to the U.S. Constitution, as it has been interpreted by the U.S. Supreme Court, puts limitations on efforts by the government—whether federal, state, or local—to regulate speech.[2] In *Yniguez v. Arizonans for Official English*, 69 F.3d 920 (9th Cir. 1995), vacated on procedural grounds 117 S. Ct. 1055 (1997), the federal Court of Appeals ruled that an Arizona initiative measure which compelled the use of English violates the First Amendment of the U.S. Constitution. Although the U.S. Supreme Court has since vacated the lower court's opinion, thereby eliminating the opinion's value as binding precedent, the analysis employed by the federal Court of Appeals provides some useful insight into the judicial analysis of an Official English Declaration.

The Arizona measure not only declared English to be the official language of the state but also prohibited the use of languages other than English during performance of government business. Maria-Kelly Yniguez was a bilingual state employee who often communicated on the job in Spanish with monolingual Spanish-speaking members of the public whom she served. Fearing her use of Spanish could subject her to discipline, she brought a lawsuit in federal court to stop enforcement of the English-only provision. The Court of Appeals concluded that the Arizona provision

---

[1](cont.) (c) *Enforcement*. The Legislature shall enforce this section by appropriate legislation. The Legislature and officials of the State of California shall take all steps necessary to insure that the role of English as the common language of the State of California is preserved and enhanced. The Legislature shall make no law which diminishes or ignores the role of English as the common language of the State of California.

(d) *Personal Right of Action and Jurisdiction of Courts*. Any person who is a resident of or doing business in the State of California shall have standing to sue the State of California to enforce this section, and the Courts of record of the State of California shall have jurisdiction to hear cases brought to enforce this section. The Legislature may provide reasonable and appropriate limitations on the time and manner of suits brought under this section.

[2]The First Amendment provides in part as follows: "Congress shall make no law ... abridging the freedom of speech, or of the press."

# 7. LEGAL IMPLICATIONS 173

violated the free speech rights of all employees and officials of the state and local government.

It is noteworthy that the court in *Yniguez* drew a sharp distinction between the Arizona measure and Official English Declarations adopted in other states. The court characterized the Arizona measure as "wholly coercive" in restricting the choice of language by government workers. In contrast, the court observed that Official English Declarations in states such as California, which do not prohibit the use of other languages, appear to be "primarily symbolic."

Two dissenting justices in *Yniguez* asserted that the Arizona measure did not violate the First Amendment because the restrictions pertained only to the language used, not the content of the message. The majority, however, concluded otherwise—that the choice of a particular language may affect the message.

A similar conclusion was reached by a federal district court in *Asian American Business Group v. City of Pomona*, 716 F.Supp. 1328 (C.D. Cal. 1989). In that case, the City of Pomona had passed an ordinance that required business signs containing "foreign alphabetical characters" to devote at least half of the sign area to "English alphabetical characters." When an association of Asian American businesses sued in federal court to challenge the constitutionality of the ordinance, one question the judge had to decide was whether, for purposes of the First Amendment, a restriction on the language used is equivalent to a restriction on the content of a message. Judge Takasugi concluded that: "Since the language used is an expression of national origin, culture and ethnicity, regulation of the sign language is a regulation of content. ... Choice of language is a form of expression as real as the textual message conveyed." The judge ruled that the ordinance violated the freedom of speech.

Although state laws restricting language use have been rarely examined by the U.S. Supreme Court, that high court has similarly struck down government efforts to require speakers to use only English. In *Meyer v. Nebraska*, 262 U.S. 390 (1923), a Nebraska law prohibited the teaching of foreign languages before the 8th grade, thereby mandating English-only instruction in the lower grades. The court found the law unconstitutional in that it deprived the students of the opportunity to acquire knowledge, it deprived foreign language teachers of their livelihood, and it interfered with the power of the parents to control their children's education. In so ruling, the court declared that use of a particular language should not be forced:

> The protection of the Constitution extends to all, to those who speak other languages as well as to those born with English on the tongue. Perhaps it would be highly advantageous if all had a ready understanding of our ordinary speech,

but this cannot be coerced by methods that conflict with the Constitution. (262 U.S. at 401)

## Equal Protection

The Equal Protection Clause of the Fourteenth Amendment to the U.S. Constitution requires that persons in similar circumstances be given similar treatment.[3] The courts have held that the government may pass legislation applying only to certain classes of people as long as the classification is related to a legitimate purpose, but if the classification is based on race, national origin, or other "suspect" criteria, the legislation must be narrowly tailored to further a compelling governmental interest.

In *Asian American Business Group v. City of Pomona*, the judge found the business sign ordinance unconstitutional on the additional ground that it violated the Equal Protection Clause of the Fourteenth Amendment. The judge concluded that the ordinance's restriction on the use of a foreign language was, by implication, national-origin discrimination, even though the ordinance did not refer to national origin directly. The judge accepted the city's argument that the ordinance's stated purpose—facilitating identification of commercial structures in event of emergencies—was a compelling governmental interest. But the judge found that the ordinance could have accomplished this purpose in other, nondiscriminatory ways.

The lesson of this case, therefore, is that legislation directed at language minorities will be closely examined by the courts and will be invalidated if the separate treatment of foreign language speakers cannot be justified. Indeed, in *Yniguez v. Arizonans for Official English*, the court noted that because language is so closely related to national origin, the adverse impact of a restriction on the use of language falls almost entirely on language minorities. Further, the court rejected all of the proponents' justifications for requiring only English: protection of democracy by encouraging unity; encouraging a common language; promoting efficient and effective performance of government duties. The court found that none of these goals were served by the prohibition against using languages other than English. Consequently, the court, although basing its ruling on the First Amendment, commented that the Arizona measure may violate the Equal Protection Clause as well.

## The Equal Employment Opportunity Act

The First and Fourteenth Amendments shield the populace from actions by the government, but they have no effect on conduct of private individuals

---

[3]The Fourteenth Amendment provides in part as follows: "No state shall make or enforce any law which shall abridge the privileges or immunities of citizens of the United States; nor shall any state ... deny to any person within its jurisdiction the equal protection of the laws."

# 7.   LEGAL IMPLICATIONS                                                      175

or corporations. Title VII of the Civil Rights Act of 1964, sometimes called the Equal Employment Opportunity Act (42 U.S.C. § 2000e–2), was therefore enacted to provide protection from discriminatory conduct of employers, both public and private. Title VII makes it unlawful for an employer to discriminate on the basis of, among other things, race or national origin. The question not explicitly addressed by the statute, however, is whether discrimination on the basis of language constitutes discrimination on the basis of national origin. This question has arisen in two contexts: foreign-accent discrimination and English-only rules at the workplace.

***Accent Discrimination.***   The Equal Employment Opportunity Commission (EEOC), which is the administrative agency charged with enforcement of the Act, has promulgated guidelines that define national origin discrimination to include "the denial of equal employment opportunity ... because an individual has the ... linguistic characteristics of a national origin group" (29 C.F.R. § 1606.1). The EEOC has issued many rulings finding employment discrimination on the basis of foreign accent (see Hall, 1991, for a compilation of EEOC decisions on foreign-accent discrimination). Similarly, the courts have ruled that discrimination on the basis of a foreign accent is national-origin discrimination unless the accent interferes with the employee's ability to perform the duties of the job (also see Hall for a compilation of court decisions on foreign accent discrimination). The following is a sampling.

In *Carino v. University of Oklahoma*, 750 F.2d 815 (10th Cir. 1984), the court found employment discrimination when the basis for an employee's demotion was the employee's accent. Donaciano Carino, a native of the Philippines and a naturalized citizen of the United States, was employed as supervisor of the dental laboratory at the University of Oklahoma College of Dentistry. Less than a year after Carino was hired, he was reclassified as a senior dental lab technician because certain dental college faculty believed Carino was unsuitable as a supervisor on account of his accent. Carino brought a lawsuit in federal court claiming employment discrimination, and the federal district court judge found Carino's demotion attributable to his noticeable Filipino accent. The judge also found that Carino's accent would not interfere with the duties required of a dental lab supervisor. Hence, the judge found Carino had made his case of national origin discrimination. On appeal by the university, the federal Court of Appeals found no error in that decision.

More recently, in *Xieng v. People's National Bank of Washington*, 844 P.2d 389 (Wash. 1993), the court similarly found national origin discrimination in the denial of a promotion to an employee with an accent. Phanna Xieng, a Cambodian refugee, worked as a loan coordinator for a bank in the State of Washington and received positive performance evaluations, but he was consistently passed over for promotion. He then brought suit in Washington state court against the bank for national origin discrimination, and the judge found that the bank's reason for not promoting Xieng was his foreign accent; that his accent did not interfere with his job performance, nor would it have interfered with his job performance in the new position had he been promoted. Hence, the judge found the bank had unlawfully discriminated against Xieng. On appeal, the Washington Supreme Court upheld these findings.

In contrast, in *Al-Hashimi v. Scott*, 756 F.Supp. 1567 (S.D. Ga. 1991), the court found no violation of Title VII where the employee's job performance was inadequate. Hassan Mohammed Al-Hashimi, who was born in Iraq, had worked for over 20 years as a tenured professor at Paine College in Georgia. When a new college president took over in 1988, Al-Hashimi was fired, and he sued the university for employment discrimination, alleging that the reason for his dismissal was his foreign accent. The federal district court judge found, however, that the actual reason for the termination was Al-Hashimi's poor teaching performance—his failure to keep up with a common syllabus, his failure to prepare for class, and his failure to make himself understood to students. The court's acceptance of the latter reason as a justification for dismissal implies a finding that Al-Hashimi's accent interfered with his performance of his teaching duties.

Likewise, in *Fragante v. City and County of Honolulu*, 888 F.2d 591 (9th Cir. 1989), cert. denied 494 U.S. 1081, the court found no national origin discrimination where the job required good communication skills. Manuel Fragante, a Filipino immigrant, applied for a clerk's job with the Honolulu Division of Motor Vehicles, but he was not selected because of his heavy Filipino accent. When Fragante brought suit alleging national origin discrimination, the federal district court judge found that the ability to communicate clearly and effectively was a legitimate occupational qualification for the clerk's job, and the judge dismissed the lawsuit. On appeal, the federal Court of Appeals agreed that the county had a legitimate reason for rejecting Fragante's application. However, the court added a word of caution:

> Accent and national origin are obviously inextricably intertwined in many cases. It would therefore be an easy refuge in this context for an employer unlawfully discriminating against someone based on national origin to state falsely that it was not the person's national origin that caused the employment or promotion problem, but the candidate's inability to measure up to the communication skills demanded by the job. We encourage a very searching look by the district courts of such a claim. (888 F.2d at 596.)

An interesting twist on accent discrimination arose in *Williams v. Frank*, 757 F.Supp. 112 (D. Mass. 1991), where Raymond Williams, who is Black,

# 7. LEGAL IMPLICATIONS 177

claimed employment discrimination after he was fired from his job as a window clerk for the U.S. Postal Service. The court found that various acts of misconduct on the job constituted a legitimate basis for the decision to discharge Williams. Williams argued, however, that the Postal Service's reasons were a mere pretext for racial motivation, and as proof of the pretext, Williams offered evidence that his supervisors made fun of his Southern accent. The court rejected the argument, emphasizing that the supervisors' remarks had been about Williams' way of speaking, not about his race. In the court's words, "Southernness is not a protected trait" (757 F.Supp. at 120).

The apparent conclusion to be reached from this case is that accent discrimination is unlawful only insofar as it reflects discrimination based on foreign origin. Dialectic variations among native English speakers will not be given the same legal protection as phonological varieties arising from foreign language interference.

***English-Only Rules.*** At the root of the rulings in accent discrimination cases is the equation of discrimination on the basis of accent with discrimination on the basis of national origin. In contrast, the courts have not been inclined to find national origin discrimination when an employer imposes an English-only rule at the workplace.

In one of the earliest appellate cases on the subject, the federal Court of Appeals concluded that an English-only rule is not national origin discrimination. In *Garcia v. Gloor,* 618 F.2d 264 (5th Cir. 1980), cert. denied 449 U.S. 1113, Hector Garcia, a bilingual, native-born American of Mexican descent, was employed as a salesman for Gloor Lumber Company in Brownsville, Texas. The lumber company had many Spanish-speaking customers, and Garcia was hired for his bilingual skills. Nevertheless, the company had a rule prohibiting employees from speaking Spanish on the job unless they were communicating with Spanish-speaking customers, and Garcia was fired after a company official overheard him respond in Spanish to a question asked by another Mexican American employee assisting a customer. The court ruled that there is no right, at least among bilinguals, to use a language of choice: "If the employer engages a bilingual person, that person is granted neither right nor privilege by the statute to use the language of his personal preference."

Shortly after *Garcia v. Gloor* was decided, the EEOC issued its guidelines, which specifically address the validity of English-only rules:

> The primary language of an individual is often an essential national origin characteristic. Prohibiting employees at all times, in the workplace, from speaking their primary language or the language they speak most comfortably, disadvantages an individual's employment opportunities on the basis on national origin.

It may also create an atmosphere of inferiority, isolation and intimidation based on national origin. (29 C.F.R., § 1606.7(a))

Accordingly, the EEOC guidelines provide that a blanket rule requiring English to be spoken at all times is presumed to be national origin discrimination, but a limited rule, requiring English to be spoken at certain times or under certain circumstances, is permissible if the employer can show a business necessity for it (29 C.F.R. § 1606.7(b)).

Since the issuance of those guidelines, the EEOC has rendered several decisions in cases involving English-only rules in the workplace (see Thomas, 1988, for a compilation of EEOC decisions). The courts, however, have not been entirely accepting of the EEOC's view that English-only rules are a form of national origin discrimination.

In *Jurado v. Eleven-Fifty Corp.*, 813 F.2d 1406 (9th Cir. 1987), the court upheld an English-only rule, finding a legitimate business reason for it. Valentine Jurado was a radio announcer of Mexican American descent, bilingual in Spanish and English, who worked as a disc jockey for a radio station. For several years he broadcast in English only, but at the request of his program director, Jurado began to use some "street" Spanish words and phrases in an effort to attract Hispanic listeners. Later, a new program director decided the bilingual format was confusing the listeners, and he instructed Jurado to stop speaking Spanish on the air. Jurado refused to give up his bilingual presentation, and he was eventually fired. He then brought a lawsuit claiming employment discrimination, but the court concluded that the English-only order was limited to on-air time and was related to the radio station's programming decision. Hence, the court ruled that the English-only directive was business related and not discriminatory. Moreover, the court found that Jurado had the ability to conform to the English-only rule but voluntarily chose not to observe it.

Later, in *Dimaranan v. Pomona Valley Hospital*, 775 F.Supp. 338 (C.D. Cal. 1991), opinion withdrawn from publication, the court found justification for an English-only rule in the tensions created when some employees speak a separate language. Adelaida Dimaranan, a native of the Philippines, was employed as assistant head nurse in the mother/baby unit of a hospital. Dissension between Filipina and non-Filipina nurses on the evening shift of the unit led the hospital nursing supervisors to request that Tagalog not be spoken on the unit. Dimaranan, however, continued to use Tagalog, and hostilities among the nurses continued to divide the unit. At her next yearly performance evaluation, Dimaranan received poor ratings and was told she would be terminated unless she showed improvement in her ability to lead her staff. Dimaranan then filed an employment discrimination suit, claiming her poor performance review was in retaliation for her continued use of Tagalog.

## 7. LEGAL IMPLICATIONS

179

The federal district court judge found that the No Tagalog directive did not violate Title VII. The court reasoned that the language restriction was limited: it applied only to the evening shift of the mother/baby unit, and it applied only to the use of Tagalog. Further, the court found the rule justified as a response by management to the conflicts among identified staff nurses on the unit. The non-Filipina nurses believed Dimaranan showed favoritism toward Filipina nurses, and they attributed to this favoritism Dimaranan's use of Tagalog. Moreover, the court emphasized that, as in *Jurado*, the employee was fluently bilingual and could easily have complied with the rule.

Similar workplace tensions were present in *Garcia v. Spun Steak Co.*, 998 F.2d 1480 (9th Cir. l993), cert. denied 114 S.Ct. 2726. Spun Steak Company, a meat processing plant, employed several Spanish-speaking workers with varying degrees of proficiency in English. After receiving complaints that Priscilla Garcia and Maricela Buitrago made derogatory racist comments in Spanish about two coworkers, one of whom is African American and the other Chinese American, the company established an English-only policy. Garcia and Buitrago eventually received warning letters for speaking Spanish during working hours, and they brought a lawsuit to challenge the English-only rule.

In rejecting the workers' claim of discrimination, the federal Court of Appeals took an approach quite different from that taken by courts in precedent cases. The court rejected the EEOC's guidelines concerning English-only rules, finding nothing in Title VII to justify the EEOC's conclusion that English-only rules are presumed to be discriminatory. Specifically, the court ruled that Title VII does not confer on employees any right to express their cultural heritage at the workplace, nor any right to converse in the language with which they feel most comfortable. Instead, the court held that the workers were required to prove that the English-only rule had an adverse impact on them, and the court found that the workers had failed to prove their case. Following the reasoning of the *Jurado* case, the court concluded that a bilingual employee, who is able to comply with an English-only rule, is not adversely affected by it and therefore does not suffer discrimination.

The court in *Spun Steak* did acknowledge that an English-only rule could have an adverse impact on workers who speak no English. But there was only one such employee at the Spun Steak Company, and she testified that she was not bothered by the rule, as she preferred not to make small talk on the job. Further, there was evidence she was allowed to speak to her supervisor in Spanish. The court therefore found insufficient evidence that she had been adversely affected by the English-only rule.

The only case to find an English-only rule invalid under Title VII is *Gutierrez v. Municipal Court*, 838 F.2d 1031 (9th Cir. 1988), rehearing denied en banc, 861 F.2d 1187, vacated as moot, 490 U.S. 1016 (1989), but because the decision was vacated by the U.S. Supreme Court, it lacks precedential value. It is, however, the only ruling to consider the effect of California's Official English Declaration. The employer in that case, the Los Angeles Municipal Court, had argued that its English-only rule was required by the California Constitution, but the court rejected the argument, reasoning that the Official English Declaration of the California Constitution is "primarily a symbolic statement" intended to govern the language of official communications, not private conversations among public employees.

## RIGHT TO RECEIVE COMMUNICATIONS IN OTHER THAN ENGLISH

### Constitutional Rights

So far the courts have not found a constitutional right to receive communications in a language other than English (Zall & Stein, 1990). For example, the courts have ruled that the constitution does not obligate the government to provide a bilingual voting system (*Castro v. State of California*, 2 Cal.3d 223 (1970)) or bilingual education (*Guadalupe Org. v. Tempe Elem. School Dist.*, 587 F.2d 1022 (9th Cir. 1978)). Further, the courts have held that neither welfare-termination notices (*Guerrero v. Carleson*, 9 Cal.3d 808 (1973), cert. denied 414 U.S. 1137), Social Security notices (*Soberal-Perez v. Heckler*, 717 F.2d 36 (2d Cir. 1983), cert. denied 466 U.S. 929), nor civil service examinations (*Frontera v. Sindell*, 522 F.2d 1215 (6th Cir. 1975)) need be given in Spanish.

An exception exists for court interpreters in criminal cases. In *U.S. ex rel. Negron v. New York*, 434 F.2d 386 (2d Cir. 1970), the federal Court of Appeals held that the Sixth Amendment's guarantee of a right to confront and cross-examine witnesses gives to criminal defendants the right to an interpreter during court proceedings. In a later case, however, *Jara v. Municipal Court*, 21 Cal.3d 181 (1978), cert. denied 439 U.S. 1067, the California Supreme Court concluded that this right did not extend to participants in civil litigation.

### Federal Statutes

Although there is no recognized constitutional right to bilingual communications, Congress has enacted certain federal statutes that mandate communications in other than English:

# 7. LEGAL IMPLICATIONS

*Voting.* The Voting Rights Act of 1965, which outlawed literacy tests for Blacks, also outlawed English proficiency tests for Puerto Ricans (42 U.S.C. §§ 1971, 1973b(e)). The 1975 amendment to that Act requires more affirmative steps: bilingual ballots and voting materials where at least 5% of the voters are a single-language minority (42 U.S.C. § 1973aa–1a(b)).

*Education.* The Equal Education Opportunity Act of 1974 requires school districts to take whatever action is necessary to meet the educational needs of language minority students (20 U.S.C. § 1703(f); see also *Lau v. Nichols*, 414 U.S. 563 (1974)).

*Health Care.* Other federal legislation requires bilingual services in federally funded migrant and community health centers and in federally funded drug and alcohol treatment programs (42 U.S.C. §§ 254b (j) (3) (K), 4577(b)).

These federal statutes establish a "floor" of bilingual services that state governments may not ignore ("Official English," 1987). Hence, the presence of the Official English Declaration in the California Constitution has no effect on these federal mandates. Even the restrictive Arizona measure examined in *Yniguez v. Arizonans for Official English* permitted the use of other languages as required by federal law.

## California Statutes

At present, California has various statutes which require that state services be provided in languages other than English (American Civil Liberties Union, 1992). For example, all state agencies are required to employ sufficient numbers of bilingual persons in public contact positions to ensure provision of bilingual information and services. And written materials explaining governmental services must be available in a language other than English if the language is spoken by at least 5% of the people served by the office (Gov't Code, § 7290). Emergency (911) services must be multilingual (Gov't Code, § 53112). Applications for and information about various government benefits (unemployment, disability, worker's compensation, food stamps, public assistance, Medi-Cal) must be available in Spanish (Unempl. Code, § 316; Labor Code, §§ 124, 139.6; Welf. & Inst. Code, §§ 18915, 10607, 14191). Property tax exemption forms and instructions must be provided in Spanish (Rev. & Tax. Code, § 255.8). And the summary of motor vehicle laws put out by the Department of Motor Vehicles must be published in Spanish (Veh. Code, § 1656(b)).

The difficult question is whether the Official English Declaration in the state constitution renders these statutes invalid such that the state could be compelled to withdraw presently existing bilingual programs ("Official

English," 1987). That issue has not yet been decided. On the one hand, the words of the Official English Declaration suggest that official communications, such as those coming from governmental offices, must be in English. On the other hand, the Official English Declaration does not explicitly prohibit the use of languages other than English. The stated purpose of the Declaration is to "preserve, protect and strengthen the English language," leading the courts to conclude that the Official English Declaration is simply a "symbolic statement."

## Private Labeling

Another difficult issue is whether there is a right of language minorities to receive communications in their native language from private, nongovernmental sources. In certain limited situations, state statutes require the parties to private commercial transactions to furnish information in a language other than English, such as residential leases (Civ. Code, § 1632), automobile financing contracts (Civ. Code, § 1632), home solicitation contracts (Civ. Code, § 1689.7), consumer credit contracts (Civ. Code, § 2945.3), mortgage default notices (Civ. Code, § 2924c), foreign labor contracts (Bus. & Prof. Code, § 9998.2), and advertisements containing 900 numbers (Bus. & Prof. Code, § 17539.6).

In *Ramirez v. Plough, Inc.*, 6 Cal.4th 539 (1993), the California Supreme Court was asked to decide whether drug manufacturers (or other producers of potentially hazardous materials) must place warning labels on their products in languages other than English. The mother of Jorge Ramirez purchased St. Joseph's Aspirin for Children for her son, who developed Reye's syndrome soon after taking it and was permanently disabled. Because she does not speak or read English, Jorge's mother did not read the label warning of the link between aspirin and the disease. Jorge and his mother sued the aspirin manufacturer, Plough, Inc., and the question for the court was whether Plough had an obligation to print the warning label in Spanish as well as English. The California Supreme Court ruled it did not, that Plough was not required to do any more than was called for by federal and state drug-labeling laws.

The court concluded that the task of deciding when information should be provided in a language other than English was one more appropriately addressed by the legislature, not the courts. And the court noted that the legislature had already undertaken that task, enacting various laws requiring materials in languages other than English (see federal statutes and state laws cited earlier). Yet federal regulations implementing the Food, Drug, and Cosmetic Act, although encouraging labeling to meet the needs of non-English-speaking consumers, require labeling only in English. Similarly, the California health statutes require cautionary statements only in

## 7. LEGAL IMPLICATIONS 183

English. The court inferred, therefore, that the legislature has deliberately chosen not to require warnings in other than English.

The lower court had concluded that because Plough knew Hispanics were an important part of the aspirin's market and the product was advertised on Spanish radio and television, a jury could find that Plough should have expected Spanish speakers to purchase their products and should have labeled the aspirin accordingly. In this ruling, the lower court followed an earlier decision by a federal district court sitting in Florida, *Stanley Industries, Inc. v. W. M. Barr & Co., Inc.*, 784 F.Supp. 1570 (S.D. Fla. 1992), which held that a jury should have been allowed to decide whether a combustible oil product, heavily advertised in Miami's Hispanic media, should have carried a Spanish label or a pictorial cautionary symbol. The California Supreme Court, however, ruled that the issue should not be resolved on a case-by-case basis, as an open-ended rule would impose a costly and onerous burden on manufacturers to print warnings in multiple foreign languages. Further, the court noted that Jorge's mother had never heard, seen, or relied on any advertising for St. Joseph's Aspirin for Children either in Spanish or in English.

One argument made by Plough was that the Official English Declaration eliminates any obligation to issue warnings in languages other than English. The California Supreme Court, however, did not address the argument and indeed gave no mention to the Official English Declaration. Apparently, the court found the provision largely irrelevant to its analysis.

### CONCLUSION

One commentator has identified three orientations toward minority languages (Ruiz, 1990): language-as-problem, language-as-right, and language-as-resource. So far, the United States has given little attention to the view of language-as-resource; the policy debates have focused on language-as-right versus language-as-problem (Adams & Brink, 1990; Crawford, 1992). Indeed, the two approaches are ultimately inconsistent. The proponents of Official English Declarations take the language-as-problem approach, advocating the use of English only with a view toward incorporation of language minorities into the mainstream. Opponents of the English-only movement, on the other hand, affirm the value of language pluralism and view language as a right.

The tension between these two orientations has not yet been resolved. On the one hand, Congress and the state legislature have granted certain statutory rights to language minorities—rights to be free from discrimination in the workplace and rights to receive some communications in their native tongue. Yet the courts have declined to extend those rights broadly;

the courts have generally not found a right to use one's primary language in the workplace or a right to receive translations other than those specified by legislation. It is noteworthy, however, that in attempting to delineate the rights of language minorities the courts so far have not found the Official English Declaration to be significant.

## REFERENCES

Adams, K., & Brink, D. (Eds.). (1990). *Perspectives on official English*. New York: Mouton de Gruyter.

American Civil Liberties Union. (1992). Bilingual public services in California. In J. Crawford (Ed.), *Language loyalties* (pp. 303–311). Chicago: University of Chicago Press.

Chen, E. M. (1992). Language rights in the private sector. In J. Crawford (Ed.), *Language loyalties* (pp. 269–277). Chicago: University of Chicago Press.

Crawford, J. (Ed.). (1992). *Language loyalties*. Chicago: University of Chicago Press.

Hall, T. M. (1991). When does adverse employment decision based on person's foreign accent constitute national origin discrimination in violation of Title VII of Civil Rights Act of 1964. *American Law Reports Federal, 104,* 816–856.

McLeod, R. G. (1993, April 28). Census finds many speak foreign language at home. *San Francisco Chronicle,* p. A3.

"Official English:" Federal limits on efforts to curtail bilingual services in the states. (1987). *Harvard Law Review, 100,* 1345–1362.

Piatt, B. (1992). The confusing state of minority language rights. In J. Crawford (Ed.), *Language loyalties* (pp. 228–234). Chicago: University of Chicago Press.

Ruiz, R. (1990). Official languages and language planning. In K. Adams & D. Brink (Eds.), *Perspectives on official English* (pp. 11–24). New York: Mouton de Gruyter.

Thomas, T. A. (1988). Requirement that employees speak English in workplace as discrimination in employment under Title VII of Civil Rights Act of 1964. *American Law Reports Federal, 90,* 806–812.

Zall, B. W., & Stein, S. M. (1990). Legal background and history of the English language movement. In K. Adams & D. Brink (Eds.), *Perspectives on official English* (pp. 261–271). New York: Mouton de Gruyter.

# 8

# Language Rights Theory in Canadian Perspective

Joseph Eliot Magnet
*University of Ottawa*

Canadian language policy aspires to forge a stable political system out of Canada's multilingual population. Canada regulates language use in order to divert overheated competition between Canada's English- and French-speaking communities into manageable pathways where highly charged conflict may be blunted and controlled. This chapter argues that although Canada has developed processes for managing linguistic conflicts, Canadian language policy has been ineffective in communicating its goals and in inspiring acceptance. If Canada's language policy is to achieve acceptance, it must articulate principles that command respect at the high level at which the policy endeavors to operate. This chapter advances duality and accommodation as the fundamental principles of Canada's language policy.

## THE NEED FOR A LANGUAGE RIGHTS SYSTEM

### Statistical Portrait

The English and French languages predominate on Canada's soil. English is the language used in the home by 68% of Canadians. French is the language used in the home by 23% of Canadians (Statistics Canada, 1993b). Closer scrutiny of Canadian linguistic demography reveals two virtually unilingual territories joined along a narrow bilingual strip. French is concentrated in Quebec (Joy, 1992; Statistics Canada, 1993a).[1] English is concentrated in the other provinces.[2] These largely unilingual populations intersect along the "bilingual belt," a narrow corridor of territory leading from Moncton, through eastern and northern New Brunswick into southern Quebec, along the Ottawa River through northern Ontario, and onward to Sault Ste. Marie. Most of Canada's bilingual persons, approximately 16% of the total Canadian population, inhabit this area (Statistics Canada, 1993a).[3]

Canada's linguistic composition has been evolving in an unmistakable, 100-year-old trend that sees the language communities increasingly concentrate on separate territories. French has increased its hold on Quebec and the adjacent peripheries of Northern Ontario and New Brunswick, and under current conditions this trend will continue. English has expanded in the remaining Canadian provinces, and under current conditions this trend will also continue. This tendency toward linguistic separation has speeded up in recent decades.[4]

## Competition Between Canada's Language Communities

*Regional-Economic Competition.* All large political systems engender economic and political competition between regional subdivisions, and Canada is no exception. However, in Canada regional competition has an additional feature: Regional distinction is made even more unique because, as we have seen, Canada's regions have distinctive linguistic identities. In Canada, therefore, because the commonplace competition of regional interests is superimposed on a division of linguistic identities, it is possible to perceive normal regional competitions as contests of English against French. This makes regional economic competition in Canada at times supercharged; the competition of English against French tends to be perceived as intensely political and all-pervasive. The feelings generated by this competition become fierce. For example, the competition between Manitoba and Quebec companies for a federal government contract to maintain fighter aircraft quickly degenerated into English and French race-baiting. When the contract was awarded to the Quebec bidder despite

---

[1]Eighty-three percent of Quebeckers use French at home. Fifty-eight percent of Quebeckers speak only French.

[2]Ninety-eight percent of that population use English at home. More than 90% speak only English (Joy, 1992). The numbers exclude northern New Brunswick and Quebec.

[3]Eighty-six percent of the bilingual persons in Canada live in the bilingual belt (Joy, 1992). Of the Canadian population, 16.3% qualifies as bilingual (Statistics Canada, 1993a). This has increased steadily from 13.4% in 1971.

[4]For example, from 1986 to 1991, nearly twice as many Anglophones left Quebec than entered it. For more detail, see Commissioner of Official Languages (1990).

# 8. LANGUAGE RIGHTS THEORY 187

a lower tender from the Manitoba company, the English-speaking company complained that the French cheated by using their political power in Ottawa ("Quebec's CF-18 Triumph," 1986; Waddell, 1986). Canadians are capable of carrying on this imagined rivalry between English and French everywhere in their political life, even where it has little rational application, as for example, in majority–minority relations in the overwhelmingly English-speaking provinces (Magnet, 1995). The competition is perceived as a zero-sum game—one community wins; the other community loses.

***Assimilation.*** The competition between English and French communities in Canada has an additional dimension. Canadian demography places the English and French *languages* in contact. The sociology of language well understands that when diverse languages come into contact, unique effects are produced. The most important of these effects is "language shift," which may be defined as the switching from the language habitually used by a speaker to the language better understood by that speaker's audience. Language shift occurs as a result of the need to communicate in a commonly understood language. Over time, language shift leads to assimilation of weaker languages by stronger languages (Fishman, 1972; Veltman, 1997, chapter 12, this volume). Canadian history offers a potent illustration of how this works. Outside of Quebec, the weaker French language has been assimilated by the stronger English language for over 125 years, to the point where most provincial French-speaking communities are diminished and some provincial French-speaking communities have ceased to exist.[5] More recently, a similar process has been eclipsing the weaker English language inside of Quebec.[6]

***Symbolic Overtones of Competition.*** Canada's bilingual character is symbolically charged. Bilingualism is an essential feature of Canadian national identity, a reference for national loyalty, pride, and patriotism. Like the flag, the national anthem and other overarching symbols of nationhood, Canada's bilingual composition portrays the national personality. Ontarians who complain loudly about the official languages policy at home proudly trumpet their limited French on Caribbean Islands. When properly managed, the image of Canada's bilingual character resonates positively in the Canadian psyche as a potent symbol of Canada, and as such it has potential to strengthen the nation. When mishandled, official languages

---

[5]For example, there were 10,000 French-speaking residents in Saskatchewan in 1981, whereas there were only 7,000 10 years later. Similar trends are found in Alberta, Prince Edward Island, Nova Scotia, and Manitoba (Statistics Canada, 1992).

[6]The English-speaking population of Quebec shrank 30% between 1971 and 1991, from 13.1% to 9.2% of total Quebec population. This decline is attributable to emigration, not assimilation. Between 1981 and 1986, 41,000 more Anglophones left Quebec for other parts of Canada then came to Quebec from other provinces ("Language in Canada," 1989).

policy allows language conflict to smoulder too long, igniting passions that contribute to national destruction.

## FUNCTION OF CANADA'S LANGUAGE RIGHTS SYSTEM

Some of the worst conflicts in history are based on language competition, which tears countries apart. It becomes particularly supercharged where economic competition is superimposed on linguistic identity or overlays linguistic competition (Fishman, 1986). Canada's situation is not unique. All countries must design processes and institutions that aspire to keep potentially sociopathic forms of competition healthy and manageable, and to prevent them from degenerating into destructive manifestations.

This is Canada's experience. Canada's Constitution was born in the attempt to unite two powerful language communities—two nations—in a single state. Canada's federal system proceeds directly from this effort. "I thought a Legislative Union would be preferable," Attorney General John A. MacDonald (1907) stated in the Canadian Parliament in 1865, on the motion to adopt the "Quebec Resolutions":

> But ... we found that such a system was impracticable. In the first place, it would not meet the assent of the people of Lower Canada, because they felt that in their peculiar position—being in a minority, with a different language, nationality and religion from the majority ... their institutions and their laws might be assailed, and their ancestral associations, on which they prided themselves, attacked and prejudiced; it was found that any positions which involved the absorption of the individuality of Lower Canada ... would not be received with favor by her people. ... So that those who were, like myself, in favor of a Legislative Union, were obliged to modify their views and accept the project of a Federal Union as the only scheme practicable. (pp. 40–41)

Language rights were inserted into Canada's Constitution in 1867 to broker the relationship between the English and French linguistic communities where the communities would come into conflict in majority–minority settings (Constitution Act, 1867, §. 133). Language rights were subsequently expanded to define the status of the English and French languages (Canadian Charter of Rights and Freedoms, §. 16). Canadian language rights strive to create fair processes for the participation of both communities in the machinery of government, and attempt to moderate the effects of linguistic difference in the operation of the governmental machine.[7]

---

[7]In *Mahe v. A.G. Alberta* (1990), in speaking of minority language educational rights guaranteed by §. 23 of the Canadian Charter, Chief Justice Dickson stated: "The general purpose of section 23 is clear: it is to preserve and promote the two official languages of Canada, and their respective cultures by ensuring that each language flourishes, as far as possible, in provinces where it is not spoken by the majority of the population."

# 8. LANGUAGE RIGHTS THEORY 189

## CANADA'S LANGUAGE RIGHTS SYSTEM

### The System

Canada's language rights system comprises a network of heterogeneous components institutionalized in all sectors of government. The components include international, constitutional and domestic laws;[8] regulatory and watchdog agencies;[9] government structures;[10] service institutions;[11] and institutionalized political conflict.[12]

---

[8]International Law: *International Covenant on Civil and Political Rights* (1966); Constitutional Law: *Constitution Act, (1867)*, §. 133; The Manitoba Act, (1870), §. 23; The Northwest Territories Act (1875), §. 110; Constitution Act (1982), §§. 16–23; Domestic Law: Official Languages Act, S.C. (1988), c. 38; Official Languages of New Brunswick Act (1973); An Act Recognizing the Equality of the Two Official Linguistic Communities in New Brunswick (1981); *Charter of the French Language* (1988); *Criminal Code* (1985), §§. 530(1)-(5); Courts of Justice Act (1984), §§. 135–136; French Language Services Act (1990). There is a multitude of provincial legislation containing explicit language requirements, most of which reinforce the dominant position of the English language and impact negatively on effective operation of the system of official bilingualism. In this regard, legislation in British Columbia and Ontario is cited and reviewed by Magnet and Magnet (1986). For example, British Columbia requires competency in English for mine workers, power engineers, private investigators, doctors, pharmacists, veterinarians, and practical nurses. It also requires that records be kept in English pertaining to employee wages and holidays, and concerning potential employees. The province examines in English candidates for licensure under the Real Estate Act (1979), §§. 3–4; the Notaries Act (1979), §. 4; the Mortgage Brokers Act (1979); and the Pesticide Control Act (1979), §§. 4, 8. Training for many professions in British Columbia must be done at specified institutions, where instruction is offered only in English. Certain lengthy prescribed forms are available only in English and must be completed prior to licensure or registration to carry on certain businesses, such as community care facilities, veterinary laboratories, travel agencies, or motor dealerships (Magnet & Magnet, 1986).

[9]Official Language Commissioner, established under Federal and New Brunswick legislation (Official Languages Act, 1970, §§. 19–34); Office de la Langue Française, established under Quebec's Charter of the French Language (1977), §§. 122, 158, 186; Standing Joint Committee of the Senate and House of Commons on Official Languages Policy and Programs.

[10]Certain government departments have separate French and English language structures. Manitoba, for example, has two Assistant Deputy Ministers of Education with separate responsibilities for English and French language education; Ontario has an Office of Francophone Affairs in the Cabinet Office.

[11]Certain institutions service principally official language minorities. Université d'Ottawa, for example, under §. 4(c) of the University of Ottawa Act (1965), has as one of its objects and purposes "to further bilingualism and biculturalism and to preserve and develop French culture in Ontario." Similar functions are served, whether legislatively or administratively, by institutions such as Collège St.-Boniface (Manitoba), Royal Victoria Hospital, McGill University, the Protestant School Board of Greater Montreal (Quebec), and others.

[12]The government of Canada provides funds to minority language associations in all provinces and also to La Fédération des francophones hors Québec. These are hybrid entities, providing some services, but their chief impact is as political lobbies on the provincial and federal governments. As such, the associations regularly come into conflict with organized and spontaneous majority opinion. The conflicts are often spectacular, as was the case with La Société Franco-Manitobaine during the language rights crisis of 1983–1984, and La Fédération des Acadiens de la Nouvelle-Écosse during the Acadian School battles in 1985. These conflicts are built in, or institutionalized, as a result of the creation and maintenance of the minority language associations and the endowment of them, sometimes by statute, of political lobby purposes.

The language rights system is a crucial manifestation of Canada's binational character. The English and French linguistic communities share central institutions of the Federal State. Cabinet, House, Senate, Supreme Court, and bureaucracy are forged from representatives of both language communities in numbers roughly proportionate to their sizes.[13] The Canadian Constitution declares English and French to be the official languages of Canada, equal in status, rights and privileges. The Parliament, courts, and civil administration of the Federal State are obliged to function in both languages, as are important sectors of central institutions in the Provinces of Quebec, Manitoba, and New Brunswick. Canadians have the right to communicate with, and be served by, the Federal State and the Province of New Brunswick in the official language of choice. The two language communities are equitably entitled to jobs in the civil administration, and to use their language there as the language of work. Minority language education for children is guaranteed to citizens where numbers warrant.[14]

Protection of the English and French linguistic communities in the machinery of the Federal and certain provincial governments is an enduring feature of Canadian constitutional development. This tradition was extended and reinforced as Manitoba, Alberta, Saskatchewan, and the Northwest Territories joined the Federation (Northwest Territories Act, 1877, §. 110).[15] The tradition was preserved and strengthened when Canada moved to adopt a constitutional amending formula in 1949,[16] and when

---

[13]The legal and constitutional requirements are: Cabinet, constitutional convention—Re Resolution to Amend the Constitution (1981), and Dawson (1987); House—Constitution Act (1867), §§. 37 and 51; Senate, Constitution Act (1867), §. 22; Supreme Court, Supreme Court of Canada Act (1985), §. 6 (this provision is constitutionally entrenched by Constitution Act, 1982, §. 41); Bureaucracy, Official Languages Act (1985), §. 39. This last provision is especially clear on the principle:           PART VI
PARTICIPATION OF ENGLISH-SPEAKING AND
FRENCH-SPEAKING CANADIANS
Commitment to equal opportunities and equitable participation
39. (1) The Government of Canada is committed to ensuring that
(a) English-speaking Canadians and French-speaking Canadians, without regard to their ethnic origin or first language learned, have equal opportunities to obtain employment and advancement in federal institutions; and
(b) the composition of the work-force of federal institutions tends to reflect the presence of both the official language communities of Canada, taking into account the characteristics of individual institutions, including their mandates, the public they serve and their location.

[14]Canadian Charter of Rights and Freedoms, s. 16 (declaration of equal status); §. 18–19, Constitution Act (1867), §. 133, Manitoba Act (1870), §. 23 (Parliament, legislatures, court and civil administration to be bilingual); Official Languages Act (1985), §. 39 equitable participation in civil administration); Canadian Charter, §. 23 (minority language educational facilities); §. 20 (Federal and New Brunswick governmental services).

[15]This provision was carried forward when the modern day provinces of Alberta and Saskatchewan were created from the Territories (R. v. Mercure, 1988; Manitoba Act, 1870, §. 23).

[16]S. 91-1 B.N.A. Act, 1867 withholds from the Federal Parliament power to amend the Constitution "as regards the use of the English or the French language."

# 8. LANGUAGE RIGHTS THEORY 191

Canada patriated its Constitution in 1982.[17] Canada's constitutional tradition of protecting English and French language minorities was broadened significantly, and given new implementing machinery by the official languages policy in a statute adopted by Parliament in 1969 (*Official Languages Act*, 1970) and renovated in 1988 (*Official Languages Act*, 1988).

These constitutional provisions, and the regulatory regimes that implement them, originate in the 19th-century political compromises between English and French communities that made Canadian Confederation possible. History teaches that linguistic communities develop complicated relations, and Canada is no exception. Notwithstanding that Canada has a fractious history of linguistic intolerance punctuated by periodic crises (Magnet, 1995), relations between Canada's English and French communities do benefit from the often remarked restraint of the Canadian personality. Interethnic relations are also enhanced somewhat by legal institutions designed to eradicate the xenophobic fear that gives rise to sociopathic forms of ethnic competition (*Canadian Human Rights Act*, 1985; *Human Rights Act*, 1979, 1986; *Human Rights Code*, 1990; *Saskatchewan Human Rights Code*, 1978). Canadians understand that Canada's political unity is entangled with the constitutional position of the English and French languages because of power and *realpolitik*: Either of the linguistic communities can fracture the country (Trudeau, 1968). A central underpinning of Canada's language rights system is the intent to capture the loyalty of the language communities for the benefit of the Federal State. The system aspires to make each community feel that the machinery of government emanates from them.

The Canadian Charter of Rights and Freedoms entrenches important components of the language rights system. Sections 17 to 20 of the Charter guarantee five separate language rights: (a) the language of the legislature, (b) the language of statutes, (c) the language of legislative records and journals, (d) the language of the courts, and (e) the language of government services.

*The Language of the Legislature.* Section 17 of the Charter of Rights and Freedoms provides that "everyone has the right to use English or French in any debates or other proceedings of Parliament." In *Jones v. A.G.N.B.* (1975), Chief Justice Laskin interpreted similar wording in Section 133 of the Constitution Act (1867). Section 133, said Chief Justice Laskin, "provid[es] a guarantee to members of the ... Legislature ... that they are entitled to use either French or English in parliamentary or legislative assembly debates."

---

[17]Sections 16–23 of the Charter broadened the constitutional language rights of Canada's English and French language communities.

***The Language of Statutes.*** Section 18 of the Charter of Rights and Freedoms states that "the statutes … of Parliament shall be printed and published in English and French and both language versions are equally authoritative." This requires a bilingual enactment process, as well as the use of both languages in the products of that process. In the *Manitoba Language Rights Reference*, [1985] 1 S.C.R. 721, the Supreme Court of Canada outlined the requirements of the bilingual enactment process. There must be simultaneity of the use of English and French throughout the process of enacting bills into law. This means that both languages must be used simultaneously at all stages of the progress of a bill through the legislature, from introduction at first reading through to Royal Assent.

***The Language of Records and Journals.*** Section 18 of the Charter of Rights and Freedoms requires bilingualism in the "records and journals of Parliament." The constitutional command "impos[es] an obligation of the use of English and French in the records and journals." (*Jones v. A.G.N.B.*, 1975)[18] Section 18 was derived from section 133 of the Constitution Act (1867). The meaning of the "records and journals" clause of section 133 was considered by Chief Justice Deschênes in *Blaikie v. A.G. Que.* (1978) in reasons specifically approved by the Supreme Court of Canada. Chief Justice Deschênes held that the phrase "records and journals" embraces five separate items: minute books, journals, votes and proceedings, bills, and laws adopted.

***The Language of the Courts.*** Section 19 of the Charter of Rights and Freedoms stipulates that "either English or French may be used by any person in, or in any pleading in or process issuing from, any courts established by Parliament." This creates "a constitutionally based right to any person to use English or French" (*Jones* v. *A.G.N.B.*, 1975) in court pleadings, processes and oral argument (*Blaikie* v. *A.G. Que.*, 1979).

Section 19(1) applies to "any Court established by Parliament," whereas Section 19(2) applies to "any court of New Brunswick." The analogous language in Section 133 of the *Constitution Act* (1867) is to "all or any of the Courts of Quebec." The Supreme Court made clear in *Blaikie* that such provisions are not limited to section 96 courts (whose judges are federally appointed), but extends also to "Courts established by the Province and administered by provincially-appointed Judges." No Federal, Quebec, New Brunswick, or Manitoba court, therefore, is exempt from the discipline of these provisions.

---

[18]In the *Manitoba Language Rights Reference*, 1985, the Supreme Court stated that the commands of section 133 "are obligatory" in the sense that "they must be observed."

# 8. LANGUAGE RIGHTS THEORY

*Language of Government Services.* The Charter of Rights and Freedoms provides for the language of Federal and New Brunswick government services. Section 20 requires bilingual capability in all federal institutions at their "head or central offices" and at "other offices" if "there is a significant demand" for bilingual services, or if "the nature of the office" suggests that a bilingual capability would be "reasonable."[19] This provision entrenches section 9 of the federal Official Languages Act (1969), but on a substantially broader base. Under the Official Languages Act (1969), regional offices were required to provide bilingual capability in areas of significant demand only "to the extent ... feasible."[20]

*Language of the Private Sector.* The right to use English or French in private discourse arises from the fact that government is restrained from interfering with individual language choices, such as freedom of expression. Freedom of expression is protected by Section 2(b) of the *Charter of Rights and Freedoms*, analogous sections of the provincial Human Rights Codes, and certain obligations Canada has incurred under the international system for the protection of human rights. The Supreme Court has interpreted these guarantees as disentitling governments from restricting the use of English and French (*Devine* v. *Quebec*, 1988; *Ford* v. *Quebec*, 1988).

## The Actors

Canada's language rights system is a formidable agglomeration of power involving all elements of the governmental structure. Like all concentrations of governmental power, the system attracts groups and individuals seeking to promote their self-interest. As a consequence, many actors seek access to the language rights system as its various components are placed in motion. The system allocates power and resources, including jobs and governmental services, which all want. The system also impacts on the survival of Canada's linguistic communities because it is designed as a counterweight to demographic forces. So operation of the system tends to be highly charged politically. Actors in the system seek to maximize their interests in an environment of sometimes great volatility.

The official languages policy attracts exploitation by the politically opportunistic. Little politicians try to make political hay by exploiting the antagonisms that inhere in longstanding competition between the lan-

---

[19]"Any offices" of New Brunswick government institutions are bound by the same requirements attaching to federal head offices (Charter, §. 20(2)).

[20]Section 22(b) of the 1988 amendment to the *Official Languages Act* (1988) now states that "every federal institution has the duty to ensure that any member of the public can communicate with and obtain services ... in either official language ... [in] any of its other offices or facilities ... in Canada or elsewhere, where there is significant demand for communications with and services from that office or facility in that language."

guage communities. Opportunists encourage the communities to fear or attack each other ("Doern Warns of Turmoil," 1984; "Maverick Quits Manitoba," 1984).

The system seeks to moderate this conflict and make it more manageable. To this end the system diverts highly charged intergroup competition into bureaucratic processes and cumbersome legal procedure. In theory, bureaucratic and legal channels buy time while steam goes out of charged feelings. Enforcement of strict bureaucratic and judicial lines try to make most forms of race baiting unprofitable for the little politician. This is Canada's solution to overheated linguistic competition: ultrageneral legal guarantees and bureaucratic processes mediated by political and legal elites to the end of better intergroup relations in the Canadian state (Lijphart, 1977).

## CANADA'S RECORD WITH ITS LANGUAGE RIGHTS SYSTEM

Canada has now had almost 30 years of experience with the official languages policy. During this time, Canadian governments adapted many of their administrative practices to the discipline of the policy and in so doing refined, renovated, and operated a complex system of linguistic guarantees. In the same period, and for the first time, the Supreme Court of Canada expounded a modest official languages jurisprudence.

Management of linguistic conflict in Canada is an extremely delicate task, requiring as much artistic as bureaucratic skill. A by-product of the official languages policy is that highly competitive energies are subjected to institutional control. This creates charged feelings and symbolic meanings. Substance and symbol combine together in the pathways of control in a sometimes volatile mix, which on occasion detonates.

After considering the considerable experience with and adaptation of the official languages policy, it must be concluded that Canada is not conspicuously successful at managing relations between the linguistic communities. The official languages policy remains controversial—more controversial than at its inception in 1969. The Citizens' Forum on Canada's Future (1991) reported that "the majority outside Quebec express severe opposition to the implementation of Canada's policy on official languages, which they often see as unnecessary and irrelevant: "Bilingualism has failed" (p. 65). The policy has brought the federal government into serious conflict with the Government of Quebec. Contemporaneous with federal official languages efforts, Quebec legislated a distinct official *language* policy (Charter of the French Language, 1988; Official Language Act, 1974).

## 8. LANGUAGE RIGHTS THEORY 195

Quebec's policy collided with federal initiatives at critical junctures,[21] producing flashpoints of confrontation throughout the federation. Ottawa has failed to win the support of the other provinces to the federal view. The other provinces have refused to make significant progress in the channels cut by Ottawa. At least some of the current centrifugal pressures on the Canadian Federation implicate official languages policy to a significant degree, whether as cause or effect.

The competitions are also unfair in every Canadian jurisdiction, excluding the federal and New Brunswick governments. The numerically larger community controls the legislature. For obvious reasons, this control advantages it in the economic struggle. Control of the legislature also benefits the numerically larger community in the linguistic struggle. Legislative control gives the larger community control over the instruments of language policy. Canada's experience demonstrates that language policy can have a dramatic impact on linguistic competition. Quebec's *Bills 22* and *101* limited the availability of English language education and the ability to use English within the private marketplace. The legislation was a spectacular success in its own terms. Quebec resolutely attacked the size of the English community, and shriveled it—all through the manipulation of language policy (Magnet, 1995).

Although it is possible to imagine all components of the system of official bilingualism working together harmoniously in pursuit of high-priority public policies, that is not the Canadian reality. The system rarely operates smoothly. Its erratic functioning has produced several spectacular national crises, driving major Canadian communities apart, reverberating in interprovincial and federal–provincial conflict and, on occasion, threatening to incinerate the basis of the national compromises on which Canada's federal system is constructed (Magnet, 1995). These clashes are the result of structural difficulties with the language rights system itself.

It is possible that federal official languages policy would succeed better if more carefully managed by governmental actors. Good management requires a clear vision of the overarching purposes of the policy, including its symbolic overtones. This presupposes the existence of an intelligible network of principles and doctrine.

Yet there is no clear body of principles or doctrine relating to official languages policy. The Commissioner of Official Language (1993) has "criticized the absence of effort on the part of successive federal governments to

---

[21]By declaring French the only official language of Quebec (*Charter of the French Language*, §. 1); by repealing the guarantees of the *Constitution Act (1867)* and the Federal *Official Languages Act* respecting the use of English in the Legislature and courts (§. 7–13); by requiring all intergovernmental communications to be only in French (§. 16); by making French the language of commerce and business, including the only language to be used in signage (chapter VII); by limiting English education to the historic Quebec English (chapter VIII).

clarify and explain, let alone defend, Canada's language policy" (p. 9). Important actors responsible for administering the system view language rights as lacking any principled basis at all. Mr. Justice Jean Beetz, for a majority of the Supreme Court of Canada, considered official language rights as the unprincipled consequence of political compromise, lacking any seminal foundation, and presumably incapable of spawning a coherent juridical doctrine (*MacDonald* v. *City of Montreal*, 1986). Implicit in Justice Beetz's ruling is the view that language rights conflicts are best left to the rough-and-tumble of the political arena, free from traditional purposive exposition by the courts. The Court made clear it would not be a partner in spurring the reform of bureaucratic and legal machinery for regulating linguistic conflict (*MacDonald* v. *City of Montreal*, 1986.[22]; *Société des Acadiens du Nouveau-Brunswick Inc.* v. *Association of Parents for Fairness in Education* "SANB", 1986; As a consequence, the Supreme Court pulled back from its earlier attempt to expound a principled language rights doctrine. The absence of clear and generally accepted language rights doctrine makes implementation and acceptance of Canada's official languages policy much more difficult.

The language rights system requires an intelligible network of principles to attract citizen understanding and loyalty to guide the authorities who operate its various components and to check exploitation by the unscrupulous. Although one would expect articulation of principle to be a constant occupation of judicial and bureaucratic actors in the system, this has not been the case. It is only recently, since the 1965 *Report of the Royal Commission on Bilingualism and Biculturalism*, that language controversy has generated substantial legislative activity, and litigation. As noted by the Commissioner of Official Languages, proponents of the legislation have not met their burden of explanation. They have failed to lay suspicion to rest. The Courts have not bridged the doctrine gap. The resulting political fallout has fractured the coherence of doctrine necessary to operate the system.

One result of the failure to create attractive and inspiring doctrine is that the courts now explain language rights as lacking any principle at all (*MacDonald* v. *City of Montreal*, 1986; *S.A.N.B.* v. *Assoc. of Parents*, 1986). Some academic commentators try to explain language rights with highly refined philosophical theory (see next section for details). Common to this approach is a tendency to ignore the national security dimension that called the official languages policy into being, and the political struggle for power, resources, and survival that continues to surround it on all sides.

---

[22]The earlier attempt appears in the Court's opinion *Reference re Manitoba Language Rights*, 1985.

## PRINCIPLES UNDERLYING THE LANGUAGE-RIGHTS SYSTEM

### Réaume and Green's Principle of Linguistic Security

Réaume and Green (1989) have developed an academically appealing framework for explaining language rights. They say that the principle of "linguistic security" justifies language rights. "To have linguistic security in the fullest sense is to have the opportunity, without serious impediments, to live a full life in a community of people who share one's language" (p. 782; Réaume, 1992). Linguistic security implies "the knowledge that one's language group may flourish and that one may use the language with dignity" (Green, 1987, p. 658). Linguistic security is said to be provided when a speaker is given a secure environment in which to make choices as to language use and in which ethnic identification can have a positive value. The principle of linguistic security, Réaume and Green (1989) said, seeks a free and fair context in which linguistic minorities may derive individual and collective benefits from language use. In such an environment, minority language speakers would be relieved of pressures to abandon their language. The purpose of language rights, the argument concludes, is to create and maintain this environment.

The principle of linguistic security ignores well-understood sociolinguistic phenomena. Réaume and Green (1989) assumed the existence of a "linguistically secure" environment within which individuals may freely live a life within the minority language community. This overlooks the important fact that minority languages are inevitably eroded by majority languages where two or more linguistic communities come into contact (Fishman, 1972; Lachappelle & Henripin, 1982; Veltman, 1983, chapter 12, this volume).[23] Depending on the conditions, contact between languages results in weaker languages being absorbed by stronger languages at rapid rates, approaching 50% in the first generation and 90% in the second generation. There is no known state where overwhelmingly weaker languages are protected from these effects by legal regimes of bilingualism. History has never produced and cannot produce a linguistically secure environment when languages are in contact.

Canada itself is a good example of this phenomenon. For almost 30 years, Canada has administered a robust policy of official bilingualism. Throughout the course of the policy's operation, the weaker French minorities have continued to decline at brisk rates. No tinkering with this regime could have or could now alter this phenomenon. No meddling with an official lan-

---

[23]The Supreme Court of Canada referred approvingly to other aspects of Fishman's sociology of language theory in *Ford v. Quebec* (1988).

guages policy of the Canadian variety could produce linguistic security outside of Canada's bilingual belt. In order to arrest the decline of Canada's language minorities with a view toward creating the state of linguistic security foreseen by Réaume and Green (1989), it would be necessary for Canada to intervene in language planning massively—to coordinate its immigration, economic, demographic, mobility, fertility, and mortality policies with single-minded concentration on language objectives. To conceive that, in Canada's pluralistic society, any Canadian government would act in this way is to take a rapid journey to the other side of the reality principle.

The principle of linguistic security is objectionable for a second reason: It is one-dimensional. The theory of linguistic security seeks to justify language rights on the basis of a single motivating factor. As such, the theory does not account for the complex interactions of the many players within the various components of the system. The theory of linguistic security fails to recognize that language rights do not exist solely for the benefit of linguistic minorities, nor is the linguistic security of the individual minority necessarily the governing consideration in language rights theory.[24] There is a multiplicity of players within the language rights system including the federal government, Quebec, anglophone minorities in Quebec, anglophone majorities in other provinces, francophone minorities outside of Quebec, bilinguals, allophones, and unilinguals. Each of these players have interests to advance in official languages policy. Although some of these interest may seem more legitimate than others to some observers, it is crucial to realize that the system of language rights in Canada seeks to keep the forces emanating from the powerful players in check—to keep peace in the family—to the end of promoting good intercommunity relations and protecting the great seam that binds the Canadian state together. Linguistic security as a single-minded, one-dimensional motivating principle must give way to a more multifaceted approach.

A theory of language rights must also take into account the political realities that the language rights system intends to regulate. Conflict is endemic in the relations between Canada's linguistic communities. Canada's language rights system institutionalizes such conflict because the system presupposes that institutionalization will make the conflict more manageable. Language rights channel what might otherwise be uncontrollable conflict into bureaucratic and legal procedures. All contenders are invited to wage a more refined political struggle. It is for this reason that the federal government funds linguistic minority political lobbies and court challenges in each province. Channeling the various players into political and legal streams is meant to blunt and moderate their conflict. Of course,

---

[24]This is a point made by the Supreme Court of Canada in the *Manitoba Language Rights Reference, supra* note 49. The Court stated that Manitoba language rights were for the benefit of *all* Manitobans, including the Franco-Manitoban minority.

# 8. LANGUAGE RIGHTS THEORY 199

the institutionalization of political and legal channels by these funding measures implies a certain level of conflict. The point is that the language rights system is premised on the inevitability of such conflict. Its contribution is to control it as much as possible, to channel it into manageable political and legal processes in order to prevent it from escaping into unmanageable intercommunal conflict that threatens to tear apart the foundation on which the Canadian state is erected.

The principle of linguistic security would delegitimate actors whose viewpoint is antagonistic to linguistic minorities. This is unrealistic. Quebec is such an actor,[25] and her viewpoint cannot be factored out of the debate. The same is true of some of the provinces with anglophone majorities. This is the paradox of Canada's linguistic demography: English and French are simultaneously majority and minority languages. Viewpoints emanating from the language communities are charged with competition. Those viewpoints cannot be delegitimated or ignored. They must be accommodated in the sense that, *without altering the basic foundations of the system*, their interests must be heard and fairly considered so as to keep language conflict manageable.

## Toward a New Conceptualization of Canada's Language Rights System

The largest object of the Canadian Constitution is the creation of the Canadian State. As considered earlier, Canada was formed out of two nations as a binational state. Binationality (or duality) is a fundamental inspiration of Canada's system of governance. Canada provides institutional machinery, through the official languages policy, to make the binational (or dual) features of the state work better. Canada also portrays the state symbolically, by refracting the official languages policy through the prism of duality. The official languages policy should thus be trumpeted for what it is: an important referent point for Canadian identity and loyalty.

***Duality.*** "Duality" and "distinct society" are different surface manifestations of the same underlying concept. The constitutional origin of distinct society is in the *Report of Quebec's Royal Commission on Constitutional Problems* of 1956. The *Report* observed that French Canadian culture differed from English Canadian culture. French Canadian culture was communal, based on the family and parish, the civil authorities being responsible for integrating all efforts toward common community goals. English Canadian culture was individual and based on personal ideas of happiness, the civil

---

[25]For example, the Quebec government intervened in *Mahe v. Attorney General (Alberta)*, (1990) against the French linguistic minority of Alberta. Similarly, the Franco-Manitobans intervened in *Quebec (Attorney General) v. Collier* (1983) against Quebec's position on language.

authorities being responsible to free individuals for personal pursuits in the belief that enlightened self-interest would ultimately maximize benefits (Quebec, 1956). Ten years later, the Royal Commission on Bilingualism and Biculturalism (1967) observed that Quebec was "a distinct society" because "it has a considerable number of economic institutions" that allow it to act collectively, as formerly it did through the parish (cited in Magnet, 1995, pp. 84–85).

These ideas have many incarnations. The range of their meanings can be discerned in the political declarations of various Quebec Premiers since the Quiet Revolution. A theme that runs throughout all these declarations is the concept of a binational Canada. Quebec premiers ornament the idea of Canada with great rhetorical flourishes about how the Canadian state resulted from the creative act of two linguistic communities, two cultural communities, two nations. Some of the classic formulations of these ideas were in the 1965 speeches that Premier Jean Lesage delivered to the Canadian Club:

> Quebec, as the cornerstone of French Canada, is asking for the equality of Canada's two founding ethnic groups. It is seeking a status that respects its special characteristics. (Lesage, 1965a)

> Quebec, because of its language, its culture, its links with the international French language community, its economic, social and political institutions, its vitality, its desire to survive and especially to flourish, has all the characteristics of a true society. (Lesage, 1965b)

Premier Daniel Johnson (1968) varied the same theme in this way:

> The object of the Constitution must not solely be to federate territories, but also to associate as equals two linguistic and cultural communities, two founding peoples, two societies, two nations in the sociological sense of the term. A Canadian constitution must be the product of an agreement between the two nations that make up the people of Canada, and must recognize the principle of the legal equality of the two cultural communities.

More recently, the notion that Quebec forms a "distinct society" within Canada was put forth in the Meech Lake and Charlottetown Constitutional Accords of 1987 and 1992. The Charlottetown Accord recognized that Quebec's distinctness "includes a French-speaking majority, a unique culture and a civil law tradition" (*Consensus Report on the Constitution*, 1992). Both accords recognized Quebec as a distinct society, acknowledged Quebec's role to preserve and promote its distinct identity, and required that the distinct society recognition influence interpretation of Canada's Constitution. The Charlottetown Accord would also have committed Canadians and their governments to the vitality and development of official language minority communities throughout Canada.

## 8. LANGUAGE RIGHTS THEORY                                                    201

In recent years, the proponents of a renovated Canadian Constitution have been struggling to make duality, distinct society, and vital official language communities fundamental principles of the Canadian constitution. These principles intend to assist Canadians to manufacture the necessary political ententes for the French and English language communities to share a single state. Canada's official languages rights are one of the important settlements inspired by those principles. It would be well for the bureaucratic, judicial, and academic expositors of the official languages policy to explore duality as a primary interpretational principle of Canada's official languages guarantees, and through careful pronouncements to endeavor to embed it deep into Canadian constitutional rhetoric and practice.

**Accommodation.**    Throughout history, Canada's language rights system aspired to reinforce national unity by a tradition of compromise and accommodation, usually at the elite level. We may call this impetus of the system "the principle of accommodation." The principle of accommodation is a technique for managing intergroup conflict. The principle of accommodation invites all actors to the table, and keeps them there talking, lobbying, regulating, and legislating. It is a means of funneling all competing interests into the system where they may be balanced against competing claims, moderated, adjusted, and accommodated.

The principle of accommodation premises that certain elements of the language rights system will be rigidly enforced. These elements are not negotiable in the sense that they are constitutionally entrenched (even if to date the Courts have been less than faithful enforcers of the constitutional guarantees). Above these minimum guarantees the principle of accommodation is flexible. The principle is capable of rationalizing competing interests of actors in the system in order to keep charged political conflict between the language communities manageable.

The principle of accommodation recognizes the multiplicity of players in the system, including the federal government, Quebec, the anglophone linguistic community of Quebec, the anglophone linguistic majorities of the other provinces, the francophone linguistic minorities outside of Quebec, bilinguals throughout Canada, allophones, and unilinguals concerned by extension of the system. Each of these players has interests in language rights. A stable system of language rights endeavors to accommodate all players, in the sense that their views must be heard, rationalized, and—*without altering the minimum guarantees of the language rights system*—accommodated. All players must be kept at the table in order to promote the system's symbolic features, and to keep language conflict manageable.

Mr. Justice Gerald LeDain of the Supreme Court of Canada referred to something akin to this principle when, in commenting *ex cathedra* on the

Court's judgment in *Reference re Manitoba Language Rights* (1985)[26] he described the Court's unusual order in that case as "a boldly creative act of judicial statesmanship." Justice LeDain thought such an act of judicial statesmanship was required because of the "delicate problems of legal theory and judicial policy" that the unusual case implicated in the relations between the Court and the Manitoba government and legislature. He alluded also to the additional problem of encouraging or compelling the Manitoba government to respect its bilingualism obligations (LeDain, 1994). *Reference re Manitoba Language Rights* (1985) presented the Court with the spectacle of a headstrong Manitoba government, propelled by the overwhelming weight of English majority opinion in the Province, wilfully violating the constitutional language rights of the Franco-Manitoban minority, and having done so for approximately 100 years (Magnet, 1994). In this situation the Court did not conceive of its task as single-minded enforcement of the language rights of the Franco-Manitoban minority. Rather, the Court conceived of its task as one of "protecting the ... language rights of all Manitobans, including the Franco-Manitoban minority" (*Reference re Manitoba Language Rights*, 1985), by a boldly creative act of judicial statesmanship. The Court searched for an accommodation between politically aroused communities that *refrained from altering the minimum guarantees of the language rights system*.

## CONCLUSION

Canada lacks a clear, concise explanation of the principles underlying its official languages policy. Government has not filled this void. Given the Supreme Court's ruling that language rights are the products of political compromise devoid of principle, the Courts have backed themselves into a doctrinal corner. It is unlikely that the judges will be able to escape into clear doctrine or stirring symbolism in this generation. Academic doctrine remains equally unsatisfactory. The commentators toil in the tradition of explaining the work of the courts, which preoccupies them with a dead-end jurisprudence. Or they levitate in ultratheoretical logicalizations, cut loose from the propulsion driving official languages policy—good intercommunal relations and national stability.

The minority language communities pay a high price for the failure to develop satisfactory official languages doctrine. They experience daily helter-skelter judicial and bureaucratic administration of their language rights. The Canadian Federation also pays a high price for the doctrinal failings. One of Canada's potent national symbols—a banner of the desire of Canada's two national communities to do great things together in a

---

[26]Justice LeDain's comment appeared in a later article (LeDain, 1994).

# 8. LANGUAGE RIGHTS THEORY 203

binational state—is sullied, delegitimated, treated as a dirty little secret which history has made Canadians to suffer.

I offer duality and accommodation as principles inspiring Canada's language rights system—as bedrock principles. Duality informs the institutional machinery that invites two nations to share a single state. Accommodation accepts that a dual state overflows with intercommunal competition. Accommodation urges overheated linguistic competition into bureaucratic and legal processes where its sociopathic dimensions can be blunted and moderated, and its legitimate competing claims tested against each other, adjusted, and accommodated.

Duality and accommodation strive to keep language activists committed to the Canadian state. Duality and accommodation provide the operators of the language rights system with doctrine that history teaches best serves to keep language conflict manageable. Duality and accommodation provide the operators of Canada's official languages policy with doctrine that enhances the symbolic features of language rights. Duality and accommodation imbue language rights with the spirit of a big Canada, open and inviting to both national communities, in which the communities recognize and affirm themselves, their nation, and their state.

## REFERENCES

*An Act Recognizing the Equality of the Two Official Linguistic Communities in New Brunswick.* S.N.B. 1981, c. O–1.1.

*Blaikie v. A.G. Que.* (1978). C.S. 37 (Que. S.C.), 85 D.L.R. (3d) 252, at 258, aff'd in [1979] 2 S.C.R. 1016.

*Canadian Human Rights Act,* R.S.C. 1985, c. H–6.

*Charter of the French Language,* R.S.Q. 1977, c. C–11, *as am.* S.Q. 1988, c. 54.

Citizens' Forum on Canada's Future. (1991). *Report.* Ottawa: Supply and Services.

Commissioner of Official Languages. (1990). *Annual report 1990.* Ottawa: Supply and Services.

Commissioner of Official Languages. (1993). *Annual report 1993.* Ottawa: Supply and Services.

*Consensus Report on the Constitution.* (1992, August 28). Ottawa: Supply and Services.

*Constitution Act.* (1867), 30 & #1 Vict., c. 3 (formerly *British North America Act,* 1867).

*Constitution Act.* (1982). Being Schedule B of the *Canada Act 1982* (U.K.), c. 11.

*Courts of Justice Act.* (1984). S.O. 1984, c. 11.

*Criminal Code,* R.S.C. 1985, c. C–34.

Dawson, R. M. (1987). *The government of Canada* (5th ed.). Toronto: University of Toronto.

*Devine v. Quebec.* (1988) 2 S.C.R. 790.

Doern Warns of Turmoil. (1984, June 6). *Winnipeg Free Press.*

Fishman, J. A. (1972). *The Sociology of language: An interdisciplinary social science approach to language in society.* Rowley, MA: Newbury House.

Fishman, J. A. (1986). Bilingualism and Separatism. *Annals, AAPSS, 487.*

*Ford v. Quebec,* (1988). 2 S.C.R. 712.

*French Language Services Act,* R.S.O. (1990). c. F.32, *as am.* S.O. 1993, c. 27, Sch.

Green, L. (1987). Are language rights fundamental? *Osgoode Hall Law Journal, 25,* 639.

*Human Rights Act,* R.S.B.C. (1979). c. 22.

*Human Rights Act,* R.S.N.B. (1986). c. H–11.

*Human Rights Code*, R.S.O. (1990). c. H. 19, *as am.* S.O. 1993, c. 27, Sch.

*International Covenant on Civil and Political Rights* (1966). *Canada Treaty Series, 47* (1976).

Johnson, D. (1968). Opening speech. Reprinted in *Le gouvernement du Québec et la Constitution.* Quebec City: Office d'information et de publicité du Québec.

*Jones v. A.G.N.B.* (1975). 2 S.C.R. 182.

Joy, R. J. (1992). *Canada's official languages: The progress of bilingualism.* Toronto: University of Toronto Press.

Lachapelle, R., & Henripin, J. (1982). *The demolinguistic situation in Canada: Past trends and future prospects.* Montreal: Institute for Research on Public Policy.

Language in Canada. (1989). *Canadian Social Trends, 12.*

LeDain, J. (1994). Jean Beetz as judge and colleague, *Révue Juridique Thémis, 28,* 721.

Lesage, J. (1965, September 22). Speech delivered to the Canadian Club.

Lesage, J. (1965, October 1). Speech delivered to the Canadian Club.

Lijphart, A. (1977). *Democracy in plural societies.* New Haven, CT: Yale University Press.

MacDonald, J. A. (1907) Speech in the Provincial Parliament of Canada. Reprinted in H. E. Egerton & W. L. Grant (Eds.), *Canadian constitutional development* (pp. 362–363). Toronto: Musson.

*MacDonald v. City of Montreal.* (1986). 1 S.C.R. 460.

Magnet, J. E. (1995). *Official languages of Canada.* Montreal: Les Editions Yvons Blais.

Magnet, S., & Magnet, J. E. (1986). Mobility rights: Personal mobility and the Canadian economic union. In M. Krasnick (Ed.), *Perspectives on the Canadian economic union* (Vol. 60). Toronto: University of Toronto Press.

*Mahe v. A.G. Alberta.* (1990). 1 S.C.R. 344.

*Manitoba Act.* (1870). S.C. 1870 (3d. Sess.), c. 3., reprinted in R.S.C. 1970, App. II at 247 (No. 8).

Maverick quits Manitoba NDP over French-rights issue. (1984, March 8). *Montreal Gazette.*

Meech Lake Accord. (1987, June 3). Meeting of the First Ministers on the Constitution.

Mortgage Brokers Act, R.S.B.C. 1979, c. 283.

Northwest Territories Act. (1877). R.S.C. 1886, c. 50.

Notaries Act. R.S.B.C. (1979). c. 299, *as rep.* S.B.C. 1981, c. 23, *as am.* S.B.C. 1985, c. 68.

Official Languages Act. R.S.C. 1970, c. O–2, *as am.* R.S.C. 1985, c. 31, *as am.* S.C. 1988, c. 38.

*Official Languages Act,* S.Q. 1974, c. 6.

*Official Languages Act,* S. C. 1988, c. 38.

*Official Languages of New Brunswick Act,* R.S.N.B. 1973, c. O-1.

*Pesticide Control Act,* R.S.B.C. 1979, c. 322.

Quebec. (1956). *Report of the Royal Commission of Inquiry on Constitutional Problems.* Quebec City: Author.

*Quebec (Attorney General) v. Collier.* (1983). C.S. 366 (Que. S.C.).

Quebec's CF-18 Triumph. (1986). *Maclean's, 99*(1).

*Re Resolution to Amend the Constitution.* (1981). 1 S.C.R. 753.

Real Estate Act, R.S.B.C. (1979). c. 356, *as am.* S.B.C. 1984, c. 26.

Réaume, D. (1992). *The right to linguistic security: Reconciling individual and group claims.* Paper presented at the Language Rights Conference, University of Ottawa.

Réaume, D., & Green, L. (1989). Education and Linguistic Security in the Charter. *McGill Law Journal, 34,* 777–782.

*Reference re Manitoba Language Rights.* (1985). 1 S.C.R. 721.

Royal Commission on Bilingualism and Biculturalism. (1967). *Book I: General Introduction.* Ottawa: Queen's Printer.

*Saskatchewan Human Rights Code.* R.S.S. (1978). c. S–24.1.

*Société des Acadiens du Nouveau-Brunswick Inc. v. Association of Parents for Fairness in Education,* [1986] 1 S.C.R. 549.

Statistics Canada. (1992). *Home language and mother tongue.* Ottawa: Queen's Printer.

## 8. LANGUAGE RIGHTS THEORY                                                    205

Statistics Canada. (1993a). *The Daily*. Ottawa: Queen's Printer.
Statistics Canada. (1993b). *Home language and mother tongue*. (Cat. No. 93–317). Ottawa.
*Supreme Court of Canada Act*. R.S.C. (1985). c. S-26.
Trudeau, P. E. (1968). *Federalism and the French Canadians*. Toronto: MacMillan.
University of Ottawa Act. (1965). S.O. 1965, c. 137.
Veltman, C. (1983). *Language shift in the United States*. New York: Mouton.
Waddell, C. (1986, November 1). Jet repair contract stirs bitterness. *Globe and Mail*.

# IV

# Educational Perspectives

Education usually plays a major part in language policy in modern countries. Canada and the United States are no exceptions. Prime examples are French and English as mediums of instruction in schooling for francophones outside of Quebec and anglophones in Quebec as related to the Official Languages Act and the Charter of Rights and Freedoms in Canada, and the various allocations of federal funding in the United States for special language treatment in education for minority language or Limited English Proficiency children in schools. However high profile some provisions may be currently, there is always a broad range of issues percolating along—some localized, some involving specific groups of people, some attracting very little attention. The winds of local, national, and international change stir some of them up from time to time. Stakeholders appear in each with a variety of vested interests. It seems that solutions to what are perceived to be language problems are usually couched in either/or terms rather than both/and. In other words, solutions are generally proposed or at least understood in such a way that benefit to one party is seen to be a loss to another. When it comes to public education, matters concerning the power of the majority language over a minority language are often deflected into debates on the limitations of public funds. However, other factors than resources sometimes drive discussion and action.

In Part IV, Wiley (chapter 9) and Burnaby (chapter 10) have turned their attention to quite different areas of the language policy in education field. Wiley's chapter provokes reflection on the motives behind our stances in current language debates by reminding us of our history. He provides a comprehensive picture of the ways in which the German language has been treated in the United States and Canada up to the period just after World

**207**

War I. This portrait makes us think about our own potential for prejudice and bigotry as we read about how our forebears were influenced by racial attitudes and international politics to create conflict and act repressively in situations that have many parallels to our present one. Although German was a large presence in the linguistic mix of both countries at the turn of the century, these acts of repression have virtually eliminated it as a domestic language today. Not only public schools but universities and religious organizations were deeply affected in the process.

Wiley focuses on the historical difficulties experienced by immigrants and citizens in maintaining and using the languages of their heritage, whereas Burnaby turns in a different direction to consider how new immigrants to Canada and the United States are provided with opportunities to learn English as a majority language. Her account reaches back only as far as the 1960s and focuses on current policies and programs in place in both countries. The range of potential learners is narrowed to adults, but those from any language and educational background are considered. Her emphasis is on the structure of Canadian policies and how these compare and contrast with those of the United States. However, as Wiley points out, one cannot appreciate current policies without understanding their historical roots, which can shape them as much as current political and social movements. Thus contrasts between Canadian and American colonial periods, constitutions, and immigration histories are reflected in differences that exist in the present. Although there are undoubtedly lessons that each country can learn from the other, any attempts by one to emulate the other will inevitably encounter structural differences that are hard to work around.

In the circumstances described by Wiley, governments actively moved to suppress the minority language. Although elementary, secondary, and postsecondary education were important focuses of the policies, education itself was not the central issue. Thus, the press and religious institutions were involved as well. The real target was people of a specific nationality, and language became a symbol of that nationality. Governments created policies where none had been before in order to act on a people that had not previously been seen as a threat. In Burnaby's chapter, the focus is directly on education. In Canada in the 1960s, the federal government chose to offer training in official languages to immigrant adults to help integrate them into the economy. Now, in the 1990s and in much more straightened circumstances, the federal government is trying to find ways to withdraw that support and give the matter back to the provinces and nongovernmental organizations who dealt with it on their own before. Any disputes about the presence of the immigrants themselves are concentrated on employment and racism; the profile of language training is low. The language itself is not at issue, just access to it through training.

## IV. EDUCATIONAL PERSPECTIVES

Many other features of language policy in education could be compared between Canada and the United States. Indeed, suggestions about a number of them come up in other chapters in this book. The strategies for analysis used in the two chapters in Part IV provide important frameworks for addressing other situations. First, it is not possible to truly make sense of current issues of language in education without understanding the historical acts and processes that have formed present situations and which shape our unconscious attitudes. Second, policies, legislation, and constitutions form a complex framework that restricts any new policy development and resource allocation.

# 9

# The Imposition of World War I Era English-Only Policies and the Fate of German in North America

Terrence G. Wiley
*California State University, Long Beach*

### OVERVIEW

For over three centuries German immigrants have been arriving in North America. In the United States, those of German ancestry now comprise a principal component of the national population. They have also been an important factor in growth in the Canadian population. Yet today, with the exception of a few tourist-oriented German enclaves in urban areas, and save for the persistence of a small number of deutschephones in some rural areas, the German language and culture have left only a faint mark on the dominant culture. Given the extent of German migration to North America, the question can be raised as to why the influence of the German language and German culture is not more apparent.

A popular answer is that Germans easily assimilated because they saw the value of learning English and "American" ways. A detached analysis of data related to language shift and language loss across generations supports the view that linguistic assimilation into English has been routine.

211

Although a considerable amount of empirical data supports this view, a careful review of the historical experience of German Americans—not to mention that of many other groups—indicates that there is much more to their story. Just as there are push-and-pull factors that have influenced immigration, so too are there similar factors that have affected the linguistic and cultural assimilation of those of German origin. However, to frame issues only in terms of English linguistic assimilation is to overlook an important aspect of language minority experience, namely the development and maintenance of bilingualism and biculturalism.

As I have argued elsewhere (Wiley, 1996a, 1996b; Wiley & Lukes, 1996), the ideological dominance of English monolingualism influences the way in which many scholars from the United States and other English dominant countries frame their research questions about language minorities. When researchers assume that an intergenerational shift to English is inevitable, they often narrow the scope of their research questions to a focus on the acquisition of English and thereby fail to consider bilingualism and biculturalism as legitimate alternatives to monolingualism and monoculturalism. Thus, strong empirical arguments have been made for the unidirectional shift from other languages toward English (e.g., Veltman, 1983). Given the preoccupation with the rate of assimilation to English, there has neither been much concern for documenting the development of societal bilingualism nor for analyzing the forces that work against it.

In exploring the fate of German in the United States, this analysis utilizes a historical-structural approach (Tollefson, 1991; Wiley, 1996a). This approach assumes that the formation of language policies and language attitudes are best studied within broad historical sociopolitical and socio-economic contexts. In developing this discussion, the pioneering work of Leibowitz (1969, 1971, 1974) has also been influential in underscoring the need for an analysis of language policy across multiple domains including education, religion, and the popular media.[1]

Language policies have rarely been implemented strictly as ends in themselves; rather, they have been used as means to achieve other purposes. They are often instruments of social control in struggles between groups. As Leibowitz (1974) noted, policies imposed during periods of major political extremism have been used to settle old scores and have had consequences well beyond the era of their imposition. In developing these conclusions, this chapter challenges popular myths (Wiley, 1986) that (a)

---

[1]Macías' (1992) work on indigenous language policies has also been contributory, as it underscores some of the limitations of the dominant immigrant paradigm which frequently assumes that linguistic assimilation is an inevitable rite of passage (see Kloss, 1971, and Wiley & Lukes, 1996, for further discussion of the immigrant paradigm). Finally, Leibowitz (1969; see also McKay & Weinstein-Shr, 1993) called attention to the persistence of English language and literacy policies as "gatekeepers" to social access and economic participation.

# 9. WORLD WAR I ERA ENGLISH-ONLY POLICIES 213

former language minority groups eagerly learned English and gladly surrendered their native languages in exchange for assimilation; and (b) that their willing submission to Anglification and Americanization led to national unity and cultural harmony.

These myths are confronted by concentrating on the historical development of German as an immigrant minority language in the United States and then by analyzing the impact—both immediate and long term—of anti-German language policies of World War I in both the United States and Canada. Legal ramifications of the imposition of English-only policies and other restrictionist policies are explored, and the implications of the German American experience for other language minority groups are briefly considered.

As McClymer (1982) has noted, the major events of the World War I era are typically studied singularly with each separately being seen as a radical departure from normalcy. Among the important events of the era were:

> The antihyphenism (immigrants were commonly called "hyphens") of the 1916 presidential campaign, the sedition and espionage prosecutions of 1917–18, the Red Scare of 1919–20, the immigration restriction laws of 1921 and 1924, and the "American Plan" of antiunionism of the early and mid-1920s ... , the growth of the American Legion, [and] the rebirth of the Ku Klux Klan (p. 97)

McClymer added: "However abnormal these events may seem when seen in isolation" they were "part of the general politicization of culture which the period of 1914–25 bequeathed to the rest of twentieth century America" (p. 97). Its mark is still evident in popular attitudes and ideologies toward language and cultural diversity as the rage of "official English" initiatives of the late 1980s and the anti-immigrant initiatives of the 1990s, and recent manifestations of "Hispanophobia" (Crawford, 1992a) bear witness.

## GERMAN AS AN IMMIGRANT-MINORITY LANGUAGE: 18TH CENTURY TO WORLD WAR I

From a historical perspective, languages in North America can be categorized as indigenous, old colonial, later immigrant, and creoles resulting from language contact.[2] Indian languages fall into the first category. English, Spanish, French, German, Russian, Swedish, and Dutch, for example, are called "colonial" because they were the languages spoken by colonists

---

[2] African American language during the colonial period is probably best categorized with creoles. Enslaved African Americans were involuntary immigrants (see Ogbu & Matute-Bianchi, 1986, and Gibson & Ogbu, 1991, for further discussion of this term). Unlike European colonists, African Americans were subjected to policies of forced language eradication of the native tongues as well as a policy of "compulsory ignorance" with respect to English literacy (see Weinberg, 1995).

**214** WILEY

(see Fishman, 1966; Molesky, 1988; and Ricento, 1996). Further distinctions may also be made between old imperial languages, that is, colonial languages with armies, and other colonial languages. Spanish, for example, was an official imperial language imposed on conquered peoples in the Spanish colonial empire, whereas English was a dominant—but unofficial—imperial language used for official purposes throughout the English colonies—even though "England's policy-makers did not consider language problems in their determination of policies for their New World colonies" (Heath, 1992, p. 20; see also Heath, 1976, 1981).

## German in the Colonial Period

Because German was not an imperial language in North America, its development is similar to that of other minority immigrant languages. German colonists were linguistic minorities who immigrated to colonies dominated by the English. The earliest German settlement in the colonies was established in 1683 (Conzen, 1980). Thirteen Mennonite and Quaker families "from the German town of Krefeld" arrived in Philadelphia and "founded the community of Germantown" (Castellans, 1992, p. 15). The majority of the early German immigrants to North America (immigrating from the late 17th through the 18th centuries) were religious refugees. Their education was largely sectarian and privately funded, and German was typically the primary language of instruction (Leibowitz, 1974).

Prior to the American Revolution some sentiment was expressed, most notably by Benjamin Franklin, against German reluctance to use English. In a 1753 letter to a member of Parliament, Franklin (1753/1992) complained, "Few of their children in the Country learn English; they import many Books from Germany." Franklin's ethnic and class biases were evident as he stated:

> Those [Germans] who come hither are generally the most ignorant Stupid Sort of their own Nation, and as Ignorance is often attended of Credulity when Knavery would mislead it, and with Suspicion when Honesty would set it right; as few of the English understand the German Language, and so cannot address them either from the Press or Pulpit, 'tis almost impossible to remove any prejudices they once entertain. (p. 19)

Evidence suggests that Franklin's prejudices against the Germans and their language were rooted in social and economic considerations. Earlier, in 1732, he had failed in an effort to launch his own German-language newspaper, and he dropped other German-language publishing ventures due to the success of a German competitor (Crawford, 1992b). Franklin had also introduced German along with French in 1749 as an elective in his Academy (Moore, 1937). He also had reservations about the "pacifist

# 9. WORLD WAR I ERA ENGLISH-ONLY POLICIES 215

disinclination" of Germans to fight Indians (Crawford, 1992b, p. 9). In later years Franklin dropped his stridency toward the use of German. Quite expectedly, despite his protestations, German continued to be used in areas where German immigrants were concentrated.

## German in the Revolutionary and Early Republican Periods

During the American Revolution, as Heath (1992) and Crawford (1992b) have noted, the Continental Congress had liberally translated important documents into German and French believing that Enlightenment "ideas of political liberty were universal, after all, and there was no reason to restrict their expression to English" (Crawford, 1992b, p. 9). In the early years of the Republic, German was in an analogous position to that of Spanish in the United States today. Germans were highly concentrated in some regions of the new country, with the largest concentration in southeastern Pennsylvania (Gilbert, 1981). According to Crawford (1992c), by "1787 German Americans represented a proportion of the population comparable to that of Hispanics today (8.6 percent versus 9.0 percent)." Moreover, "They took pride in the German language and culture, resenting Ben Franklin's efforts to 'Anglify' their children." Recognizing the reality of linguistic and cultural diversity among the Republic's new citizens, the Framers of the Constitution "declined to give English official status in our Constitution or to stop printing public documents in German." According to Crawford this was no oversight: "The prevailing view, then and throughout most of our history, was that a democratic government has no business telling the people how to talk" (p. 177). However, despite the framers' original intentions, Molesky (1988) noted that "silence of the Constitution on language matters has had two opposing ramifications" (p. 35). For some, it seems to encourage toleration for minority languages whereas leaving open the question of language minority rights, whereas others have interpreted its silence on language matters as opening for language restrictionism and the imposition of English-only policies (see also Piatt, 1992).

## The Early 19th Century (1800 to 1835)

The early 19th century was marked by language tolerance and by official recognition of language choice (Macías, 1992). Following the end of the Napoleonic wars, of which the War of 1812 was only a part, German immigration to the United States increased. However, unlike the German religious refugees of the 18th century, those of the newer generation were more likely to be political refugees. The majority sought farmland and settled in the—then—western states of Indiana, Illinois, Ohio, Wisconsin,

Minnesota, Michigan, Iowa, and Missouri. Because Germans tended to be the majority in many regions of these states, the German language was maintained, and school laws were usually agnostic on the issue of language of instruction (Kloss, 1977; Leibowitz, 1971, 1974; Macías, 1992). German was also widely used as the language of schooling because most teachers in these areas spoke German (Macías, 1992).

## The Mid-19th Century (1836 to the Civil War)

By the 1830s, mass immigration was increasing partly in response to structural changes in the U.S. economy. Many immigrants were economically hard-pressed on arrival and became concentrated in the urban areas of the Northeast. The newly arrived:

> Down-and-out immigrants often looked like the dregs of humanity. In their first years here they were weighed down by poverty. Driven by want and by the desire for familiar languages and faces, those who stayed in cities moved into the ghettos that developed in the 1830s and 1840s (Pitt, 1976, p. 281)

Such was New York's Kleindeutschland, which was the home of some 100,000 Germans. Economic competition between groups was often manifested in interethnic social conflict (Macías, 1992).

During this period, language became more salient as an identifier of group membership. "Rather than being taken for granted as part of being an immigrant, it became one of the markers of being an immigrant" (Macías, 1992, p. 5). Language prejudice was exacerbated by religious bigotry. Anglo-Saxon Protestants considered Germans notorious "Sabbath breakers" who sacrilegiously enjoyed beer drinking, theater, music, and dancing on Sunday, as was the custom in Europe (Pitt, 1976). Facing stigmatization for their "foreign" languages and manners and lacking integration in their adopted land, Germans and other immigrants formed mutual aid societies and developed their own social and educational infrastructures. German immigrants "made the strongest efforts to retain their Old World ways. German ghettos supported their own churches, schools, restaurants, libraries, and beer halls. The 40 German-language newspapers in the U.S. in 1840 had increased to 133 by 1852" (p. 281).

Gradually, language tolerance and the right to language choice were no longer taken as given. The first major linguistic challenge came in Ohio during the late 1830s when an attempt was made to end instruction in German. Germans responded at the polls by backing Democratic candidates and used their political clout to ensure the continued use of German—but not to the exclusion of English. As a result, in 1837 German was put on an equal basis with English. In 1840 German Americans also

# 9. WORLD WAR I ERA ENGLISH-ONLY POLICIES

succeeded in the having German-language instruction allowed in the first German public school in 1840 (Leibowitz, 1974; see also Schlossman, 1983).

Prior to the Civil War, anti-Catholic and anti-immigrant sentiment increased dramatically. "Catholic demands for state aid to parochial schools and their protests against the use of the Protestant Bible in the public schools caused violent reaction" (Pitt, 1976, p. 283). In 1844, anti-Catholic violence in Philadelphia culminated in the burning of two Catholic churches and many Irish Catholic homes. Thirteen were killed and more than 50 were injured. Because a substantial portion of the German American population was Catholic, they too became targets of ethnoreligious bigotry.

Antebellum Nativism peaked in the 1850s under the leadership of the aptly named Know-Nothing party, which, by 1854, had succeeded in electing a number of governors and congressional and state representatives. Among its more ambitious goals was a 21-year naturalization period (Pitt, 1976). Abraham Lincoln's comments regarding the party reflected the sentiments of liberals of the period when he stated: "When the Know-Nothings get control, it [the Declaration of Independence] will read all men are created equal, except *negroes and foreigners and Catholics*" (p. 284). With the coming of the Civil War, the Know-Nothing movement and its attacks on immigrants and Catholics ended.

## Late 19th and Early 20th Centuries (1870s to 1914)

After the Civil War much of the nation's politics were preoccupied first with Reconstruction and transcontinental expansion, and later with massive industrialization and then imperialism as manifested in the Spanish American War (1898). Imperialistic endeavors turned brutal as the United States forcibly put down the Philippine Insurrection (1899–1902). German immigration peaked in the last three decades of the 19th century as nearly 2.8 million[3] entered the country, but it then declined sharply in the first two decades of the 20th century when fewer than 500,000 Germans immigrated (Pitt, 1976).

Kloss (1977), in his encyclopedic study of language policies in the United States, concluded that 19th-century language policies were, for the most part, tolerance-oriented. Although Kloss marshaled a considerable body of evidence in making this case, Macías (1992) noted that there is also an indication that the tolerance was applied selectively to certain groups. He suggested that tolerance was not arbitrary; rather, it was calculated. For Germans and other European immigrants, religious bigotry and economic competition between groups were important contributing factors to inter-

---

[3]It is important to recognize that there was considerable diversity within the German immigrant population. See, for example, Rippley (1980).

group conflicts. As millions of newcomers entered the country, with the new majority coming from eastern and southern Europe, anti-immigration and anti-Catholicism reemerged as a growing force in national politics under the leadership of the American Protective Association (APA). It is important to note that widespread xenophobia and anti-Catholicism co-occurred with the rise of Jim Crowism and the resurgence of racial oppression in the South. Nativist sentiments of the time were reflected in popular magazines and newspapers, which portrayed the public schools as instruments for Anglo-Protestant acculturation. Editorials and political cartoons regularly depicted Catholic schools as tools for the Holy Roman subversion (see Apple & Apple, 1982). In terms of language politics, the period between 1880 and 1900 was significant because "it was during this period that increased repressive and exclusive language legislation was passed by state legislatures" (Macías, 1992, p. 13).

Largely because of its association with Catholic education, the German language increasingly became a target of Anglocentric school legislation in the East and Midwest during the 1880s. "As a result of the legislation requiring English as the only medium of instruction in the public schools and the anti-alien German feeling, the Germans developed large numbers of new private and religious schools" that displaced public schools (Macías, 1992, p. 14). In 1886, 65% of students receiving German instruction were being educated in parochial and secular private schools—38% were receiving instruction in Catholic schools, 23% in Protestant schools, and 4% in private schools (Conzen, 1980). Because "German instruction in the public schools was always precarious" only the parochial schools and rural schools were effective in keeping "the second generation within the cultural fold" (p. 420). Nevertheless, to compete with the loss of students to these schools, many public schools offered instruction in German.

In an effort to counter the German retreat from public education, a number of states passed laws banning sectarian books in an effort to thwart Catholic education. Between 1889 and 1890, New York, Ohio, Illinois, Wisconsin, Nebraska, Kansas, and North and South Dakota passed laws prescribing English as the language of instruction, in part because instruction in German was seen as promoting Catholicism (Leibowitz, 1971, 1974). The most noteworthy examples of the new linguistic intolerance were the 1889 Edwards Law of Illinois and the Bennett Law of Wisconsin. These laws clearly attempted to end language tolerance and the right to language choice in education by requiring both public and private elementary schools to use English as the language of instruction.

German Lutherans, who also used German as a medium of instruction, found themselves ensnared in the same anti-German language morass as their Catholic brethren. However, Protestants and Germans had long been

## 9. WORLD WAR I ERA ENGLISH-ONLY POLICIES 219

agreed that "language saves the faith" and had strived to preserve the language as long as possible (Conzen, 1980). In response to the imposition of English-only instruction, a broad coalition of German Lutherans, German and Polish Catholics, Scandinavian Lutherans, and German Free-thinkers voted in Democrats supporting anti-Edwards (in Illinois) and anti-Bennett (in Wisconsin) party platforms. In 1893 both acts were repealed (Leibowitz, 1971, 1974; see also Luebke, 1969). The success of this reversal was largely symbolic, however, as the primacy of English-only instruction had become an accomplished fact (Macías, 1992). By 1900, the public schools were making inroads in the parochial school share of the German language educational market. In that year public schools were educating 42% of students receiving German instruction—a 7% increase over 1886 (Conzen, 1980).

In addition to churches and schools, the press was another visible force in cultural and linguistic preservation. However, according to Conzen (1980), the press was also a force for assimilation because—in addition to using the native language—it also provided information about the dominant culture and how to adapt to it. During the 1880s, German publications accounted for about 80% of the foreign-language press in the United States. "The total peaked at almost 800 in 1893–1894" (p. 420). However, given the decline in immigration, by 1900, German publications had declined to 613.

By the early 20th-century, a number of factors were shaping language policies. Urbanization and industrialization were increasing and public schooling was being extended. Macías (1992) contended that another significant factor was the increasing consolidation of federal control over regional or local ethnic areas. He argued that tolerance-oriented language policies occurred where the federal government's controls were weak. However, more restrictive policies were likely to be implemented where there was an increase in federal control, a rural to urban shift in population, and an increase in migration to an area by English speakers.

## THE FATE OF GERMAN DURING WORLD WAR I

### Culture Wars 1914 to 1917

As noted, German immigration had been declining since the 1880s. Many among the German-American population were assimilating culturally and linguistically into the dominant society. However, at the outbreak of war in Europe, German and other foreign languages were widely used in some areas of the country, particularly in the Great Plains states. In some localities of Nebraska, "German was used more than English," and the ability to speak a foreign language was even considered an important qualification of a good store clerk (Manley, 1959, p. 114). According to Conzen (1980; also see Holli, 1981; Luebke, 1968), the outbreak of war in Europe rekindled ethnic pride and interest in ancestral homelands. "Indeed, the heightened ethnic consciousness of the war years was a boon to German newspapers' and organizations' previous dependence upon a constituency that was rapidly assimilating" (p. 422). The German press proudly took a pro-German stance and editorialized for U.S. neutrality. In 1914, U.S. support for the allies was far from a given. The United States had, after all, fought two wars (the American Revolution and the War of 1812) against England, and England had toyed with the notion of recognizing the South during the Civil War. Moreover, a sizable minority of the U.S. population (about 13%) was either first (2.5%) or second generation (10.5%) German according to the 1910 census.

Initially, there were pro-German mass demonstrations, collections for war relief, and lobbying for arms as well as loan embargoes in German American communities, and German Americans worked to defeat Wilson's reelection as his pro-British sentiments became more evident (Conzen, 1980; Holli, 1981). Nevertheless, Conzen (1980) concluded that for most German-Americans, pro-German activity "was a confirmation rather than a betrayal of their status as full American citizens" (p. 422).

In cities with large immigrant populations such as Chicago, for example, the war in Europe generated "culture wars" among immigrant populations. In 1914, according to Holli (1981), only 750,000 of Chicago's 2.4 million were native-born according to a school census. First- and second-generation Germans (about 400,000) constituted the largest ethnic block. The city also had a large number of Austrians (nearly 59,000) as well as other groups of Irish, Russian-Jewish, and Swedish origin—many of whom had little sympathy toward the Allies. However, there were also some 230,000 of Polish origin and 45,000 of English-origin whose loyalties were with the Allies.

Pro-German sentiment was initially flaunted by many German Americans. When war was declared in Europe, a throng of 5,000 German Americans jubilantly marched to the offices of Chicago's major dailies. Holli (1981) noted that pro-German chauvinists tended to depict the war in ethnically offensive terms by characterizing it as a war between "Slavs and Teutons" and "Western Civilization versus Russian barbarians." Even more inflammatory were their references to "natural serf races," "half-Asiatic barbarians," and backward "hordes of the Muscovite" (p. 411). A number of incidents of interethnic violence occurred amidst the highly volatile climate.

Optimistic about the outcome of the war, hopeful German Americans argued for compulsory German language instruction, believing destiny would ordain it as a world language. However, as the war in Europe raged

## 9. WORLD WAR I ERA ENGLISH-ONLY POLICIES

on, and as the United States moved from a neutral to an increasingly pro-Allies stance, it became apparent that their aspirations would not be realized.

### U.S. Entry Into the War and the Impact of Entholinguistic Intolerance

When the United States entered the war against Germany in 1917, most German Americans were unprepared for the onslaught that was about to befall them. Although the majority of "German-American newspapers and associations quickly declared their loyalty" to the United States, "a storm of anti-Germanism raged between the fall of 1917 and spring 1918" (Conzen, 1980, p. 422; see also Luebke, 1974, for a detailed history of the period).

German Americans became ensnared in both mass hysteria and the attempt of the federal government to ready the U.S. population for "total war." German Americans were blamed and suspected for acts of sabotage. "Certainly German agents were after the food supply as well as the utilities. … And the entire state [of Colorado] was warned [by the *Denver Post*] that sausages (frequently German-made) might contain ground glass" (Dorsett, 1974, p. 281). Among one of their more insidious alleged plots, German Americans were accused of conspiring to subvert Native Americans from their patriotic duty of joining the armed services. When Native Americans in Colorado, Utah, Wyoming, and Nevada opposed the draft, their opposition was not seen as being based "on an understandable disdain for a government that had confiscated their lands. On the contrary, German agents had infiltrated the tribes" (p. 283).

Amidst this climate of purported national vulnerability, state governments were asked to create state councils of defense. According to Manley (1964), in Nebraska, as in other states, the Council of Defense "had been envisioned principally as an agency to mobilize the state's economic resources"; however, it soon became clear that the principal work of the council would involve investigations of loyalty and patriotism. In Nebraska, where more than quarter million of the state's population of about 1.2 million were either German-born (some 57,000) or of German descent (about 201,000), the council had an ample number of "suspects" on which to conduct its work. Several of its members argued that in dealing with "hesitating patriots" the Council "operated under a 'higher law' than the Constitution; that the decisions and actions of the State Council were not subject to judicial review"; and that witnesses interrogated by the counsel had no right to counsel, cross-examination, nor "knowledge of the charges brought" (p. 2).

State councils of defense had several popular targets: schools, universities, churches, and unions. In each case use of the German language was seen as proof of disloyalty. According to Manley (1964), in a confrontation with the Lutheran Missouri Synod the Nebraska State Council argued:

> [It] believed that "the foreign language papers, the sectional school training ... and the Germanic propaganda emanating from pulpits occupied by Kaiser agents" explained the "disloyalty" of the German Lutherans. These "Nebraska caesars"—that is, the German Lutheran pastors—must be curbed and their use of the German language ended. A proper patriotic spirit could never be secured so long as the German language continued to be widely used. (pp. 8–9)

The Nebraska Council applied the same logic regarding the connection between language and loyalty to a number of contexts. For example, it announced that "instruction in schools, worship services in churches, [and] conversations in public and over the telephone must be in English" (Manley, 1964, p. 9). In Jefferson County the local council ordered telephone operators to "cut off parties" who used German (Manley, 1959, p. 114). Cedar County patrons were admonished to refrain from using German so as not to "cause irritation or misunderstanding," and they were issued permits for the use of foreign languages under threat of revocation for abusive overuse (p. 115).

Manley (1959) noted that libraries were another popular target of ethnolinguistic intolerance, and—in some cases—the dominant press itself that led the attack on freedom of expression. In late 1917, for example, the *Lincoln Star*, an ever-zealous advocate for the cause of Americanization, initiated a drive to purge from the Nebraska State Library Commission some 1,000 German-language books. The commission determined that the books were primarily of interest to elderly German Americans. A reporter from the *Star* examined the books and noted that many had been printed in German, which was taken as proof of their propaganda value for Germany because they "were not American books with American ideals translated into German" (Manley, 1959, p. 126). In November of 1917, the Nebraska State Council of Defense voted unanimously to have all German books removed from the public libraries.

Wilcox (1993) observed that universities were also "a favorite target for zealots, who were anxious to believe that faculties harbored political liberals and radicals. Professors at several universities were dismissed on account of their perceived lack of support for America and the Allies" (p. 59). At the University of Michigan most of the German program was dismantled when six of its professors were removed. Wilcox contended that at the heart of the incident "was a conflict over how much ideological diversity Americans would allow in public universities" (p. 60). At Michigan, the German professors were ousted by a coalition of extremist professors who acted in concert with powerful alumni. Together they were able to influence the regents and administration to remove the German faculty. Wilcox con-

## 9. WORLD WAR I ERA ENGLISH-ONLY POLICIES 223

cluded that the World War I era attack on professors of German foreshadowed the academic purges of the 1950s.

As the wave of ethnolinguistic restrictionist efforts swept the country, some 18,000 persons in the Midwest alone were fined for language violations (Crawford, 1995). According to Luebke (1980), in many communities mob rule lead to German Americans being threatened and beaten; some were tarred and feathered; others had their homes and buildings painted yellow as a sign of disloyalty:

> In Texas a German Lutheran Pastor was whipped after he allegedly continued to preach in German. … In South Dakota a county council of defense itself became the object of mob threats when it met to consider the question of granting permits to pastors of German churches to give synopses of their sermons in German at the close of English-language services. In Nebraska a German Lutheran pastor of a Church in Papillion was beaten by a mob. … Schools and churches were ransacked for German-language books. In South Dakota, Yankton high school students were praised for having dumped their German-language textbooks into the Missouri River as they sang the "Star-Spangled Banner." The burning of German-language books as part of super-patriotic exercises occurred in Oakland, Hooper, and Grand Island, Nebraska. In Boulder, Colorado a German-book-burning rally was sponsored by the University of Colorado preparatory school. Early in September 1918, the Lutheran parochial school in Herington, Kansas was destroyed by fire by super-patriots. (pp. 9-10)

In reflecting on the climate of intimidation that it had helped to create, the Nebraska Council of Defense rationalized that "if foreign languages could be abolished … the alien population would be removed from its tenuous and dangerous position" (Manley, 1964, p. 13). In the true spirit of repression, the Council reasoned that it would be better if the removal of German from churches and schools were voluntary in order to "appease 'the ever-increasing prejudice against everything German' which threatened to result in disorder and violence" (p. 14). Pressure for "voluntary" rejection of German took the form of character assassinations, releases from employment, and the boycotting of German-owned business—some 285 of which were boycotted in Colorado alone (Dorsett, 1974).

In Colorado, "jails were full of people who allegedly made pro-German statements or were suspected of spying," and some "were held … for days, and even weeks without due process of law" until they were cleared by the federal Secret Service (Dorsett, 1974, p. 288). Anticipating more stringent measures to be taken against the Japanese in World War II, superpatriotic citizens of Mesa County, Colorado, proposed converting a local Indian school into an interment camp for German Americans. Although their recommendation was not acted on, Ft. Douglas in Utah was used to intern a number of aliens suspected of being national security threats.

Manley (1959) concluded that attacks on German language and culture also had significant consequences for other ethnolinguistic groups. "Restrictions were being placed upon people who had always exhibited the highest patriotism, even though they did not speak English" (p. 165). In Plainview, NE, a resident complained that his Danish-speaking mother, who had been a generous contributor to the Liberty Loan drives, "was now denied the comfort of her religion" (p. 164). Those of Swedish descent likewise suffered. C. A. Lennquist, who headed a home for children, protested to the Council that "to deprive an immigrant of his language was the same as 'digging out his eyes'" (p. 168). Unmoved, the Nebraska Council stayed the course, and its members expressed satisfaction that the state "would soon be *swept clean* of the German language" (p. 172; emphasis added). In the end, the eradication of one's ancestral language became an essential component of Americanization and the rite of passage into the Anglo-American fold—at least for those who would be allowed to assimilate.

The psychological impact of ethnolinguistic repression is impossible to calculate. However, the plea of one Nebraskan woman is telling. Writing directly to President Wilson in 1918, she implored: "'I beg you with all my heart not to make us destroy our language which we have learned from parents and grandparents'" (cited in Manley, 1959, p. 115).

## The Assault on Religious Expression

Those who steadfastly tried to retain their language for religious reasons were especially vulnerable to persecution. Luebke (1980) noted that in several Midwestern states German-speaking Mennonites were viciously attacked for their resolute maintenance of German as well as for their pacifism. In 1918, police narrowly rescued a Mennonite from a mob who had begun hanging him. Elsewhere, Mennonite students were severely ostracized. In the summer of 1918, "some of the most conservative Mennonites of the Great Plains states decided that their status within the United States had become intolerable" (p. 10), and more than 1,500 left the United States seeking refuge in the prairie provinces of Canada.

Zealots were not satisfied with mere ethnolinguistic restrictionism—they demanded public patriotic demonstrations of loyalty. According to Manley (1959), Lutheran ministers and their congregations were singled out and put under intense scrutiny to demonstrate their loyalty. In April of 1918, five Lutheran pastors were denounced for refusing to participate in a Lancaster Council of Defense patriotic rally held in Lincoln. In retaliation the Council threatened to use its influence "against those who had declined to participate" (p. 153). The fanaticism of the attack was noted by the *Nebraska State Journal*, which compared the incident to the New England witch-hunt hysteria.

## 9. WORLD WAR I ERA ENGLISH-ONLY POLICIES

The attempt to coerce Lutheran pastors into patriotic stances compromised their religious views because many felt obligated to maintain the principle of separation of church and state. The Missouri Synod published a pamphlet in its defense that stressed the historical posture of the church. It noted that German Lutherans had fled to the United States in 1838 to escape persecution in their homeland, that the majority of Lutherans were American-born, and that the church had not attempted to rationalize German wartime acts such as the sinking of the Lusitania (Manley, 1959).

Some congregations resisted the imposition of English because many of their members—especially the elderly—could not understand English. In a modest accommodation, the Nebraska State Council moved to allow one day of foreign-language religious service per week. However, given the Anglophone opposition to foreign-language use, "the State Council advised ministers who were offering foreign-language services for older members of their congregations not to advertise or promote the special services" and care was taken to ensure that English-speaking persons would not attend these meetings (Manley, 1959, p. 164).

The impact of repression on language shift among Germans and speakers of other European immigrant languages was significant. The use of English "accelerated rapidly in the churches as elsewhere; in 1917 one-sixth of the Missouri Synod Lutheran Churches held at least one English service a month, while at the end of the War, three-quarters were doing so" (Conzen, 1980, p. 23).

### Impact on the German-Language Press

Although the German-language press had been gradually declining for several decades, wartime repression greatly accelerated its descent. "The total number of German-language publications declined from 554 in 1910 to 234 in 1920; daily circulation was only about a quarter of its 1910 level" (Conzen, 1980, p. 423). After the United States entered the war, county councils of defense requested German Americans to cancel their subscriptions (Manley, 1959); "In October, 1917, the United States Post Office Department created a system for licensing foreign-language publications. Before [books or periodicals] could be circulated, translations of each were to be filed with local postal authorities" (p. 120). In Nebraska such requirements became part the state's sedition act. According to Section 6:

Any person, firm or corporation in the State of Nebraska who shall publish, within the State of Nebraska, any newspaper, magazine, book, pamphlet, or other printed matter in whatever form, in any language other than the English language, shall as soon as printed, file a copy thereof with the State Council of Defense. In addition to such a copy there shall also be filed with the State Council of Defense a copy of any translations thereof into the English language required or furnished to the Post Office Department of the Federal Government. (cited in Manley, 1959, p. 304)

State councils of defense carefully reviewed the German-language press for signs of disloyalty. In Nebraska, a history professor was retained to scrutinize the press. Many in the state argued that all foreign-language newspapers should carry English translations. In response, Walter Roskcky, president of the Foreign Language Press Association countered that the "Nebraska Press Association had been unable to name a specific act of disloyalty on the part of the foreign newspapers," and he cautioned: "'Let us remember that it is a SYSTEM we are fighting, NOT A PEOPLE'" (Manley, 1959, p. 125; emphasis in original).

## The National Debate on German Language Instruction

During the war, writers in the popular press argued over the merits of "dropping German altogether" from school programs (Goodrich, 1918, p. 197). Given the popular support for eliminating the German language from the curriculum, it is important to ask where educators stood. According to Luebke (1980), "Many educators lent their authority to the war on German-language instruction in the schools" (p. 5). Prominent educational journals and educational associations such as the National Education Association (NEA) lent their weight to the attack on German and support for English-only policies. The NEA even pressed Congress to pass the Smith-Townes Act, which required states to be denied federal funds unless they enforced laws imposing English as the language of instruction (Burnell, 1982).

Some educators veiled their attacks in psuedo-objectivism. For example, Gordy, in a 1918 article for the *Educational Review*, began:

There is at the present time much discussion among school officials concerning the advisability of continuing the study of the German language in our schools.

In order to come to a sane decision on this problem as with any problem, it becomes necessary to weigh the pros and cons accurately and without prejudice. (p. 257)

In detailing his "accurate" and "unprejudiced" view, Gordy explained that "the German mind while alert for progress, is overwhelmingly egotistic, sordid, and has been stimulated, in its last frantic states by the dread[ed] *disease*—Teutomania" (pp. 260–261; emphasis added). As a would-be linguist, Gordy observed that German, as "a language lacking in euphony savors of the animalistic and does not produce a certain mental polish and refinement of nature essential to civilized people" (pp. 261–262). Like many of his contemporaries, he believed that "it would be

## 9. WORLD WAR I ERA ENGLISH-ONLY POLICIES

impossible to study German without being influenced to a certain extent by German thought" (p. 262). In a final appeal to feigned rationality, Gordy concluded: "Let us weigh these facts sanely and let us decide that modern civilization has no need of the products of a people who are the Huns of modern times" (p. 263).

For many educators, merely dropping German from the curriculum was an insufficient remedy for the lingering ill effects of German-language instruction. In 1918, L. D. Coffman (1918), dean of the College of Education at the University of Minnesota, writing in an NEA publication, contended that "what the root is to the tree ... the German language is to Germany" and that the "sinister influence of German Kultur" was part of a conspiracy of "many un-American schools and many un-American teachers" (p. 62). Coffman depicted German teachers as having utilized every opportunity to develop "an affection for Germany which the war, in many instances, has been unable to disturb" (p. 63). To reverse the alleged German indoctrination, Coffman prescribed Americanization imparted through English:

> What these teachers did and were doing for Germany all teachers in the future must do for America. Their patriotism must be of the simon-pure quality. They must be familiar with and teach the facts about foreign lands, but the ideals they seek to implant must be American ideals, and the language of the graded schools in which these ideals are imparted must be the English language. (p. 63)

Taking advantage of the national "emergency" as an opportunity to promote teacher education, Coffman further argued that teacher training could no longer be left to local discretion, because "the welfare and safety of the country demand federal recognition of teacher training" (p. 64). In an effort to gain status and resources for teacher education, the field was linked to the noble purpose of national self-defense. Coffman exhorted: "The nation must understand that teaching is a form of high patriotic service, and that the education of the masses is as necessary for social solidarity and security as for social progress" (p. 65). Teacher competence was to be measured by patriotism and the ability to promote Americanization through English-only instruction.

Not all educators agreed, and a stubborn minority argued against basing educational language policy solely on the contemporary political situation. "Their words were written in the educational periodicals and on the pages of the newspapers of the day" (Moore, 1937, p. 30). In South Dakota, for example, Commissioner of Education P. P. Claxton steadfastly held to the position that:

> "We cannot afford to eliminate the German language entirely. ... I want it definitely understood that my opinion is not influenced by the entrance of the United States into War. I do not believe our present relations with the German

empire should affect in any way the policy of our schools in regard to German instruction." (cited in Moore, 1937, p. 31)

## Official Actions Against German-Language Instruction

Despite Claxton's protest, and those of a minority of others, "by the middle of the school year 1917–1918, the tide of anti-German language feeling was approaching its height" (Moore, 1937, p. 34) and the assault on German-language instruction was in high gear. In Nebraska, the Council of Defense recruited a professor of Slavic languages from the University of Nebraska to survey the extent of foreign language use in the schools. Among her revelations were that some 12,000 children were attending parochial schools where German was taught or used. More startling to the council was that several superintendents reported that some schools began the day with the singing of the German anthem and more than 100 "failed to display the American flag" (Manley, 1964, p. 9).

In December of 1917 both the teaching and the use of all foreign languages—not just German—was banned in Nebraska. Privately, it was admitted that the "State Council actually had no legal basis for requiring any school to ban German. But ... a 'well defined sentiment' in the state demanded that all schools use only 'the language of our country'" (Manley, 1964, p. 12). That "well defined sentiment" has been more aptly described as "disrespect for the law" (Luebke, 1980, p. 9). When local school boards moved too slowly, Americanizers resorted to burglary. German textbooks were stolen from Seward high school (Manley, 1959).

Despite the general climate of repression generated by the war, it is important to note that in some areas German instruction remained popular. For example, as late as April of 1918, twice as many Trenton, New Jersey students were enrolled in German courses as in French or Spanish courses (Moore, 1937). Given language loyalty to German it is important to see official English-only language polices, and those restricting German and other foreign languages, as important instruments of social control. In this regard, Leibowitz (1974) noted that in the early 1900s the Federal government urged states to pass statutes mandating English as the language of instruction in both public and private schools. Federal urging in this area demonstrates that the national government was not a neutral bystander in matters of educational language policy. According to Leibowitz, in 1903, 14 states had a statutory requirement imposing English as the language of instruction. On the eve of World War I in 1913, 17 states had such a regulation. By 1923, a total of 34 had imposed the requirement. Thirty-one states passed new, or additional, educational language policies between 1917 and 1921, according to Edwards (1923). In 15 of those states the imposition of English-only policies was explicitly linked to restrictions on

## 9. WORLD WAR I ERA ENGLISH-ONLY POLICIES 229

other languages. Many states made it illegal to teach foreign languages in the lower grades, usually either below Grade 6 or Grade 8.

Despite encouragement from the federal government, constitutionally the primary responsibility for educational policy resides in the authority of the states, and during the war they, in turn, allowed considerable discretion to local districts in the administration of policies. Thus, there was no uniform pattern for excising German from the schools. In a reflective study undertaken less than 20 years after the war, Moore (1937) observed:

> The variation in the method and in the extent of this delegation of authority by the state to the local district is one explanation for the differences which appear in the methods used to eliminate the study of the German language in the secondary schools. For example, in California, the study of German was eliminated by resolution of the State Board of Education; in Louisiana, the device used was legislative enactment; in South Dakota, the same objective was attained under the direction of the State Council of Defense; in Iowa, elimination was accomplished by the direction of the State Superintendent of Public Instruction. In the majority of the states, however, the authority to eliminate German as a study was vested entirely in the hands of the local community. (pp. 29–30)

The brunt of the anti-German statutes was felt in the primary grades; however, there was also a detrimental effect at the secondary level. In March 1918, the *Literacy Digest* undertook a survey of secondary schools around the country to determine how many had dropped German language study. Of the 1,017 schools reporting, 149 (about 15%) indicated that they had eliminated German (Moore, 1937). However, in areas where the attack on German had been more vicious, students shunned German as an elective. Burnell (1982) noted that in 1918 the University of Michigan (which had fired six of its German-language faculty) sent out a survey to 200 Michigan high schools. In 166 schools, German was not selected by a single student. This was especially remarkable in a state where 11% of the population claimed German ancestry.

By the early 1920s the combination of a hostile social climate and the force of official restriction had a disastrous impact on German language enrollments. As Gilbert (1981) documented, nationally U.S. school enrollments in German had increased from 10.5% in 1890 to a record high of nearly 24% in 1915, but then plunged to less than 1% in 1922. Comparatively, instruction in French rose from about 10% in 1915 to over 15% in 1922. Between 1915 and 1948 the percentage of high school students studying German had dropped from nearly one fourth of all students to less than 1% (Leibowitz, 1971). State data reveals similar declines. In Michigan in 1915, for example, over 96% of the high schools offered German compared to only 7.5% in 1920 (Burnell, 1982). Because many high schools dropped German-language instruction, university admission requirements for foreign-language prerequisites were likewise relaxed or amended.

## Americanization and Anglification: Panaceas of Assimilation or Placebos for Intolerance?

During the war years many states and local governments passed Americanization laws requiring adults to take prescribed courses in Americanization. Pundits, politicians, and academics debated the extent to which various European-origin groups could be assimilated as well as the merits of Americanization. Eastern and southern Europeans were deemed less meltable by Anglo-Saxon chauvinists and, thus, less likely candidates for Americanization. Nevertheless, a wave of Americanization efforts swept the country. Its many supporters argued that it was indispensable for promoting assimilation and national security.

However, against the popular tide of Americanization there were some advocates of cultural pluralism. The most notable of the day was Horace Kallen who, writing in *Nation* in February 1915, argued against both Americanization and Anglification. He contended that the United States "need not be held to a monolingual standard for English was to the nation what Latin was to the Roman Empire," that is, a "language of the upper and dominant class, not necessarily the masses or the provinces" (cited in Holli, 1981, p. 420). Kallen insisted that each group "naturally would have its own emotional life, its own language, and its intellectual forms in a 'true Federal State' ... [i.e.], a federation or commonwealth of nationalities." Possibly ahead of his time, Kallen's voice was little more than an echo amidst the clamor for Anglification and Americanization.

Across the nation school districts offered civics and English classes for the foreign-born, and businesses and labor unions organized similar classes (McClymer, 1982). In Colorado, "aliens, naturalized citizens, and children of foreign-born parents were required to attend" Americanization classes and "sign oaths of loyalty to the United States government" (Dorsett, 1974, p. 292). Further, residents of foreign birth or parentage were forced to join the America First Society and sign its pledge: "I pledge myself to be, first of all, an American; to promote with all my power a knowledge of the language, the history, the government and the ideals of this country, and to support her by every word and act in her struggle for the freedom of mankind."

"The signing of the armistice on 11 November 1918 ended the war against Germany, but the war against German language and culture in the United States continued with scarcely any diminution" (Luebke, 1980, p. 11). The continuation of the assault came as no surprise because "both

## 9. WORLD WAR I ERA ENGLISH-ONLY POLICIES 231

Democratic and Republican candidates had insisted on 'patriotic education' after the war" (Manley, 1964, p. 15). The Red Scare which followed the war also ensured that the movement for Americanization would continue. In April of 1919 the *Chicago Tribune* boldly proclaimed, "Only an agile and determined immigrant possessed of overmastering devotion to the land of his birth can hope to escape Americanization by at least one of the many processes now being prepared for his special benefit" (McClymer, 1982, p. 98). Regarding this xenophobic atmosphere for singularity, McClymer observed:

> In so overheated a climate, no deviation from the newly, and narrowly, defined "American way" could be regarded as trivial; some patriotic organization or other was sure to launch a campaign to eradicate it. The General Federation of Women's Clubs, for example, became convinced that immigrant mothers were a "reactionary force" and determined to "carry the English language and American ways of caring for babies, ventilating the house, preparing American vegetables, instead of the inevitable cabbage" (p. 98)

The Americanization movement continued well into the mid-1920s. Despite its heady goal of total Americanization, the endeavor was not particularly effective, either for teaching English, or in preparing immigrants for citizenship. The movement was largely decentralized and many local programs lacked sufficient resources (McClymer, 1982). Thus, its major impact was essentially ideological. Americanization was probably more successful in stigmatizing cultural and linguistic diversity than in facilitating assimilation. By the late 1920s and early 1930s, it had succeeded in contributing to intergenerational conflict in many ethnic families by weakening respect for the language and culture of parents in the eyes of children who were less than fully assimilated (Montalto, 1982b). Its excesses led to the establishment of an intercultural education movement that sought to reinstill a sense of cultural pride for a generation of students left in a cultural limbo in the wake of the Americanization movement (see Montalto, 1982a, for a detailed account; see also Wiley, 1993).

### THE IMPACT OF LANGUAGE RESTRICTIONISM AND REPRESSION IN THE UNITED STATES

Facing official policies aimed at eradicating the use of German harassment from state councils of defense, the ultranationalistic press, mobs, and even law enforcement, many German Americans attempted the equivalent of an ethnic lobotomy. Names were changed from Mueller to Miller (Dorsett, 1974). The very word "German" had become so despicable that a Massachusetts report on children's health reported data on Liberty Measles rather than German Measles (Moore, 1937). "It was a time to submerge all signs

232 **WILEY**

of German-ness, and the German community never recovered" (Beltramo, 1981, p. 352).

In the 1910 U.S. census, over 2.3 million people claimed to have been German-born as opposed to less than 1.7 million in 1920 (Conzen, 1980). This was a striking decline even when considering mortality and out-migration. State data are even more revealing. Burnell (1982) observed that in Nebraska nearly 14% of the population had identified itself as being of German origin in 1910; however, only 4.4% made similar claims in 1920. In Wisconsin, the disappearance of Germans was even more conspicuous as the 1920 data reported only 6.6% of the population as being of German origin compared to nearly 29% in 1910. Burnell concluded:

> No other North American ethnic group, past or present has attempted so forcefully to officially conceal their [sic] ethnic origins. One must attribute this reaction to the wave of repression that swept the Continent and enveloped anyone with a German past. (p. 22)

In ethnically diverse cities like Chicago, public demonstrations of the extent of one's Americanization factored in to interethnic rivalries. Holli (1981) observed that many Polish, Czech, and Slavic Americans began self-consciously distancing themselves from their "hyphenated" status. Some conspicuously began referring to their ancestral homelands as "motherlands"—rather than their "fatherlands" in an effort to distance themselves from expressions that were analogous to those in German. Increasingly, during the interethnic "culture wars" a demonstration of Americanization became a means of enhancing the status of one's ethnic group over that of others. However, even Teddy Roosevelt, who frequently attacked "hyphenated Americans," exempted Greek Americans.

## Meyer v. Nebraska (1923): The Official Status of English Versus the Salience of Language Rights

In 1919, Nebraska passed a law that was similar to those of other states which prohibited foreign language instruction through Grade 8. As noted, most states applied such restrictions to either Grades 1 through 6 or 1 through 8 in an effort to make foreign languages inaccessible during those ages when children would have the best opportunity for acquiring them. In 1923 all such statutes were declared unconstitutional (Piatt, 1992; see Edwards, 1923, for a contemporary reaction). The case that brought the decision to a head was *Meyer v. Nebraska*, 262 U.S. 390 (1923; see Crawford, 1992b, for text of case). Meyer taught in a parochial school in Hamilton County, Nebraska. He was convicted and fined for using a German Bible history book as a text for reading based on the Nebraska statute. Meyer lost in an appeal to the Nebraska Supreme Court. The Nebraska court reasoned

# 9. WORLD WAR I ERA ENGLISH-ONLY POLICIES          233

that teaching ancestral languages to children of immigrants was unfavorable to national safety and self-interest. However, in 1923 the Supreme Court overturned the decision, arguing that in peacetime no threat to national security could justify the extremity of the Nebraska law. The Court argued the Nebraska statute violated the Due Process Clause of the Fourteenth Amendment. It ruled in favor of Meyer by a 7–2 margin (see Crawford, 1992b; Murphy, 1992).

Nevertheless, for advocates of freedom of language choice and language rights,[4] the ruling established a shallow precedent. From the Court's perspective, the significant issue in the case was the defense of individual liberties—not language rights for their own sake. The right to use languages other than English was important only in its association with other more fundamental protections. Oliver Wendell Holmes' dissent was most foreboding as he argued that all citizens of the United States should be required to speak a common tongue (Murphy, 1992). The Court's majority did not object to his position. Rather, it affirmed it by arguing that "the power of the state to compel attendance at some school and to make reasonable regulations for all schools, *including a requirement that they shall give instructions in English is not questioned*" (cited in Norgren & Nanda, 1988, p. 188, emphasis added; see also Crawford, 1992c). Thus, far from establishing the salience of languages rights, the Court's decision affirmed the official status of English-language instruction.

Following the *Meyer* decision there was no rush to reestablish German-language instruction to its pre-war levels. Many communities waited a number of years before bringing German instruction back because a "legacy of repression" persisted (Burnell, 1982, p. 14).

## THE FATE OF GERMAN IN CANADA AND
## THE UNITED STATES COMPARED

The German-origin population in North America extends across national boundaries. Although there are few studies that have addressed immigrant experiences and impact of language policies on them from a comparative perspective,[5] Burnell (1982) has demonstrated the importance of studying the impact of World War I from such a perspective. His principal focus is the "cross-cultural impact of a single event on a linguistic minority residing on either side of an international frontier" (p. 1). Burnell chronicled many

---

[4]See Macías (1979) for an overview of issues related to language rights.
[5]Language policies are frequently analyzed within the contexts of national boundaries. Although their work is not specially related to immigration, Phillipson (1992) and Tollefson (1991) provided important examples of cross-national analyses of language policies and the impact of English as the dominant world language.

similarities in the wartime experience of German Canadians with their kindred in the United States. However, he also underscored one significant difference in Canadian language politics, that is, the official status of French and its numerical dominance in Quebec.

On the eve of World War I, German Canadians constituted a "small but cohesive" group that was concentrated in the "Berlin (later Kitchener)—Waterloo districts of Ontario," where they constituted about 20% of the population and in Manitoba, Saskatchewan, and Alberta, where they comprised at least 10% of the population (Burnell, 1982, p. 1). At the time, English- and French-speaking Canadians accounted for around 70% of the population, compared to German speakers, who comprised less than 6%.

Burnell (1982) observed that bilingual schools in Canada flourished in areas where Germans were concentrated, especially in rural areas and in localities infused with new immigrants, just as they did in the United States. In 1890, German Canadians had won the right "to receive instruction in German reading, grammar, and composition" on the request of a parent or guardian (p. 3). This right was a matter of considerable controversy for Anglophones primarily because of their distrust of the quality of French bilingual schools.

With the outbreak of war, "an atmosphere of anti-Germanism ... pervaded nearly every aspect of Canadian life" just as it did in the United States, and German-language instruction was likewise excised from much of the Canadian curriculum (Burnell, 1982, p. 3). German professors at the University of Toronto were suspended just as their colleagues were in the United States. When compulsory education was mandated in Manitoba in 1916, a clause was added that prohibited second-language instruction.

In drafting legislation to end bilingual education in Canada:

> Research questions on the efficacy of learning a second language were simply not addressed. At that time there was a paucity of data on whether children whose mother tongue was not English would be more likely to succeed in school (Burnell, 1982, p. 7).

This was the case even if they were entitled to bilingual education. English-only policies were implemented in Alberta and Saskatchewan; however, an exception was made to accommodate speakers of French. Burnell concluded that English-only policies were intended to keep Canadian Anglo children from learning a second language, which, in fact, became the case in areas dominated by languages other than English.

Finally, concerns over bilingual education were linked to fears of "Bolshevism" (Burnell, 1982, p. 6) just as anxieties regarding diversity were tied to the Red Scare in the United States. However, Mennonites, Amish, and other insular religious groups were generally "not perceived as a threat to

## 9. WORLD WAR I ERA ENGLISH-ONLY POLICIES

the larger Canadian society" and received more favorable treatment than they did in the United States (p. 8).

### CONCLUSION: IMPLICATIONS OF THE IMPOSITION OF ENGLISH-ONLY POLICIES AND AMERICANIZATION

Following World War I, Burnell (1982) noted that "anti-German feeling was largely replaced by an anger directed toward all symbols of foreign influence" (p. 14). Nevertheless, it is also important to recognize that more than xenophobia was at work. For those of European origin, the force and breadth of the attack on diversity may have been new; however, a careful review of the experiences of indigenous peoples as well as other peoples of color indicates that the English-only movement was concerned with far more than just language. In this regard, Tamura (1993), in an analysis of the relationship between the English-only movement and the anti-Japanese campaign in Hawaii between 1915 and 1940, contended:

> The English-only effort was an integral part of the Americanization crusade. ... Underlying the crusade was the doctrine of Anglo-Saxon superiority—the conviction that American traits derived from the English, and that the future of American democracy depended upon the survival of the English language and the dominance of the Anglo-Saxon "race." (p. 37)

To contemporary ears the notion of an Anglo-Saxon "race," as opposed to a German or Italian race, may sound peculiar. However, during the early 1900s, those of European origin were frequently classified into Nordic, Alpine, and Mediterranean races (Hakuta, 1986). In the European racial pecking order, Nordics were at the top and Mediterranians (Greeks and Italians) at the bottom. Nordic supremacists of the time considered Italians to be a "superior sort of Chinaman" (Wyman, 1993, p. 100). The war encouraged some to make even finer distinctions between "Anglo-Saxons" and "Huns."

Throughout the war years, language was both a marker of foreigner status and an instrument of racialization within the European-origin population. According to Miles (1989), racialization is "a process of delineation of group boundaries and an allocation of persons within those boundaries by primary reference to (supposedly) inherent and/or biological (usually phenotypical) characteristics. It is therefore an ideological process" (p. 74). During the World War I era, linguistic, religious, and cultural differences functioned like physical differences in defining intergroup boundaries of race. In a sense they helped to establish a two-tiered racial classification system: One tier defined race within the European-origin population on the basis of language, religion, culture—and to a lesser degree on physical differences; the other defined race between Europeans and all others largely on the basis of physical differences and secondarily on the basis of language and culture.[6] However, as German Americans and other European-origin groups assimilated willingly, or through coercion, into the English-speaking fold and adopted the Anglo-dominate culture, color and other physical differences persisted as the primary determinants of race between those of European origin and all others. As the second and third generations of European immigrants became linguistically homogenized through Anglification, there was less concern among Anglo-dominated, European-origin peoples regarding language as a marker of "racial" differences.

In reflecting on the significance of the wartime attack on German Americans and other European-origin language minorities, it is apparent that they shared many similar experiences to those which have more often plagued peoples of color. Much of that experience has, however, been forgotten, or repressed, in the collective memories of European-origin peoples. Subsequently, many among their third- and fourth-generation descendants have come to assume that their grandparents and great-grandparents all willingly deserted their ancestral tongues and cultures.

However, the degree of commonality in the experience of discrimination encounter by German Americans and other European-origin language minorities compared to that of linguistic minorities of color can also be overstressed. Dorsett (1974), for example, noted the similarities in the loss of due process and attack on civil liberties experienced by German Americans of the World War I era and Japanese Americans during World War II. He concluded that "our wretched treatment of Japanese-Americans was not an accidental aberration that grew out of wartime hysteria. Furthermore, it was not simply an extreme case of white America's degradation of a non-white minority"; rather, he locates it in the "propensity to bury the Bill of Rights" (p. 293).

It is important to acknowledge these similarities; nevertheless, the differences in treatment between groups should not be overlooked. First, it is important to note that Dorsett's comparison is across time, that is, German Americans of the World War I era compared to Japanese Americans of the World War II period. It is, however, perhaps more instructive to compare the experiences of the two groups during the same period. In this regard, Tamura's (1993) analysis of Americanization and English-only policies in Hawaii during World War I and its aftermath is useful. First, she observes that—at least on its surface—the attack on the Japanese American population in Hawaii had much in common with the mainland

---

[6]It could also be argued that there is a third tier of group boundary delineation that is based largely on social class wherein wealth allows some members of a stigmatized group to negate, or transcend, some restrictions imposed on the basis of perceived physical differences and other dimensions of diversity.

## 9. WORLD WAR I ERA ENGLISH-ONLY POLICIES 237

attack on German Americans. To illustrate, Tamura noted that there was an attempt to suppress the Japanese-language press and to abolish Japanese-language schools. However, despite these similarities, she contended that the English-only movement had less to do with language than with race and national origin. This became even more apparent after World War I. The significant difference between the treatment of the two groups is that there was no systematic endeavor to segregate German Americans from Anglo-Americans, as was the case for Japanese Americans in the years following the war.

It is only through a careful comparative analysis of the differential impact of Americanization and the imposition of English-only policies that we can understand the processes of both assimilation and exclusion. The work of Leibowitz (1969, 1971) represents a pioneering example of the comparative analysis of the imposition of English-only policies and English literacy requirements on various groups, such as African Americans, German Americans, Native Americans, Japanese Americans, Puerto Rican Americans, and Mexican Americans. He demonstrates how the English-language instruction requirement and anti-foreign-language requirements masked discriminatory intentions against these groups on the basis of religion, race (defined here as a socioideological construct based on perceived physical differences between groups), and national origin usually in contexts of intergroup political and economic competition. Americanization and English-only policies also had a significant impact on other groups, such as those of Mexican origin (see Olneck & Lazerson, 1980). Examples such as these point to the need for further cross-group comparisons regarding the impact of the imposition of English-only policies and Americanization, especially because even today it is frequently argued that such policies are in the best interests of all children. Many of the studies that we do have (see also Menchaca & Valencia, 1990; Weinberg, 1995) suggest that, despite the similarities in the rhetoric regarding the need for Anglification, English-only policies had a substantially differential impact across groups, especially when racial differences were considered significant by the dominant group.

The ideology of Americanization and Anglification promised structural assimilation, that is, social mobility, allowing the "entrance of immigrants and their descendants into the social cliques, organizations, institutional activities, and general civic life of the receiving society" (Weiss, 1982, p. xii). However, for many groups Americanization and English-only policies reneged on that promise by assigning generations of minority children to segregated and inferior schools even as it was claimed that mandated conformity was ostensibly for their own good.

# REFERENCES

Apple, J. J., & Apple, S. (1982). The huddled masses and the little red school house. In B. J. Weiss (Ed.), *Education and the European immigrant: 1840–1940* (pp. 17–30). Urbana: University of Illinois Press.

Beltramo, A. F. (1981). Profile of a state: Montana. In C. A. Ferguson & S. B. Heath, (Eds.), *Language in the USA* (pp. 339–380). Cambridge, England: Cambridge University Press.

Burnell, J. B. (1982, March). *The decline of German language and culture in the North American heartland, 1890–1923.* Paper presented at the Annual Meeting of the Comparative and International Education Society, New York. (ERIC Document Reproduction Service, No. ED 228 135)

Castellans, D. (1992). A polyglot nation. In J. Crawford (Ed.), *Language loyalties: A source book on the official English controversy* (pp. 13–18). Chicago: University of Chicago Press.

Coffman, L. D. (1918). Competent teachers for American children. In *National Educational Association: Addresses and proceedings of the fifty-sixth annual meeting* (pp. 62–66). Washington, DC: Secretary's Office of the National Education Association.

Conzen, K. N. (1980). Germans. In S. T. Thernstrom, A. Orlov, & O. Handlin (Eds.), *Harvard encyclopedia of American ethnic groups* (pp. 404–425). Cambridge, MA: Belknap Press of Harvard University Press.

Crawford, J. (1992a). *Hold your tongue: Bilingualism and the politics of "English Only."* Reading, MA: Addison-Wesley.

Crawford, J. (Ed.). (1992b). *Language loyalties: A source book on the official English controversy.* Chicago: University of Chicago Press.

Crawford, J. (1992c). What's behind official English? In J. Crawford (Ed.), *Language loyalties: A source book on the official English controversy* (pp. 171–177). Chicago: University of Chicago Press.

Crawford, J. (1995). *Bilingual education: History, politics, theory, and practice* (3rd ed.). Los Angeles: Bilingual Education Services.

Dorsett, L. W. (1974). The ordeal of Colorado's Germans during World War I. *Colorado Magazine, 51,* 277–293.

Edwards, I. N. (1923). The legal status of foreign languages in the schools. *Elementary School Journal, 24,* 270–278.

Fishman, J. A. (Ed.). (1966). *Language loyalty in the United States.* The Hague, Netherlands: Mouton.

Franklin, B. (1992). The German language in Pennsylvania. In J. Crawford (Ed.), *Language loyalties: A source book on the official English controversy* (pp. 18–19). Chicago: University of Chicago Press. (Original work published 1753)

Gibson, M. A., & Ogbu, J. U. (Eds.). (1991). *Minority status and schooling: A comparative study of immigrant and involuntary minorities.* New York: Garland.

Gilbert, G. G. (1981). French and German: A comparative study. In C. A. Ferguson & S. B. Heath (Eds.), *Language in the USA* (pp. 257–272). Cambridge, England: Cambridge University Press.

Goodrich, C. G. (1918). Shall we teach German in our public schools? *Outlook, 119,* 195–197.

Gordy, H. M. (1918). The German language in our schools. *Educational Review, 56,* 257–263.

Hakuta, K. (1986). *Mirror of language: The debate on bilingualism.* New York: Basic Books.

Heath, S. B. (1976). Colonial language status achievement: Mexico, Peru, and the United States. In A. Verdoodt & R. Kjolseth (Eds.), *Language and sociology.* Louvain, Belgium: Peeters.

Heath, S. B. (1981). English in our language heritage. In C. A. Ferguson & S. B. Heath (Eds.), *Language in the USA* (pp. 6–20). Cambridge, England: Cambridge University Press.

Heath, S. B. (1992). Why no official tongue? In J. Crawford (Ed.), *Language loyalties: A source book on the official English controversy* (pp. 20–31). Chicago: University of Chicago Press.

## 9. WORLD WAR I ERA ENGLISH-ONLY POLICIES 239

Holli, M. G. (1981). Teuton vs. Slav: The Great War sinks Chicago's German Kultur. *Ethnicity,* *8*, 406–451.

Kloss, H. (1971). Language rights of immigrant groups. *International Migration Review, 5*, 250–268.

Kloss, H. (1977). *The American bilingual tradition.* Rowley, MA: Newbury House.

Leibowitz, A. H. (1969). English literacy: Legal sanction for discrimination. *Notre Dame Lawyer, 25*(1), 7–66.

Leibowitz, A. H. (1971). *Educational policy and political acceptance: The imposition of English as the language of instruction in American schools.* (ERIC Document Reproduction Service No. ED 047 321)

Leibowitz, A. H. (1974, August). *Language as a means of social control. The United States experience.* Paper presented at the VIII World Congress of Sociology, University of Toronto, Toronto, Canada. (ERIC Document Reproduction Service No. ED 093 168)

Luebke, F. C. (1968). The German-American alliance in Nebraska, 1910–1917. *Nebraska History, 49*, 165–185.

Luebke, F. C. (1969). *Immigrants and politics: The Germans of Nebraska: 1880–1900.* Lincoln: University of Nebraska Press.

Luebke, F. C. (1974). *Bonds of loyalty: German-Americans and World War I.* DeKalb: Northern Illinois University Press.

Luebke, F. C. (1980). Legal restrictions on foreign languages in the Great Plains states, 1917–1923. In P. Schach (Ed.), *Languages in conflict: Linguistic acculturation on the Great Plains* (pp. 1–19). Lincoln: University of Nebraska Press.

Macías, R. F. (1979). Choice of language as a human right—Public policy implications in the United States. In R. V. Padilla (Ed.), *Bilingual education and public policy in the United States. Ethnoperspectives in bilingual education research* (Vol. I, pp. 39–75). Ypsilanti: Eastern Michigan University.

Macías, R. F. (1992). *"Cauldron-boil & bubble"—United States language policy towards indigenous language groups.* Unpublished paper, Linguistic Minority Research Institute, University of California at Santa Barbara.

Manley, R. N. (1959). *The Nebraska State Council of Defense: Loyalty programs and policies during World War I.* Unpublished masters thesis, University of Nebraska.

Manley, R. N. (1964). Language, loyalty and liberty: The Nebraska State Council of Defense and the Lutheran churches, 1917–1918. *Concordia Historical Institute Quarterly, 37*(1), 1–16.

McClymer, J. F. (1982). The Americanization movement and the education of the foreign-born adult, 1914–1925. In B. J. Weiss (Ed.), *Education and the European immigrant: 1840–1940* (pp. 96–116). Urbana: University of Illinois Press.

McKay, S. L., & Weinstein-Shr, G. (1993). English literacy in the U.S.: National policies, personal consequences. *TESOL Quarterly, 27*(3), 399–419.

Menchaca, M., & Valencia, R. R. (1990). Anglo-Saxon ideologies in the 1920s–1930s: Their impact on the segregation of Mexican students in California. *Anthropology & Education Quarterly, 21*, 222–249.

Miles, R. (1989). *Racism.* London: Routledge.

Molesky, J. (1988). Understanding the American Linguistic Mosaic: A historical overview of language maintenance and language shift. In S. L. McKay & S. C. Wong (Eds.), *Language diversity: Resource or problem? A social and educational perspective on language minorities in the United States* (pp. 69–107). Cambridge, MA: Newbury House.

Montalto, N. V. (1982a). *A history of the intercultural educational movement, 1924–1941.* New York: Garland.

Montalto, N. V. (1982b). The Intercultural Education Movement 1924–41: The growth of tolerance as a form of intolerance. In B. J. Weiss, (Ed.) *Education and the European immigrant: 1840–1940* (pp. 142–160). Urbana: University of Illinois Press.

Moore, W. H. (1937). *The conflict concerning the German language and German propaganda in the public schools.* Unpublished doctoral dissertation, Stanford University, Stanford, CA.

Murphy, P. L. (1992). *Meyer v. Nebraska.* In K. L. Hall (Ed.), *The Oxford companion to the Supreme Court of the United States* (pp. 543–544). New York: Oxford University Press.

Norgren, J., & Nanda, S. (1988). *American cultural pluralism and the law.* New York: Praeger. (See especially chapter 10: Language, culture, and the courts, pp. 185–199)

Ogbu, J. U., & Matute-Bianchi, M. E. (1986). Understanding sociocultural factors: Knowledge, identity, and school adjustment. In *Beyond language: Social and cultural factors in schooling for language minority students* (pp. 73–142). Los Angeles: Evaluation, Dissemination & Assessment Center, California State University.

Olneck, M. R., & Lazerson, M. (1980). Education. In S. Thernstrom, A. Orlov, & O. Handlin (Eds.), *Harvard encyclopedia of American ethnic groups* (pp. 303–319). Cambridge, MA: Harvard University Press.

Phillipson, R. (1992). *Linguistic imperialism.* Oxford, England: Oxford University Press.

Piatt, B. (1992). The confusing state of minority language rights. In J. Crawford (Ed.), *Language loyalties: A source book on the official English controversy* (pp. 229–234). Chicago: University of Chicago Press.

Pitt, L. (1976). *We Americans* (Vols. 1 & 2). Glenview, IL: Scott, Foresman.

Ricento, T. (1996). Language policy in the United States. In M. Herriman & B. Burnaby (Eds.), *Language policies in English dominant countries: Six case studies* (pp. 122–158). Clevedon, England: Multilingual Matters.

Rippley, L. V. J. (1980). Germans from Russia. In S. T. Thernstrom, A. Orlov, & O. Handlin (Eds.), *Harvard encyclopedia of American ethnic groups* (pp. 425–430). Cambridge, MA: Belknap Press of Harvard University Press.

Schlossman, S. L. (1983). Is there an American tradition of bilingual education? German in the public elementary schools, 1840–1919. *American Journal of Education, 91*, 139–186.

Tamura, E. H. (1993). The English-Only effort, the anti-Japanese campaign, and language acquisition in the education of Japanese Americans in Hawaii, 1915–1940. *History of Education Quarterly, 33*, 37–58.

Tollefson, J. W. (1989). *Alien winds: The reeducation of America's Indochinese refugees.* New York: Praeger.

Tollefson, J. W. (1991). *Planning language, planning inequality: Language policy in the community.* New York: Longman.

Veltman, C. (1983). *Language shift in the United States.* Berlin: Mouton.

Weinberg, M. (1995). *A chance to learn: A history of race and education in the United States.* Cambridge, England: Cambridge University Press.

Weiss, B. (Ed.) (1982). *American education and the European immigrant, 1840–1940.* Urbana: University of Illinois Press.

Wilcox, C. (1993). World War I and the attack on professors of German at the University of Michigan. *History of Education Quarterly, 33*(1), 60–84.

Wiley, T. G. (1986). The significance of language and cultural barriers for the Euro-American elderly. In C. L. Hayes, R. A. Kalish, & D. Guttmann (Eds.), *The Euro-American elderly: A guide to practice* (pp. 35–50). New York: Springer.

Wiley, T. G. (1993). Back from the past: In search of models of multicultural education. *Journal of General Education, 42*(4), 280–300.

Wiley, T. G. (1996a). Language planning and language policy. In S. McKay & N. Hornberger (Eds.), *Sociolinguistics and language teaching* (pp. 103–147). Cambridge, England: Cambridge University Press.

Wiley, T.G. (1996b). *Literacy and language diversity in the United States.* Washington, DC/McHenry, IL: Center for Applied Linguistics/Delta Systems.

## 9. WORLD WAR I ERA ENGLISH-ONLY POLICIES                                    241

Wiley, T. G., & Lukes, M. (1996). English-Only and standard English ideologies in the United States. *TESOL Quarterly, 3*, 511–530.

Wyman, M. (1993). *Round-trip to America: The immigrants return to Europe, 1880–1930*. Ithaca, NY: Cornell University Press.

# 10

# ESL Policy in Canada and the United States: Basis for Comparison

Barbara Burnaby
*Ontario Institute for Studies in Education*
*University of Toronto*

English is dominant in the United States and in most of Canada, both of which have a great deal of non-English-speaking immigration. Therefore, English as a second language (ESL) provisions are important to both countries. Given similarities and differences between the two countries it would be useful to compare them in terms of lessons learned about ESL in order to enhance both systems. However, it has proven extremely difficult to describe comprehensively the actual implementation of either system at a national level due to the complexity of policies, funding mechanisms, and means of delivery. According to Chisman, Wrigley, and Ewen (1993), "The ... pattern of [ESL] service [in the United States] is so disorganized and complex that no one really knows how it works; no one can provide satisfactory answers to many of the most elementary questions about service and funding" (pp. 1–2). The situation in Canada is similar. Fortunately, there are now a few large scale studies that are beginning to fill in the gaps in both countries (Burnaby, 1992b; Chisman et al., 1993; Cumming, 1991; Cumming, Hart, Corson, & Cummins, 1993). In addition, it has not been possible to do more than estimate the extent to which these systems are meeting the needs or demands of the target populations (Ashworth, 1992; Burnaby, 1992b; Chisman et al., 1993; Churchill, 1986).

243

Although this incomplete understanding of the two systems is an uncertain basis for comparison, this chapter addresses ways in which the two systems are unlike each other in order to pave the way for future discussion on their similarities. It will cover four areas: (a) how the role of francophones in Canada is different from that of any language minority in the United States; (b) how some government structures that relate to ESL policies in Canada are different from those in the United States; (c) how immigration in Canada is different from that in the United States; and (d) how literacy or adult basic education (ABE) provisions are organized differently in relation to ESL in the two countries.

## SALIENT FACTORS

Canada and the United States inherently and currently have a number of characteristics that ultimately influence their ESL policies. With respect to demographics, Canada has a land mass somewhat larger than that of the United States but, at about 28 million, about one tenth the United States population. The physical size in relation to the population tends to encourage immigration:

> For America, faced with a 1,900-mile border with Mexico, the issues of undocumented immigration and temporary workers were especially important, but the same was not true for the United States's northern neighbor. Canadians also had to take into account their shared southern border with a very large, highly developed economy and their economic, cultural, and political ties to the evolving British Commonwealth. (Chiswick, 1992, p. 5)

History and its relatively small population size puts Canada in a somewhat different strategic position from that of the United States in the world economic and political scene. However, like the United States, Canada experienced a baby boom after the second world war. As a result, there was a large number of young people coming into the labor market in the 1970s and 1980s, but that excess has turned to scarcity in the 1990s, and Canada, like the United States, is looking to immigration to help deal with the labor market and other economic consequences (Chiswick, 1992).

Regarding language and culture, Canada has two dominant groups: francophones, about one quarter of the total population who live mainly in Quebec but have longstanding communities elsewhere in the country; and anglophones, who predominate in the rest of the country. These two groups take center stage in national politics, whereas Aboriginal peoples and other linguistic and cultural minorities have considerably lower profiles. The country is officially bilingual: Quebec is officially French speaking, New Brunswick is officially bilingual, and the rest of the provinces and the

# 10. ESL POLICY IN CANADA AND THE UNITED STATES                                245

Yukon Territory are monolingual English. The official languages of the Northwest Territories are English, French, and seven Aboriginal languages. Four provinces—Ontario, Manitoba, Quebec, and New Brunswick—have parallel French and English school systems. On all these factors except for the monolingual English provinces, Canada is significantly different from the United States, where English is the dominant language in all states and there is, as yet, no national official language.

Both Canada and the United States presently exist in an international environment that affects immigration and local attitudes:

> Starting in the 1960s they [Canada and the United States] explicitly modified their policies to include third world, eastern hemispheric newcomers. Growing racial and ethnic tolerance, economic forces, lobbying, and international factors all played roles in shaping the ways these two North American countries similarly developed greater openness in their immigration policies. (Chiswick, 1992, pp. 4–5)

In sum, from the broadest perspective, Canada is like the United States in being a prosperous North American country attractive to immigrants, and influenced by the baby boom, the world recession and other international pressures. Unlike the United States, it has a minority population with a lot of political power, two official languages, and a small population in a large land mass.

## LANGUAGE PRIORITIES IN AN OFFICIALLY BILINGUAL COUNTRY

The structure of the Canadian government was created by The British North America Act of the British Parliament in 1867. In 1982, this act was "repatriated" as The Constitution Act of the Parliament of Canada, with an associated Charter of Rights and Freedoms. The critical factor in the repatriation has been that Quebec has not signed its agreement to this new constitution with the effect that French–English relations have stayed high on the national agenda, eclipsing virtually everything else political for months at a time on several occasions. The point here is that contention of status between English and French has been able to overwhelm issues regarding other minority populations, although the Aboriginal groups were able to get closer to the table in the recent rounds of constitutional discussions since the late 1980s.

In 1969, Canada declared itself officially bilingual. The Official Languages Act focuses only on English and French and those who speak those languages as mother tongues. Therefore, issues of specific concern to people who speak Aboriginal languages or other nonofficial languages are not directly addressed. According to the terminology of the Act, "language minorities" are anglophones in Quebec and francophones in the rest of the country. Also, the Act has to do almost exclusively with federal activities and jurisdictions, although it monitors provincial, territorial, and other local language initiatives. As a result of the Act, there is a Standing Committee of the House of Commons on Official Languages, and an Office of the Commissioner of Official Languages. The main activities include ensuring equitable service and language of work in both official languages in the federal public service, parliamentary institutions, the armed forces, and crown corporations, as well as transfer payments to the provinces and territories for language education in primary and secondary schools[1] (mother-tongue-medium schooling for "language minorities," English as a subject in French-medium schools, and French as a subject in English-medium schools). In some ways, the Act has considerable impact on the daily lives of Canadians; for example, all goods must be labeled in both languages. However, the intention of the Act is not to make everyone bilingual but to ensure equitable services.

The Official Languages Act exerts a great deal of influence on the political agenda, drawing attention and resources away from the language needs of those residents who speak neither official language. In the schools especially, initiatives to assist non-official-language-speaking students to learn the language that is the medium of instruction are complicated by the schools' programs to offer instruction in the second official language.

For the purposes of any discussion of Canadian ESL policies from the U.S. perspective, it is unfortunate that the Canadian official language policy is as intrinsically interesting as it is to the field of comparative education and sociolinguistics, because it attracts attention away from the ways in which Canada deals with residents who speak neither English nor French. This population was completely ignored by Vaillancourt (1992) and almost completely by Churchill (1986) in their respective comparative studies. Both studies focused on national policies (and Churchill only on elementary and secondary education), and because a great deal of the Canadian initiative for official language training for non-official-language-speaking adults and virtually all of it for schoolchildren is undertaken by the provinces, it is not (well) documented or scrutinized.

The comparison between francophones in Canada and linguistic minorities in the United States is not apt because the groups are significantly dissimilar. According to Bloom and Grenier (1992):

Canada and the United States have similar economic structures, and English is the majority language in both countries. The countries' linguistic minorities,

---

[1]This is one of the rare examples of the federal government being fiscally involved with public schooling.

## 10. ESL POLICY IN CANADA AND THE UNITED STATES 247

however, have little in common. Three important differences deserve mention. First, Canada's major linguistic minority—a French-speaking population—is not an immigrant group. The major linguistic minority in the United States—a Spanish-speaking population—is predominantly an immigrant group [see, however, Churchill, 1986, pp. 44–45]. Second, although the French-speaking population in Canada is a minority group nationally, it is a majority in Quebec, a major province. In contrast, the Spanish-speaking population in the United States is a minority both nationally and in every state and SMSA. Finally, French is an official national language in Canada whereas Spanish is not an official language in the United States. (pp. 382–383)

The authors go on to demonstrate that the gap between the earnings of francophone men is decreasing in Canada since 1970 relative to those of anglophone men but that Spanish-speaking men in the United States show an increased gap between their earnings and those of English-speaking men.

On the other hand, studies comparing the role of knowledge of the official languages in Canada and of English in the United States to economic and other factors of *immigrants* in both countries (Boyd, 1992; Chiswick, 1992; Chiswick & Miller, 1992) show that the United States and Canadian immigrant populations are very similar. Therefore, it makes sense in this discussion to focus on provisions for *nonofficial* language minorities in Canada as comparable to linguistic minorities in the United States.

McManus (1992), commenting on Vaillancourt's 1992 paper, indicated some useful policy directions to which to attend:

In Canada, he [Vaillancourt] claims, the federal government's role in language policy derives from its role as the arbitrator between the two language groups, while in the United States it derives from the federal government's role as the defender of individual civil rights. In recent decades, however, U.S. affirmative action and civil rights policies have tended to define and defend protected groups rather than individual persons. Thus, the only remaining distinction is that *in Canada only two groups are protected* [italics added], while in the United States the number of protected groups is limited only by the ethnic, racial, and sexual composition of the population. Practical policy implications follow: in Canada allophone [non-official-language-speaking] immigrants are encouraged to acquire English or French, but in the United States, because of a tendency to protect minority group rights, there is less official encouragement to acquire English. (p. 301)

The significance of these matters here is that Canada, unlike the United States, has "the French fact" to take into account on the national political scene so that issues of non-English, non-French linguistic and cultural minorities have an extra hurdle to jump to get on the national agenda. Hispanics in the United States have a powerful lobby, but nowhere near the power of the Canadian francophones with entrenched constitutional language rights.

ESL in Canada and the United States has much in common if the teaching of English to francophones is set aside. Churchill (1986), comparing the "coverage and effects" of national school programs for linguistic minorities in all the OECD countries, reported that "only a small portion of the target population [in the United States] is reached by bilingual and bicultural programmes." He continued:

> The most optimistic results are found in the Canadian case study [which reported on the programs under the Official Languages Act and not on ESL or FSL for immigrant children]. The fact that the latter refers to an established minority and the others [minority populations in some other OECD countries] to "new" minorities makes it unlikely that the role of regulatory measures is the main causal factor. *The status of the minority appears, rather, to determine in large measure the regulatory approach adopted.* The overall impression derived from the studies is that the indigenous and new minorities are poorly covered in most instances, and that the nature of the provision is not clear. (p. 103)

Chisman et al. (1993) agreed that status is a major issue in ESL in the United States:

> In large part, the disappointing performance of ESL service in this country is due to the fact that ESL for adults is, and long has been, a neglected backwater of our educational system. It is a poorly supported, low-status activity to which most educators and policy makers give only passing attention. (p. 1)

In any event, immigrants in Canada who want access to English in Canada have to deal not only with their low status position but also with the fact that French–English issues have a more central and entrenched place in the national attention than do their own issues.

## GOVERNMENT STRUCTURES AFFECTING LANGUAGE ISSUES

Three points are made here about differences in the Canadian and U.S. governments as they affect ESL. One concerns a preoccupation in Canada over division of power between the federal and provincial governments; another addresses the role of the courts in affecting legislation and policies; and a third looks at strategies for accountability for government funding.

### Federal/Provincial Relationships

According to The British North America Act and The Constitution Act, powers are divided between the federal government and the provinces. These divisions have been highly significant in the conduct of Canadian political affairs. In 1867, the federal government, among many other things, got partial jurisdiction over immigration (and all that now entails), certain

## 10. ESL POLICY IN CANADA AND THE UNITED STATES 249

aspects of the national economy (that now include national employment policies), and Aboriginal affairs. The provinces, among other powers, got education. These powers are jealously protected by the respective parties and have evolved over the years. For example, a fairly potent force on the federal scene is the Council of Ministers of Education of Canada, a body that coordinates provincial responses to the federal government when education issues are raised:

> In the Canadian constitutional system, the Federal government is severely limited in the means of action at its disposal for affecting educational policies: the case study [of the education of linguistic and cultural minorities in Canada] describes the use of financial incentives within a negotiated framework as the prime means for fostering bilingualism policies in the provinces. (Churchill, 1986, p. 64)

The first example given here relates to how the federal government got involved in adult ESL despite provincial jurisdiction over education. There is nothing in federal legislation that even suggests that people who speak neither English nor French have the *right* to support in learning one of those languages. However, there is considerable legislation that impinges on, and some programs that relate directly to, issues of language for residents of Canada who do not speak either of the official languages.

In the economic, population, and immigration boom of the 1960s, the federal government wanted to exercise some control over the labor force. Although it was not permitted constitutionally to get involved with education,[2] it succeeded in getting involved with training of adults in skills related to work.[3] It began by passing acts whereby it would purchase training seats from provincial institutions. Thus, the provinces still controlled the training itself but officials in federal employment offices chose the students. Students' tuition fees were covered and they were given a training allowance to support them while they studied. The provinces had not, up to that time, had much of a system of public, nonuniversity postsecondary institutions, but, in considerable part to take advantage of this federal program, community colleges expanded across the country at that time. The program involved various levels of academic upgrading and prevocational training for a wide variety of occupations for all Canadians.

A large part of this program was language training for adult immigrants. Although circumstances varied from province to province, immigrants who were selected by federal officials could get about 24 weeks of full-time language training with a subsistence allowance. On the whole, only inde-

---

[2]The provinces are still exclusively responsible for ESL and French as a second language for children who do not speak an official language (Flaherty & Woods, 1992).

[3]The succession of federal acts has been The Technical Vocational Training Assistance Act of 1960, The Occupational Training for Adults Act of 1967, The National Training Act of 1982, and The Labour Force Development Strategy of 1989.

pendent class immigrants (those selected on the basis of the point system) got seats with training allowances. The purpose of the program was explicitly to "unlock" their occupational skills for the labor market. Most of the training was general purpose, classroom-based language training, but at least one province used some of the training program to offer English in the workplace.

Over the years, there has been considerable controversy over this sought-after program. The community colleges in urban, immigrant-receiving areas developed large ESL sections to handle the trainees, but some were criticized for keeping their teachers on temporary contracts; for using unqualified teachers; for providing general, regimented programs that did not respond to varieties of student need; for excluding potential students who were ineligible for the federal funding but who wanted the same kind of training on a fee-paying basis; and for exploiting this lucrative program to support less profitable facets of their activities. In the 1970s, selection of students by federal officials targeted the "head of the household" so that many women were excluded. Also, candidates had to be deemed by officials to be destined for the labor market so that many women and older people (mostly immigrants from the family or assisted relative classes) were excluded (Boyd, 1992). The program was legally challenged under the Charter of Rights and Freedoms for being discriminatory to women (Doherty, 1992), but the program was discontinued before a decision was reached. The skills (e.g., language assessment, intercultural communication) of the federal officials who were the gatekeepers to the program were considered to be inadequate (e.g., Belfiore & Heller, 1992).

Because of its labor-related objectives, this program was administered from the Employment side of Employment and Immigration Canada. In 1986, in response to some of these criticisms, the Settlement Branch of the Immigration side of Employment and Immigration Canada launched a pilot language training program aimed specifically at immigrant women not destined for the laborforce. It called for proposals from educational institutions, and especially from nongovernmental organizations (NGOs) already involved in immigrant settlement activities, to mount 1-year projects to provide language training with support, if needed, for child minding (not daycare, which is highly regulated) and transportation. The training would be part time and with no training allowances. In doing this, it took a significant step over the line of provincial responsibility for education because it would be federal, not provincial, officials who would make decisions about which proposals to fund and would monitor the projects. In order to counteract possible provincial objections, an advisory council was to be set up in each participating province or region with representation from the federal and provincial governments and suitable

## 10. ESL POLICY IN CANADA AND THE UNITED STATES 251

NGO groups where appropriate. It was in federal interests to take this step because it would break the hold the provinces had on the federal government to buy seats exclusively from the community colleges with their "expensive," unionized teaching force.

This pilot, which became the Settlement Language Program (SLP), has been remarkable in its demonstration of at least some of the kinds of potential learners who have not been reached by other kinds of programs.[4] Each project was unique: some attracted immigrants who had been in the country for as many as 20 years; others attracted isolated and older people; still others in areas where there is not much immigration reached the kinds of learners that would be served by other federal and provincial programs in high immigration areas; many appealed to people who were not literate in their mother tongue. In an assessment of the first year of the pilot (Burnaby, Holt, Stelzer, & Collins, 1987), it was found that all of the participants (even the senior citizens) wanted to be considered as destined for the laborforce.

A year or so later, another small pilot program, Language at Work (LAW) was initiated on a similar basis for workplace and language skills training combined for immigrant women. Although the SLP and LAW were considered to have the advantage of providing well-targeted training by organizations that are in good touch with the community, concerns relate to the stress on small organizations to maintain and juggle various sources of funding for short-term projects, lack of consistency or standards, the qualifications of staff (in some situations), and the ability of federal officials to make informed judgements about funding and evaluating the projects.[5] Chisman et al. (1993) noted the same values and concerns about parallel United States agencies providing ESL.

For a perspective on the relative sizes of these programs, note the following from Immigration Canada (1992b):

In 1990/91, 92 per cent ($99M of $107.3M) of federal language training funds provided full-time institutional training related to labour market needs. The two other language training programs, the Settlement Language Program (SLP) and Language at Work (LAW), primarily targeted immigrant women. They offered only part-time training and accounted for a relatively small portion of federal funding.

At present, EIC [Employment and Immigration Canada]-funded language training programs only reach some 28 per cent of newly arrived adult immigrants in need of language training. (p. 2)[6]

---

[4]NGOs and school boards had been dealing with some of this through localized initiatives.
[5]But at least federal officials do not make all the judgements about which individual clients can enter the classes.
[6]It is not clear on what basis this figure was determined.

Since the new immigration plan announced by the federal government in 1990, language training and other settlement services have been included as part of a settlement-oriented package. It originally proposed to replace all previous federal language training (including the employment-related program) with a new program including Language Instruction for Newcomers to Canada (LINC; 80% of the language training dollars) and Labour Market Language Training (LMLT; 20%). However, LMLT was moved soon after to an employment-based training program. Funding levels for this initiative are supposed to be 60% higher than previous federal language training expenditures. However, Canadian citizens and refugee claimants are not eligible, and no training allowances for students are available. "Visa-ready" immigrants awaiting final processing overseas are also to be served (Immigration Canada, 1993a).[7] The plan was to increase the proportion of newly arrived adult immigrants receiving language training from the 1990 level of about 28% to about 45% in 1995 (Immigration Canada, 1991).[8]

LINC works like the SLP in that individual NGOs, educational institutions, and private organizations can apply for funds to deliver a LINC program through a one-year contract. It is not clear how a full range of programs in any one area are coordinated. Potential LINC students go to be assessed at an A-LINC center, where their language skills are tested and rated at 1 of 12 national ESL benchmark levels, including ESL literacy (Citizenship and Immigration Canada, 1996). If they score at the lower levels (below about 3 or 4), they are counseled about appropriate LINC programs in their area. LINC curricula matching for the lower benchmark levels are developed cooperatively to fit with provincial standards. Child-minding and transportation may be funded as well in LINC programs. There is a limit on how much time a student will be allowed in the program.

A major concern expressed about LINC is the exclusion of refugee claimants and citizens. Immigration Canada (1993b) indicated that 117,000 people claimed refugee status from 1989 to 1992. Although a streamlined refugee status adjudication system was put in place in 1989 to clear up the backlog of claimants, there are still thousands of them in the country. Immigrants who have become citizens have also been excluded from LINC. On the basis of 1986 Canadian census data, Pendakur (1992) indicated:

> Roughly half the immigrants unable to speak English or French arrived in Canada prior to 1980; almost one third arrived prior to 1970 ... It should be noted that the size of the group is likely to increase because while the number of persons unable to speak an official language remained relatively stable between 1981 and

---

[7]Canada, unlike the United States, has not conducted its own overseas language training and cultural orientation before this.

[8]It is not clear how these percentages were determined.

## 10. ESL POLICY IN CANADA AND THE UNITED STATES 253

1986, increasing immigration from non-English–French speaking countries will likely change this situation. This in turn will serve to increase the demand for federally and provincially funded language training programs. (p. 161)

Boyd's (1992) figures showed that there is also a proportionately large group of this sort in the United States. According to Cumming (1991) " … research has suggested that some immigrants to Canada, particularly women, only consider themselves able to pursue language studies after they have established a secure home life and economic position, a point which may be 3 to 10 years after their initial immigration" (pp. 8–9; see also Cumming & Gill, 1991; Seward & McDade, 1988). In Canada at least, a high percentage of these people will have taken out Canadian citizenship. Clearly, the federal government is leaving responsibility for them to the provinces.

In sum, the federal government eased itself over the federal/provincial boundary where education is on the provincial side. First, it called adult issues "training" in order to get jurisdiction and the provinces agreed as long as they got to control the training itself through federal seat purchase of training even if federal personnel chose the students. Then the federal government took another major step in tendering contracts directly with private groups, NGOs, and educational institutions for federal ESL programs. In doing so it not only got away from provincial measures of control (such as having to run the program through provincially designated institutions) but it also refocused its expenditures by eliminating training allowances for students and restricting the program to noncitizens. This LINC strategy is now the main federal ESL funding approach for adult ESL learners. In this discussion, an essential factor is that the federal funding is entirely independent from provincial ESL programs, which vary according to immigration levels in each province but are extensive in many.

In contrast, Chisman et al. (1993) said of the United States:

Most, but not all, funding for adult ESL service is provided through intergovernmental programs: federally initiated programs to which states, and sometimes localities, contribute funds and for which they also develop policies within a federal policy framework. The federal Adult Education Act is the source of intergovernmental funding for ESL most commonly identified, but JOBS, JTPA, vocational education and a host of smaller programs also fall into this category. (p. 79)

They note divided responsibility (which means both sides can shirk), lack of national uniformity, and problems of concentrating the effort where it is most needed as the main weaknesses of this structure. In the Canadian situation with separate federal and provincial programs, coordination is a real challenge, but at least each side knows where its jurisdiction is. The issue of uniformity is being addressed at least within the LINC program through the levels system, and federal control over LINC contracts gives the federal government power over where to concentrate the funding in various areas of the country and among various groups. Provinces must fill in where federal programs leave gaps.

A second short example of federal/provincial relations over education is provided here. It has been included because it illustrates how the Canadian division of powers has largely kept the Canadian federal government out of nonofficial minority language education and its relationship with ESL. In 1971, several years after The Official Languages Act was made law, the federal government declared itself to be, by policy, multicultural. The policy was passed as legislation in 1988. Clearly aimed at calming the backlash among nonofficial language and cultural groups over the declaration of official languages, the multiculturalism policy pledged to promote respect and support for all the languages and cultures in the country. There was some money attached to the policy and provinces expanded "heritage" language programs for the teaching of nonofficial languages in schools. Resistance was demonstrated in many areas to having heritage language classes as a regular part of the curriculum (Ashworth, 1992; Cummins & Danesi, 1990; d'Anglejan & De Koninck, 1992), and they remain largely as an add-on in most jurisdictions (Ashworth, 1992; Toohey, 1992). Federal assistance through transfer payments to provinces for heritage language programs was cut off in 1990, but many provinces continue to support them (Canadian Education Association, 1991). Although the multiculturalism policy and Act encouraged the learning of the official languages, they were never associated with fiscal support for official language training programs.

This policy and Act are about as close as Canada has gotten federally to the Bilingual Education Act in the United States with respect to the use of minority languages in education. However, Canadian heritage language programs are not linked to issues of children being at risk concerning learning English (or French); their intention is to offer children the opportunity to learn a language that is present in the community. The assumption is that most children in such classes will be learning their ancestral language, but other interested children are usually not excluded. Criticisms of the programs include that they largely aim at the beginning level of learning the languages and do not capitalize on the nonofficial language skills that children bring with them from their homes (Burnaby, 1987; Toohey, 1992).

These two illustrations are provided to show how the federal and provincial governments have to dance with one another over the issue of federal interests versus provincial control over education. The central point is that there is no federal legislation and funding in Canada that is comparable to those such as the Adult Education Act, the Bilingual Education Act, or the

## 10. ESL POLICY IN CANADA AND THE UNITED STATES 255

Johnson–O'Malley provisions in the United States. Although it is acknowledged that these measures in the United States are not comprehensive in their coverage of learners in need according to their definitions, they do represent some federal power of intervention. The Canadian federal government has to be much more subtle in its means of supporting such issues.

### The Role of the Courts

The next point is brief because its full delineation requires major legal discussions more fully covered elsewhere in this volume (see Fettes, Magnet, and Schmidt). The passing of the Constitution Act and particularly the Charter of Rights and Freedoms in 1982 marked a turning point in Canada. Up to that point the legislative and justice systems of Canada did not make much room for Canadians to challenge government policies or laws in court. However, the Charter of Rights and Freedoms has provided a template against which to make such challenges. As noted earlier, the federal government's policy in choosing immigrants for federal language training programs was challenged in court after 1982. It is not clear what other cases related to ESL for immigrants might be forthcoming. However, up until this point, the Canadian courts have not played a role, as they did, for example, in the *Lau v. Nichols* case in the United States, in changing in any way the provision of ESL.

### Strategies for Control Over Programs

A further difference between the Canadian and U.S. government structures is the contrast between the ways in which funding for language programs are distributed and monitored. A government funding body can either restrict or be lenient about the initial terms of service and the way the service is provided. The negotiated character of the federal–provincial relationship (and that of colleges and school boards with the provinces) in Canada has permitted a considerable degree of useful flexibility in ESL program development. Inevitably, what one gains in flexibility one tends to lose in comprehensiveness. There have been no national standards for student outcomes until the LINC benchmarks (Citizenship and Immigration Canada, 1996), which now can be applied not only to LINC students but also to students in any provincial or local ESL programs at higher language skill levels. However, ESL teacher qualifications are not nationally standardized, and programs have not been evaluated comparatively, much less competitively. With respect to control over services, Canadian programming is quite different from that of the United States. Churchill (1986) compared the Canadian federal-provincial grant formula for public education under the Official Languages Act to the Bilingual Education Act in the United States on the extent of freedom from central control (high, medium, or low): (a) at the initiation of service; (b) choice of population and numbers served; (c) choice of mode of service; and (d) accountability and inspection after grant. He assessed the Canadian program as having a high degree of freedom from central control on all four factors, whereas has sees the Bilingual Education Act as high at the initiation of service, medium on choice of population and mode of service, and low on accountability and inspection. In general, Canadian programs have not been held strictly accountable. From a public perspective, as well, it is impossible to track funds as they are transferred to the provinces, and from the provinces to, for example, a college, and within the college to a specific program. Until the initiation of the LINC program, only programs like the SLP, where federal monies go directly to the delivery agency, have been fiscally accountable in the public view.

With the advent of LINC and the benchmarks in Canada, a major change is the attempt to standardize language training across the country. Teachers who believe in learner-centered curriculum are already worrying about how such standardization will relate to their principles (Goldstein, 1993). Delivery agencies at least have their say in the type of program they propose. LINC level 1 is supposed to address ESL literacy, but it also includes all learners at the basic fluency level. Only in large immigrant receiving centers where there are special classes for ESL literacy can they be treated separately. Thus, ESL literacy learners are often excluded again as they were before. Federal policies on how the different LINC contracts are chosen in relation to need are not public. Chisman et al. (1993) said of U.S. language programs:

> While they [ESL teachers and coordinators] support the establishment of evaluation standards that would lead to greater program accountability, they fear that the recent national emphasis on such standards will result in systems of evaluation and accountability based on standardized tests. (p. 57)

By contrast, Canadian ESL teachers are so unused to such accountability measures that they are concerned even about the prospect of benchmarks, much less standardized tests as measures of accountability. The point here is that accountability of Canadian ESL programs seems to have been much less regulated on the basis of national standards of whatever sort than those in the United States, and that ESL practitioners on both sides of the border are wary about the impact of such standards.

In sum, ESL provisions in Canada and the United States are differently influenced by respective national government structures, relations between the courts and legislatures, and normal practices relating to accountability for government funded programs. Although there are positive and nega-

# 10. ESL POLICY IN CANADA AND THE UNITED STATES 257

tive implications related to these factors on both sides, it is important to appreciate the differences when comparing policies in the two countries.

## IMMIGRATION POLICIES

The phrase "a nation of immigrants" often is used to describe the birth and continued vitality of United States life. It is an even more appropriate depiction of Canada. With a population roughly one-tenth that of the United States, Canada had until recently an immigration flow approximating one-quarter of all movement into the North American continent. Nearly one in five of the Canadian population is foreign born, compared with about one in twenty in the United States.

Both countries share a similar history of legal migration flows and immigration policies. In the decades following World War II, migrant flows to both countries shifted from European countries to third world countries, and they now include substantial family-based migration. These changes in migration composition reflect fundamental alterations in North American immigration legislation. Starting in the 1960s, both Canada and the United States revised postwar immigration policies, discarding national origin as the main criterion of admission and instead invoking social, humanitarian, and economic criteria. (Boyd, 1992, p. 305)

Hawkins (1989) listed the 10 basic principles of the 1976 Immigration Act, the framework for immigration legislation that is still largely in place:

Enriching the cultural and social fabric of Canada, taking into account its federal and bilingual character; family reunion; federal–provincial–municipal and voluntary sector collaboration in immigrant settlement; the fostering of trade, commerce, tourism, cultural and scientific activities, and international understanding; non-discrimination in immigration policy; economic prosperity in all Canadian regions; the health, safety, and good order in Canadian society; and the exclusion of persons likely to engage in criminal activity. (p. 71)

For various reasons, numbers of immigrants to Canada have fluctuated over the years. In the 1970s and 1980s, the totals ranged from a high of 218,465 in 1974 to a low of 84,302 in 1984. According to the World Refugee Survey of 1992, Canada has the highest proportion among the countries surveyed of resettled refugees in its population (1 refugee to every 82 in the general population compared with 1 to 171 in the United States; Immigration Canada, 1992a). In 1990, the federal government announced a new immigration plan with the goal of bringing in 220,000 immigrants in 1991 up to about 250,000 per year in increments until 1995. Objectives for the implementation of the plan included improvements in support for the integration of immigrants into Canadian society (Employment and Immigration Canada, 1992). These improvements include substituting the LINC

**258** BURNABY

programs for all previous federal ESL training along with some other changes.

Immigration classes are family class, refugees, independent immigrants, assisted relatives, business immigrants, and retirees. In 1967, a point system was set up to evaluate applicants for some immigrant classes; it has been revised several times but the principle structure remains. Hawkins, writing in 1989, described:

> Numerical weights are attached to a set of 10 factors (9 in the earlier version) which attempt to assess the qualifications of an applicant for landed immigrant status in the broad areas of *education, training* and experience, occupation and intended destination, age, *knowledge of English and/or French* [italics added], personal suitability, and the presence or otherwise of relatives in Canada ... Members of the family class and retired persons are not selected according to these criteria. Three of the 10 factors do not apply to assisted relatives. Convention refugees are assessed by means of the point system, to enable immigration officers to learn about their background, qualifications, and experience, but are not given a point rating. (p. 77)

There are targets set each year for the number of immigrants in each class and quotas for some (Employment and Immigration Canada, 1993). Family class, which has no selection criteria (the point system), normally represents the largest group of immigrants (84,000 out of 206,000 in 1991; Immigration Canada, 1992a). Over several decades, immigrants have overwhelmingly chosen to settle in major urban centers such as the greater Toronto area, Vancouver, and Montreal[9]; to counteract this imbalance, immigrant applicants with certain occupational skills can strengthen their case by voluntarily agreeing to settle for a specified period of time in a particular area of the country (Immigration Canada, 1993b).

Two points of contrast between Canada and the United States are especially significant. Both are reflected in the ten principles for immigration given in the Hawkins (1989) quote earlier. One concerns Canada's emphasis on economics in immigration relative to that of the United States:

> Economics was more important for shaping immigration policy in Canada than in the United States, and American policies were more closely tied to foreign policy questions than were Canadian ... Canada has a different governmental structure and a stronger tradition of immigration recruitment than has the United States. For example, immigration has been dealt with in the same ministry as manpower or employment matters in Canada, whereas most immigration issues are handled by the Justice Department in the United States. (Chiswick, 1992, p. 5)

One form this Canadian emphasis has taken has been the use of the point

---

[9]See Chisman et al. (1993, pp. 8–9) for comparable distribution figures for immigrants in the United States.

## 10. ESL POLICY IN CANADA AND THE UNITED STATES                    259

system for selecting some classes of immigrants, and one set of points were for skills in one of the official languages. Chiswick (1992) noted:

> Although the United States 1990 Immigration Act is narrowing the gap [between the United States and Canada] in the proportion of visas issued on the basis of the applicants' skills, when these amendments were being debated in Congress the proposal to include English-language fluency in the selection criteria was defeated. (p. 10)

Does the use of the Canadian point system mean that Canadian immigrants are more fluent in English or French than United States immigrants are in English? Chiswick and Miller's 1992 study of the role of language in the United States and Canadian immigrant labor market shows that employed immigrant men in Canada have a slightly higher rate of fluency, but that comparison is risky given that the Canadian and United States censuses use rather different measures of language skills.[10]

The second point concerns differences between the Canadian and United States government structures. Given the importance of balance and negotiation between the federal and provincial levels in Canada, it is not surprising that the immigration principles stress collaboration among various sectors. Such a balance is reflected in federal interests in shouldering only part of the costs of immigrant settlement.

> The [federal] government's increased funding represents a significant commitment. However, EIC [the Employment and Immigration Commission] never has and never will act as the sole provider of language training. EIC is counting on sponsors and on training providers to continue to make other opportunities available. The federal government wants overall training opportunities increased. It does not want its increased expenditures to replace existing sources. (Immigration Canada, 1992c, p. 1)

This balance also means that provinces can negotiate to take over some of the power in administering immigration intake and services. Since 1978 (the Cullen-Couture Agreement followed by the Canada–Quebec Accord in 1991), Quebec has taken control of some aspects of immigration and virtually all aspects of settlement in its jurisdiction. This is because immigrants historically have turned to English rather than French even in Quebec. Because the birthrate in Quebec is very low, the province is concerned with supporting its francophone culture by immigration that

---

[10]Nakamura and Nakamura (1992) compared wage rates of immigrant and native-born men in Canada and the United States and concluded:

We have found that, on average, the hourly wage rates of immigrant workers as compared with native workers in Canada are higher than is the case in the United States. This is consistent with our finding that, compared with the native populations, *immigrant workers in Canada have more education on average than is true for immigrant workers in the United States.* (p. 161; emphasis added)

# 260 BURNABY

will integrate into French rather than English society (d'Anglejan & De Koninck, 1992):

> The federal government retains responsibility for establishing immigration levels and general classes of immigrants, admitting immigrants and granting permanent resident status, while Quebec gains sole responsibility for selecting independent immigrants destined for Quebec and for integration services for permanent residents of Quebec. Additionally, the Accord compensates Quebec for the federal withdrawal from settlement and integration services. (Immigration Canada, 1991, p. 15)

Given this circumstance, virtually none of the discussion in this chapter on federal policies (other than financing levels) applies to the administration of French language training to immigrants in Quebec.

In sum, immigration to Canada is higher proportionally than that in the United States, and therefore it creates a greater pressure on the population. It seems that Canadian entrance requirements for official language fluency for certain immigrant classes, which are not required of applicants to the United States, do not have a significant impact on the overall ESL situation in Canada relative to that in the United States. Quebec has taken over immigration to that province to the extent that it controls who it will take in and provides its own language and settlement services so that immigrants there are focused on the French language and Quebec culture. Because Quebec is the third largest immigrant receiving province, this provision makes a considerable impact in Canadian immigration.

## ESL AND ADULT BASIC EDUCATION

Literacy has not been mentioned thus far, but is important because of the close link between literacy and ESL in the United States. In Canada, adult basic education (ABE; below Grade 9 level), not aimed especially at immigrants, was initially included in the federal adult training program for the workforce in the 1960s. In the early 1970s, this level was removed from the program. NGOs have been much more active than any other group of delivery agencies in basic literacy work. Provincial school boards and colleges, through direct program delivery, have increasingly become involved in noncredit ABE in the 1980s, while ministries of education, through distance education, and school boards, through part-time and full-time credit classes, have stepped up their efforts in secondary level upgrading and accreditation.[11] In many parts of the country, literacy teaching developments led to much closer cooperation between government educational institutions and community NGOs serving literacy learners.

---

[11]Canadian institutions do not generally use the GED as a goal or a standard.

## 10. ESL POLICY IN CANADA AND THE UNITED STATES                    261

In the 1980s, international economic pressures created a concern in the private sector about the skills of its workforce (Burnaby, 1992a). A private corporation (Creative Research Group) sponsored a limited test of adult literacy skills in 1987, then in 1990 the federal government released the results of an extensive survey/test of adult literacy (Statistics Canada, 1991). Both were loosely based on the United States National Assessment of Educational Progress literacy study (Kirsch & Jungeblut, 1986). The results indicated that about 20 to 25% of the sample were functionally illiterate. Unfortunately for present purposes, "the data [in the Canadian study] were not cast to allow the conversion of the NAEP results to the Canadian scheme" (Statistics Canada, 1991, p. 53), but the results appear to be fairly comparable.

In the mid-1980s, one province and the federal government took the unprecedented step of putting adult literacy on their agenda; the other provinces soon followed. The federal government established the National Literacy Secretariat, which is now housed in the Human Resources Development Canada and provides funds for research, promotion, and coordination; it does not fund direct service. Although the level of activity is very low relative to that of other federal programs, it is highly significant that the issue is officially recognized as something more than a problem of the marginalized.

Immigrants to Canada tend to be more *and* less well educated than native born Canadians; in other words, there is a greater gap between the less and more educated in the immigrant group. The numbers of immigrants with low levels of education in their mother tongue have been growing for more than a decade (Klassen & Burnaby, 1993). Analyses of the federal literacy study data showed that immigrants as a group did not contribute greatly to the overall illiteracy levels in the country but that some groups of immigrants, particularly women, were particularly at risk (Boyd, 1991; Jones, 1992). Academic studies (e.g., Boyd, 1992; Cumming & Gil, 1992; Klassen, 1987) have shown that immigrants with low levels of literacy in their first language have considerable and specific internal and external barriers to access to ESL and other kinds of training.

It has been a major criticism of general ESL policy and provision that ESL literacy learners are not accommodated. Issues of training for immigrants who do not speak an official language and who are not literate in their first language are normally considered to be an ESL rather than an adult literacy concern in Canada nonetheless (Burnaby, 1992b). Bilingual ESL and mother-tongue literacy programs, developed at local levels in high immigrant density areas, are dealing with some of the demand. One federal strategy for reducing the specific problems of immigrants with low levels of education has been, recently, to try to use the point system to lower the numbers of such immigrants admitted. This approach, however, will not affect the main groups of ESL literacy immigrants, that is, those who are not evaluated on the basis of points. Boyd (1992) showed that the ESL literacy group in both Canada and the United States is predominated by women and that women more than men face external barriers to access to ESL training.

One further point here is that, under some conditions, immigrants (not necessarily those with low levels of education) have taken major advantage of expanded provisions of literacy classes since the mid-1980s to meet their ESL needs (Burnaby, 1992b). Chisman et al. (1993) noted that the same trend is happening in the United States: "The demand for ESL services is overwhelming our adult education system: most people would probably be surprised to learn that about half of what is often called 'adult literacy' instruction in the United States consists of ESL" (p. 2).

In light of changes to the Adult Education Act in 1988 and the National Literacy Act of 1991 in the United States, some discussion is needed of differences in Canada and the United States on the distinction between ESL and literacy in service provisions. Undoubtedly, many of the same factors influenced Canada to create new immigration and laborforce training policies at about the same time as the United States put the National Literacy Act into law in 1991. Chisman's 1989 report on the federal role in literacy—which includes ESL—in the United States and was apparently influential in the development of the National Literacy Act, outlines similar concerns to those of Canadians worried about the role in the economy of adult literacy (e.g., DesLauriers, 1990; Drouin, 1990; Economic Council of Canada, 1990) and to those of Burnaby (1992a) about ESL in her national overview. As in the United States (Chisman, 1989), ESL service delivery in Canada is better organized than that for adult literacy.

The definition of literacy in the Act broadly encompasses economic, social, and personal development goals for all legal residents of the United States, and the interests of a number of federal departments are subsumed (e.g., reflected in programs like family literacy and literacy in prisons). Canada's new measures address ESL, citizenship, and literacy for potential citizens (with some specialized, laborforce-oriented ESL for highly trained newcomers) in one program administered from a single section of one department, and literacy and training, but not ESL explicitly, for economic and personal development of all residents in another program administered from another section of the same department. The federal ESL program in Canada promises more coordination and flexibility than before, but imposes eligibility restrictions concerning citizenship status and fluency levels; the United States Act is potentially almost infinitely inclusive.

# 10. ESL POLICY IN CANADA AND THE UNITED STATES 263

In practice, the Canadian program may prove to be too restrictive to meet real needs, and the United States Act too general to be cohesive or accountable. Indeed, Chisman et al. (1993) thought that the United States linkage of ESL with ABE is unworkable ("Unless and until adult ESL can be recognized as a highly distinctive [from ABE] educational service that deserves priority in its own right, there is little chance for progress in its work"; p. 17). The Canadian provinces or others will have to provide ESL for all residents after their first year or so in the country, whereas the U.S. provisions allow for federal support much more widely. Various programs under the umbrella of the U.S. Act put money in the hands of the states and other bodies, whereas the Canadian federal ESL program provides only for direct contracting between the federal department and individual delivery agencies. Although the initiatives in both countries go some distance toward consolidating funding and providing leadership at the national level, the new National Institute for Literacy and state literacy resource centers in the United States are likely to provide for coordination and research that is not anticipated through the Canadian program thus far.

In light of differences between Canada and the United States discussed early in this chapter, one can speculate on some reasons for these contrasts in policy. Concerning comments made earlier about the United States tending to support individuals' rights, the Act certainly leans in the direction of support for a basic good for all residents. On the other hand, Canada's new ESL policy carefully avoids making promises to its citizens in general. Canada's higher immigration rate proportionate to the total population could justify a specific focus on immigrants. Provincial control over education and the negotiated character of federal/provincial relationships might account for the federal government's leaving all but initial language training in the hands of the provinces. Also, the greater split in Canada between provincial control over education and federal control over immigration probably motivates the division of ESL from literacy to some degree. Finally, provincial control over education has probably been the major reason why Canada federally has not created national level institutions on topics, such as ESL or literacy, related to training. On the other hand, federal powers in the area of economic development permitted it at one point to consider establishing an institute concerned with the credentialing of immigrants.

## CONCLUSION

It has not been the intention of this chapter to make a great deal of the differences between Canada and the United States with respect to ESL in their respective countries. It is clear even from this contrastive discussion that there is more in common between nonofficial language speakers in Canada and language minorities in the United States than there are differences. However, in order to clear the decks for a good Canada/U.S. comparison of ESL policies, we need to acknowledge certain things. The first is that the teaching of English to francophones or French to anglophones in Canada should be left outside of the discussion of ESL to minority language speakers, because that area of language teaching has an entirely different status. A second is that nonofficial language speakers in Canada have a particular political challenge, relative to that of their U.S. counterparts, in order to get their voice heard because the French–English debate takes up a great deal of the Canadian political consciousness. Xenophobia in the United States may present a comparable barrier (Chisman et al., 1993), but there is no way of equating the two problems. A third matter is structural differences between Canadian and United States governments with respect to federal and provincial/state relations, the role of the courts in challenging legislation, and policies for controlling contracts for educational services. In addition, immigration plays a different role in Canada as a geographically large country with a small population. Canada has a larger proportion of immigrants and refugees than does the United States. However, language restriction on admitting some immigrants to Canada does not seem to make much difference, and Canada may be moving from an economic focus on immigrant settlement toward a more justice-oriented model like that of the United States. Finally, Canada has separated ESL (including ESL literacy) from adult basic education. The United States has taken the opposite direction. There are problems with both these approaches, which could benefit from mutual study of the situations in both countries.

## REFERENCES

Ashworth, M. (1992). Views and visions. In B. Burnaby & A. Cumming (Eds.), *Socio-political aspects of ESL in Canada* (pp. 35–49). Toronto: OISE Press.

Belfiore, M. E., & Heller, M. (1992). Cross-cultural interviews: Participation in decision-making. In B. Burnaby & A. Cumming (Eds.), *Socio-political aspects of ESL in Canada* (pp. 223–240). Toronto: OISE Press.

Bloom, D., & Grenier, G. (1992) Earnings of the French minority in Canada and the Spanish minority in the United States. In B. Chiswick (Ed.), *Immigration, language, and ethnicity: Canada and the United States* (pp. 373–409). Washington, DC: The AEI Press.

Boyd, M. (1991). Gender, nativity, and literacy: Proficiency and training issues. In Statistics Canada (Ed.), *Adult literacy in Canada: Results of a national study* (pp. 85–94). Ottawa: Minister of Industry, Science and Technology.

Boyd, M. (1992). Gender issues in immigration and language fluency. In B. Chiswick (Ed.), *Immigration, language, and ethnicity: Canada and the United States* (pp. 305–372). Washington, DC: The AEI Press.

## 10. ESL POLICY IN CANADA AND THE UNITED STATES    265

Burnaby, B. (1987). Language for Native, ethnic, and recent immigrant groups: What's the difference? *TESL Canada Journal, 4,* 9–27.

Burnaby, B. (1992a). Adult literacy issues in Canada. In R. B. Kaplan (Ed.), *Annual review of applied linguistics XII* (pp. 156–171). Cambridge, England: Cambridge University Press.

Burnaby, B. (1992b). Official language training for adult immigrants in Canada: Features and issues. In B. Burnaby & A. Cumming (Eds.), *Socio-political aspects of ESL in Canada* (pp. 3–34). Toronto: OISE Press.

Burnaby, B., Holt, M., Steltzer, N., & Collins, N. (1987). *The Settlement Language Training Program: An assessment* (Report of behalf of the TESL Canada Federation). Ottawa: Employment and Immigration Canada.

Canadian Education Association. (1991). *Heritage language programs in Canadian school boards.* Toronto: Canadian Education Association.

Chisman, F. (1989). *Jump start: The federal role in adult literacy.* Southport, CT: The Southport Institute for Policy Analysis.

Chisman, F., Wrigley, H. S., & Ewen, D. T. (1993). *ESL and the American dream.* Washington, DC: The Southport Institute for Policy Analysis.

Chiswick, B. (1992). Introduction. In B. Chiswick (Ed.), *Immigration, language, and ethnicity: Canada and the United States* (pp. 1–12). Washington, DC: The AEI Press.

Chiswick, B., & Miller, P. (1992). Language in the immigrant labour market. In B. Chiswick (Ed.), *Immigration, language, and ethnicity: Canada and the United States* (pp. 229–296). Washington, DC: The AEI Press.

Churchill, S. (1986). *The education of linguistic and cultural minorities in the OECD countries.* Clevedon, England: Multilingual Matters.

Citizenship and Immigration Canada. (1996). *Canadian language benchmarks: English as a second language for adults, English as a second language for literacy learners* (Working Doc. 1996). Ottawa: Supply and Services Canada.

Creative Research Group. (1987). *Literacy in Canada: A research report* (prepared for Southam News, Ottawa). Toronto: Creative Research Group.

Cumming, A. (1991). *Identification of current needs and issues related to the delivery of adult ESL instruction in British Columbia.* Victoria: British Columbia Ministry of International Business and Immigration.

Cumming, A., & Gil, J. (1991, April). *Learning language and literacy among Indo-Canadian women.* Paper presented at the annual meeting of the American Educational Research Association, Chicago.

Cumming, A., & Gil, J. (1992). Motivation or accessibility? Factors permitting Indo-Canadian women to pursue ESL literacy. In B. Burnaby & A. Cumming (Eds.), *Socio-political aspects of ESL in Canada* (pp. 241–252). Toronto: OISE Press.

Cumming, A., Hart, D., Corson, D., & Cummins, J. (1993). *Provisions and demands for ESL, ESD, and ALF programs in Ontario schools.* Toronto: Modern Language Centre, Ontario Institute for Studies in Education.

Cummins, J., & Danesi, M. (1990). *Heritage languages: The development and denial of Canada's linguistic resources.* Toronto: Our Schools/Our Selves Education Foundation and Garamond Press.

d'Anglejan, A., & De Koninck, Z. (1992). Educational policy for a culturally plural Quebec: An update. In B. Burnaby & A. Cumming (Eds.), *Socio-political aspects of ESL in Canada* (pp. 97–109). Toronto: OISE Press.

DesLauriers, R. C. (1990). *The impact of employee illiteracy on Canadian business.* Ottawa: Human Resource Development Centre, Conference Board of Canada.

Doherty, N. (1992). Challenging systematic sexism in the National Language Training Program. In B. Burnaby & A. Cumming (Eds.), *Socio-political aspects of ESL in Canada* (pp. 67–76). Toronto: OISE Press.

Drouin, M-J. (1990). *Workforce illiteracy: An economic challenge for Canada.* Montreal: The Hudson Institute.

Economic Council of Canada. (1990). *Good jobs, bad jobs: Employment in the service economy.* Ottawa: Supply and Services Canada.

Employment and Immigration Canada. (1992). *Annual report 1991–1992.* Ottawa: Minister of Supply and Services Canada.

Employment and Immigration Canada. (1993). *A new immigration program for the 1990s.* Ottawa: Minister of Supply and Services Canada.

Flaherty, L., & Woods, D. (1992). Immigrant/refugee children in Canadian schools: Educational issues, political dilemmas. In B. Burnaby & A. Cumming (Eds.), *Socio-political aspects of ESL in Canada* (pp. 182–192). Toronto: OISE Press.

Goldstein, T. (1993). Working with learners in LINC programs: Asking ourselves some questions. *Contact: Newsletter of the Association of Teachers of English as a Second Language of Ontario, 18,* 12–13.

Hawkins, F. (1989). *Critical years in immigration: Canada and Australia compared.* Kingston and Montreal: McGill–Queen's University Press.

Immigration Canada. (1991). *Annual report to Parliament: Immigration plan for 1991–1995: Year two November 1991.* Ottawa: Minister of Supply and Services Canada.

Immigration Canada. (1992a). *Annual report to Parliament: Immigration plan for 1991–1995: Year three 1993.* Ottawa: Minister of Supply and Services Canada.

Immigration Canada. (1992b). *New immigrant language training policy.* Ottawa: Employment and Immigration Canada.

Immigration Canada. (1992c). *Questions and answers of the new immigrant language training policy.* Ottawa: Employment and Immigration Canada.

Immigration Canada. (1993a). *Immigration consultations 1993: The federal immigrant integration strategy in 1993: A progress report.* Ottawa: Employment and Immigration Canada.

Immigration Canada. (1993b). *A new immigration program for the 1990s: Background.* Ottawa: Employment and Immigration Canada.

Jones, S. (1992). Literacy in a second language: Results from a survey of everyday life. In B. Burnaby & A. Cumming (Eds.), *Socio-political aspects of ESL in Canada* (pp. 203–220). Toronto: OISE Press.

Kirsch, I. S., & Jungeblut, A. (1986). *Literacy: Profiles of America's young adults* (Final Report No. 16–PL–01). Princeton, NJ: The National Assessment of Educational Progress.

Klassen, C. (1987). *Language and literacy learning: The adult immigrant's account.* Unpublished master of arts thesis. Toronto: University of Toronto.

Klassen, C., & Burnaby, B. (1993). "Those who know": Views on literacy among adult immigrants in Canada. *TESOL Quarterly, 27,* 377–398.

McManus, W. (1992). Commentary on part three. In B. Chiswick (Ed.), *Immigration, language, and ethnicity: Canada and the United States* (pp. 299–302). Washington, DC: The AEI Press.

Nakamura, A., & Nakamura, M. (1992). Wage rates of immigrant and native men in Canada and the United States. In B. Chiswick (Ed.), *Immigration, language, and ethnicity: Canada and the United States* (pp. 145–166). Washington, DC: The AEI Press.

Pendakur, R. (1992). Labour market segmentation theories and the place of immigrant speaking neither English nor French in Canada. In B. Burnaby & A. Cumming (Eds.), *Socio-political aspects of ESL in Canada* (pp. 160–181). Toronto: OISE Press.

Seward, S., & McDade, K. (1988). *Immigrant women in Canada: A policy perspective.* Ottawa: Canadian Advisory Council on the Status of Women.

Statistics Canada. (1991). *Adult literacy in Canada: Results of a national study.* Ottawa: Minister of Industry, Science and Technology.

## 10. ESL POLICY IN CANADA AND THE UNITED STATES

Toohey, K. (1992). We teach English as a second language to bilingual students. In B. Burnaby & A. Cumming (Eds.), *Socio-political aspects of ESL in Canada* (pp. 87–96). Toronto: OISE Press.

Vaillancourt, F. (1992). An economic perspective on language and public policy in Canada and the United States. In B. Chiswick (Ed.), *Immigration, language, and ethnicity: Canada and the United States* (pp. 179–228). Washington, DC: The AEI Press.

# V

# Focus on Context

The kinds of policies discussed in this book are, when all is said and done, only the statements and actions of governments. They exist in contexts where many other forces make their own statements and take their own actions. The focus of Part V is on the iterative impacts that individuals and groups on the one hand and governments on the other have on each other where action on language is concerned. Such discussions really cut governments down to size in terms of their actual effectiveness, at least where regulating language is concerned. Even where governments can be shown to have had a devastating effect on specific languages and their use (see, e.g., Crawford, chapter 6, this volume), such effects would not have been possible if it were not the case that public opinion in the majority population was generally at least as racist as the policies themselves (see also Wiley, chapter 9, this volume). Thus, it is essential in a book on language policy to attend to the reactions and interactions of various stakeholders as well as to the ideals stated in the policies themselves.

Because language has a pervasive influence on virtually all aspects of human life, the authors of chapters in this section (and elsewhere in the book) raise a broad range of matters in discussing the effects of language policy. For example, in chapter 11 Cartwright shows that, even in our age of almost limitless communication across distances, geography can play an important role in the implementation of language policies. The "border lands" between the concentration of francophones in Quebec and that of anglophones in the rest of Canada have been the site of a high proportion of the struggle after the declaration of the *Official Languages Act*. (See also Crawford's chapter for a discussion of the effect of the reservation system on indigenous languages.)

**269**

In line with authors in previous parts of this volume (e.g., Magnet, chapter 8; Crawford, chapter 6; and Miner, chapter 7), two authors in Part V mention the role of economics in one way or another in relation to language policy. Cartwright notes the ire of ratepayers in various parts of Ontario when policy requires or even implies that their tax dollars might be spent on the interests of a linguistic minority. Veltman (chapter 12) mentions that anglophone parents, by sending their children to French immersion programs in hopes of better jobs for the children in the future, have been responsible for one of the larger shifts in individual bilingualism since the *Official Languages Act*.

Veltman and Ricento (chapter 13) take penetrating looks at the history and demographics of English language use relative to that of other languages in the United States in order to bring into question the need for declaring English the official language. Both point out that, unlike French as a community and "national" language in Canada, English is under no kind of threat at all. Indeed, as Wiley shows in chapter 9, English is more universally used now than in any other time in the history of the United States. This immediately raises the question of the purpose an official declaration of English would serve.

Whatever the stated purpose of legislation or policy, there is always also the matter of enforcement. If there was a need for policy in the first place, then a change in behavior is implied that must be brought about. Cartwright describes in detail how one implementation policy was ineffective. His outline of the gradualism policy of the Ontario government with respect to the federally declared official languages created bad feelings on both sides—anglophone and francophone. The cautious approach was perhaps more dangerous to governments than a bold one might have been. Veltman shows the various effects of federal and provincial policy on English and French, suggesting that the policies were only one factor in a tide of other social factors that have influenced language behavior. Ricento anticipates the impact of a declaration of English as official language in the United States, most of which he predicts will be negative in majority/minority relations. He also notes, with Miner (chapter 7), that it may not have much effect at all in many aspects of life, although he points out more negative possibilities than Miner.

With enforcement often comes resistance. Cartwright documents how resistance on both sides of an issue can foil the cautious attempts of governments to keep both sides happy while implementing language change. Canada's own versions of "English-only" groups emerged in reaction to policies intended to mediate between two language groups. Ricento gives examples of repressive responses by authorities in enforcing the letter of the law when social reality did not match the principle. And

## V. FOCUS ON CONTEXT 271

Veltman tells of citizens voting with their feet and in their homes in commonsense responses to language policies (see also Crawford, chapter 6, this volume).

Part V, Focus on Context, highlights major themes throughout the book which indicate that language policy is embedded in the context of the real lives of individuals and groups. Without an appreciation of historical antecedents, we cannot comprehend the network of legal and social relationships that have created the situation in the first place. Without studies of demography, geography, economics, cultures, and spirituality, we cannot understand or predict language behavior. Laws, court decisions, and government spending influence language and its use, but only if they are in sympathy with the many other factors in life that are touched by language.

# 11

# French-Language Services in Ontario: A Policy of "Overly Prudent Gradualism"?

Don Cartwright
*The University of Western Ontario*

In the late 1960s, the Report of the Royal Commission on Bilingualism and Biculturalism (RCBB, commonly known as the B. and B. Commission) recommended that French and English receive official status for all the functions of the Parliament and Government of Canada and in the operation of all federal institutions. Similar official-languages status was recommended for the provinces of New Brunswick and Ontario. This policy was founded on the concept of institutional bilingualism whereby services are made available through government agencies according to the linguistic request of the recipient. It was not the intention of the Commission that official-languages status would be interpreted as a move to enforce individual bilingualism. To clarify this it was stated in the general introduction to the Report, "A bilingual country ... is a country where the principal public and private institutions must provide services in two languages to citizens, the vast majority of whom may very well be unilingual" (Canada, RCBB, 1967, p. xxvii). The members of the B. and B. Commission also based their guidance for French-language services throughout the country on the principle of personality, whereby services are available to individuals according to their choice, because they believed that the francophone

273

populations beyond Quebec were an important linkage between French and English Canada, a symbolic force for political integration.

Two additional reasons for recommending such status for Ontario and New Brunswick were based on the number of francophones who lived in these provinces, and on their geographic contiguity with Quebec that, at the time, was already bilingual (Canada, RCBB, 1967, p. 96). New Brunswick accommodated the Commission and declared official-languages status for English and French in 1969; Ontario did not. Instead this provincial government opted for a program of French-language services through the bit-by-bit approach, or as it was designated by editorialists in the Quebec newspaper *Le Devoir*, a policy of "overly prudent gradualism" (Leclerc, 1990).

There have been politicians in Ontario from all parties who have proclaimed that official-language status for French is the proper culmination of a policy of gradualism. It is argued here, however, that gradualism may have placed such status beyond attainment. In developing this argument, the processes of gradualism in selected domains are discussed to demonstrate that the time taken to develop services may have taken us past the point when it would have been prudent to declare French as an official language in Ontario. Furthermore, sociolinguistic developments elsewhere in Canada and the work of the lobbyist group Alliance for the Preservation of English in Canada (APEC) have exacerbated the problems of gradualism. Beyond the domains that have already attained province-wide application in services, Franco-Ontarians must be content to receive government services in French within designated areas with significant francophone populations.

## "OVERLY PRUDENT GRADUALISM": FRENCH-LANGUAGE SERVICES IN ONTARIO

When the French language received official status in Canada in 1969, it was through the Official Languages Act of the Government of Canada, which had no application in areas of provincial jurisdiction. To facilitate the application of the Act, and to encourage the lower levels of government to emulate bilingual services provided in federal offices and agencies, the territorial concept of bilingual districts—borrowed from Finland—was incorporated. In 1973, the role of bilingual districts was explained to representatives of the Ontario government by members of the second federal Bilingual Districts Advisory Board (BDAB), the body appointed to recommend the location of districts, but the concept was rejected by the provincial group. These people stated that it was the provincial government's position that "it was wiser to attempt to meet the demand for bilingual services where it arose by pragmatic and practical decisions rather than by creating

# 11. FRENCH-LANGUAGE SERVICES IN ONTARIO

bilingual districts" (Canada, BDAB, 1973, Vol. 13, Folio 19). Although the government of Ontario would not condone the concept of bilingual districts at this time, it was "attempting to supply services" (Canada, BDAB, 1973) in a functional manner without drawing attention to such activities through the formal declaration of districts and their attendant boundaries. It was stressed that this would be done in specific regions where there was a geographical concentration of francophones. "Wherever feasible" was the common phrase that was to guide services in the courts, in education, and in other kinds of services. The provincial government, ever fearful of a backlash from the anglophone majority, would proceed slowly and cautiously in these domains. The premier of Ontario, when discussing bilingual districts in the Legislative Assembly, declared, "The need for bilingual districts must be related to the type of service to be provided for each jurisdiction" (Ontario, Legislative Assembly, 1971, p 1109). It is clear that gradualism would also accommodate a process of selectivity for services in French which would "meet the needs" of the francophone community. The trend in court services is a good example of this selectivity at work.

## THE JUDICIARY

The areas of eastern and northern Ontario that are close to Quebec are considered to be part of Canada's bilingual belt (Joy, 1972). It was in these borderlands that the program for the gradual bilingualization of the provincial courts began. In the mid 1970s, the attorney general's office authorized a pilot project for French-language services in the provincial court, criminal division, in Sudbury, Ontario. This city is situated within the borderlands in northern Ontario and is considered a significant central place for Franco-Ontarian activities in this region; the human resources were also at hand to support this project for French and bilingual trials. The attorney general may have believed that this would be an inconspicuous place to begin his program. About 16 months later, the same court services were extended to several urban centers in the borderlands of both eastern and northern Ontario (see Fig. 11.1). These cities and towns were central places for "designated areas," a territorial specification that was incorporated into amendments to the Judicature Act and the Juries Act in 1977, and that guaranteed French-language services in the criminal division of the provincial court. Such territorial designation accommodated a large proportion of the francophone population of Ontario, but it also suited the provincial policy of gradualism for French-language services (Graham & Thomas, 1987).

Unlike the territorial component in federal language legislation, these areas were not newly created judicial territories but were aligned with existing counties and districts, the standard units for the areal administration of judicial services. The provincial ministry was actually aided in its areal selection by the recommendations contained in the report of the first Bilingual Districts Advisory Board (Canada, BDAB, 1971). The concept of designated areas for court services was not considered to be synonymous with bilingual districts, however, because only specific services were to be provided; the federal areas would have embraced all government services.

In 1978, the Criminal Code was amended to allow criminal cases to be tried in French beyond the originally designated areas, in effect, incorporating the entire province. The significance of this change was that prov-

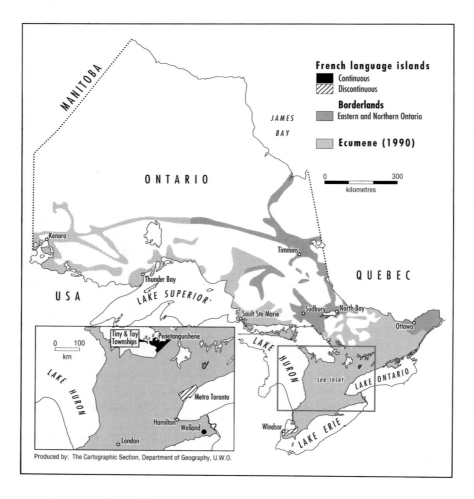

FIG. 11.1. Major concentrations of French mother-tongue population, Ontario, 1990.

## 11. FRENCH-LANGUAGE SERVICES IN ONTARIO 277

ince-wide status applied only to cases that were to be held before a judge, because a bilingual team could travel to the accused. If a trial were to be held before a judge *and* jury, it could be done only within the designated areas. When an accused who selected such a French-language trial was incarcerated elsewhere in the province, he or she was given the right to be transferred to a designated area where bilingual jurists would be available.

The next phase was announced by the attorney general in November 1981, when French-language services were extended to the civil courts in the designated areas that would accommodate most of the French-speaking citizens of the province. Similar services were extended to the provincial court, family division, small claims, and provincial offenses courts. The government could now claim that a broad range of civil court services were available in French in designated areas that would accommodate 83% of the Franco-Ontarian population. By 1987, these court services were also extended to the entire province but, as with criminal cases, only when tried before a bilingual judge. Trials before judge and jury were still held in a designated area "because of the difficulty of empanelling such a jury in some parts of the province" (Ontario, Legislative Assembly, 1989, p. 4935).

The Courts of Justice Act (1984) had confirmed the legal status of French as one of the two official languages of Ontario's courts, although as Braen (1988) pointed out, English was still the language of usage and dominance in certain and specified instances. This, too, was eventually addressed by the provincial government when, in 1989, section 136 of the Courts of Justice Act was amended through Bill 62. Under the former legislation, trial documents that were filed in French had to be accompanied by a translation. Legal proceedings such as motions on points and procedure, pre-trial hearings and submissions on costs that were made in French were to be translated into English. The amendments in Bill 62 allowed such filings and proceedings to be submitted and conducted in French without an accompanying translation (Ontario, Legislative Assembly, 1989, pp. 4935–4944). Each party now had the right to have his or her own documents in his or her own choice of the two languages, but, as in the choice of trial before judge *and* jury, this could be done in *designated* court offices that were specified in schedule 2 of the amending act. Although trial by bilingual juries is available in 12 designated areas[1] in the province, bilingual documents (described earlier) are accommodated in only 8 of the designated areas, "because there are the court officials there who are capably bilingual and can receive those documents" (p. 4974). It was the declared intention of the attorney general to extend this service to the remaining designated areas of the province as the bilingual capacity of the court offices developed.

---

[1] There were 49 judicial areas in the province of Ontario at the time that the Courts of Justice Act was amended in 1989.

Roy McMurtry, the attorney general who orchestrated most of the changes in court services, was frequently complimented for his efforts to introduce and extend French-language services into the provincial judicial system, a personal commitment that contrasted markedly with that of many of his colleagues in the cabinet. The spokesperson on justice matters who sat in the opposition in the Legislative Assembly, a member of the provincial parliament from a bicultural electoral district in the city of Ottawa, was also enthusiastic about the attorney general's program, but is reported to have complained, "When they proceed to grant important minority rights, they do it so quietly" (Carriere, 1992, p. A1). This was generally referred to as the quiet victory guided by a minister who was aware that, with the election of the separatist Parti Québeçois in Quebec in 1976, the whole issue of French-language services beyond Quebec was very sensitive.

The gradualism of French-language rights before the courts of Ontario has been consistent since Premier Davis made his declaration of policy in 1971, even though there have been several changes in provincial governments since then. Although party spokespersons may see the entrenchment of French in the constitution as an official language with English, as the only fair and reasonable culmination of policy when they sit in the opposition, when they win an election and form the government the policy of gradualism seems to become prudent after all. Perhaps the fear of backlash is endemic only on the government's side of the Assembly.

## EDUCATION

If the development of bilingual courts in Ontario can be described as a quiet victory for French-language services, advances in the educational domains must be described as volatile. Because of the nature of the institution, French-language services in the courts were bound to hold less attraction for the press. It was the language of instruction for schools and minority-language facilities that have been more contentious, an occurrence that is not unique to Ontario (Mallea, 1989). In the discussion that follows, distinctions are made among educational instruction, facilities, school governance, and school boards in this domain of French-language services. One must make such distinctions because accommodation has been gained and rights received piecemeal over several decades.

French-language education in Ontario was severely restricted after the third grade of elementary school by the notorious Regulation 17 (1912). This remained the law of the province for 30 years, although in 1927 the ministry allowed the French language to be used in some elementary schools, particularly Catholic schools and mainly in eastern Ontario (Brault, 1965; Mougeon & Heller, 1986). "These schools operated in isolation: they were

## 11. FRENCH-LANGUAGE SERVICES IN ONTARIO                                    279

not part of the English-language system of education in the province, and they lacked the planning, the guidance, and the coordination essential to an adequate educational regime" (Canada, RCBB, 1968, p. 51). Provision of services in this domain, it is clear, was strictly through limited functional arrangements.

Boards of education were not granted permission to open French-language secondary schools until 1968. Before that, French-language instruction was provided in only a few subjects at the secondary level. Under the new legislation (Bill 141), French-language schools could be established wherever the number of students could provide a viable unit. The basis of "wherever numbers warrant" was stated in the legislature, phraseology that lacked the specificity of designated areas. Some school boards responded positively to the spirit of the bill and established French-language facilities relatively quickly. Many francophones, however, found the wording of the legislation too vague, and several school boards were accused of failing to provide educational services to which the local francophones were entitled; it was these, of course, that received the publicity. The minority had little recourse if the educational services were inadequate or lacking; consequently the provincial government was required to step in on several occasions and direct the construction of French-language high schools. Designated areas, which seemed to service the provision of French-language services in the courts fairly well, were not incorporated into the educational system:

> In some areas it may only be possible to provide one class of Francais and perhaps one or two other subjects in French. In other areas a complete arts and science program and some commercial subjects could be started. The intent of the legislation is, however, that a divisional board will provide the fullest program possible. (Ontario, Legislative Assembly, 1968, p. 3641).

Bill 141 was important legislation for Franco-Ontarians, but it was also a cause of much confusion and a contributor to community conflict. Two examples are taken from Sturgeon Falls in northern Ontario, between North Bay and Sudbury, and Essex County in southwestern Ontario, near Windsor, to illustrate this discord.

In 1970, French-speaking parents in the district that was served by the Sturgeon Falls high school requested a French-language secondary school under the auspices of Bill 141. This issue generated division in the community not only between francophones and anglophones, but also among members of the Franco-Ontarian population. Spokespersons from the anglophone population who opposed the plan for two, unilingual secondary schools did so on the basis of costs and a refusal to recognize that a threat to the French language and culture existed in their community. (How could their language and culture be threatened when Sturgeon Falls was 75%

French-speaking?) Some francophones believed that there was a need for French-speaking students to learn English at school and, therefore, one bilingual school would be adequate. Those who supported this solution feared the effects that a French-language school could have on the marketability of graduates who would enter the labor force lacking "the necessary terminology" to qualify for jobs in Ontario's industrial sector (Helm, 1989, p. 183). Before the issue was resolved with the construction of two unilingual schools, a culmination of direct provincial involvement and funding, the conflict received national attention and became a cause célèbre for all Franco-Ontarians. "What had begun as a dispute between the district school board and a group of its ratepayers—reached a much wider audience. ... The town which had shone as an example of Canadian unity now was torn apart by the issue of educational segregation" (p. 197).

Essex County, near the city of Windsor, was the location of similar conflict and again the local ratepayers who opposed the issue cited costs and perceived lack of "need" for a French-language secondary school by the local minority. The conflict became so intense that it was eventually necessary for the Minister of Education to intervene directly. This only intensified local differences as those who were opposed to the minority school resented what they considered a violation of local autonomy by the Minister (Rosser, 1977). One regional newspaper, with the largest circulation in southwestern Ontario, summarized this in an editorial statement: "It is terribly sad that this controversy was allowed to brew for eight years without corrective provincial action. Essex has become something of a national scandal. It didn't need to be" (Heine, 1977, p. 6).

Thus, the policy of gradualism applied not only to the provision of French-language services but also to corrective measures when legislation that was vague and ambiguous contributed to local competition for resources. Throughout the late 1970s and early 1980s, numbers required to create a "viable" class for French-language instruction and the vagueness of wording in the act "may establish" were removed and clarified respectively (Gill, 1983). For example, in section 258 of the Education Act, 1980, the term "may establish" was used to describe the responsibility of a local board in providing secondary schools, or classes in secondary schools, for the use of the French language in instruction. Similarly if numbers did not warrant such classes, the board "may enter into an agreement" with a neighboring school board to accommodate local pupils who wished to receive their secondary education in the French language. With the incorporation of the Charter of Rights and Freedoms into the Canadian Constitution in 1981, the "may" was abolished and "rights to receive" was incorporated for French and English-language minority education (Mougeon & Heller, 1986). This section of the Charter also refers to entitle-

## 11. FRENCH-LANGUAGE SERVICES IN ONTARIO 281

ment beyond rights to receive instruction and declares that minority-language educational facilities must also be provided out of public funds.

In deference to the potential costs of this instruction, and the facilities, the phrase "wherever numbers are sufficient" was included in this section of the Charter. The vagueness of this statement was tested in several court cases across the nation. In Ontario, the government requested that the Ontario Court of Appeal clarify the Education Act of 1980 in the context of section 23 of the Charter. The Court declared that the Educational Act was in conflict with the Charter of Rights and Freedoms and provided guidelines to correct this. For French-language facilities, the Court granted no discretionary powers to school boards, and the numbers that the provincial government required for minority-language instruction (25 pupils in primary schools and 20 pupils in secondary schools) were considered to be unconstitutional as they were too rigid and arbitrary. The government responded by introducing amending legislation in December 1984 (Bill 119) which stipulated that the minimum number required to receive minority language instruction would be "one," and school boards would be required to provide facilities within their jurisdiction or purchase access to such facilities from a neighboring board (Ontario, Standing Committee on Social Development, 1984).

Plans to guarantee francophone parents the right to elect their own members (trustees) to represent francophone interests on local school boards were announced in March 1983. Approximately 40 boards in the province would be affected because the legislation would apply only to those school boards where there were at least 500 French-speaking students or where such students accounted for 10% of the student population. With these stipulations, school governance was approaching the designated areas concept that had been employed for services in the provincial courts. These plans were stalled when every school board affected by the proposal objected to the change in trustee representation. The provincial government responded to this by referring to the decision of the Ontario Court of Appeal which had ruled that the provincial Education Act conflicted with the Charter on school governance, because the content of French-language education was at the discretion of local boards that received only guidance on matters of minority education from advisory committees. The right to school governance, the court declared, was subsumed in the right to educational facilities for minority language instruction (Terrien & Johansen, 1990). Amending legislation to accommodate the court's decision on school governance finally received third reading in the Legislative Assembly in 1986 but did not become fully operative until 1988, 5 years after the initial amendments had been introduced. To make the amending legislation accord with Ontario's guarantee of a French-language education for *all* francophone students, designated areas implied in the 500 and 10% limits were dropped and the election of French-speaking trustees to all public and separate school boards offering French-language instruction was incorporated.

Franco-Ontarian associations had been requesting greater input by francophone ratepayers in the operation of their school system for many years. In his annual report for 1983, the federal Commissioner of Official Languages expressed their sense of frustration: "Of what use are minority-language rights that are, so to speak, in the gift of the majority" (p. 183)? Under the amendments to the Education Act, the new minority-language trustees elected to local boards would have exclusive jurisdiction in matters of program, recruitment, and assignment of teachers for those children who were enrolled in the French-language classes. The changes, however, fell short of establishing full French-language boards of education. It was not until April 1988 that the provincial government tabled a bill in the Legislative Assembly to create a French-language school board in Ottawa–Carleton, thereby satisfying a demand first made more than 10 years earlier. When this amending legislation received third reading in the Legislative Assembly the minister declared: "The government believes the Ottawa-Carleton region should have such a French-language board because of the very special and unique circumstances in the national capital area" (Ontario, Legislative Assembly, 1986, p. 2373).

The uniqueness of the national capital area was recognized in 1969 by the federal government when it declared the area to be the only official bilingual district under the Official Languages Act of Canada. Although this declaration applied only to federal offices and agencies, it was anticipated that the provincial government of Ontario would follow the example of the Government of Canada and provide similar status in areas of provincial jurisdiction. In the realm of jurisdiction over their own schools, Franco-Ontarians had to wait almost 20 years for this grand gesture, a right that anglophones in Quebec have possessed for decades. Similar status has since been applied to a French-language board of education for metropolitan Toronto and, through regulation, to Russell–Prescott counties in eastern Ontario (Ontario, Legislative Assembly, 1990).

The progression in French-language educational services from specific geographical areas to a province-wide application was accelerated by the Charter of Rights and Freedoms, and was not the culmination of the provincial government's gradualist policy. This federal legislation was an important instrument in moderating local conflicts such as those that emerged in Essex County and Sturgeon Falls over access to French-language schools. In the realm of school governance for Franco-Ontarians, however, the policy of gradualism prevails. The creation of other French-

## 11. FRENCH-LANGUAGE SERVICES IN ONTARIO 283

language boards of education is now in limbo while the provincial government reviews the entire structure and role of local boards of education. This delay in an application of policy for school governance that, it seemed, would emulate the pattern of school services in French is generating further ethnic conflict that will involve the United Nations Commission on Human Rights. Before we discuss this new issue, it is necessary to investigate an assault that the provincial government must endure from another organization that previously concentrated its attack on federal language policies.

### FRENCH-LANGUAGE SERVICES ACT
### AND THE WORK OF APEC

When the French Language Services Act (Bill 8) of Ontario was introduced in 1986, the concept of designated areas was again incorporated and applied whenever the minority formed 10% of the total population or, in metropolitan areas, where the total number of francophones reached 5,000 or more. The legislation, which came into effect in November 1989, gives members of the provincial Legislative Assembly full rights to use English or French in debates and proceedings; and ministries, agencies, boards, and commissions of the provincial government are legally required to provide the full range of their services in French within 23 designated areas (see Fig. 11.2). These have been delimited so that 82% of the Franco-Ontarian population is accommodated.[2] The development of judicial services in French has been peaceful compared to those for schools and other government services in Ontario, and it may be that the latter are interrelated. Lobbyists who are against the extension of French-language rights in Canada have frequently used conflict and competition over French-language schools to foment reactions against Bill 8 in several communities. The Alliance for the

---

[2]When the census data for 1991 were released by Statistics Canada, representatives of the francophone population in London, Ontario claimed eligibility for designated-area status because the "French-speaking" population of the city exceeded 5,000, the required number for metropolitan centers. To justify their claim, the representatives used the following mother-tongue populations (single and multiple responses): French only; English and French; English, French, and nonofficial language; French and nonofficial language. Mother tongue is defined for the census as "the language(s) first learned as a child and still understood." It is essential to note that this is *not* the definition of a "speaking" population. No mention is made in the French Language Services Act or in the compendia to the act how the minority population in a designated area is to be defined other than 10% of total population (rural) or 5,000 francophones in urban areas. In the compendia, however, it is stated that "services will be offered where 10% or more of the population is French-speaking" (Archives of Ontario, R.G. 149, I-7-B-2. Paper #31 Compendia, Bill 8). When home-language data are compiled from the same census populations mentioned earlier ("language(s) used most often in the home"), the number of francophones "speaking" French for London is 2,100 in 1991. In June 1994, Ontario's minister responsible for francophone affairs announced that London would become the twenty-third designated area under the act thereby ignoring the conundrum of a mother-tongue population versus a "speaking" population.

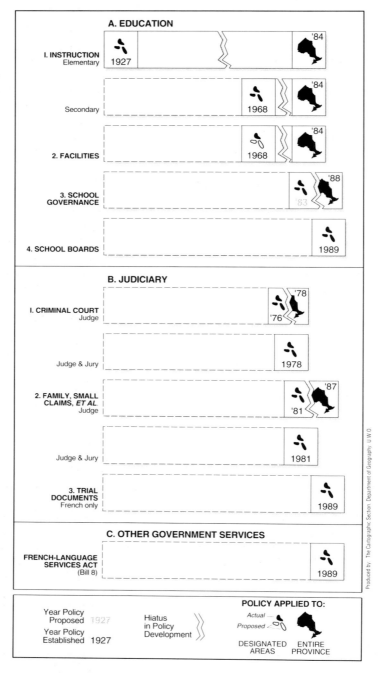

FIG. 11.2. Territorial stages for French-language services in Ontario.

## 11. FRENCH-LANGUAGE SERVICES IN ONTARIO

Preservation of English in Canada (APEC) is the most vociferous and effective of the antibilingual groups.

APEC was founded in Halifax, Nova Scotia, in 1977, but moved its headquarters to Toronto in 1980. This organization is dedicated, outwardly, to the removal of official bilingualism throughout Canada, and uses as its motto: "One language unites, two languages divide." In this it concurs with its counterpart in the United States, U.S. English, an organization with which there is some contact and interaction. As a lobby group, APEC attacks language policies and programs throughout the country, but its members have been particularly active among municipalities within Ontario. This organization has been relentless in its attacks against the French Language Services Act with warnings to those living in designated areas that anglophones will have no opportunities for access to, or promotion in, civil service positions unless they become fluent in French. Bilingual people from the provinces of Quebec and New Brunswick will be brought to Ontario to fill jobs that are classified as bilingual in the designated areas (*APEC Newsletter*, September 1989). In the issue of their newsletter dated August 1989 under the title "Bill 8—Chaos in Eastern Ontario," APEC stated:

"The District Health Council of eastern Ontario has made recommendations that are totally unacceptable to English-speaking people living there. What is this council recommending? Bilingualism for ' … all key administrative and senior personnel of local health facilities.' This is tantamount to saying that these people are to be hired in Quebec. To tell English-speaking Canadians that there is an area of Ontario where they may not seek employment is a denial of their status as Canadian citizens." (p. 4)

Such a statement ignores the increasing number of bilingual anglophones throughout the province, and particularly among the younger age cohorts in eastern Ontario (Cartwright, 1988). But such factual errors and innuendoes are regular techniques employed by this organization.

Fears of "invasion" by bilingual Quebecers is a constant theme circulated in eastern and northern Ontario by members of APEC. An internal memo in the Office of Francophone Affairs, Toronto, described APEC as having stirred up particularly strong anti-French sentiments in North Bay and Sudbury, two cities within designated areas in northern Ontario. In eastern Ontario, French-speaking Quebeckers, APEC claims, will be brought in to fill the jobs in various provincial offices and the provincial parks along the St. Lawrence River because unilingual local residents will no longer be qualified. As more and more francophones move into the area, they will demand more and more rights and services. Such warnings by APEC were reported in local newspapers and in others outside Ontario.

APEC used the requests for domain exclusivity by Franco-Ontarians as examples of an "artificial need for the use of French in Ontario" (*APEC*

*Newsletter*, November/December, 1988, p. 4) and a move toward segregation that they referred to as apartheid, Ontario style. Funding by the provincial government for a new French-language community health center was interpreted as the "segregation of people with French blood in their veins from the rest of us" (*APEC Newsletter*, November/December 1988, p. 4). And when municipalities with a predominantly French-speaking population established the Francophone Association of Municipalities of Ontario as an affiliated body of the Association of Municipalities of Ontario (AMO) to "promote the use of French-language services in the province, the professional development of its members and the sharing of human and material resources" (*APEC Newsletter*, April 1991, p. 4) this was not interpreted as an opportunity to promote the use of the mother tongue beyond the home, but just more evidence that one aim of the leaders of the Franco-Ontarians is complete segregation from English-speaking people (*APEC Newsletter*, April 1991).

Under Bill 8, municipalities are specifically excluded from any responsibilities to provide their own services in French. Those with sizeable Franco-Ontarian populations, however, may opt into the act if they wish to provide some services in French in addition to the full range of services already guaranteed in English. About 33 municipalities within the designated areas have decided to offer bilingual services. In spite of this, APEC has actively agitated among municipal councils within and adjacent to designated areas, claiming that the provincial government can and is planning to amend the act to force municipalities to provide services in French at local expense. During municipal elections in the autumn of 1988, APEC members fomented anguish and distress among many municipal councillors on this issue. The outcome was described in an editorial in a Toronto newspaper: "about 120 muddle-minded Ontario municipalities harkened to the Alliance's anti-French arguments and asked the provincial government to hold a referendum on bilingualism" ("The Fearful, Anglophones, " 1988, p. A6). Of greater impact, however, were the 27 municipalities, many in or very near the designated areas, that, through the ballot or council vote, have claimed a status of either "official" unilingualism (English) or an unwillingness to spend funds to provide French-language services. Under the Canadian system of government, municipalities have no authority to make such official unilingual declarations. These administrative units are creatures of the provinces and cannot legislate in fields that come under provincial jurisdiction. APEC (1990) conceded that these were municipal "resolutions": "These resolutions have no operative effect at all. The intent of the resolutions is to send a message. We believe that the Ontario government has received that message" (*APEC Newsletter*, November 1990 [insert]). The members of APEC were elated at these

## 11. FRENCH-LANGUAGE SERVICES IN ONTARIO 287

resolutions; what did not concern them were the messages that Quebec received.

Two municipalities that received national publicity for their unilingual declarations were the municipalities of Sault Ste. Marie and Thunder Bay with populations of 85,000 and 113,000, respectively. Both cities are in designated areas under Bill 8 and are situated close to the borderlands illustrated in Fig. 11.1. Resolutions adopted by both councils were, in part, a reaction against a request from local francophone parents for separate, elementary and secondary, French-language schools—an issue that has nothing to do with the French Language Services Act—and, in part, as a stated reaction of resentment against Quebec's unilingual-sign law, Bill 178 (see later discussion). Nevertheless, the French Language Services Act, with the urging of local APEC members, was used as the catalyst to declare English the official language in both urban centers. Municipal councils throughout Quebec debated and condemned these actions as insulting and hostile. In one community in that province the mayor was quoted as saying, "We should tip our hats to these people; they are doing something to help move Quebec closer toward separation" (Seguin, 1990, p. A5), and in the French-language press:

> Le 29 janvier dernier, Sault-Sainte Marie devenait le 26e municipalité ontarienne a se déclarer officiellement unilingue anglaise, déclenchant une vive agitation dans toute les couches de la société, non seulement ontarienne et canadienne-française, mais l'ensemble pays. (Cantin, 1990, p. S2)[3]

In such a way, the municipal declarations in Ontario, particularly those with a sizeable francophone population within and near the borderland with Quebec, have contributed to the growing chasm between French and English Canada.

That an organization such as APEC was able to influence municipalities near and within the designated areas is due, in part, to the ignorance of many local citizens and their elected representatives on the contents of Bill 8 or its intent. It was discovered during field research in eastern Ontario that many of the latter had not read the legislation. The government of Ontario is not blameless either and has been criticized for drafting legislation that many found confusing. An editorial in *The Glengarry News*, a weekly newspaper in eastern Ontario, provided an example of the complaint that was expressed in other local newspapers within the borderland and at many council meetings:

> If there is any censure to be laid on the government it is for drafting a bill that is

---

[3]"Last January 29th, Sault Ste. Marie became the 26th municipality in Ontario to declare itself officially unilingual in English, releasing a lively tumult in all levels of society, not only Ontarian and French Canadian, but the whole country."

excessively vague and open to varying interpretations. This ambiguity has created an opportunity for those who oppose the extension of French-language services as a matter of principle, or even from personal prejudice, to cry doom and predict all kinds of dire repercussions for English-speaking Ontarians ... the government will have to do something ... to clarify what the law means in its actual implementation. ("Tilting," 1987, p. 4)

This confusion was confirmed in the report of the task force that investigated the state of municipal services in French in Ontario (1988). It was stated that the authority which the provincial government could exercise over services that had been delegated to the municipalities was not clearly defined and, therefore, there was uncertainty over language services for such delegated authority. Furthermore, although the provincial government offered subsidies to the municipalities for French language courses, translation, bilingual road signs, and rental of simultaneous interpretation services, the task force discovered that many did not know that these funds were available. Other councillors who were aware of the program expressed fear that the province would use the subsidies as a form of pressure to force municipalities to introduce French-language services. This is illustrated in the minutes-of-council for a municipality that is situated within a designated area in the borderland: "The inference could be taken that the province will allow municipalities to maintain their autonomy only if they respect local realities, obviously as identified by the province, and adapt to social policies as set by the province" (Council of the Corporation of the Township of Charlottenburg, Ontario, 1988).

Further confusion was created when the government of Ontario produced a map, shortly after Bill 8 was promulgated, to illustrate the 22 designated areas (see Fig. 11.3). This map, produced unfortunately in some urgency in 1989, also provided ammunition to the APEC arsenal of statements regarding loss of jobs for unilingual anglophones and a gradual invasion of the provincial borderland by bilingual Quebeckers. The areal extent of the designated areas was exaggerated and extended beyond the limits of those explicitly listed in the schedule of the act. For example, the whole of the Districts of Kenora and Thunder Bay and the County of Renfrew have been illustrated as "designated areas," whereas the schedule in Bill 8 lists only one township in the first, one town and six townships in the second, and one city and two townships in the latter as officially designated areas. Similar cartographic errors were made in central and southwestern Ontario. By illustrating areas according to political divisions rather than by the permanently inhabited areas (the ecumene), the image is created of a vast francophone-occupied area in the province. Such a cartographic image played into the hands of APEC directly when they warned citizens through their regular newsletters:

## 11. FRENCH-LANGUAGE SERVICES IN ONTARIO

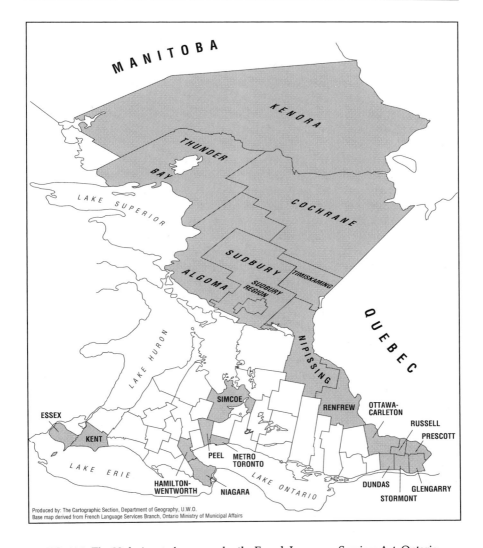

FIG. 11.3. The 22 designated areas under the French Language Services Act, Ontario.

1. Of the creation (through the act) of an artificial need for the French language in Ontario and attendant costs to the taxpayer (*APEC Newsletter*, March 1991, p. 2).
2. That the act was only a preliminary to a declaration of French and English as official languages in Ontario (*APEC Newsletter*, March 1991, p. 2).

3. That francophones will take over the administrative positions in government agencies, offices and institutions throughout the borderland (*APEC Newsletter*, April 1991, p. 3).
4. That Franco-Ontarians will attain political influence far beyond that warranted by numbers (*APEC Newsletter*, November 1989, p. 2).
5. Of the trend toward power in the federal civil service, in the borderland of Ontario, and in influence in Toronto (*APEC Newsletter*, October/November, 1987, p. 4; June 1990, p. 3).

The cartographic error was recognized and corrected when the provincial government issued a revised map of the designated areas in 1990 (see Fig. 11.4). Although the government assigned designated-area status to regions of Franco-Ontarian concentration for specific court and other provincial services, APEC has used such status, particularly in the borderlands, as an example of a francophone invasion of the province. This is an interpretation of a borderland that has also been employed by some members of U.S. English in the southern United States. One member, in a letter to U.S. Secretary of State Henry Kissinger in 1985, warned that continued Mexican immigration into the United States could produce a "Chicano Quebec" in the area bordering with Mexico (Martinez, 1988, p. 159).

Although APEC originally proselytized under the banner "In Defence of the English Language," a subheading that they used on their monthly publication until August 1988, there may be a hidden agenda, clues to which surface occasionally in their newsletters. Readers of APEC's publication are advised to boycott specific products that carry labels in which the French language is written before English or in which product information is provided in French only. In the January 1990 issue of the newsletter, readers were advised to boycott Zellers Department Stores because the head office of the company is in Montreal. If this lobbyist is concerned only with legislated bilingualism and the preservation and entrenchment of English, why does he attack a company because of the location of its head office? As this organization grows, elements of a hidden agenda may become more prevalent and more obvious as it did with their counterpart in the United States, U.S. English.

## DUAL PRESSURES ON THE PROVINCIAL GOVERNMENT

Members of APEC have taken the policy of gradualism which was originally intended to eliminate, or at least minimize, a backlash from the English-speaking majority in Ontario, and interpreted it as having a hidden agenda of official-language status for French. The services that have been extended in the courts, education and through the French-Language Serv-

## 11. FRENCH-LANGUAGE SERVICES IN ONTARIO

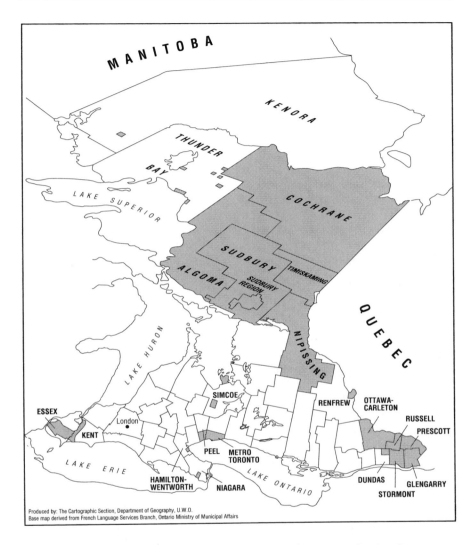

FIG. 11.4. The 23 designated areas under the French Language Services Act, Ontario (modified delimitation, 1996).

ices Act have been described by APEC as insidious, iniquitous, divisive and discriminatory:

> We have had an insidious program of "Backdoor Bilingualism" where the government introduces French-language services gradually without making Ontario people aware of what it is doing. The ultimate goal is to reach that level of

French-language services when the government can say, "nothing will change by declaring Ontario officially bilingual" (*APEC Newsletter*, December 1986, p. 1)

The provincial government was vulnerable to this charge of "backdoor bilingualism" because when French-language services were being allocated, members of the Legislative Assembly chose not to enlighten Ontarians on the processes of cultural erosion that Franco-Ontarians were constantly battling.

These lobbyists have been dismissed by many as a right-wing fringe group of bigots and racists. Their membership grows annually, however, and they are well organized with regional organizations throughout the province that hold monthly meetings; and they are very successful in obtaining newspaper coverage of their events. This publicity, coupled with the shortage of information on the government's long-term agenda for French in the province, has created unease among many local administrators who recognize the current trend in Canada of transferring costs for social services to the lower levels of government, from federal to provincial to municipal.

The French Canadian Association of Ontario (ACFO) may have fueled the apprehensions of local administrators and added unwanted pressure to the provincial government's language policy when, in the autumn of 1991, representatives asked to have the French Language Services Act extended beyond the designated areas and embrace the entire province. A positive response has not been received by ACFO and this seems to have added to the frustrations over the school governance issue that fermented throughout the late 1980s and early 1990s and erupted in May 1994. Two Franco-Ontarians have applied for a judgement from the United Nations Human Rights Commission that the rights of French-speaking Canadians in the province have been systematically denied. In their submission, the representatives are reported to have demanded an end to the repression of education rights and to "the subtle but all too devastating linguistic-cleansing measures that are the very root of our cultural genocide, whether they be perpetrated consciously or unconsciously" (Wills, 1994, p. B8). They maintain that both the federal and Ontario governments have violated the International Covenant on Civil and Political Rights which Canada has signed. Part of the violation is the failure of the province to grant francophones full management of their schools, and therefore they have asked the U.N. committee for "a declaration acknowledging that Ontario's francophone minority has in the pursuit of its development, the same individual and collective rights as those enjoyed by the anglophone majority" (Wills, 1994, p. B8). In this action the representatives are being fully supported by ACFO.

## DISCUSSION

There is no doubt that a positive declaration on individual and collective rights of Franco-Ontarians from the U.N. Commission should, in the opinion of their representatives, culminate in official status for French in the province. The reasons for taking such a drastic approach against the policy of gradualism, which successive governments have embraced, can be conceptualized through instrumentalist and constructivist systems of analysis. Instrumentalists devote their analysis to the uses that are made of ethnicity, in political and social competition, by activists who exploit a nascent or established solidarity (Young, 1993). They embrace the notion that ethnic groups are calculating, are self-interested, and seek to maximize their share of material and symbolic resources through forces that are latent in community identity. The devices that are used to claim greater share of these resources are the "instruments" that can produce substantive results. The appeal to the U.N. Commission and the requests for extended government services beyond the current designated areas by ACFO, when linked to the province-wide status of rights for French-language services in education and the judiciary, become significant instruments that may project government services in French beyond designated areas and into the principle-of-personality status. The move to a declaration of "official" status for French could be seen as a very short and logical step from this province-wide status for government services.

To appreciate why the francophone representatives have taken this route, we may also apply a constructivist analysis to their venture. Constructivists believe that identities are socially constructed and are in need of constant reconstruction. These identities can be used to mobilize individuals along ethnolinguistic lines. For the Franco-Ontarians the traditional institutions of parish and family have weakened as significant elements in cultural continuity. At one time, many enjoyed regular contact and interaction with francophone neighbors in a rural environment with little need to extend beyond their area. This, too, has lost its impact on the culture as the range of interaction has been extended with improved transportation and communication. The isolation factor is no longer the boundary against the penetration of English. With changing contacts, exogamy has become more prevalent, and this has contributed markedly to language transfer (Castonguay, 1982). The migration of younger cohorts from regions of numeric strength to urban centers that can have a high potential for assimilation has also motivated the constructivist agenda.

Faced with cultural erosion in some domains, activists among the minority must struggle for new domains that will sustain identity and the vigor of the language. They must strive to have that identity accepted as an authentic part of the heritage of Ontario with language status at the provincial level no less than equivalent to that at the federal level and in New Brunswick. The symbolism inherent in this is important to ethnolinguistic vitality and to the rehabilitation of lapsed francophones. With enhanced status, the potential for minority language usage in the private sector could increase.

There are social scientists who will argue against this agenda particularly if the representatives of Ontario's francophones are in earnest over their fears of "cultural genocide." Several researchers have demonstrated that the Franco-Ontarian population has experienced the culturally erosive process of language shift. This process can be defined as the change from the habitual use of one language to that of another by members of a minority, and it has two components—intergenerational and intragenerational language shift (de Vries, 1994; Fishman, 1991). Intragenerational language shift is measured by the comparison between an individual's mother tongue and his or her home language whereby identical responses to the two questions from the census indicate language maintenance and different responses are assumed to indicate language shift. Intergenerational language shift occurs in the context of home–family–neighborhood when communication between adults and children in minority domains takes place in the language of the majority. This can happen in informal (the family) and formal (the school) domains.

According to de Vries (1994), most of the quantitative work on language shift in Canada has dealt with intragenerational language maintenance and shift. He has used this technique to demonstrate that about half of the French mother-tongue population in Ontario appears to have shifted to English home language between 1971 and 1986. He claimed, "It is reasonable to deduce that even the sizeable francophone regional minorities in Ontario are increasingly becoming vulnerable to language shift to English, despite the gradual improvements in the language rights granted by the government of Ontario" (p. 64).

Mougeon and Beniak (1994) have measured both forms of language shift in Ontario and have reached a conclusion similar to de Vries'. They emphasized, however, that one must differentiate between a slow and gradual process in language shift and one that is sudden and rapid. With the former, language shift is not considered an inexorable process and, indeed, it may be reversed to a process of maintenance. They are encouraged that the shift to English among Franco-Ontarians has taken place gradually and that institutional support for the mother tongue has made it possible and attractive for francophones to maintain their language. They are heartened by the range of community organizations—social, cultural, and economic—in francophone areas, but more so by the positive responses among the younger

## 11. FRENCH-LANGUAGE SERVICES IN ONTARIO

generations to three types of cultural activities—music, poetry, and theater in French. "There is a sense and hope that these activities will serve as new rallying points for the assertion and cultivation of Franco-Ontarian cultural and linguistic distinctiveness" (Mougeon & Beniak, 1994, p. 122).

Fishman (1993) emphasized that policies which are intended to reverse language shift should be applied at this local scale:

> If intergenerational mother-tongue transmission is being aimed at, there is no parsimonious substitute for focusing on the home–neighbourhood–community processes which bind together adults and children—in early bonds of intergenerational and spontaneous affect, intimacy, identity and loyalty. (p. 80)

This "arena" in itself will not guarantee reversal of language shift, but he believed it is a necessary condition before other domains—schools, workplace, mass media, and government services—can provide instrumental reinforcement for the ethnolinguistic minority. If too much attention is directed to the status domains, such as government services, without sufficient intergenerational mother-tongue continuity at the local level, the reversal of language shift may be thwarted and intergroup conflict can emerge because the majority must bear most of the costs for these services. In Canada, recent political developments seem to have entrenched such reaction by the majority.

In spite of the words of encouragement for Franco-Ontarians that political parties provide regularly, the policy of gradualism may have taken us beyond the optimum time to declare two official languages in Ontario and, thereby, achieve the gesture toward national unity envisaged by the B. and B. Commission in the 1960s. Legislation that was passed in Quebec to secure the cultural integrity of the French language has gradually been accommodated in Ontario, but when the government of Quebec felt compelled to override a decision by the Supreme Court of Canada to protect the provision of outdoor signs in French only (Bill 178), it produced expressions of regret and outrage throughout English Canada.

Two attempts have been made to amend the Constitution Act of 1982 and thereby secure Quebec's endorsement of this legislation; the Meech Lake Accord in 1990 and the Charlottetown Accord in 1992, both of which failed in nationwide referenda. Subsequently, province-wide support for sovereignty in Quebec went above 50% in every poll taken for two consecutive years (Reid, 1993). The year following the defeat of the Charlottetown Accord, the people of Quebec voted so strongly for a new federal party, the Bloc Québécois, that it secured enough seats in the House of Commons to form the official opposition. This party has one objective—to win a separatist vote in Quebec. Several months later, in a provincial election, the Parti Québécois, whose objective is also a sovereign Quebec, defeated the incumbent Liberal government by a narrow margin in the popular vote. Both parties developed strategies to gain support for the referendum held in October, 1995 on independence for Quebec. The sovereignists narrrowly lost this vote. These developments have generated a gulf between French and English Canada that has not lessened at the time of writing.

The policy of gradualism may have been successful in helping most Ontarians to avoid the unwelcome task of making an immediate decision for or against social legislation, but with this policy the government also lost the opportunity to educate the population on the need for such legislation. Now this population may no longer be in a mood to accommodate official-language status for French in Ontario. Formal status for French, in my opinion, will in the long run do less for the sustenance and development of the Franco-Ontarian culture than a continuation of the functional organization of territory whereby services are provided in designated areas of numerical strength and geographic concentration. One can support province-wide status for French-language education at the elementary and secondary levels because of the significance of this institutional development to ethnolinguistic vitality. Majority support for services in other domains is likely to develop when it can be demonstrated that the "designated areas," where these will be applied has historical, demolinguistic, and socioeconomic justification. Argue for minority-language services and sustenance on the basis of these strengths, and we are more likely to defuse groups like APEC and maintain the support of the majority—another significant variable in ethnolinguistic vitality.

Several social scientists have discussed the futility of a federal policy that attempted to thrust the whole of Canada toward "bilingual" status. In his review of Richard Joy's book *Canada's Official Language Minorities*, Lachapelle (1978) discussed the territorial concentration of Canada's two largest linguistic groups, and concluded that this concentration would continue in the future. He stated that any linguistic policies that failed to take this into account would run a strong risk of "chasing shadows and hence being doomed to failure" (p. 40). McRoberts (1989) also contended that the country has moved inexorably toward "twinned unilingualism ... with only a 'bilingual belt' straddling the borderlands of Quebec and Ontario and Quebec and New Brunswick" (p. 146). It may be argued, however, that it was the existence of the bilingual belt which, in part, frustrated any attempt to develop a federal policy founded on the principle of territoriality in the late 1960s. The B. and B. Commission, and subsequently the federal government, seemed to be baffled by these borderlands in which the cultural features of French and English Canada overlap. McRoberts pointed out that the Commission failed to conceive a scheme in which a minority language would be recognized for specific purposes

## 11. FRENCH-LANGUAGE SERVICES IN ONTARIO                    297

while the majority language retained preeminent status. The government of Ontario is in a position to learn from this omission. Rather than work toward official-language status for French in the province, the policy of gradualism could culminate with guarantees provided for specific purposes, thereby recognizing the geographic and demographic realities of the province. The counsel for language policy offered by Williams (1991) is applicable in Ontario:

> One can do as great a disservice to a language minority by exaggerating its capacity to act and to fulfil state expectations, as one can by denying the legitimacy of its claims and neglecting the requisite provision of resources so as to allow language reproduction. (p. 21)

The majority of the Franco-Ontarian population is situated in or near the borderlands illustrated in Fig. 11.1. These people enjoy a geographical concentration and critical mass that allows them to support and sustain a number of organizations and institutions, which have been essential in the unending efforts to maintain their cultural identity. Their geographical proximity to Quebec, the heartland of francophone culture in North America, permits an interaction that has also been significant to the cultural sustenance of these borderlanders. For the francophones in the language islands, several of the spatial and demographic characteristics of the aforementioned are absent, particularly the opportunity for regular interaction with Quebec. The local minority-language institutions have provided the scaffolding for cultural continuity. An attempt by the provincial government to foster empathy among a local majority to compensate for weaknesses that are developing in the scaffolding of their neighbors has greater opportunity for success, if planned and executed intelligently, than a policy of official language status that embraces the entire province.

### REFERENCES

Alliance for the Preservation of English in Canada (APEC). (1986, December). Language referendum needed. *APEC Newsletter, 9*(8).

Alliance for the Preservation of English in Canada (APEC). (1987, October/November). Government policy. *APEC Newsletter, 10*(7).

Alliance for the Preservation of English in Canada (APEC). (1988, November). Apartheid Ontario style. *APEC Newsletter, 11*(8).

Alliance for the Preservation of English in Canada (APEC). (1989, August). Bill 8—chaos in eastern Ontario. *APEC Newsletter, 12*(6).

Alliance for the Preservation of English in Canada (APEC). (1989, September). Aftermath of Ontario's Bill 8, the French language services act. *APEC Newsletter, 12*(7).

Alliance for the Preservation of English in Canada (APEC). (1989, November). Nothing to worry about, Mr. Premier? *APEC Newsletter, 12*(9).

Alliance for the Preservation of English in Canada (APEC). (1990, June). Social fabric undergoing change. *APEC Newsletter, 13*(4).

Alliance for the Preservation of English in Canada (APEC). (1990, November 18). [Letter from Ronald Leitch to Preston Manning, insert]. *APEC Newsletter, 13*(9).

Alliance for the Preservation of English in Canada (APEC). (March, 1991). President presents brief. *APEC Newsletter, 14*(3).

Alliance for the Preservation of English in Canada (APEC). (1991, April). Francophone association of municipalities of Ontario. *APEC Newsletter, 14*(4).

Alliance for the Preservation of English in Canada (APEC). (1991, April). Rights or privileges? *APEC Newsletter, 14*(4).

Braen, A. (1988). Statut du français et droits de la minorité francophone en Ontario, *Revue Générale de Droit, 19*, 493–506.

Brault, L. (1965). *Histoire des comtés unis de Prescott et de Russell*. L'Original: Conseil des Comtes Unis.

Canada, Royal Commission on Bilingualism and Biculturalism. (1967). *Preliminary Report* (Book 1). Ottawa: The Queen's Printer.

Canada, Royal Commission on Bilingualism and Biculturalism. (1968). *Education* (Book 2). Ottawa: The Queen's Printer.

Canada, The Bilingual Districts Advisory Board. (1971). *Report*. Ottawa: The Queen's Printer.

Canada, The Bilingual Districts Advisory Board. (1973). *Running record* (Vol. 13, Folio 19). Ottawa: Public Archives of Canada.

Canada, Commissioner of Official Languages. (1983). *Annual report*. Ottawa: Ministry of Supply and Services Canada.

Cantin, A. (1990, March 10). La declaration d'unilinguisme. *Le Droit*, p. S2.

Carriere, V. (1992, January 8). Bilingual courts: Even critics happy. *The Globe and Mail*, p. A1.

Cartwright, D. G. (1988). Linguistic territorialization: Is Canada approaching the Belgian model? *Journal of Cultural Geography, 8*, 115–134.

Castonguay, C. (1982). Intermarriage and language shift in Canada, 1971–1976, *Canadian Journal of Sociology, 18*, 263–278.

Council of the Corporation of the Township of Charlottenburg, Ontario. (1988, September 20). [Minutes of special meeting].

de Vries, J. (1994). Canada's official language communities: An overview of the current demolinguistic situation, *International Journal of the Sociology of Language, 105/106*, 37–68.

The fearful anglophones [Editorial]. (1988, September 19). *The Globe and Mail*, p. A6.

Fishman, J. A. (1991). *Reversing language shift: Theory and practice of assistance to threatened languages*. Clevedon, England: Multilingual Matters.

Fishman J. A. (1993). Reversing language shift: Successes, failures, doubts and dilemmas. In E.-H. Jahr (Ed.), *Language conflict and language planning* (pp. 69–81). Berlin: Mouton de Gruyter.

Gill, R. M. (1983). Federal and provincial language policy in Ontario and the future of the Franco-Ontarians, *Annual Review of Canadian Studies, 13*, 13–43.

Graham, W. C., & Thomas, C. (1987). Bilingual practice in the province of Ontario: Some observation. In R. H. Matas & D. J. McCawley (Eds.), *Legal education in Canada* (pp. 547–561). Montreal: Federation of Law Societies of Canada.

Heine, W. C. (1977, March 10). Abdication. *London Free Press*, p. 6.

Helm, T. (1989). *The struggle for French-language education in Sturgeon Falls, West Nipissing, Ontario: A community of contradictions*. Unpublished master's thesis, Trent University, Peterborough, Ontario.

Joy, R. J. (1972). *Languages in conflict: The Canadian experience*. Toronto: McClelland and Stewart.

Lachapelle, R. (1978). Minorities concentrate, so should policy. *Reports on Confederation, 1*, 40.

Leclerc, J.-C. (1990, February 1). Le langage du Sault-aux-racistes. *Le Devoir*, p. 8.

Mallea, J. R. (1989). *Schooling in a plural Canada*, Clevedon, England: Multilingual Matters.

Martinez, O. J. (1988). *Troublesome border*. Tucson: The University of Arizona Press.

## 11. FRENCH-LANGUAGE SERVICES IN ONTARIO 299

McRoberts, K. (1989). Making Canada bilingual: Illusions and delusions of federal language policy. In D. P. Shugarman & R. Whitaker (Eds.), *Federalism and political community: Essays in honour of Donald Smiley* (pp. 141–169). Toronto: Broadview.

Mougeon, R., & Beniak, E. (1994). Bilingualism, language shift, and institutional support for French: The case of the Franco-Ontarians. *International Journal of the Sociology of Language, 105/106,* 99–126.

Mougeon, R., & Heller, M. (1986). The social and historical context of minority French language education in Ontario. *Journal of Multilingual and Multicultural Development, 7,* 199–227.

Ontario. Legislative Assembly. (1968, May 30). *Debates* (pp. 3637–3677).

Ontario. Legislative Assembly. (1971, May 3). *Debates* (pp. 1103–1174).

Ontario. Legislative Assembly. (1986, July 10). *Debates* (pp. 2297–2400).

Ontario. Legislative Assembly. (1989, December 18). *Debates* (pp. 4905–4996).

Ontario. Legislative Assembly. (1990, December 20). *Debates* (pp. 2957–3024).

Ontario, Standing Committee on Social Development. (1984, October 29). (pp. S49–S75).

Reid, S. (1993). *Lament for a nation: The life and death of Canada's bilingual dream.* Vancouver: Arsenal Pulp.

Rosser, B. (1977). *Bicultural conflict in a language island: Essex County, Ontario.* Unpublished bachelor of arts thesis, Department of Geography, The University of Western Ontario, London, Ontario.

Seguin, R. (1990, February 7). Resolution spurs anger, frustration. *The Globe and Mail,* p. 5.

Terrien, J., & Johansen, D. (1990). Minority language education rights: Section 23 of the charter (89–6E). Ottawa: Library of Parliament, Research Branch.

Tilting at the same old windmills [Editorial]. (1987, July 29). *The Glengarry News,* p. 4.

Young, C. (1993). *The rising tide of cultural pluralism.* Madison: University of Wisconsin Press.

Williams, C. A. (1991). *Linguistic minorities, society and territory.* Clevedon, England: Multilingual Matters.

Wills, T. (1994, May 25). Franco-Ontarians tell U.N. they suffer oppression. *Montreal Gazette,* p. B8.

# 12

# Quebec, Canada, and the United States: Social Reality and Language Rights

Calvin Veltman
*Université du Québec à Montréal*

Much of the discussion concerning movements to favor any given language turns on the hypothesis that government action does in fact have a significant impact on social reality. This is a popular thesis in both the United States and Canada, both within and without academic circles. Nonetheless, a good deal of data suggests that social systems are inherently self-sustaining, a feature that renders them relatively impervious to governmental intervention, except in very specific circumstances. Consequently, governmental initiatives to control language behavior are generally met by adaptive strategies designed to maintain the *status quo*.

In this chapter I examine the general features of language shift in the United States and Canada, paying particular attention to the situation in Quebec. I then evaluate in a summarized manner the impact that language policies have had on language shift and retention.

## LANGUAGE SHIFT IN THE UNITED STATES

### Methodological Considerations

Due to the repeated failure of the Bureau of the Census to obtain data on the mother tongue of the American population, few data are available in the United States at the national level that would permit us to assess the rate and extent of language shift, either for Spanish-speaking Americans or for members of other language groups. Although the census has collected data concerning the knowledge and use of English and other languages, no analysis of language shift can be performed without knowing the mother tongue of individuals (Veltman, 1991, 1992).

Attempts to develop rates of language shift using ethnic origin as the point of departure are doomed to failure, given the fact that many Americans have English for their mother tongue, irrespective of their ethnic origin.[1] Even in homes where some Spanish was spoken, an estimated 2.9 million Americans reported in 1976 that English was their mother tongue. Needless to say, people of English mother tongue should not be included in the base population for which we wish to calculate rates of language shift from Spanish to English. Rather, criteria for inclusion in or exclusion from the Spanish language group on the basis of mother tongue should first be established, after which observed language practices can be related to what we may qualify as "original" language characteristics.

The single large-scale data source that may be used to obtain rates of language shift for the American population dates from 1976, when the National Center for Education Statistics and the Bureau of the Census jointly undertook a nationwide survey of 150,000 American households known as the Survey of Income and Education (SIE). This study included a variety of language-use questions relating to household language practices, individual language use, and, notably, the mother tongue of most respondents.[2]

## General Findings

Notwithstanding popular fears to the contrary, data from the SIE indicate that immigrants to the United States rapidly learn English, appropriate it as their personal language, and integrate themselves into the English language group (Veltman, 1983, 1989). Within 5 years, rates of language shift to English begin to accelerate; after 10 years, young immigrant children show rates of language shift comparable in every way to those of native-born children in the same language group. Although rates observed for Hispanic immigrants and their children are lower than those observed

---

[1]An exception is the Navajo language group where ethnic origin, mother tongue, and Navajo language practice tend to coincide (Veltman, 1983).

[2]In fact, the Survey did not bother to obtain the mother tongue of persons born in the United States who lived in English monolingual households. The authors of the study assumed that such persons would have English for their mother tongue, an hypothesis that is clearly not true for many children of immigrants. As a result, we may assume that calculated rates of language shift likely underestimate the true rate, were all persons of a given mother tongue correctly identified.

## 12. SOCIAL REALITY AND LANGUAGE RIGHTS                                303

in other large minority language groups, the analysis reveals that most of the grandchildren of any given group of Hispanic immigrants will not speak Spanish on any regular basis (Veltman, 1989).

Even in highly segregated Hispanic communities, the movement to English is very rapid, particularly among younger immigrants and native-born Hispanics. In the state of California, over 80% of native-born persons of Spanish mother tongue aged 10–29 usually spoke English in 1976, the time of the survey; in the Northeastern states, the rate hovered around 70%.[3] Rates of language shift for native-born persons exceed 50% in every area of the country except rural Texas, where the rate of language shift to English was nonetheless over 45%.

Furthermore, based on trend analysis, the 1976 SIE reveals that rates of language shift have been rising regularly throughout the 20th century in the United States, such that younger persons in the Spanish language group have undergone greater assimilation to English than have younger ones, with still greater anglicization to come (Veltman, 1988, chapters 6 and 7).[4]

### The Sources of Language Shift

The previous analysis leads us to conclude that rates of language shift are extremely high in the United States and they would appear to be rising from one period to another. These findings suggest that the process of language shift is itself structured by other, powerful factors that have exercised increasing pressure on persons in minority language groups to both learn English and integrate into the English language group. We may think of the pressures generated by the need to attend school, to obtain a job, to enter into contact with neighbors, to purchase goods and services, to read and understand the omnipresent English mass media, and so forth. These are objective features of the environment of persons who come from minority language backgrounds, to which may be added some fundamental psychological, if not moral, values: the desire not to be ridiculed because of one's inability to speak English or the accent with which one speaks; the desire to be a person considered successful; to be thought to be a "good American." These values are so basic that they too may be considered "structural" in the sense that they are relatively permanent features of American society.

Further, increasing urbanization prevents most groups from developing autonomous ethnic-based societies such as those created by the Amish and certain groups of Mennonites in a number of American states. New immigrants increasingly settle in cities where they are more directly exposed to the structural forces that fuel rapid linguistic integration than were French

---

[3]In Los Angeles, 67.9% of all native-born persons, irrespective of age, usually spoke English; the rate was 55.3% in the greater New York area at the time of the survey.

[4]See Veltman, 1983, 1988, 1991, or 1992 for the appropriate methodological discussion.

Canadian, German, and Scandinavian immigrants of previous generations.

Because the factors which fuel such high rates of language shift are essentially *structural* in nature, it is indeed most unlikely that more recent data would reveal that the patterns observed in 1976 have changed. On the contrary, the SIE data suggest that immigrants assimilate more rapidly now than they did in the past. We may, therefore, be relatively confident that, if anything, the data collected nearly 20 years ago underestimates the rapidity and the completeness of language shift in the United States.

## Language Legislation in the United States

No data suggest that observed differences in rates of language shift can be explained by the presence or absence of language legislation. In fact, Marshall (1986) noted that Spanish services are frequently offered in states with large Hispanic populations, even where English is the official state language (Illinois); such services are generally absent in states that have no official language but have few Hispanics. In short, the actual need for Spanish language services is a better predictor of the presence of such services than is the presence or absence of an official state language.

This is a relatively important observation because it suggests that we may draw a distinction between the theoretic right to obtain services in a minority language and the actual presence of such services. In short, the theoretic denial of specific minority language rights does not prevent communities or states (in the sense of governments in general) from implementing minority language services when such action is thought to be either necessary or expedient, as for example, in announcements concerning public health and safety.

It follows, therefore, that the granting or denial by a state of individual rights with respect to the use of a minority language is essentially symbolic, that is, a public statement with respect to the social status of any given language, with little or no relationship to actual behavior in the real world (Veltman, 1986). Consequently, legislation designed to restrict the use of Spanish represents a statement that the English language group is dominant and that Spanish-speaking people need not expect a particularly warm welcome.

Needless to say, where a dominant group feels extremely confident of its position, it is not necessary to enact language legislation; its members believe (or know) that newcomers will eventually adopt their language. Where a dominant group feels that their power is slipping away, efforts may be made to "send a message" to the minority group about the continued ability of the majority to set the rules of the game, much as White Protestants did when they supported the enactment of Prohibition (Gus-

# 12. SOCIAL REALITY AND LANGUAGE RIGHTS                                    305

field, 1963). At the very least, this is a working hypothesis that may help us to understand the factors which motivate those who wish to enact English-first, English-only, English-always amendments to the Constitution.

## LANGUAGE SHIFT IN ENGLISH CANADA[5]

### General Considerations

The Canadian linguistic situation is particularly interesting when viewed from an English Canadian or an American perspective. Because English is the overwhelmingly dominant language in most Canadian communities outside of Quebec and the Acadian homeland in northeastern New Brunswick (l'Acadie), the promotion of bilingualism has generally meant the promotion of the French language in English Canada, together with some smaller support of the English language minority in Quebec.

That is to say, a minority language, French, is explicitly protected (promoted) in Canada as a result of the Official Languages Act (1968). Outside Quebec, three provinces now provide services in French to French-speaking citizens in designated areas of their provinces (Manitoba, Ontario, and New Brunswick). To English-speaking people, these arrangements seem eminently charitable, particularly when compared to the difficulties that Spanish-speaking people encounter in many of the states of the United States.

Viewed, however, from the standpoint of the dominant, French-speaking, Quebec perspective, the conception of Canada as a country that esteems and promotes two major languages relies more on the "power of positive thinking" than on fundamental differences from the United States with respect to the treatment of language minorities. That is to say, the country is thought by English-speaking people to be bilingual because the federal government has been trumpeting this idea since 1969. Wherever you go in Canada, French and English appear together on cereal boxes, in airports, and so forth; all federal government publications are issued in both languages.[6] All this language planning on the part of the federal government is designed to create the impression that Canada is a bilingual country where both English- and French-speaking citizens can live comfortably anywhere in the country in their own language.

---

[5]English Canada is defined as all of Canada with the exception of Quebec. It should, however, be noted that the Acadian region of New Brunswick is predominantly French-speaking (58%) and that assimilation to the English language group there appears to be extremely limited, if not negligible. This contrasts markedly with the French-speaking minorities in other provinces.

[6]Frequently, the French cover is on one side of the document, the English cover on the other side; there are two complete texts, one upside-down with respect to the other.

The promotion of the French language by Ottawa has been so efficient that it is widely thought that French is a necessary language to social advancement in Canada. As a result, hundreds of thousands of English-speaking Canadians have enrolled their children in French immersion programs to make sure that the average English-Canadian, English-speaking child will be able to compete successfully for federal government jobs. That the federal government has heavily financed these programs is not at all unrelated to their presumed importance and popularity.

## The Linguistic Structure of English Canada

The social structure of English Canada is in many ways similar to that of the United States,[7] at least with respect to language issues. The data reveal widespread and rapid assimilation to the English language group by all groups of immigrants in all areas of English Canada; virtually none adopt French as a usual home language.

With respect to the learning of French by English-speaking people in English Canada, it should not be expected that people would learn it so well that they would become French-speaking. Nearly all English Canadians work and play in English language institutions with English-speaking people; most English Canadians live with English-speaking spouses and play with their English-speaking children. Consequently, there is no area of social life where a second language can in fact be useful, unless one hopes to become a teacher of French, as occasionally happens in the United States as well. That is to say, the structural pressures are not conducive to the retention of French by immersion graduates (DeVries, 1985; Van der Keilen, 1995; Wesche & MacFarlane, 1995; Wesche, Morrison, Pawley, & Ready, 1990). Most immersion students do not use French in any setting outside the classroom while enrolled in such programs. Nor does the frequency of student visits to dominant French-speaking areas and the length of such contacts have a positive impact on student abilities (Hart, Lapkin, & Swain, 1991). It is no surprise that most immersion graduates do not use French in any significant way after having "graduated".[8] Since French immersion programs have no great impact in Quebec (Genesee,

---

[7]Notwithstanding the fact that English-speaking Canadians take great pains to distinguish themselves and the Canadian polity from the United States. The United States is supposed to be a linguistic "melting pot"; Canada an "ethnic mosaic," and so on. In our view, these images have nothing to do with the reality of the pervasive linguistic assimilation in both countries.

[8]Nonetheless, those in favor of bilingual education continue to tout its success. For example, after a devastating review of the literature showing that virtually none of the original objectives of French immersion programs have been attained, Wesche and MacFarlane (1995) concluded that immersion programs might be more successful "if systematic opportunities for contact with francophones and their culture were made integral features of immersion programmes" (p. 272). One might more logically conclude that the entire effort was an interesting social experiment that did not work.

## 12. SOCIAL REALITY AND LANGUAGE RIGHTS                                    307

1987), it would be extremely unlikely that they would have a significant impact in English Canada.

As may have been expected, the same structural considerations that are unfavorable to the maintenance of French among English Canadians also militate against the retention of French among French Canadians living in English Canada. Although it is somewhat difficult to assess the historical trend,[9] it would appear that rates of anglicization for persons of French mother tongue continue to rise in all parts of English Canada, including those areas in Ontario adjacent to Quebec, where the provincial government has made significant progress in the past few years in providing local services in French (Cartwright, chapter 11, this volume; Castonguay, 1994).

### Results of Language Planning in English Canada

In short, legislative action on behalf of the French language has not produced any significant changes at the local or community level that would affect the vitality or the survival prospects of the French language group in any region of English Canada. This is hardly surprising. Aside from the promotion of immersion programs, federal policy with respect to bilingualism has only applied to federal agencies or to the most superficial aspects of daily life (such as written advertising). As a result, 25 years of officially promoted bilingualism have neither had much impact on the health of French language minorities in English Canada, nor have they significantly altered the linguistic composition of the federal civil service, nor increased the use of French by civil servants (cf. Beaujot, chapter 3, this volume).

Not only has the promotion of the French language by the federal government been ineffective, it has had two negative, unintended consequences. First of all, federal language planning efforts on behalf of French have alienated other minority language groups in English Canada (see Burnaby, chapter 10, this volume). It can be readily understood that other minority language groups of equal or greater proportion in a given population vigorously resent the special status that has been conferred on the French language, particularly because observed rates of anglicization do not differ significantly between the French language group and other minority language groups in English Canada.

In addition, the promotion of French has also proved to be politically ineffective. Federal legislation with respect to bilingualism was sold to English Canada as the necessary price to be paid to put an end to Quebec nationalism. The promotion of French over the last 25 years has done nothing to reduce the importance of Quebec nationalism, which, if any-

---

[9]Given the fact that since 1971 Statistics Canada has frequently changed the wording of its language questions, the instructions given to respondents, its method of treating the data, or any combination thereof.

thing, is more important today than it was at the end of the 1960s. Many English Canadians have come to feel that there is nothing they can do to please Quebeckers, a conclusion that logically follows from an exceedingly poor diagnosis of what Quebec has really wanted all along, that is, greater political autonomy within the Canadian federation. It is foolish, if not dangerous, to think that a demand for greater autonomy could be satisfied by increased enrollments in French immersion programs in English Canada. Only the one-time charisma of Pierre Elliott Trudeau could have sold such a ridiculous idea, one that has been largely discredited in Quebec and that has led to a great deal of frustration and backlash in English Canada.

## THE LINGUISTIC SITUATION IN QUEBEC

### Geolinguistic Generalities

Aside from all the wishful thinking, what really makes Canada a bilingual country is not the presence of any given number of bilingual individuals; it is the fact that the Canadian federation includes Quebec. In point of fact, Canada was once a more bilingual country in terms of the language spoken by its citizens that it is now. The population pressure generated by high French Canadian birthrates led to emigration from Quebec throughout the latter part of the 19th century and the early part of the 20th century. Most emigrants went to the New England states and Ontario, but a certain number participated in the settlement of the Canadian West. It should be remembered that French-speaking peoples were present in sufficient numbers such that Manitoba was admitted to the Confederation as a bilingual province.[10]

The Great Depression, World War II, and rapidly falling birthrates in the French-Canadian group put an end to both demographic and territorial expansion. The French-speaking minorities living outside Quebec (and Acadia) were subjected to the structural pressures that favor language shift to English,[11] such that the proportion of French-speaking people in Canada living outside Quebec has declined progressively since 1941. The figure was 19.0% in 1941, 16.0% in 1971 and 14.9% in 1991.[12] Needless to say, given the anglicization of the French language population living outside Quebec,

---

[10]The Manitoba legislature revoked the status of French as an official language in 1871. This act, challenged by an individual citizen and underwritten by the Canadian federal government, was declared unconstitutional by the Supreme Court of Canada in the late 1970s, 100 years after the event!

[11]The assimilation of the French Canadian language group in the United States is now all but completed (Veltman, 1987).

[12]Figures are for persons of French mother tongue as reported by Lachapelle and Henripin (1980); 1991 data are estimated by assigning multiple responses equally between the multiple categories selected.

# 12. SOCIAL REALITY AND LANGUAGE RIGHTS 309

the use of French as principal home language is still more concentrated in Quebec. In 1971, 12.2% of the (active) French-speaking population lived outside Quebec, in 1991 the figure was only 10.1%. Thus, 9 in 10 French-speaking people now live in Quebec (see also Beaujot, Cartwright, chapters 3 and 6, this volume).

As English Canada has become more English, Quebec has become less so.[13] In 1871, the Census identified 20.4% of the population as being British in ethnic origin; in 1941, 14.1% of Quebeckers had English for their mother tongue, a figure that declined to 13.1% in 1971, 10.4% in 1981 and 9.2% in 1991. These data reveal a marked decline in the importance of the English language presence over the past 120 years, notably so since the Quiet Revolution of the 1960s and 1970s (Veltman, 1996).

The decline of the English-speaking population is particularly evident in the so-called "contact areas"[14] of the Ottawa River Valley and the Eastern Townships. At the time of the first Canadian census of 1871, both regions were predominantly English-speaking. Persons of French ancestry comprised 46.0% of the population of the Ottawa River Valley and 39.3% of the Townships. In 1981, approximately 85% of the former and 78% of the latter were composed of persons of French mother tongue. Anglophones are now essentially concentrated in certain well-defined neighborhoods of the Montreal metropolitan area; outside Montreal, the population is massively francophone.

## Quebec's Language Legislation

It is within this broader demographic context that Quebec nationalism can best be understood. In fact, Quebec nationalism may be seen as an outgrowth or as an adaptive response to the reorganization of the Canadian economy that has been occurring throughout this century (Veltman, 1996). A number of important factors have contributed to this reorganization, not the least of which are the opening of the Canadian West and the shifting of the population center of the country to the Great Lakes area, the rise of highly mobile modes of transportation (by truck and air), the opening of the St. Lawrence Seaway, the shifting of the center of the American economy to the industrialized cities of the Great Lakes, and so on. Under these circumstances, English-language firms moved their operations to southern Ontario, causing Montreal to lose its position as an English-speaking,

---

[13]This is also true of Acadia where the French-speaking population became more numerous than the English language group at the turn of the 20th century and now accounts for some 58% of the population. This figure has been quite stable since 1971.

[14]Areas where both English and French language groups are present. In general, contact areas include the Ontario counties on the Quebec border and Acadia in New Brunswick. Inside Quebec, three areas are identified: Loyalist settlement north of the U.S. border, in the federal capital region, and the greater Montreal region.

British-dominated city that controlled the Canadian economy (Linteau, 1992). Consequently, the English language not only lost its unique power as an important mechanism of upward social mobility, it no longer assured the dominance and prosperity of the entire region. Quebec nationalism may thus be seen as an adaptive response to the rise of Montreal as a regional center that, in order to effectively dominate its hinterland, must use French as the principal language of business.

Quebec nationalism has found its quintessential expression in the adoption of successive laws designed to promote the French language and, accordingly, French-speaking people. The laws find their basic justification in the fact that the 1971 Census of Canada revealed that three times more people from third language groups (non-French, non-English) had integrated into the English language minority as opposed to the French language majority. In addition, the data revealed that in direct language transfers between the two groups, the French majority lost more than it gained. Given the progressively weakened position of the English minority, many French Canadians felt that the time had come to resist the continued imposition of English in many areas of social life. The first major piece of legislation was brought in by Premier Bourassa's Liberal government in 1974, followed by the Parti Québécois' Law 101 in 1976.

However, given repeated, successful attacks on the constitutionality of different aspects of Law 101 and the repeal of certain measures by both Parti Québécois and Liberal governments, Quebec's language legislation has been essentially confined to two major areas: the channeling of immigrant children into French language schools; and weak, largely ineffective attempts to promote the use of French in the workplace (see Beaujot, chapter 3, this volume).

## Language Planning and the Workplace

The attempt to promote the use of French has met with adaptive efforts to minimize the impact of Law 101. The most notable failure concerns the language of work, where many firms have failed to put "francization" committees and programs in place. Furthermore, habitual forms of intergroup contacts remain current. Clerks, receptionists, and secretaries, both French-speaking and English-speaking, regularly speak English to their bilingual clients as they attempt to serve customers in the language they think the client would like to use. If the client speaks French but has even a small non-French accent of some type, most people will spontaneously speak English, whether or not the person so addressed speaks that language.

Further, nearly all jobs dealing with the public continue to require a good knowledge of English as a precondition for employment. In short, English continues to enjoy a social utility well beyond what is necessary when

## 12. SOCIAL REALITY AND LANGUAGE RIGHTS

judged by the size of the English-speaking population itself. The people, both English-speaking and French-speaking, have "conspired together" to maintain the linguistic equilibrium that existed prior to the implementation of Law 101.

There are also, however, data which show that the percentage of French-speaking people who now work in French has had a tendency to increase over time (Commission de protection de la langue française et al., 1992). Even more significant, the percentage of allophones and anglophones who now use French at work has tended to increase over time. Consequently, it would appear that the language legislation has produced some small effects on language practice at work, although it is impossible to distinguish between direct effects and indirect ones, particularly because the working population is not composed of the same people at different points in time.

### Language Planning and the Educational System

The requirement that immigrant children attend French schools was designed to create a citizenry literate in the national language. It was also hoped that French schooling would lead children to become French-speaking and integrate into the French language group. Neither objective has been fully achieved because a large number of French schools now have significant English language ghettos, the effect of which is to minimize contact with native speakers (Beauchesne & Hensler, 1987).

On the other hand, the percentages of minority language students who continue their postsecondary education in French has tended to rise somewhat over time, although the English-language junior colleges and universities continue to enroll a greater share of such students than might have been expected (Commission de protection de la langue française et al., 1992).

### General Evaluation of Language Planning

In spite of the presence of these reactive mechanisms, the social utility of the French language has improved dramatically over the past 20 years. Nonetheless, we cannot automatically attribute these changes to the direct effects of Quebec's language legislation. In fact, it would appear that the language legislation has altered the structure of migratory flows to and from Quebec, leading to the entry of a population more disposed to integrate the French language majority and to the continuing out-migration by young anglophones seeking better economic opportunities in English Canada.

It may well be, however, that symbolic statements by the Quebec government regarding the status of French have accelerated these processes, because a reexamination of census data reveals that they were set in motion in the 1960s, that is, well before language planning legislation was adopted

(Veltman, 1996). In any case, the development of state interventionism in Quebec during the Quiet Revolution was associated with the symbolic message that francophones were going to control their own destiny, irrespective of the reaction of the anglophone business elite. The language legislation of the 1970s obviously reinforced this point.

This symbolism appears to have had an impact on a number of important demographic factors. First of all, as the symbolic value of their language declines, the rate of out-migration by anglophones has increased, particularly during the latter half of the 1970s. Second, the rate of in-migration of English Canadians has also declined. Third, English-speaking immigrants from other countries may also hesitate before coming to Quebec, leaving the door open for immigrants more susceptible to policies of francization than were previous immigrant groups. All of these factors create a situation conductive to the demographic decline of the English language group, even though the status of the language they speak continues to remain rather high.

In recent studies we have conducted for Quebec's Ministry of International Affairs, Immigration and Cultural Communities, we have found that the single most important factor predicting the direction of language shift is the linguistic competence of immigrants before they arrive in Quebec. Those who know English integrate into the English language group and obtain jobs where they can largely get by on the basis of their knowledge of English. Even when they learn French, they do not use it to any significant extent. On the other hand, immigrants who know only French when they arrive in Quebec integrate into the French language group and work largely in French, irrespective of the degree to which English language skills were required (Veltman & Paré, 1993, 1995).

On the other hand, immigrants who spoke neither English nor French prior to their arrival are not only learning French as their principal second language, but are also overwhelmingly integrating into the French language group. This probably represents a significant change from the past, indicating not only that the demographic weight of the French-speaking community requires the learning and use of French, but also that the symbolic message regarding the importance of learning French and "becoming" French-speaking is not lost on the latest immigrant cohorts (Veltman & Paré, 1993).

## CONCLUSION

The Quebec findings are most interesting from a theoretical point of view. They suggest that although language planning efforts may not directly attain the goals they seek to achieve, the symbolic value assigned to the official language may serve as a clear indicator of the road to be traveled

## 12. SOCIAL REALITY AND LANGUAGE RIGHTS                                313

by language minorities, that is, the direction which language shift and linguistic assimilation is supposed to take. Although few of those present in the society at the time during which the legislation is adopted take its dispositions seriously, both potential and new immigrants tend to accept the announced framework as indicative of social reality and act accordingly. On the one hand, the social system changes only slowly because those present resist change and seek adaptive strategies.[15] On the other hand, migration flows are affected that ultimately bring people who are more amenable to the new legislation, progressively transforming the society. It would appear that Quebec's legislation has produced this indirect effect, inducing more Arab, Haitian, and Latin American immigrants to settle in Quebec while discouraging English-speaking immigrants from the United States, the United Kingdom, Carribean countries, and the Indian subcontinent.

In spite of the demographic changes occurring in Quebec, the English language minority enjoys far greater language rights than French-speaking minorities in English Canada. It also has the best opportunity to employ its language to the fullest; in fact, the actual use of English far exceeds what the law requires. Indeed, English is widely used in situations where theoretically it is forbidden, in the areas of both employment and schooling, the two areas where Quebec's language legislation remains intact. As for the language laws regulating advertising, their effects are largely symbolic because they do not control the language spoken between customers and merchants.

It is important, therefore, that we look at the entire social system before deciding that legislation of one sort or another will have an important positive or negative effect on this or that type of language practice. In our view, language practice is determined by a variety of largely demographic factors; government policy tends to be subverted by adaptive mechanisms designed to reinforce the current social and cultural system. Such intervention in the arena of language tends to be highly symbolic, throwing the weight of the State behind this or that language, offending some and exciting others, but having only a marginal effect on the basic processes that affect the size and shape of minority language communities. As we have pointed out, Quebec demography may be somewhat influenced by such symbolic factors.

On the other hand, it appears unlikely that such is the case in either English Canada or the United States. The need to learn English and become English-speaking is so strong that policies designed to preserve or protect minority languages may be expected to have little or no effect. Similarly,

---

[15]One need only think of the hundreds of children illegally enrolled in English schools under Law 101, for whom the schools received no funding and who were faced with the potential impossibility of attending high school. When the Liberal government returned to power, they benefited from an immediate amnesty.

# 314 VELTMAN

the promotion of English as a State or national language adds little or nothing to the social and economic pressures already operative on immigrants and their children.

## REFERENCES

Beauchesne, A., & Hensler, H. (1987). *L'école française à clientèle pluriethnique de l'île de Montréal* (étude no. 25, Dossiers du Conseil de la langue française). Québec: les Publications du Québec.

Castonguay, C. (1994). *L'assimilation linguistique: mesure et évolution* (étude no. 41, Dossiers du Conseil de la langue française). Québec: les Publications du Québec.

Commission de protection de la langue française et al. (1992) *Indicateurs de la situation linguistique au Québec* (édition 1992). Québec: Conseil de la langue française.

DeVries, J. (1985). *Ottawa's French immersion graduates*. Ottawa: Centre for Research on Ethnic Minorities, Carleton University.

Genesee, F. (1987). *Learning through two languages*. Cambridge: Newbury House.

Gusfield, J. (1963). *Symbolic crusade: Status politics and the American temperance movement*. Urbana: University of Illinois Press.

Hart, D., Lapkin, S., & Swain, M. (1991). *French immersion at the secondary/post-secondary interface: Toward a national study*. Toronto: Ontario Institute for Studies in Education.

Lachapelle, R., & Henripin, J. (1980). *La situation démolinguistique au Canada, évolution passé et perspectives*. Montréal: Institut de recherches politiques.

Linteau, P.-A. (1992). *Histoire de Montréal depuis la Confédération*. Montréal: Les Éditions du Boréal.

Marshall, D. F. (1986). The question of an official language: Language rights and the English Language Amendment. *International Journal of the Sociology of Language, 60*, 7–75.

Van der Keilen, M. (1995). Use of French, attitudes and motivations of French immersion students. *The Canadian Modern Language Review, 51*, 287–304.

Veltman, C. (1983). *Language shift in the United States*. The Hague, Netherlands: Mouton.

Veltman, C. (1986). Comment: The question of an official language for the USA. *International Journal of the Sociology of Language, 60*, 177–182.

Veltman, C. (1987). *L'avenir du français aux États-Unis* (étude no. 27, Documentation du Conseil de la langue française). Québec: Éditeur officiel du Québec.

Veltman, C. (1988). *The future of the Spanish language in the United States*. Washington: Hispanic Policy Development Project.

Veltman, C. (1989). Croissance et anglicisation de la population hispano-américaine. In P. Pupier & J. Woehrling (Eds.), *Langue et droit* (pp. 487–496). Montréal: Wilson & Lafleur.

Veltman, C. (1991). Theory and method in the study of language shift. In James Dow (Ed.), *Language and ethnicity* (pp. 145–168). Amsterdam: John Benjamins.

Veltman, C. (1992). The measurement of language shift. In *Le peuplement des Amériques* (pp. 23–40). Veracruz, Mexico: International Union for the Scientific Study of the Population.

Veltman, C. (1996). The English language in Quebec, 1940–1990. In J. Fishman, A. Conrad, & A. Rubal-Lopez (Eds.), *The status of post-imperial English* (pp. 205–237). New York: Mouton de Gruyter.

Veltman, C., & Paré, S. (1993). *L'adaptation linguistique des immigrants de la décennie 1980*. Montréal: Direction des communications du ministère des Communautés culturelles et de l'Immigration, Gouvernement du Québec.

Veltman, C., & Paré, S. (1995). *L'enquête de 1993 sur la pratique linguistique des immigrants*. Montréal: Direction des communications du ministère des Communautés culturelles et de l'Immigration, Gouvernement du Québec.

## 12. SOCIAL REALITY AND LANGUAGE RIGHTS

Wesche, M., & MacFarlane, A. (1995). Immersion outcomes: Beyond language proficiency. *The Canadian Modern Language Review, 51*, 250–274.

Wesche, M., Morrison, F., Pawley, C., & Ready, D. (1990). French immersion: Post-secondary consequences for individuals and universities. *The Canadian Modern Language Review, 46*, 430–451.

# 13

# Partitioning by Language: Whose Rights Are Threatened?

Thomas Ricento
*University of Texas at San Antonio*

One of the arguments frequently made by those who support efforts to make English the official language of the United States is that bilingualism is often destablizing, that it can lead to civil strife, chaos, and national disunity. In the popular press and in literature distributed by organizations such as U.S. English, Canada is often portrayed as a country whose policy of official bilingualism has led to the separatist movement in Quebec in recent years, and that unless we in the United States declare English the official language, the unity of the United States and the welfare of its citizens will be adversely affected.

These are strong claims. Similar claims about the damaging effects of bi- and multilingualism are also made in regard to India, Belgium, and Sri Lanka, where, it is argued, competition among official languages has adversely affected each of the named polities. In the United States, bilingual education programs, bilingual ballots, and bilingual media are seen as promoting separatism and removing the need for non-English speakers to assimilate, which in the past has always meant essentially giving up one's cultural and linguistic identity and adopting an "American" identity.

Are these claims valid? And if they are, what lessons can be drawn from the Canadian experience, if any? Who will gain and who will lose if English is elevated to an official status in the United States? Whose rights are threatened?

**318**                                                                                          **RICENTO**

In this chapter, I present evidence from a study of 170 countries suggesting linguistic heterogeneity is *not* associated with civil unrest. I then compare the history and evolution of language policy in Canada and the United States, demonstrating that the rationales and goals of official language policies are very different in the two countries. Next, I briefly consider the negative effects federal official English legislation would have in the areas of education, voting, public services, and government agencies. I conclude by arguing that in the United States, English is the undisputed dominant national language needing no protection from competing languages, whereas linguistic duality and cultural pluralism are "facts" in Canada, enshrined in the Charter of Rights and Freedoms.

## LINGUISTIC HETEROGENEITY AND CIVIL STRIFE

First, let me briefly respond to the claim that bi- or multilingualism is somehow a bad thing and responsible for civil strife and other maladies in countries such as India, Sri Lanka, and Belgium.

Joshua Fishman, who has studied language and ethnicity extensively over the years in many countries and contexts, conducted a number of studies (Fishman, 1990, provides a summary of these studies) that found little evidence of separatism resulting from providing minority groups with governmental services in their own languages. He found that the roots of separatism lie in minority–majority relations broadly conceived, not in language. Factors contributing to separatism are a history of repression, economic domination, and nondemocratic central control. Problems popularly attributed to bilingualism are really problems of social and economic development and control, superimposed on linguistic, racial, and religious differences. Fishman found, based on a study of 62 linguistically heterogenous countries, that tolerance and generosity toward linguistic minorities promote good majority–minority relations and lead to a stable polity; attacking a minority's ability to use its own language results in social pathology, uncontrollable political conflict, and widespread difficulties.

Fishman (1989) used a statistical analysis to study the possible effect of linguistic heterogeneity on civil strife and per capita gross national product. He utilized databanks developed by political scientists in the United States for 170 countries, covering 238 different economic, political, social, cultural, historical, geographic, and demographic variables. The variable "linguistic heterogeneity" was operationalized as the proportion of the population claiming as its own the major mother tongue of any given country: The smaller that proportion, the greater the degree of linguistic heterogeneity; the larger that proportion, the smaller the degree of linguistic heterogeneity. Four different indicators of civil strife for which records are kept include:

## 13. PARTITIONING BY LANGUAGE

(a) magnitude and frequency of conspiracy against the established government; (b) magnitude and frequency of internal warfare due to revolution, sedition, or secession; (c) magnitude and frequency of internal turmoil (riots, strikes, protests); and (d) a composite average of the aforementioned three. Fishman found that out of 230 possible predictors of civil strife, only 13 make truly independent contributions that yield a multiple correlation of .82, and linguistic heterogeneity is not one of the 13 optimal predictors.

As far as the correlation between per capita gross national product and linguistic heterogeneity is concerned, linguistic heterogeneity has a correlation with per capita gross national product that would explain about 10% of the worldwide interpolity variation. However, when this variable is correlated with all other possible predictors of per capita gross national product, it really explains nothing at all about per capita gross national product. Fishman (1990) noted that the inescapable implication of the findings is that lingua francas and bilingualism enable many polities to attain higher per capita gross national product and avoid civil strife regardless of their degree of linguistic heterogeneity. Further, polities that are low in per capita gross national product and high in civil strife are, on the whole, characterizable as such regardless of their degree of linguistic heterogeneity, some of them being linguistically very homogeneous. So the claim that bi- or multilingualism is itself destablizing is not supported.

## CANADA: BACKGROUND

Those in the United States who use the Canadian situation to support official English legislation often tell only part of the story. In order to get a clearer picture, we need to understand Canada's past and how its status as an officially bilingual nation came about.

The Canadian Constitution, according to Magnet (1990), "resulted from a political compromise between Catholic francophones and Protestant anglophones in 1867" (p. 53). Canada's Constitution recognized the right of francophones to protect their language and culture from being absorbed by the anglophone majority. Under the Canadian Constitution, the provincial government of Quebec, like other provinces, controlled local matters, including language. Linguistic minorities in all provinces, both anglophone and francophone, were able to use either French or English in important governmental transactions; as other provinces joined the federation, the tradition of protecting the language and denominational rights of linguistic and religious minorities by special constitutional collective rights was continued where, prior to confederation, these groups had enjoyed such autonomy. Canada's linguistic diversity was doubly protected. Anglophones and francophones controlled the provincial governments where each was predominant. Where significant minorities existed, they were protected by a constitutional obligation for bilingualism at the federal level, and, in significant cases, at the provincial level as well. Provision was made for bilingual municipal notices, proclamations, electoral forms and voters' notices. Minorities remained secure.

The great Canadian compromise was shaken when, in 1885, the predominately French-speaking western Metis revolted over government refusal to respect their land claims. This provided the pretext for political action on the part of politicians who hoped to overturn the status quo of linguistic and cultural tolerance. As Dalton McCarthy, a conservative Member of Parliament, put it in 1889: "The race and language issue gave the politician something ... to live for; we have the power to save this country from fratricidal strife, the power to make this a British country in fact as it is in name" (cited in Magnet, 1990, p. 54). In 1890, the province of Manitoba stripped all public support from Catholic schools, and passed the Official Language Act, abolishing constitutional guarantees for French in the province. Education in French was abolished in Ontario in 1912, and antagonism continued for the next half century.

By the 1960s, although Quebec as a whole had caught up in its socioeconomic development with the rest of Canada, many Quebec francophones felt resentful of their subordinate linguistic and economic status vis-à-vis anglophones (Bourhis, 1994). In response to this perception, language planning activity in Quebec grew in the 1960s and 1970s. Fearful of being marginalized economically and politically, francophones elected the Parti Québécois to power in Quebec City in 1976. In the wake of this election, and prompted in part by severe civil unrest in Quebec during the 1960s, the federal government in Ottawa made efforts to protect and promote French in order to reestablish and refortify minority rights envisaged in the Canadian Constitution. The federal Official Languages Act (1969) made both French and English official languages and assured equitable participation of francophones in the federal civil service and guaranteed federal services in French (Magnet, 1990).

However, for many Québécois, this was too little, too late. In 1974, the Quebec government adopted Bill 22, which declared French to be the official language of Quebec and established the primacy of French in public administration, utilities, professions, labor, and education (Bourhis, 1994). Choice with regard to schooling was restricted; children without an adequate knowledge of English were required to attend French schools. Another Bill (101), passed by the Parti Québécois government in 1977, made French the *only* official language of Quebec. The bill was passed in response to the growing encroachment of the English language and culture within the province. Whereas francophones viewed Bill 101 as both a symbolic and

# 13. PARTITIONING BY LANGUAGE    321

pragmatic vehicle for the economic and political control of their future, anglophones saw Bill 101 undermining their legitimate rights enshrined at the federal level as English-speaking citizens of Quebec. One of the major results of the legislation was to virtually eliminate the economic disparity between the French- and English-speaking Québécois.

In 1982, several additions to the Canadian Constitution were passed, including one that put both English and French as official languages of the country in the Constitution itself rather than in legislation. The Province of Quebec never agreed to the new constitution, which led to the compromise constitutional amendments known as the "Meech Lake Accord." Among the provisions was the recognition of Quebec as a "distinct society" within Canada, and the coexistence of the French and English languages as a "fundamental characteristic of Canada."

The provincial legislatures were given until June 23, 1990 to sign on to the provisions. In 1988, tensions mounted after Quebec reinstated a ban on commercial signage in English, and ignored a Supreme Court ruling that the ban was unconstitutional. The issue of provincial authority to regulate their linguistic heritage was raised in the wake of the controversy in Quebec. The provinces of Newfoundland and Manitoba failed to approve the Meech Lake Accord by the deadline of June 23. A further attempt, the Charlottetown Accord, failed in a national referendum in 1992.

## Canada and the United States: Parallel or Divergent Cases?

Many would argue the lesson from Canada is that official language policies which tend to exclude or marginalize significant linguistic minority groups are divisive, and do little to promote intergroup harmony. "French-only" policies, like "English-only" policies, in Canada or in the United States, have not advanced the goals of tolerance and support for minority language users. Yet, such a conclusion would be only partially justified if one considers the status of, for example, French in Canada compared to that of Spanish in the United States.

Some parallels can be drawn between the passage of Bill 101 and the current move in the United States to declare English the official language, via a constitutional amendment. Much like California, New York, Florida, and southwestern states (Arizona, New Mexico, Texas), Quebec has experienced demographic change in the last 20 years, from out-migration to other parts of Canada, and in-migration particularly from countries in Asia, Europe, and the Caribbean. By the early 1970s, 20% of Quebec was non-French-speaking. In addition, a dramatic decline in the French Canadian birthrate and the continued English domination of the Quebec economy was cause for concern; in the United States, no similar threat to the economic domination of the English-speaking group has been experienced as a result

322                                                                RICENTO

of increased immigration from Asia and the Americas. Francophones (especially in Quebec) perceive their way of life will be threatened unless steps are taken to preserve it. Evidence provided by Beaujot and Veltman in this volume appear to validate that concern. The same cannot be said for the status of English speakers in the United States, where the status of English has never been challenged or in danger of usurpation by a competing language. English was no more threatened in 1790, when 8.7% of the population recorded in the first national census spoke German, than it is today with 9% of the population speaking Spanish (Crawford, 1992).

Another difference is that nowhere in the continental United States is there such a large, homogeneous linguistic group concentrated in one area as there is with francophone Québécois in Canada. The exception is Puerto Rico, where some 80% of the population is functionally monolingual in Spanish (Resnick, 1993). However, Puerto Rico is a commonwealth and quasi-independent; Spanish is the language of government and education in Puerto Rico, and it is unlikely that, even in the event it achieves statehood, English will be imposed as the only official language. Furthermore, Puerto Rico represents only about 1% of the total U.S. population, whereas about 25% of Canadians reside in Quebec.

## THE "ENGLISH AS THE OFFICIAL LANGUAGE" MOVEMENT IN THE UNITED STATES

The rights of non-English-speaking minorities in the United States have, in the past, been curtailed by the imposition of literacy tests for voting, immigration, and naturalization. English has been imposed as the language of instruction by state legislatures, and even the teaching of foreign languages was at one time outlawed in a number of U.S. states. The *Meyer v. Nebraska* (1923) Supreme Court decision found a 1919 Nebraska statute that forbade teaching in any language other than English to be unconstitutional, and in 1927, the Court upheld a ruling by the Ninth Circuit Court of Appeals, which had found similar laws in 22 other states to be unconstitutional (Tamura, 1993). Restrictive immigration laws passed in the 1920s favored immigration from Northern Europe. This policy was changed in 1965 with the passage of the Immigration and Nationality Act; under its terms, immigration from the Americas and Asia increased dramatically. Demographic changes in the U.S. population, coupled with an ethnic revival movement, affirmative action programs, and bilingual education programs, apparently created anxieties among a portion of the dominant population. One of the responses to this change in American society was a movement to declare English the official language of the United States. In 1981, Senator S. I. Hayakawa, a Canadian immigrant of Japanese ancestry,

## 13. PARTITIONING BY LANGUAGE 323

introduced a constitutional amendment to declare English the official language of the country in order to counter the bilingual education and voting measures that "threaten to divide us along language lines" (cited in Crawford, 1992, p. 4). Although the proposed amendment did not advance beyond the committee stage, the effect on the national "debate" was profound. Whereas before 1969 only two states (Illinois and Nebraska) had passed laws naming English as the sole official language, by 1990 17 states had passed laws or constitutional amendments making English their official language; as of 1996, 22 states have laws regarding the status of English (including officially bilingual Hawaii).

Although bills declaring English the official language of the U.S. government were introduced in every Congress since 1981, it was not until Republicans had won a majority of the seats in the 1994 midterm elections that a bill was voted on, and passed. On August 1, 1996, the U.S. House of Representatives passed HR 123, dubbed The English Language Empowerment Act, by a vote of 259 to 169. The bill repealed the federal requirement, as stipulated in the Voting Rights Act, as amended in 1975, that bi- or multilingual voting ballots be provided in jurisdictions with significant numbers of voters whose first language is other than English. The bill would require the federal government to conduct all official business only in English (although the prohibition against non-English languages applies only to written communication), with certain exceptions in teaching languages, international relations, public health and safety, and some judicial proceedings. The Senate failed to act on a similar measure; hence, English as the official language is still not the law of the land.

During the 1996 Presidential election year, the U.S. Senate majority increased from 53–47 to 55–45, and by most accounts, the ideological composition of that body has moved in a more conservative direction. With majorities in both houses of Congress, Republicans are likely to consider this issue in the current (105th), and possibly in future sessions of Congress. Opinion polls conducted over the past several years suggest the majority of Americans support officialization of English,[1] although it is not clear whether respondents understand the implications of such legislation. Furthermore, attitudes vary according to region, ethnicity, and political affiliation, among other variables. Results from a telephone survey of 1,300 registered voters in San Antonio, Texas, conducted by the author in summer

---

[1]In the General Social Surveys (1994), 890 respondents (60% of the 1,474 who answered the question) answered the following question in the affirmative: Do you *favor* a law making English the official language of the United States, meaning government business would be conducted in English only, or do you *oppose* such a law? However, in related questions, 898 respondents (61% of the 1,474 who answered the question) believed election ballots should be printed in some other languages in addition to English, and 948 respondents (64% of the 1,474 who answered the question) indicated they were either strongly or somewhat in favor of bilingual education.

# 324                                                                RICENTO

1996, found that only 48% of the respondents supported official English, 37% opposed it, and 15% were undecided (N = 388; African American = 8.2%, Mexican American/Hispanic = 19.2%, Native American = 1.8%, White/Anglo American = 57.7%, Other = 4.9%%, 8.2% refused). White/ Anglo Americans, African Americans, and Republicans supported official English to a greater degree than did Mexican Americans/Hispanic Americans and Democrats.

In order to assess the impact such legislation would have on non-English speakers, we need to look at current laws and see how they might be overturned or overridden by a constitutional amendment, or by a Congressional bill making English the official language of government. At least four areas would be negatively impacted: education, voting, public services, and government agencies.

## Education

Although HR 123 (unlike other official-English bills introduced in the 104th Congress) did not eliminate federal support for bilingual education, official-English advocates claim that the interests of minority-language speakers will be best served if bilingual education programs are curtailed or eliminated and replaced with structured immersion programs. But will they? The use of students' native (non-English) language for instructional purposes (including bilingual education) was recommended under the Lau Remedies as the most appropriate means of addressing minority language students' needs in the elementary grades. These guidelines were drafted after the *Lau vs. Nichols* (1974) Supreme Court decision found that English-only instruction to non-English speakers violated Title VI of the Civil Rights Act of 1964. The Court did not specify the precise form remediation should take, but the principle was affirmed that equal educational opportunity is denied when non-English-speaking children are taught in a language they cannot understand. Although bilingual education programs have not been uniformly successful, it is not clear that structured immersion will be any more successful. At any rate, the entire matter of what is the most appropriate way to service the educational needs of language minority students is not advanced by attacks on bilingual education. Of greater concern is the fact that only a small percentage of students eligible for federally funded bilingual education programs are enrolled (about 15% in 1990–1991). About 500,000 limited English proficient (LEP) students are receiving no English language instruction. The central issue is a lack of appropriate educational programs for English-language learners, not an excess of so-called bilingual education programs.

If a law or an amendment to the U.S. Constitution were passed making English the official language of the United States, it could undermine local

# 13. PARTITIONING BY LANGUAGE

efforts to promote two-way, or developmental, bilingual programs and strengthen support for weak transitional bilingual programs, in which students are quickly exited to mainstream English-only classrooms, often before they are ready to do academic work in English. This would result in even greater problems for English-language learners, and would move the clock back to a time when students who spoke non-English languages in school were punished and humiliated. In Arizona, Mendoza (1986) found that less than half of low-achieving limited English proficient language minority students were, in fact, currently enrolled in bilingual or ESL programs (cited in Brandt, 1990). Will making English the official language improve the educational opportunities for English-language learners in Arizona? Will their dropout rate suddenly improve? Who will benefit? The idea that structured immersion programs should replace developmental bilingual programs reflects an ideological commitment to English monolingualism, rather than a rational assessment of best educational practice based on reputable research, which suggests that late-exit bilingual programs, in which students have been taught primarily in their native language (in this case, Spanish), for at least 5 years, produces the most sustained achievement (Ramírez, Yuen, Ramey, 1991; Thomas & Collier, in press).

## Voting

Here, the potential for damage may be even greater. Large numbers of voters who depend on assistance, materials, or both in languages other than English would be cut off from the electoral and political process. In 1975, Congress found that Hispanics, Asian Americans, American Indians, and Aleuts had been discriminated against by longstanding English-only provisions, and so they amended the Voting Rights Act. Congress recognized the fundamental right of suffrage as a prerequisite to preserving all other rights. Under the provisions of the Voting Rights Act, language minority voters can receive oral assistance and voting materials in a language they can understand. Passage of English-only laws, such as HR 123, would destroy this right, effectively disenfranchising a large number of Hispanic and Asian voters. Based on surveys conducted in San Antonio and East Los Angeles between November 1981 and January 1982, Brischetto and de la Garza (1983) concluded that "the availability of bilingual ballots and coordinated voter registration drives may account for … unexpectedly high levels of voting-related participation among older Spanish monolinguals" (p. 29).

## Public Services

In some states where English-only ordinances or statutes have been approved by voters, public services in non-English languages were terminated. After voters approved an antibilingual ordinance in Dade County, Florida, on November 4, 1980 (Ordinance 80–128), signs throughout the county were posted only in English, all public meetings and documents had to be in English (translations in other languages were prohibited), and advertisements to lure Latin American tourists had to be printed in English even though they appeared in Central and South American newspapers (Tatalovich, 1995). The ordinance was repealed by unanimous vote of the Dade County Commission in 1992, reflecting a change in the composition of the commission from 1980 (the 1980 ordinance had been passed by a majority White commission, whereas it was repealed by a commission composed of six Hispanics, four African Americans, and three Anglos in 1992). The passage of a largely symbolic constitutional amendment declaring English the official language of the state of Florida (1988) ratified current practice, namely that all public meetings, records, and official documents use English. Because of the political and economic power of Cuban legislators from Miami, it is unlikely that more restrictive measures under the amendment will be approved. However, official English supporters in Dade County have threatened to challenge the repeal of the 1980 English-only ordinance (Tatalovich, 1995).

Even where services in non-English languages are provided (e.g., in California, state agencies are required to hire sufficient numbers of bilingual employees to provide information and services in specified languages; Miner, chapter 7, this volume), grass-roots organizations have rallied support for ballot initiatives that would restrict such access. Federalizing the status of English as the official language could energize grass-roots organizations interested in reducing the availability of non-English languages in the public domain, especially given the current anti-immigration climate.

This attitude (anti-immigrant, anti-non-English-language) can be seen in an incident in Huntington Park, California, where municipal court employees were forbidden from speaking to each other in Spanish.[2] The late former senator S. I. Hayakawa said that employees should not even be allowed to ask "Where shall we go for lunch?" in Spanish, because this would violate Proposition 63 (the initiative that amended the Constitution of California making English the official language of the state).

In another incident, the mayor of Monterey Park, California, Barry Hatch, tried (unsuccessfully) to refuse a gift of 10,000 Chinese language

---

[2]Alva Gutiérrez, a bilingual clerk, sued to overturn an English-only policy imposed by three municipal court judges in Huntington Park, California. In deciding in favor of Gutiérrez, the 9th U.S. Circuit Court of appeals (*Gutiérrez vs. Municipal Court*, 1988) found California's official English amendment did not require an English-only policy for employees. The court found the official English provision to be "primarily a symbolic statement" and irrelevant in deciding the case. However, the decision was dismissed in 1989 by the U.S. Supreme Court, not on its merits, but because the lawsuit was judged to be moot because the plaintiff had quit her job and accepted a cash settlement (Crawford, 1992).

## 13. PARTITIONING BY LANGUAGE                                    327

books from the government of Taiwan for the city library because English is the approved legal language (Crawford, 1992).

Restricting English in publicly funded domains influences behavior in the private domain as well. In Denver, Colorado, another "official English" state, a restaurant worker was asked to translate an item on the menu into Spanish for a customer, and was fired by the manager, who cited the recently enacted "English-only" law. Although courts have generally found that private-sector employers may require their employees to use only English in the workplace (see Miner, chapter 7, this volume), the potential for abuses (e.g., firing persons because they translate a menu item) is great, and some individuals and groups could be disproportionately affected because of their native language or ethnicity.

In Arizona, U.S. District Court Judge Rosenblatt ruled, in *Yniguez v. Mofford* (1990), Arizona's official English statute unconstitutional. He found the law so broadly worded that it would prohibit the use of any language other than English by all officers and employees of all political subdivisions in Arizona while performing their official duties. The court found that state employees might be barred from commenting on matters of public concern in a foreign language, and legislators might not be free to speak to their constituents in a language other than English. The decision was appealed to the U.S. Supreme Court, and on March 3, 1997, the Court vacated the District Court's ruling as moot, because the Spanish-speaking employee had left her state job before the appeals court's 1994 ruling (Greenhouse, 1997). The decision leaves open the possibility for a U.S. Supreme Court ruling sometime in the future on the constitutionality of official English laws.

### Government Agencies

Many government workers are required to use foreign languages to execute their duties. A list of workers who might be affected, compiled by EPIC (English Plus Information Clearing House), includes agricultural inspectors, Immigration and Naturalization Service agents, soldiers, census takers, diplomats, tax collectors, public defenders, park rangers, librarians, customs agents, Peace Corps workers, prison guards, scientists, Bureau of Indian Affairs officials, court interpreters, CIA staff, federal employees in Puerto Rico, Agency for International Development personnel, and many others. Although it is true that HR 123 excludes from the "English only" provision "actions, documents, or policies necessary for (i) national security issues; or (ii) international relations, trade, or commerce," as well as other specific activities, including interpreters in the Bureau of the Census and in criminal trials, the potential for confusion and uneven application is very great, given the indeterminacy and overlap of various governmental and nongovernmental domains and activities. A new bureaucracy would have to be created just to determine which activities and agencies are exempt among the various governmental and quasi-governmental agencies, commissions, and departments.

Also, although most of the official English bills recently considered in Congress exempt criminal proceedings from the non-English prohibition, interpreters for witnesses with limited or no proficiency in English in civil suits would continue to be optional. Only in actions in which the United States has initiated a civil lawsuit is the English-only requirement waived under provisions of HR 123. The adverse effects on the operation of governmental agencies at federal, state, or local levels would be great. In states such as New Mexico, Arizona, Texas, and California, large groups of immigrants who depend on transitional bilingual services while they are in the process of acquiring English would be affected, and these people would be further segregated from the political, economic, and social mainstream. It is not clear who would benefit if English were to become the de jure official language of the United States. To claim that the civil rights of English speakers are threatened by the existence of non-English-language government services does not seem to correspond to reality. And yet, official English laws would generally prohibit government from making or enforcing an official act that required the use of languages other than English, and persons who felt discriminated against because they communicate in English could sue. Do the rights of English speakers really need special protection because a relatively small number of non-English speakers may require translators and special services while they are acquiring the ability to function effectively in a new (English) language and culture? According to U.S. English and similar groups, they do. The facts indicate otherwise. Based on data from the 1990 decennial U.S. census, nearly 32 million U.S. residents older than 5 years of age speak a language other than English at home. Of that number, only 5.8 million (about 2.5% of the U.S. population) report they speak English "not well" or "not at all."

## CONCLUSION

The fundamental difference between the approaches to bilingualism in Canada and the United States is that in Canada language policy has been directed toward group rights rather than individual rights. Canada has evolved a tradition of cultural pluralism and linguistic duality, enshrined in the Charter of Rights and Freedoms. In contrast, in the United States, bilingualism (official or otherwise) has not been a goal of social policy, but rather a means to ease the assimilation process for immigrants. Language in the United States is not generally viewed as a fundamental constitutional right, but bilingualism and bilingual services are a *means* by which funda-

# 13. PARTITIONING BY LANGUAGE

mental rights are protected and enforced (Trasvina, 1990). As Justice McReynolds put it in the *Meyer v. Nebraska* (1923) case (262 U.S. 390):

> The protection of the Constitution extends to all, to those who speak other languages as well as to those born with English on the tongue. Perhaps it would be highly advantageous if all had ready understanding of our ordinary speech, but this cannot be coerced by methods which conflict with the Constitution—a desirable end cannot be promoted by prohibited means.

States have typically made bilingual services available to ensure that the rights of non-English speakers will not be abridged just because they are not proficient in English. There is usually no expectation that such services will be permanent, or that bilingual services will be maintained just to ensure the perpetuation of language communities. In Canada, the collective rights of groups are protected in order to maintain cultural and linguistic pluralism. Canada is similar to Belgium and Switzerland in this respect, but quite different from the United States. In Canada, group rights are promoted; in the United States, language differences are generally tolerated (although not always), and only when individual rights protected by the Constitution or statute are abrogated because of differences in language or language skills (e.g., literacy) are remedies applied. This has been the case in regard to education policy, voting rights, translation, and government services.

Declaring English the official language of the United States would reduce or eliminate political, social, and educational access for large numbers of citizens, as well as newly arrived immigrants in the process of adapting to their new culture. The rights of non-English speakers would be jeopardized to the benefit of no one, and the very premise of toleration of differences—cultural and linguistic—that has attracted millions of immigrants to American shores over the past 200 years, and enabled the United States to prosper—economically and culturally—would be undermined.

## REFERENCES

Bourhis, R. (1994). Ethnic and language attitudes in Quebec. In J. W. Berry & J. A. Laponce (Eds.), *Ethnicity and culture in Canada: The research landscape* (pp. 322–360). Toronto: University of Toronto Press.

Brandt, E. (1990). The official English movement and the role of first languages. In K. Adams & D. Brink (Eds.), *Perspectives on official English: The campaign for English as the official language of the USA* (pp. 215–228). Berlin: Mouton de Gruyter.

Brisschetto, R. & de la Garza, R. (1983). *The Mexican American electorate: Political participation and ideology. The Mexican American Electorate Series, Hispanic Population Studies Program* (Occasional Paper No. 3). San Antonio and Austin, TX: Southwest Voter Education Project and the Hispanic Population Studies Program of the Center for Mexican American Studies.

Crawford, J. (1992). *Hold your tongue: Bilingualism and the politics of "English only."* Reading, MA: Addison-Wesley.

Fishman, J. A. (1989). Cross-polity perspective on the importance of linguistic heterogeneity as a "contributing factor" in civil strife. In J. A. Fishman (Ed.), *Language and ethnicity in minority sociolinguistic perspective* (pp. 605–626). Clevedon, England: Multilingual Matters.

Fishman, J. A. (1990). Empirical explorations of two popular assumptions: Inter-polity perspective on the relationships between linguistic heterogeneity, civil strife, and per capita gross national product. In G. Imhoff (Ed.), *Learning in two languages: From conflict to consensus in the reorganization of schools* (pp. 209–225). New Brunswick, NJ: Transaction.

*General Social Surveys, 1972–1994: Cumulative Codebook.* (1994, November). Conducted for the National Data Program for the Social Sciences at National Opinion Research Center, University of Chicago.

Greenhouse, L. (1997, March 4). Justices set aside reversal of "English only" measure. *New York Times*, p. A8.

Magnet, J. E. (1990). Canadian perspectives on official English. In K. Adams & D. Brink (Eds.), *Perspectives on official English: The campaign for English as the official language of the USA* (pp. 53–61). Berlin: Mouton de Gruyter.

Mendoza, N. (1986, February 6). Bilingual education [op-ed page]. *Phoenix Gazette.*

Ramìrez, J. D., Yuen, S. D., & Ramey, D. R. (1991). *Final report: Longitudinal study of structured immersion strategy, early-exit, and late-exit transitional bilingual education programs for language-minority children.* San Mateo, CA: Aguirre International.

Resnick, M. C. (1993). ESL and language planning in Puerto Rican education. *TESOL Quarterly 27*, 259–273.

Tamura, E. H. (1993). The English-only effort, the anti-Japanese campaign, and language acquisition in the education of Japanese Americans in Hawaii. *History of Education Quarterly, 33*, 37–58.

Tatalovich, R. (1995). *Nativism reborn? The official English language movement and the American states.* Lexington: The University Press of Kentucky.

Thomas, W. P., & Collier, V. P. (in press). *School effectiveness for language minority students.* Washington, DC: National Clearinghouse for Bilingual Education.

Trasvina, J. (1990). Bilingualism and the Constitution. In K. Adams & D. Brink (Eds.), *Perspectives on official English: The campaign for English as the official language of the USA* (pp. 281–284). Berlin: Mouton de Gruyter.

# 14

# Conclusion:
# Myths and Realities

Barbara Burnaby
*Ontario Institute for Studies in Education*
*University of Toronto*

Thomas Ricento
*University of Texas at San Antonio*

We had several purposes in mind when we commissioned the chapters that comprise this volume. First, we wanted to demonstrate that the study of language policy is a multidisciplinary and interdisciplinary enterprise. The contributors to this volume come from the disciplines of demography, education, history, law, linguistics, political science, and sociology; however, the research and analysis presented here is interdisciplinary, providing expanded and integrated frameworks within which questions are posed and explanations provided. Second, we hoped that the individual work of these researchers taken together would provide not only new insights but also contribute to theory building in the still-emerging field of language policy studies. At the very least, we believed the work presented in these chapters would stimulate discussion while providing concrete data, information, and analysis to aid policy developers in their decision-making processes in the United States, Canada, and similarly situated countries. We hope we succeeded in achieving these goals, at least to some reasonable degree.

Although few of the chapters are direct comparisons between the two countries, the topics chosen by the authors in response to the purposes of the book provide examples and arguments that cover many critical issues

331

of importance for decision making in the language policy arena. These include: historical and political profiles of both countries; language status information and the levels of analysis required to determine it (e.g., social, cultural, political, demographic); policy types (official, de jure, de facto, juridical, implicit, accidental); policy domains ( territorial, federal, provincial, local, etc.); types/domains of bi- and multilingualism (individual, societal, governmental, including federal/provincial/state/local); functional distribution of languages and language varieties; sources of official policy (legislative, court decisions and pronouncements, administrative, executive, referenda, constitutional) and unofficial policy (local and national culture, majority/minority group relations and histories, international events, myths, religious beliefs/doctrines, theories of human nature, etc.); political processes, including nation building and nationalism, governmental structure and decision-making processes; and processes of language change (e.g., shift, drift, displacement, replacement, attrition, maintenance). We have encouraged very broad definitions of "policy" and "politics" so that consideration is given to many kinds of social actions from constitutional provisions, through legislation and funding policy, to private and small institutional activities. By exploring examples of roles language policies could play in North America and their possible impact, a rich picture emerges of an almost bewildering array of contingent factors and fragile relationships at risk. These chapters demonstrate, if nothing else, that simple language policy measures to address apparent problems are certain to have far-reaching, long-term, and completely unforeseen consequences.

As editors, we did not provide the authors with a set of questions to be addressed. However, it is clear from the material produced that there were a number of common issues in the minds of the authors. The following is a brief discussion of some of the more salient themes that run through the collection. The intention here is not to reiterate earlier arguments but to emphasize links that appear across the chapters:

1. *The Canadian experience with official languages does not support arguments to declare English the de jure official language of the United States.*
   Several authors in this volume cite public arguments made in the United States to the effect that struggles in Canada over the establishment of two official languages demonstrates that it would be prudent for the United States to declare English as its only official language. Such a declaration, according to these arguments, would forestall similar struggles in the United States between the dominant language, English, and Spanish, spoken by about 9% of the population. However, this premise is not accepted by any of the authors here; indeed, it is refuted strongly. One argument against this position is

## 14. CONCLUSION 333

that francophones in Quebec differ enough from any of the Spanish-speaking minorities in the United States to keep the Canadian and U.S. situations from being parallel. Ricento (chapter 13) and Schmidt (chapter 2) point out factors of difference between Canadian francophones and U.S. language minorities (principally Spanish speakers), including the geographic concentration of francophones in Canada, smaller economic inequalities between anglophones and francophones in Canada than between anglophones and Hispanics in the United States (see also Burnaby, chapter 10), constitutional provisions for dualism in Canada (see also Magnet, chapter 8), and more complete social organizational structures in Canadian francophone communities than in U.S. minority-language communities. Also, Hispanics were absorbed into the United States in the Treaty of Guadalupe Hidalgo (1848), and were historically ascribed the status of colonized peoples, rather than as partners in nation building; this contrasts with the main francophone population in Canada, which is viewed by the dominant (anglophone) culture as a "founding" people, entitled to claim equality with anglophones as far as their cultural aspirations are concerned. In both countries, indigenous peoples (whose presence on the North American continent precedes that of the dominant European groups) have taken a back seat to the interests and aspirations of the dominant European origin groups.

The effect of these differences between the two countries is that Canada is working on a separate social and political issue from that of the United States as it struggles to make official bilingualism work. Magnet, Schmidt, and Ricento (chapter 13) emphasize that Canada's choice of two official languages reflects a certain reality rooted in history and present conditions. This provision for the rights of a group other than the majority is not the result of a recent political upheaval simply created by a minority large enough to flex its political muscles; all the factors noted earlier are involved. As Burnaby and Fettes (chapter 5) suggest, this relationship between francophones and anglophones in Canada does not demonstrate a strong tendency on the part of the Canadian majority toward pluralism embracing all linguistic minorities; only the French are in a position to insist that their rights be protected. Indeed, Cartwright (chapter 11) and Beaujot (chapter 3) suggest that even francophones outside of Quebec are highly vulnerable. Without a minority group in the position of the francophones in Canada, the United States is occupied with the question of the role of all minority languages in national unity issues (although most attention is focused on the largest group, Spanish speakers). There is no reason to suppose that if Canada did not have the "French fact," its "deep values," as described for the United States by Ricento (chapter 4), would be different from those of the United States. But given that the "French fact" exists, Canada must be circumspect in its rhetoric about languages to minimize invidious comparisons between the rights for French and those for other minority languages. In sum, comparing Canada's Official Languages Act to the movement to declare English the only official language of the United States is to a considerable degree comparing apples and oranges. Canada has to come to terms with the same problems that the United States does in terms of its many linguistic minorities, but the special French–English relationship distracts from this focus.

2. *The movement to have English declared as the (only) official language in the United States disregards internal evidence that it is likely to be ineffective and create more intergroup problems.*

Schmidt, Ricento (chapter 4), Wiley (chapter 9), and Veltman (chapter 12) point out that the implicit and explicit rationale for declaring English the official language in the United States is that such monolingualism is needed for national unity. This rationale is challenged on several fronts in the chapters of this volume. There are two sides to this matter: (a) does getting official status enhance the power of that language; and (b) does suppressing nonofficial languages reduce ethnic conflict?

Veltman, using indicators from the Canadian experience, shows that the symbolic power of being an official language (French) is not enough to make much difference against a language (English) with greater actual social and economic power. Although some internal migration and switches in second languages learned by immigrants has resulted from the declaration of French as an official language, the real power of English works to vitiate the effects of laws, and citizens find adaptive mechanisms to subvert policies. Thus, in his view, having English as an official language does little to enhance its position of real power. Chapter 7 by Miner adds greatly to this picture by illustrating in great detail the lack of effect that "English only" provisions have had when declared by individual states in the United States. She sees conflict between the language-as-problem orientation of the English-only advocates and the "language-as-right" stance of those who oppose English only. Although the latter has not gained any ground in court decisions, neither has "English only" established itself as a significant force.

Wiley and Ricento (chapter 13) specifically raise issues around what would be lost, in their views, if English were declared the official language in the United States. Wiley demonstrates that assimilation

# 14. CONCLUSION                                                                335

to English has not always been a voluntary process in the United States (or Canada), and that such purges of minority languages and cultures have not been a guarantee that members of these groups are afforded equal participation in society. In other words, language can be focused on as an ethnic marker and then the ethnic group can be threatened through attacks on that language, but this approach does not exhaust the ways in which the majority can put coercive pressure on minorities. Acting on language as a key marker of a "problem" ethnic group is likely not only to fail in addressing the real power issue between the majority and the minority, but also to suppress language resources in the country among minority groups and even as school subjects of instruction. Ricento takes a different approach and discusses how participation in the majority society by members of current language minorities would be hampered by English-only provisions. He details how accessibility to education, voting, public services, and government agencies would be diminished by "English only" laws. In sum then, a number of authors in this volume take the position that declaring English the official language of the United States would not effectively augment the power that English already has, that it would aggravate or at least not solve minority–majority conflicts, and that it would possibly create new areas of distress, tension, or both.

3. *Status level action on languages does not address all language conflict problems and even exacerbates some.*

   The matter of the impact of status level changes for languages is closely related to the discussion in the preceding section. Declaring Canada to be officially bilingual or the United States to be officially unilingual are assertions of language *status*. As we have just seen, there is considerable pessimism about the utility of fortifying the status of English in the United States. Several authors demonstrate the limitations of status level action in achieving social cohesiveness in either country.

   Beaujot, Crawford (chapter 6), Miner, Veltman, and Ricento all provide examples of ways in which various laws and policies adopted by Canadian and U.S. governments have failed in one way or another to enhance cohesiveness with the majority or protect minority rights, or both. Veltman, Fettes, and Cartwright make a particular point of indicating limitations to the effectiveness of language status action. Veltman emphasizes that language associated with a socially powerful group will maintain the benefit of that association despite legislation that proposes to establish some other relationship. He indicates that making French an official language in Canada has mainly affected only the marginalized and that giving English more powers in the United States would have little effect in light of the strengths it already has. Cartwright outlines factors in the implementation of the Official Languages Act and its implication in Ontario. He concludes that, in this case of minority language protection, it is not the broad declaration of official language status that matters, but specific action on language support in specific domains, taking local circumstances such as demographic mix into account. He also demonstrates the importance of educating the majority population about the intentions of language legislation so that local manifestations of the legislation are appreciated rather than seen as a threat.

Fettes provides two special perspectives to the volume. First, he points out that languages differ radically among themselves on many dimensions and therefore will not all be affected the same way under legislation. He lists factors that make the Aboriginal languages of the Northwest Territories in Canada significantly different from French. These languages were declared official, along with French, in the Northwest and Yukon Territories, with the federal Official Languages Act as the model for implementation. Fettes argues that this implementation has been ineffective because the needs for protection and development of these languages contrast greatly with those of French. His second particular contribution to the volume comes in his description of an alternative model to language status action. At the same time that the Northwest Territories chose to declare official languages and to include the local Aboriginal language among them, the neighboring Yukon Territory chose not to declare official languages at all, but to work on language change and development from the grassroots level upwards. The potential of this model for application in a number of the language situations in this volume merits investigation. In sum, evidence presented in this volume suggests status level action on languages is often not successful or even relevant in promoting the majority language or protecting minority ones. Alternatives to legislation and policy directives in resolving language issues should be sought out and explored. In light of the specific focus in this volume on Canada and the United States, a central message is that Canadian official language legislation does not present a model of language support and protection to be emulated by language minorities other than francophones in Quebec.

4. *Language legislation and policy have been used for outright repressive action against minority linguistic groups.*

This point about repressive actions taken by North American governments may seem facile, but it clearly needs to be reinforced every time

# 14. CONCLUSION

decisions about language legislation and policy are taken. As Cartwright points out in his demonstration of the need for education of the majority in order for legislation in favor of the minority to work, the majority is loath to accept, much less appreciate, the issues of minorities and to believe that it has played a complicit part in maintaining a status quo which favors its own socioeconomic interests. Crawford, Fettes, and Wiley describe specific incidences of repression of specific languages and their speakers. Veltman, Ricento, and Burnaby show how minority language groups' interests can be submerged and manipulated to the benefit of the majority despite stated intentions of linguistic evenhandedness and support. Although these authors do not emphasize the point, it is often the steps that are not taken that make the difference rather than those that are. The public needs to learn the extent of the injuries sustained by specific groups as a result not only of direct government action and inaction, but by daily interactions at institutional and interpersonal levels. Public participation in the formulation of policy is crucial, but the public's role in policy implementation in institutional settings is equally important. Veltman and Cartwright emphasize that language status legislation is a weak instrument indeed in affecting social change, but Crawford, Fettes, and Wiley show that it can have devastating effects when applied in specific ways. Public attitudes play essential roles in both undermining legislation to protect minorities and enforcing laws to repress others. At least some factions in the population might alter this behavior if they were more aware of the consequences of their actions.

5. *Languages other than the majority language are generally ignored as national resources.*

Miner specifically makes the point that although language can be seen as a problem, a right, or a resource, it has been almost totally neglected as a resource in U.S. policy. Burnaby, Schmidt, Crawford, and Wiley support this observation. Most policies concentrate on getting minorities to conform to the language of the majority. In some cases, particularly the Bilingual Education Act in the United States, minority languages are enlisted not for the sake of their own value, but as a means to hasten transition to English. Token efforts are made to teach minority languages (e.g., noted in Fettes), but Wiley describes the suppression of German taught as a foreign language. How different might the discussion in this book have been if North America saw languages as an asset in communicating with the rest of the world, let alone as a way to facilitate communication among its minority groups at home?

# IMPLICATIONS OF THE FINDINGS FOR THEORY

There are several ways in which this volume contributes to a theory of language policy and planning (LPP). First, we have shown that to be descriptively adequate and to have explanatory power, any theory of LPP must rely on multiple databases (case studies, census data, migration patterns, policy documents, and so on) and must consider social, political, economic, cultural and linguistic factors that motivate human behavior. To the extent the work in this volume has added to our understanding in these areas, it advances theory building. Second, a number of the findings and analyses presented in this volume apply rather generally. An example is the finding that in the United States and Canada, dominant language groups tend to ignore or undervalue the cultural aspirations of less dominant language groups, irrespective of official language policy that explicitly protects their rights to equal access to education, voting, and public services. This could apply to polities that are democratic or nondemocratic, "developed" or "developing." Another example of a potential universal is the central importance of economic considerations in language-policy decision making at all governmental levels; although legislation and other policy documents may trumpet a commitment to human rights, equality before the law, and other high-sounding values, economic interests and outcomes are almost always of central importance (cf. e.g., Ricento, with regard to language policy development in the United States and Magnet and Veltman on Canada). On the other hand, the popular belief that individuals in liberal democracies have equal access to the political economy or that their decision making regarding language choice is unconstrained by their membership in an ethnolinguistic group is not supported. A third candidate for a universal, related to the point made earlier, and supported by findings in this collection, is the claim that general principles of economics and sociolinguistics have as much, if not more, influence on language behavior as official-language policies do. Languages without broad-based functional utility in the political economy of a state, or without a specialized and protected niche (e.g., in religious communities or educational institutions), are especially vulnerable to displacement/replacement by dominant languages. In the absence of special protections—territorial, juridical, or legislative—or continual in-migration from other countries, minority languages tend not to thrive or survive, in the long run. Language change is also a potential result of contact situations; a number of studies on the linguistic consequences of language contact are available (cf. Silva-Corvalán, 1994, who investigated Spanish in Los Angeles, and Mougeon & Beniak, 1991, who examined French in Ontario). Schecter and Bayley (in press) have investigated the interaction of identity and language behavior among Spanish-speaking immigrant families in California and Texas.

# 14. CONCLUSION                                                                 339

These studies offer detailed ethnographic (Schecter & Bayley) and linguistic (Mougeon & Beniak; Silva-Corvalán) analyses of the processes of language shift, attrition, and change. Language policies need to take into account the implications of these and other studies if they are to be realistic in their expectations and goals.

With respect to fitting Canada and the United States within a typology of language-policy types, we defer to previous work in this area (e.g., Ferguson, 1966; Kloss, 1966, 1977; Stewart, 1972). More recently, Schiffman (1996), in providing his own scheme, noted how difficult it is to describe all the factors that enter into decision making resulting in the variety of language policies that could be enumerated. Although typologies seemed to make sense in the postcolonial era following World War II, priorities have changed in recent years, reflecting changes in national borders and the eruption of ethnic rivalries that had been contained under previous authoritarian regimes. External factors, such as access to technology and globalization of national economies, have influenced national priorities in many developing nations. Any scheme we might propose would, therefore, be of limited utility beyond North America.

The chapters in this volume have provided great detail on the types, structures, and operation of language policies in the United States and Canada, so we will not repeat them here. Data on the numbers of speakers of the various languages is widely available, and much of that information is also provided in these chapters. The important contribution of the works in this volume, we believe, is in how they illustrate the complex interworkings of language policy (agents, processes, goals), history, economics, legal/political traditions, and educational systems. A static two- or even four-dimensional model in which policy types are mapped onto descriptions of multilingual societies fails to capture this complexity. The detailed case studies in this volume on the formation, operation, and effects of policies have shown how different approaches at different times have fared. However, not all elements of this picture will remain static. Immigration from non-English-speaking/non-Western European countries to North America has far exceeded that from English-speaking/European countries in recent decades, and this trend will continue; growing ties between Western Canada and Pacific Rim countries increase the importance of nonofficial languages in economic and social life; increases in language minority populations in the United States will create additional minority/majority cities early in the 21st century, and states by 2100, based on current trends. Aboriginal groups (especially in Canada) are demanding that their rights as coequal partners with French and English be respected. All of these changes taken together suggest that the dynamics of majority–minority relations will continue to shift to the point that decision making regarding language use in public life, including education, will more and more be influenced by the interests and aspirations of new coalition majorities.

An example of a change in language-in-education policy can be seen in the very rapid expansion of two-way bilingual programs throughout the United States. The goal of these programs is to enroll equal numbers of students monolingual in English and others monolingual in a non-English language with a goal of developing true bilingual competence. In the period between 1963 and 1968, only four programs were started; in the period ending 1993, a total of 169 programs were in operation; by the 1994–1995 school year, 182 programs in 100 school districts in 18 states and the District of Columbia were running (Christian & Whitcher, 1995). Although precise updated figures were not available as of this writing, at least another 40 programs will be added to the list of two-way bilingual programs, many of which have been started since the 1994–1995 school year (C. Montone, personal communication, February 24, 1997). Although Spanish is the most frequently used non-English language in these programs by a wide margin, eight other languages are currently serving as media of instruction: Korean (4), Cantonese (3), French (3), Navajo (2), Arabic (1), Japanese (1), Russian (1), and Portuguese (1).

Another example illustrates the degree to which attempts to legitimize a "nonstandard" language variety are resisted by the dominant culture. On December 18, 1996, the Oakland, California Board of Education adopted a resolution that recognized Ebonics (also known as Black English or African American Vernacular English; AAVE) as the "primary language" of many of the district's African American students, who comprise 53% of the 52,300-student enrollment, and calls for them to be taught in their primary language (Schnaiberg, 1997). The resolution suggests that some of these students are eligible for state and federal bilingual education and ESL funding. There was an immediate and loud reaction to the resolution across the country, the effects of which continue at the time of this writing. Politicians, writers, journalists, and educators, most of whom were unqualified to judge the merits of the resolution from the perspective of linguistics or even current educational theory and practice, weighed in with their opinions. The actual thrust of the resolution was lost in the uproar. In fact, linguists are unanimous in viewing AAVE as a legitimate rule-governed variety; whether it is a language or dialect is irrelevant to the purpose of the school board's resolution, namely to ensure teachers are familiar with the nature of AAVE, and that this knowledge be invoked to help these underachieving African American students acquire standard English (not to maintain or improve their fluency in AAVE). Available empirical evidence suggests that students who come to school speaking a nonstandard

## 14. CONCLUSION                                                                    341

variety of English may be "subtly dehumanized, stigmatized, discriminated against, or denied" (from the resolution). Just as students from other nationality groups—Asian American, Latino American, and Native American—may come from backgrounds or environments where a non-English language is dominant, and require special programs to aid in the transition to the mainstream standard English classroom, African American students who come from homes where AAVE is spoken require special assistance. Much of the heated national debate has centered on one issue: Is Ebonics a language or not? This case illustrates the degree to which local educational matters that involve issues of language and identity easily become national political issues when certain "commonsense," but misinformed, orthodoxies (e.g., Black English is "bad" English, or slang) are violated.

A third example, from Canada, illustrates the way in which language becomes a focal point in relations between the Aboriginal population and the government. The 1960s saw the rise of national Aboriginal political organizations, a failed bid by the federal government to abolish the Indian Act and, soon after, a call for Aboriginal control of institutions for Aboriginal peoples, especially education (National Indian Brotherhood, 1972), but with federal fiscal responsibility. By the 1990s, this latter movement has evolved into a demand for government-to-government relations between First Nations and mainstream governmental units, and the assumption of local Aboriginal control over institutions in many communities. In this process, rhetoric about the importance of Aboriginal languages has largely been replaced by other issues such as economic development. The actual development of Aboriginal language programs in schools has not been related strongly to the configuration of events at the national level. In some northern areas where children come to school virtually monolingual in an Aboriginal language, three jurisdictions (the eastern part of the Northwest Territories and two in Arctic Quebec) have established Aboriginal language medium of instruction in the early grades. In these jurisdictions, Aboriginal people are in the numerical majority and have political control, but these factors are not the only potent ones driving such decisions. In southern areas, where school-aged Aboriginal children are often two generations away from speaking their ancestral language, Aboriginal language immersion programs are developing locally in some communities but not in others. Although local control of education undoubtedly facilitated some of these moves, it is not necessarily the only or even the leading factor in their development. Similarly, patterns of teaching Aboriginal languages as subject of instruction are not particularly related to those of Aboriginal political or administrative control. Research to determine what *is* driving these initiatives is essential to our appreciation of and preparedness for the new era of language relations that is emerging.

## CONCLUSION

Politics can never be completely separated from language, as language is a quintessential aspect of being human and politics is a principal means by which humans obtain power, control, or status. There will never be a "neutral" science of language policy as long as such an enterprise is pursued by human beings with their particular sociocultural roots and identities investigating the lives of other human beings with their particular roots and identities. The study of language and politics requires the researcher to turn the telescope/microscope on himself or herself as much as on the polity in question. We have tried to make clear our orientation with regard to fundamental issues raised in this volume: we support linguistic self-determination, that is, the idea that individuals ought to have a say about the language(s) they can speak, learn in school and maintain throughout their lives; we believe government can play a more constructive role in supporting and implementing language policies that enhance social integration while valuing the languages and cultures of all citizens; we favor approaches to language policy and planning that take into account the interests and aspirations of all ethnolinguistic groups in a nation, indigenous and immigrant, large and small. Researchers in policy science sometimes try to separate "politics" from "policy" in their investigations and theorizing; although such a distinction may serve a heuristic function, it is artificial. Cibulka (1995) noted that "the borderline between policy *research* and policy *argument* is razor thin" (p. 118). Better descriptions and taxonomies will surely advance our knowledge of "reality," but researchers must make explicit the values and goals that inform and motivate their investigations. The work in this volume offers a description of reality in the United States and Canada, and a projection of how it could be different (and better) if certain processes and policies were implemented.

## REFERENCES

Christian, D., & Whitcher, A. (1995). *Directory of two-way bilingual education programs in the United States*. Santa Cruz, CA and Washington, DC: National Center for Research on Cultural Diversity and Second Language Learning.

Cibulka, J. G. (1995). Policy analysis and the study of the politics of education. In J. D. Scribner & D. H. Layton (Eds.), *The study of educational politics* (pp. 105–125). Washington, DC: The Falmer Press.

Ferguson, C. A. (1966). National sociolinguistic profile formulas. In W. O. Bright (Ed.), *Sociolinguistics. Proceedings of the UCLA sociolinguistics conference, 1964* (pp. 309–315). The Hague, Netherlands: Mouton.

Kloss, H. (1966). Types of multilingual communities: A discussion of ten variables. *Sociological Inquiry, 36*, 7–17.

Kloss, H. (1977). *The American bilingual tradition*. Rowley, MA: Newbury House.

## 14. CONCLUSION          343

Mougeon, R., & Beniak, E. (1991). *Linguistic consequences of language contact and restriction: The case of French in Ontario, Canada.* Oxford, England: Oxford University Press.

National Indian Brotherhood. (1972). *Indian control of Indian education.* Ottawa: Author.

Schecter, S. R., & Bayley, R. (in press). Language socialization practices and cultural identity: Case studies of Mexican-descent families in California and Texas. *TESOL Quarterly.*

Schiffman, H. F. (1996). *Linguistic culture and language policy.* London: Routledge.

Schnaiberg, L. (1997, January 15). "Ebonics" vote puts Oakland in maelstrom. *Education Week,* XVI.

Silva-Corvalán, C. (1994). *Language contact and change: Spanish in Los Angeles.* Oxford, England: Oxford University Press.

Stewart, W. A. (1972). A sociolinguistic typology for describing national multilingualism. In J. A. Fishman (Ed.), *Readings in the sociology of language* (pp. 531–545). The Hague, Netherlands: Mouton.

# Author Index

## A

Adams, K., 183, *184*
Albert, L., 57, *68*, 75, *81*
Apple, J. J., 218, *328*
Apple, S., 218, *238*
Arfé, G., 5, *31*
Ashworth, M., 243, 254, *264*
Atkins, J. D. C., 156, 157, *164*

## B

Baker, C., 14, 15, 16, 28, *31*
Baker, K. A., 88, 96, *110*
Barrera, M., 58, 62, *68*
Bastarache, M., 81, *81*
Baugh, J., 105, *110*
Baxter-Moore, N., 49, 50, 52, *69*
Bayley, R., 338, 339, *343*
Beach, C., 107, *110*
Beauchesne, A., 311, *314*
Beaujot, R., 74, 76, 79, *81*, 119, 123, *147*
Beer, S. H., 6, *31*
Belfiore, M. E., 250, *264*
Beltramo, A. F., 232, *238*
Beniak, E., 294, 295, *299*, 338, 339, *343*
Bloom, D., 246, *264*
Bourbeau, R., 74, 76, 77, *81*, *83*
Bourhis, R., 320, *329*
Bouvier, L. F., 64, *68*
Boyd, M., 247, 250, 253, 257, 261, 262, *264*
Braen, A., 277, *298*
Brandt, E., 325, *329*

Brault, L., 278, *298*
Brenzinger, M., 151, *164*
Breton, A., 77, *81*
Breton, R., 66, 72, 77, *81*
Brink, D., 183, *184*
Brisschetto, R., 325, *328*
Brod, R., 104, *110*
Brooks, S., 77, 79, *81*
Brym, R. J., 59, 66, *68*
Buckley, W. F., 105, *110*
Burnaby, B., 119, 120, 123, *147*, 251, 254, 261, 262, *265*
Burnell, J. B., 226, 229, 232, 233, 234, 235, *238*
Burns, J. F., 52, *68*

## C

Caldwell, G., 74, *82*
Cantin, A., 287, *298*
Carr, J., 106, *110*
Carriere, V., 278, *298*
Cartwright, D. G., 72, 74, 78, 79, *82*, 285, *298*
Castellans, D., 214, *238*
Castonguay, C., 25, *31*, 74, *82*, 293, *298*, 307, *314*
Castro, R., 58, *68*
Chapa, J., 64, *69*
Chen, E. M., 172, *184*
Chisman, F., 243, 248, 251, 253, 256, 258, 262, 253, *265*
Chiswick, B., 244, 245, 247, 259, *265*

**345**

Christian, D., 99, *110*, 340, *342*
Churchill, S., 125, *147*, 243, 246, 249, 255, 265
Cibulka, J. G., 340, *340*
Coffman, L. D., 227, *238*
Coleman, W. D., 78, *82*
Collier, V. P., 325, *330*
Collins, N., 251, *265*
Conzen, K. N., 213, 218, 219, 220, 221, 225, 232, *238*
Corson, D., 243, *265*
Cottingham, B. E.. 121, 136, 139, *148*
Crawford, J., 90, 96, 99, 100, 101, 102, 103, 104, *110*, 158, 159, 160, 162, *164*, 183, *184*, 213, 215, 223, 232, 233, *238*, 322, 323, 326, 327, *329*
Cumming, A., 243, 253, 261, *265*
Cummins, J., 46, *68*, 96, *110*, 243, 254, *265*

**D**

D'Andrea, D., 152, *164*
Danesi, M., 254, *265*
d'Anglejan, A., 53, 54, *68*, 254, 260, *265*
Davis, K., 64, *68*
Dawson, R. M., 190, *203*
de Kanter, A. A., 88, 96, *110*
De Koninck, Z., 254, 260, *265*
de la Garza, R., 58, *68*, 323, *328*
Denison, N., 155, *164*
DeSipio, L., 58, *68*
DesLauriers, R. C., 262, *265*
de Varennes, F., 123, *148*
Deveau, A., 21, *32*
de Vries, J., 294, *298*, 306, *314*
Doherty, N., 250, *265*
Dorsett, L. W., 221, 223, 230, 231, 236, *238*
Draper, J. B., 103, *110*
Drouin, M.–J., 262, *266*
Dunn, M., 124, *148*

**E**

Edwards, I. N., 228, 232, *238*
Edwards, J., 2, 15, 18, *31*, 155, *164*
Elliott, J. L., 19, 20, 22, *31*
Epstein, N., 66, *68*, 95, 96, *110*
Ewen, D. T., 243, *265*

**F**

Falcon, A., 58, *68*
Farley, J., 159, *164*
Farrand, M., 6, *31*

Feder, D., 105, *111*
Feldman, P., 161, *164*
Ferguson, C. A., 339, *342*
Fernández, R. R., 97, 100, *111*
Fettes, M., 123, 124, 146, *148*
Fishman, J. A., 66, *68*, *69*, 145, *148*, 159, 163, *164*, 187, 188, 197, *203*, 214, *238*, 294, 295, *298*, 318, 319, *330*
Flaherty, L., 249, *266*
Fleras, A., 19, 20, 22, *31*
Foot, R., 130, *148*
Foster, M. K., 119, *148*
Francis, D. R., 56, *69*
Franklin, B., 6, 214, 215, *238*
Fredeen, S., 212, *148*
Freeman, R. D., 99, *111*
Fretz, J. W., 21, *31*
Frum, D., 56, *69*

**G**

Garcia, F. C., 58, *68*
Garcia, J., 58, *68*
Garcia, M. T., 58, *68*
García, O., 107, *111*
Gardner, L., 135, 138, 139, 140, 141, 142, 146, *148*
Gardner, R. W., 64, *68*
Gauvreau, D., 75, 76, *83*
Genesee, F., 306, 307, *314*
Gibson, M. A., 213, *238*
Gil, J., 253, 261, *265*
Gilbert, G. G., 215, 229, *238*
Gill, R. M., 280, *298*
Glazer, N., 5, 7, *31*
Goldstein, T., 256, *266*
Goodrich, C. G., 226, *238*
Gordy, H. M., 226, 227, *238*
Graham, W. C., 275, *298*
Green, L., 197, 198, *203*, *204*
Greenhouse, L., 327, *330*
Grenier, G., 75, *82*, 246, *264*
Griffiths, N. E. S., 21, *31*
Grimes, B.F., 119, *148*
Grin, F., 106, *111*
Guindon, H., 78, *82*
Gusfield, J., 304, 305, *314*
Guttman, A., 2, 3, *31*

**H**

Habermas, J., 2, 3, 4, *31*
Hakuta, K., 152, *164*, 235, *238*

# AUTHOR INDEX

Hale, K., 162, 163, *164*
Hall, T. M., 52, *69*, 175, *184*
Hamilton, A., 89, 91, *111*
Harnum, B., 126, 127, 128, 131, 132, *148*
Harrison, B., 74, 77, *82*
Hart, D., 243, *265*, 306, *314*
Hartmann, E. G., 105, *111*
Havel, V., 6, *31*
Hawkins, F., 257, 258, *266*
Hayes-Bautista, D. E., 64, *69*
Heath, S. B., 86, *111*, 156, *164*, 214, 215, *238*
Heine, W. C., 280, *298*
Heller, M., 250, *264*, 278, 280, *299*
Helm, T., 280, *298*
Henderson, S., 120, *148*
Henripin, J., 72, *82*, 197, *204*, 308, *314*
Henry, S., 46, *68*
Hensler, H., 311, *314*
Hernandez-Chavez, E., 42, *69*
Hicks, J. H., 103, *110*
Higham, J., 59, *69*, 101, *111*
Hinton, L., 152, 153, 161, *164*
Holli, M. G., 220, 230, 232, *239*
Holm, W., 153, *164*
Holt, M., 251, *265*
Huber, B., 104, *110*

## I

Imhoff, G., 88, *111*

## J

Jackson, D., 49, 50, 52, *69*
Jackson, R. J., 49, 50, 52, *69*
Jamieson, M. E., 123, 124, *148*
Jay, J., 89, 90, 91, *111*
Johansen, D., 281, *299*
Johnson, D., 200, *204*
Jones, S., 261, *266*
Joy, R. J., 186, *204*, 275, 296, *298*
Jungeblut, A., 261, *266*

## K

Kakfwi, S., 133, *148*
Kallen, E., 8, 30, *31*
Killilea, M., 3, *31*
Kinkade, M. D., 119, *148*
Kirsch, I. S., 261, *266*
Klassen, C., 261, *266*
Kloss, H., 63, *69*, 216, 217, *239*, 339, *342*
Krauss, M., 151, 152, 154, 160, *164*, *165*

Krosenbrink-Gelissen, L. E., 21, *31*
Kuijpers, W., 5, *31*

## L

Labrie, N., 4, *32*
Lachapelle, R., 72, 73, 75, 76, 79, 80, *82*, 197, 204, 296, *298*, 308, *314*
Ladefoged, P., 163, *165*
Lane, R. E., 107, *111*
Langgaard, P., 121, *148*
Lapkin, S., 306, *314*
Laponce, J. A., 55, *69*, 78, *82*
Lazerson, M., 237, *240*
Leclerc, J.-C., 274, *296*
LeDain, G., 202, *204*
Leibowitz, A. H., 42, *69*, 87, 94, 95, 103, *111*, 212, 214, 216, 218, 219, 228, 229, 237, *239*
Lemco, J., 53, *69*
Lesage, J., 200, *204*
Levine, M. V., 47, 53, 56, 64, 65, *69*
Li, P. S., 23, *31*
Lijphart, A., 194, *204*
Linteau, P.-A., 310, *314*
Lipset, S. M., 59, *69*
Loewen, R. K., 21, *31*
Luebke, F. C., 219, 221, 223, 224, 226, 228, 230, *239*
Lukes, M., 212, *241*
Lyons, J. J., 93, 94, 95, 99, *111*

## M

MacDonald, J. A., 188, *204*
MacFarlane, A., 306, *315*
Macías, R. F., 212, 215, 216, 217, 218, 219, 233, *239*
Madison, J., 89, 90, 91, *111*
Magnet, J. E., 187, 189, 191, 195, 202, *204*, 319, 320, *330*
Magnet, S., 189, *204*
Malcolm, A. H., 52, *69*
Mallea, J. R., 51, *70*, 278, *298*
Mandabach, F., 86, *111*
Manley, R. N., 219, 222, 223, 224, 225, 226, 228, 231, *239*
Marmen, L., 74, 77, *82*
Marshall, D. F., 304, *314*
Martinez, O. J., 290, *298*
Marunchak, M., 21, *31*
Matute-Bianchi, M. E., 213, *240*

McAll, C., 18, 19, 21, 25, *31*
McClymer, J. F., 101, *111*, 213, 230, 231, *239*
McConvell, P., 121, *148*
McDade, K., 253, *266*
McKay, S. L., 212, *239*
McLaughlin, D., 160, *165*
McLeod, R. G., 171, *184*
McManus, W., 247, *266*
McNaught, K., 86, *111*
McQuillan, K., 74, *81*
McRoberts, K., 18, *32*, 47, *70*, 78, *82*, 296, *299*
Menchaca, M., 237, *239*
Mendoza, N., 325, *330*
Miles, R., 235, *239*
Miller, P., 247, *265*
Molesky, J., 214, 215, *239*
Monaghan, F., 91, *111*
Montalto, N. V., 231, *239*
Moore, W. H., 214, 227, 228, 229, 231, *240*
Morrison, F., 306, *315*
Mougeon, R., 278, 280, 294, 295, *299*, 338, 339, *343*
Murphy, P. L., 233, *240*

### N

Nahanee, T., 123, *149*
Nakamura, A., 259, *266*
Nakamura, M., 259, *266*
Nanda, S., 233, *240*
Nelde, P., 4, *32*
Norgren, J., 233, *240*

### O

Ogbu, J. U., 99, *111*, 213, 238, *240*
Olneck, M. R., 237, *240*

### P

Paillé, M., 77, 79, *82*
Pal, L. A., 77, *82*
Paré, S., 312, *314*
Pawley, C., 306, *315*
Pendakur, R., 252, *266*
Phillips, A., 7, *32*
Phillips, K., 64, *70*
Phillips, S., 123, *149*
Phillipson, R., 10, 11, *32*, 233, *240*
Piatt, B., 172, *184*, 215, 232, *240*
Pinker, S., 163, *165*
Pitt, L., 45, *70*, 91, *111*, 216, 217, *240*
Polèse, M., 78, 80, *82*

Porter, R. P., 88, *111*
Pratt, R. H., 158, *165*
Purich, D. J., 52, *70*

### R

Ramey, D. R., 87, *112*, 325, *330*
Ramírez, J. D., 87, *112*, 325, *330*
Rawlyk, G. A., 21, *31*
Ready, D., 306, *315*
Rèaume, D., 197, 198, *204*
Reid, S., 295, *299*
Reitz, J. G., 79, *83*
Renfrew, C., 157, *165*
Resnick, M. C., 322, *328*
Resnick, P., 51, *69*
Reyhner, J., 157, *165*
Ricento, T. K., 13, *32*, 97, 101, *112*, 214, *240*
Rippley, L. V. J., 217, *240*
Robins, R. H., 151, *165*
Robinson, P., 74, *83*
Rogers, J., 12, *32*
Rosenau, J. N., 23, *32*
Ross, S., 21, *32*
Rosser, B., 280, *299*
Ruíz, R., 109, *112*, 171, 183, *184*
Russell, P. H., 19, 26, *32*

### S

Sapir, E., 162, *165*
Sasse, H.-J., 155, *165*
Schecter, S. R., 338, 339, *348*
Schiffman, H. F., 339, *348*
Schink, W. O., 64, *69*
Schlossman, S. L., 217, *240*
Schmidt, A., 151, 164, *165*
Schmidt, R. J., 38, *70*
Schnaiberg, L., 340, *343*
Schrock, J. R., 162, *165*
Schwartz, J., 154, *165*
Scott, G. M., Jr., 67, *70*
Seguin, R., 287, *299*
Seward, S., 253, *266*
Shkilnyk, A. M., 118, 123, *149*
Silva-Corvalán, C., 338, 339, *343*
Stanley, A., 56, *70*
Stein, S. M., 180, *184*
Steltzer, N., 251, *265*
Stewart, W. A., 339, *343*
Sundquist, E. J., 15, *32*
Swadesh, M., 152, *165*

# AUTHOR INDEX

Swain, M., 306, *314*
Szasz, M. C., 158, *165*

## T

Tamura, E. H., 103, *112*, 235, 236, *240*, 320, 322, *330*
Tatalovich, R., 324, *330*
Taylor, C., 8, 9, 23, *32*
Termote, M., 75, 76, 80, *83*
Terrien, J., 281, *299*
Thériault, J.-Y., 74, *83*
Thomas, C., 275, *298*
Thomas, T. A., 178, *184*
Thomas, W. P., 325, *330*
Tlen, D. L., 139, *149*
Tollefson, J. W., 10, 12, *32*, 212, 233, *240*
Toohey, K., 254, *267*
Tousignant, J. P., 121, 135, 139, *148*
Trasvina, J., 329, *330*
Tremblay, M., 74, *83*
Trudeau, P. E., 191, *205*
Tschanz, L., 118, *149*
Tucker, G. R., 109, *112*

## U

Uchitelle, L., 56, *70*
Uhlenbeck, E., 151, *165*

## V

Vaillancourt, F., 79, *83*, 106, *110, 111*, 246, 247, *267*
Valencia, R. R., 237, *239*
Van der Keilen, M., 306, *314*

Veltman, C., 76, *83*, 105, *112*, 152, *165*, 187, 197, *205*, 212, *240*, 302, 303, 308, 309, 312, *314*

## W

Waddell, C., 187, *205*
Walsh, M. W., 51, *70*
Weinberg, M., 92, *112*, 213, 237, *240*
Weinstein-Shr, G., 212, *239*
Weiss, B., 237, *240*
Wesche, M., 306, *315*
Whitcher, A., 99, *110*, 340, *342*
Wilcox, C., 222, *240*
Wiley, T. G., 91, 104, *112*, 212, 231, *240, 241*
Williams, C. A., 297, *299*
Williams, C. H., 4, 5, 6, 7, 8, 24, 26, 30, *32*
Williams, J., 102, *112*
Willig, A. C., 96, *112*
Wills, T., 292, *299*
Wilson, E. O., 154, *165*
Wilson, V. S., 19, *32*
Woods, D., 249, *265*
Woycenko, O., 21, *32*
Wrigley, H. S., 243, *265*
Wurm, S. A., 155, *165*
Wyman, M., 235, *241*

## Y

Young, C., 293, *299*
Young, R. A., 29, *32*
Yuen, S. D., 87, *112*, 325, *330*

## Z

Zall, B. W., 180, *184*
Zeitlin, M., 64, *70*

# Subject Index

## A

AAVE, *see African American Vernacular English*

Aboriginal, *see Native peoples and languages*

Acadia (l'Acadie), x, 18, 21, 74, 79–80, 189, 305, 308

Accent, 175–177, 303, 310
  accent discrimination, 175–177

Accommodation, xi, 14, 19–20, 23, 34, 38, 62, 72, 168, 185, 201–203, 274, 277

Acculturation, 218

Adaptive strategies, 301, 311–313

Adult basic education (ABE), 260–263

Adult Education Act (USA), 253–254, 262

Advocates for Indigenous California Language Survival, 161

Affirmative action, 6, 50, 92, 96, 247, 322

African American Vernacular English (AAVE), 340–341

African Americans, 2, 41, 62, 64, 91, 103–105, 213, 237, 324, 326

Alaska Native Language Center, 160

Alliance for the Preservation of English in Canada (APEC), 101, 274, 283–292, 296

Allophone, 50, 52–53, 55, 85, 198, 201–203, 247, 310

American Defense Society, 90

American Institutes for Research (AIR), 96

Americanization, 90, 101, 103, 213, 224, 228, 230–232, 235–237

Amish, 234, 303

Anglicization, 76, 301, 305–309

Anglo–Saxonism, 101

APEC, *see Alliance for the Preservation of English in Canada*

Assimilation, xi, 2, 5, 8, 12, 14–15, 18–19, 27, 34, 41, 43–46, 50–51, 53, 57, 59, 61–62, 65–67, 76, 88, 104–105, 154, 157–158, 161, 187, 212–213, 219, 230–231, 302–304, 308–309, 313

Australian Language and Literacy Policy, 86

## B

B. and B. Commission, *see Royal Commission on Bilingualism and Biculturalism*

Backlash/resistance, 17, 35, 67, 86–87, 95, 97, 126, 145, 158, 254, 270, 275, 290, 310

Baker, K., 88, 96

Belgium, 5, 54, 78, 317, 329

Bennett Law, 218

Bilingual districts, 48, 78, 274–276
  Bilingual Districts Advisory Board (BDAB) (Canada), 274–276

Bilingual Education Act (BEA) (USA), x, 41, 74, 76, 78, 80, 87–89, 91–100, 102, 106, 108–109, 254–255

Bilingual services, 27, 181, 193, 273, 286, 328–329

**351**

# SUBJECT INDEX

Bill (Law) 101 (Quebec), 53–56, 66, 78, 101, 310, 320–321
Bill 22 (Quebec), 53, 320
Biodiversity, 154
Bloc Québécois, 295
British North America Act, 245, 248
Buckley, William F., 105
Bureau of Indian Affairs (BIA) (USA), 157–158, 161, 327

## C

California, 9, 37, 44–45, 61, 63, 67, 92, 97, 99, 101–102, 104–105, 148, 152–153, 161, 171–173, 180–183, 211, 229, 303, 319, 328, 336, 340
Canadian West, 308–309
Catholic, 5, 50, 59, 61–62, 217–219, 278–279, 320
  anti–Catholic, 217–218
  Catholic schools, 218, 278–279, 320
Census, 24–25, 51–53, 71–72, 91, 121, 123, 130, 153, 171, 220, 231, 252, 259, 294, 301, 308–309, 322, 327–328, 338
Charter of Rights and Freedoms, 17, 27, 49, 51–52, 55–56, 117, 128, 133–134, 146, 188, 190–193, 207, 245, 250, 255, 280–282, 318, 328
Charter of the French Language/Chartre de la langue français (Quebec), 189, 194–195
Chicano, 40–42, 290
Chinese, 18, 26, 103, 105, 179, 327
  Chinese American, 179
Commissioner of Official Languages, 48, 196, 246, 280
Comparative analysis, 237
Constitution Act (Canada), 17, 117, 123, 169, 189–192, 195, 245, 255, 295
Coral Way Elementary School, 94, 98
Creole, 213
Cullen–Couture Agreement (Canada), 259
Cultural
  genocide, 42, 161, 292, 294
  pluralism, 8, 14, 16–17, 27, 30, 86, 95, 99, 114, 230, 240, 297, 316, 326
Czech Republic, 6

## D

Dade County, Florida, 104, 326

Democracy, 2–4, 6–7, 9, 14, 16, 28–30, 63, 106, 174, 235
Demographics, 72, 93, 244, 270
Denver, 221, 327
Descendants, 29, 79, 236–237
Diglossia, 158
Discrimination, x, 5, 7, 12, 16, 25, 41–42, 47, 62, 91, 102, 157, 174–179, 183, 236, 257
  accent discrimination, 175–177
  employment discrimination, 42, 175–178
Disloyalty, 221–223, 226
Domain, xi, 5, 14, 20–22, 24, 28, 54, 66, 90, 92, 102, 106, 114, 120–121, 127, 139, 145, 156, 159, 212, 274–275, 278–279, 285, 294–296, 326–327, 332, 336
Duality, xi, 34, 75, 80, 168, 185, 188, 199, 201, 203

## E

Eastern Townships, 309
Ebonics, 340–342
Education, *see also Schools*
  bilingual education, 3–4, 12, 15, 30, 34, 37, 41–46, 65, 69, 87–89, 92, 94–100, 103, 108–110, 158, 161, 180, 234, 306, 317, 322, 324–325, 340
    late-exit bilingual education, 105
    maintenance bilingual education, 15
    transitional bilingual education, 96, 325
    two–way bilingual education, 99, 109, 325, 340
  immersion programs, 44, 77, 306–308, 324–325, 341
  language education, 45, 49, 77, 188–190, 195, 219, 246, 254, 278–280, 296
  medium of instruction, 218, 246, 341
  post–secondary
    community colleges, 249–250
    junior colleges, 309
    universities, 10, 108, 198, 208, 221–222, 311, 315
  student visits, 304
  subject of instruction, 341
Edwards Law (USA), 218
EEOC, *see Equal Employment Opportunity Commission*

# SUBJECT INDEX

353

Employment and Immigration Canada, 250–251, 257–259

English as a second language (ESL), xi, 46, 93, 97, 100, 243–244, 246–257, 259–264, 325, 340

English–only/English Only, xi–xii, 12, 34–35, 43, 46, 51, 95, 97–98, 100, 102, 114, 126, 153, 155, 157–159, 171, 173, 175, 177–180, 183, 213, 215, 218–219, 226–228, 234–237, 270, 305, 325–328, 328, 334–335
   policy, 126, 158, 179, 321, 326
   rules, 157–158, 175, 177–179

English Plus, 45, 327

Equal Employment Opportunity Commission (EEOC) (USA), 175, 177–179

EEOC guidelines, 178

Equal protection clause, 97

ESL, *see English as a second language*

Ethnicity, *see also names of specific groups*, 12, 19, 21, 31, 34, 68, 71, 318
   ethnic origin, 71, 74, 190, 232, 302, 309

Europe/European, 5–6, 25, 27, 29–30, 40, 48, 58–60, 90, 105, 156–157, 165, 213, 216–217, 219–220, 230, 235–236, 257, 321–322, 333, 339

European Union, 5

Experience of conquest, 40

## F

Federal/Aboriginal relations, (chap. 5, Canada; chap. 6, USA)

Federal/provincial relations (Canada), 17, 21, 49–50, 52–57, 64–65, 77, 122, 188, 191, 194–196, 199–203, 245–257, 259, 260, 271–274, chap. 11, 305–306, 307, 314, 319–322

*Federalist, The*, 89, 91

Federation for American Immigration Reform (FAIR), 101

Fertility, 28, 72–73, 77, 101, 198

First Amendment, 46, 172–174

First Nations, *see Native peoples*

Fourteenth Amendment, 174, 233

Francisation, 52–53

Franco–Ontarian, chap. 11

Francophones, 2, 12, 28, 34–35, 46, 49–55, 57, 60–66, 75, 78, 82, 167, 189, 207, 244, 246–247, 263, 267, 272–273, 277–278, 281, 283, 290, 292, 294, 297, 306, 312, 319–320, 332–333, 336

Franklin, Benjamin, 6, 214–215

Freedom of speech/expression, 6, 172–173, 193, 222

French–Language Services Act (Ontario), 290–291

## G

General Social Surveys, 323

Geographic contact, 78, chap. 11

German, xi, 15, 18, 52, 102–104, 156, 207–208, chap. 9, 304, 322, 337
   anti–German hysteria, 103, chap. 9
   anti–German sentiment, 15, chap. 9
   enrollments in German, 103, 229
   instruction in German, 216, 218, 234
   German American, 102–104, chap. 9
   German Canadian, 233–235
   German language, xi, 207, 211, 213, 215–216, 218–224, 226–230
   German newspapers, 219
   pro-German/Teutomania, 220, 223, 226

Government
   institutions, 50, 128, 131, 193
   services, 27, 114, 117, 132, 140, 158, 191, 193, 272, 274, 282, 294–296, 328–329

Group conflict, 39, 201, 217, 282, 293

Gullah, 104

*Gutierrez v. Municipal Court* (1988), 179

## H

HR, 123, 323, 325–328

Hamilton, Alexander, 89, 91

Hawaii, 103, 112, 235–236, 238, 240, 323, 330

Hebrew, 105, 159

Hispanic, 2, 28, 96, 102, 152, 178, 183, 215, 247, 302–304, 324–326, 333

Hispanophobia, 213

Historical–structural approach, 212

Holmes, Oliver Wendell, 233

## I

Ideology, 4, 8, 11–12, 14, 16–19, 26, 68, 148, 237
   ideological dominance of English, 212

Illinois, 215, 218–219, 304, 323

Immigrant, xi, 1–2, 18–19, 24–26, 34, 44–45, 48, 50, 52–53, 59, 71, 76–80,

**354**  SUBJECT INDEX

90–91, 94–95, 97, 99, 101, 104–107, 113–115, 124, 176, 208, 211, 213–217, 220, 224–225, 231–234, 236–238, 245, 247–252, 255–261, 263–264, 302–304, 306, 310–314, 321–322, 328–329, 334, 338, 342
anti-immigrant, 213, 217, 326
immigrant languages, 115, 124, 214, 225
immigrant women, 250–251
immigration, 12, 24–25, 34, 45–46, 52, 54, 72, 76–77, 79–80, 90, 97, 100–102, 105, 135, 198, 208, 212–213, 215–217, 219, 233, 243–245, 248–249, 251–253, 257–260, 262–263, 290, 322, 326
immigration levels, 253, 259
Immigration Act (Canada), 258
Indian Act, 122, 341
Institutional completeness, 65–66, 294–295
Integration, 1, 3, 6, 8, 12, 16, 19–20, 27, 53, 61–62, 104, 130, 145–146, 216, 257, 259, 273, 303, 342
Internal migration, 74, 334

**J**

Japanese, 103, 223, 235–237, 323, 340
anti-Japanese campaign, 235–236
Japanese American, 236–237
Judiciary, 275–278, 293

**K**

Kallen, Horace, 230
Knowledge of official languages, 76
Know-Nothings, 217
Korean, 99, 340

**L**

Labor market, 19, 62, 244, 250, 259
Laborforce, 250–251, 262
Labour Market Language Training (LMLT) (Canada), 252
Language, *see also Languages and the names of individual languages*
choice, 13, 20, 156, 160, 193, 215–216, 218, 233, 338
contact, 8, 24, 213, 293, 297, 338
death, xi, 13, 114, 154–156, 163, 165
diversity, x, 86
education, *see Education*
of interaction, 76

legislation, xi–xii, 54, 79, 167–169, 218, 275, 304, 310–312, 336
loyalty, 228
maintenance, xii, 21, 88, 95–96, 106, 145, 294
minority, 16, 40, 42–44, 48–49, 64, 87–88, 91, 98, 106–109, 133, 181, 201, 212–213, 215, 244, 270, 279–280, 296–297, 305, 310, 313, 324–325, 330, 339
planning, x, 22, 54, 68–69, 106–107, 114, 124, 132, 198, 305, 307, 312–313, 318, 330
protection, 336
questions, 71, 307
retention, 71, 121, 139–140, 145, 149
revitalization, 160
rights, *see Rights*
shift, 73, 121–123, 152–153, 155, 157–159, 161, 187, 211, 225, 268, 292–293, 301–303, 308, 312–313, 338
status, xii, 89, 106, 114, 124, 248, 272, 288, 292, 294–295, 332, 335–337
tolerance, 215–216, 218
transfer, 72, 74, 293, 310
of work, 78, 128, 190, 246, 310
in the workplace, 189
Language Instruction for Newcomers to Canada (LINC), 251–253, 255–257, 265
Languages
colonial, 214
dominant, xi, 11–12, 53–54, 63, 90, 94, 98, 245, 305, 332, 338
endangered, 154, 159–161, 163
foreign, 15, 93, 95, 97, 103, 108–109, 152, 173–174, 177, 183, 219, 219, 221–223, 225–229, 232, 237, 320, 327, 337
home, 71, 73–75, 77, 80, 94, 153, 294, 306, 309
imperial, 214
indigenous, xi, 28, 90, 98, 113–114, 152–153, 156, 158, 160, 163
Indo–European, 156–157
non–official, 26, 85, 118, 245, 247, 264, 283, 334, 339
official, x–xii, 12, 24, 34, 37, 40, 45, 48–49, 53, 63, 71, 75–77, 79, 90, 92, 97, 101, 114, 118, 120, 126–127, 129, 131, 133–135, 145, 167–169, 171–172, 187–191, 193–199, 201–204, 208, 245–247, 249, 252, 254,

# SUBJECT INDEX

258, 260–261, 270, 272, 277–278, 283, 287, 295, 308, 313, 317–318, 319–328, 332–336, 338–339
second official, 246
third language groups, 308
tribal, 159
Latino, 12, 35, 37, 41–45, 57, 61, 63–67, 70, 99, 340
*Lau v. Nichols* (1974), 87, 92, 181, 255
LeDain, Justice Gerald, 201–202
Liberal Party (Canada), 17, 47
Liberalism, 8, 26, 59, 65
Limited English Proficiency (LEP), 27, 44, 96–97, 207, 324–325
LINC, *see Language Instruction for Newcomers to Canada*
Linguistic
  access, 37, 40, 42–45, 48–49
  assimilation, 57, 67, 89, 158, 211–212, 306, 313
  confederation, 41, 52, 54–55, 66
  duality, 27, 75, 314, 328
  hegemony, 1
  heterogeneity, 318–319
  identity, 73, 188, 317
  relativity, 163
  security, 197–199
Literacy, 42, 103, 107, 109, 114, 120, 124, 129, 160, 181, 213, 237, 244, 252, 256, 260–264, 322, 329
LMLT, *see Labour Market Language Training*
Louisiana Creole, 103
Lutheran, 218–219, 222–225
  Lutheran Missouri Synod, 222

## M

Manitoba, 51–52, 57, 119, 186, 189–190, 192, 194, 196, 198–199, 202, 234, 245, 305–306, 320–321
Mennonite, 21, 214, 224, 234, 303
Mexican American, 42, 61–62, 98, 104, 177–178, 237, 324
*Meyer v. Nebraska* (1923), 92, 157, 232, 322–323, 329
Miluk, 159
Mixed marriages/exogamy, 23, 291
Mob rule, 223
Monolingualism, 12–13, 15, 30, 38, 43–44, 50–54, 99, 101, 104, 109, 146, 153, 172, 212, 230, 245, 302, 322, 325, 334, 339, 341

Montreal, 52, 74, 76–78, 80–82, 189, 196, 258, 288, 309–310
Mortality, 72–73, 198, 232
Mother tongue, 15, 71–77, 79, 93, 117, 205, 234, 245, 251, 261, 284, 294–295, 301–303, 307–309, 318
Multicultural policy, 24, 50
  multiculturalism, ix–x, 2, 8, 16–27, 29–30, 48, 51, 82, 117, 146, 254
  Multiculturalism Act (Canada), 17, 30
Multilingualism, xii, 39, 51, 89, 106, 317–319, 332

## N

National identity, 17–18, 66, 100–101, 109, 187
National origin, 7, 26, 94, 173–178, 237, 257
National Policy on Languages (Australia), 86
National unity, xii, 1–13, 24, 28, 39–40, 44, 201, 213, 295, 331–332
Nationalism, 4, 10, 19, 39, 47, 55, 86, 332
Native American Languages Act (USA), 164
Native peoples and languages, 29
  Aboriginal, xi, 34, 113–115, chap. 5, 244–245, 249, 336, 339, 341
  Apache, 119
  Arapaho, 159
  Arawak, 155
  Athapaskan, 119
  Cree, 28, 119, 120
  Dene/Athapaskan, 119–120, 125, 129–132, 135
  First Nations, 18, 27–28, 71, 118–119, 121–124, 135, 137, 140–143, 145–146, 341
  Haida, 119
  Inuit, 28, 51, 118–120, 125–126, 129–130, 132, 137
  Iroquoian (Mohawk), 119
  Kutenai, 119
  Micmac, 199, 120
  Montagnais/Naskapi (Innu), 28, 119
  Native American, 98, 103–104, 151–154, 157, 159–162, 164, 324–325
  Navajo, 99, 113, 119, 153–154, 158–160, 302, 340
  Northern Ute, 159
  Ojibway, 119
  Pasqua Yaqui, 159
  Red Lake Band of Chippewa, 159

Salish, 119
Sioux (Dakota, Assiniboine), 119
Tohono O'odham, 159
tribal, 159
Wakashan, 119
Yupik, 152
Nativism/-ist, 34, 59, 92, 100, 218
Nebraska, 15, 92, 173, 218–219, 221–226, 228, 232–233, 322–323
New Brunswick, 28, 46, 74, 79, 147, 186, 189–190, 192–193, 195, 203–204, 244–245, 271–272, 285, 294, 305
NGO, 250–253, 260
No official language, 304
Non-official language, 117
Northwest Territories, xi , 52, 123, 125, 127–128, 130–131, 133, 144, 189–190, 245, 336, 340

## O

Office of Civil Rights (USA), 96
Official bilingualism, 55, 79, 145, 189, 195, 197, 285, 317, 332
Official English, 11, 45–46, 171–174, 180–184
Official English Declaration (California), 171–173, 180–184
Official Languages Act (Canada), 52, 86, 117, 127, 129, 132–133, 144, 167, 190, 193, 195, 207, 245–246, 248, 254–255, 274, 282, 305, 320, 334–336
Ontario, 24, 28, 46, 51–52, 71, 74, 79, 186, 189, 234, 245, 265, 268, 271–290, 292–297, 305, 307–308, 310, 320, 335, 338
Ottawa River Valley, 186, 309
Oyster Bilingual School, 98, 100

## P

Parliament of Canada, 204, 245
Parti Québécois, 17, 53–54, 129, 278, 295, 308, 317, 320
Patriation, 49, 62, 123, 135, 245
Pluralist, 4, 12, 16, 19, 34, 37, 41–43, 45–55, 57, 63, 66, 107, 163, 198
Point system, 257–258, 261
Political culture, 2, 4, 59–60, 66, 86, 98, 100, 106–107
Politics of recognition, 3–4, 29

Population size, 244
Press, 17, 21, 218–220, 225–226, 237, 292, 293
Private sector, 22, 65, 78, 108, 260
Professors, 222, 234
Prohibition, 304
Proposition 187 (California), 97
Proposition 63 (California), 326
Publications, 95, 103, 219, 225, 305
Puerto Rico, 62, 322, 327

## Q

Quebec, xii, 2–3, 9, 12, 17, 19, 24, 27–28, 34–35, 38, 40, 44, 46–48, 50–57, 61–68, 72–80, 85–86, 90, 101, 125–126, 186–190, 192–195, 198–201, 207, 233, 244–247, 259–260, 272–273, 276, 280, 283–286, 288, 293–296, 303, 305–311, 316–320, 336, 340
Quebec nationalism, 19, 308–310
Quiet Revolution, 40, 46, 61, 79, 85, 200, 309, 311

## R

Race, ix, 12, 15, 21–22, 62, 91–92, 104–107, 152, 158, 174–177, 181, 186, 192, 194, 220, 230, 235–237, 240, 274, 290–291
  racial classification, 235
  racialization, 235
  visible minorities, 23, 25, 71
RCBB, see Royal Commission on Bilingualism and Bilculturalism
Refugee, 22, 175, 214–215, 252, 257–258
  refugee claimants, 252
Rights
  civil rights, 6, 8, 12, 15, 40–42, 45, 86, 92, 247, 328
  group, 5–6, 8, 27, 247, 328–329
  human, 4, 6, 31, 110, 193, 338
  individual, 4–6, 27, 263, 304, 328–329
  language, ix, 51, 56, 126, 138, 169, 188–191, 193, 195–199, 201–203, 233, 247, 276, 280–281, 293, 304, 313
Roosevelt, Theodore, 90–91, 232
Royal Commission on Bilingualism and Biculturalism (RCBB, B. and B. Commission), 47, 78–79, 200, 273–274, 279, 295–296

# SUBJECT INDEX

## S

Sault Ste. Marie, 186, 285
Schools, 15, 20, 34, 41–44, 50, 53, 56, 62, 65, 76–79, 92–93, 95–96, 98–103, 108–119, 120, 122–124, 130, 133–134, 136–137, 139, 141–142, 152–153, 156–161, 163, 181, 207–208, 216–223, 226–230, 232–234, 236–240, 245–246, 248, 251, 254–255, 260, 276–281, 287, 292, 295–296, 303, 310–311, 313, 320, 325, 330, 335, 340–342
    Protestant schools, 218
    school systems, 245
Segmentalist perspective, 77
Settlement services, 251, 260
SIE, *see Survey of Income and Education*
Sign law (Bill 178, Quebec)/signage, 126, 195, 287, 295, 321
Social
    control, 13, 212, 228, 239
    justice, x, 1, 6, 8, 13, 19, 25, 29, 114, 163
    mobility, 24, 78, 237, 310
    reality, 24, 270, 301, 313
    status, 304
Sovereignists, 294
Spanish detention, 102
Supreme Court (Canada and USA), 46, 64, 87, 92, 97, 172, 176, 180, 182, 190, 192–194, 196, 198, 202, 232, 295, 308, 321–322, 324, 327
Survey of Income and Education (SIE), 300–304
Symbolism, 33, 145, 202, 294, 312

## T

Taiwan, 327
Tanton, John, 45, 101

Teacher education/training, 160, 227
Texas, xii, 46, 61, 85, 93, 99, 102, 223, 303, 317, 321, 324, 326, 338
Thunder Bay, 51, 287–288
Title VI (Civil Rights Act, USA), 100, 108, 324
Title VII (Elementary and Secondary Education Act, USA), 94–95, 102
Treaty of Guadalupe Hidalgo (USA), 333
Trudeau, Pierre Elliot, 17, 47–51, 56, 64, 85, 117, 123, 191, 308

## U

United Kingdom, 5, 313
U.S. English, 45, 95, 101, 285, 290, 317, 328

## V

Values, x, 3, 20, 24, 39, 47, 66, 81, chap. 4, 118, 122, 124, 141, 145–146, 154–155, 157, 159, 162, 251, 303, 333, 338, 342
Voting Rights Act (USA), 42, 92, 97, 104, 108, 181

## W

Warning labels, 182

## X

Xenophobia, 92, 218, 235

## Y

*Yniguez v. Mofford* (1990), 327
Youth, 43, 74, 156, 220
Yukon Territory, 123, 125–126, 135–149, 245, 336